THE MATTER OF MOTION

Luigi Aloysius Galvani (1737–1798)
Courtesy of the Wellcome Institute Library, London.

THE MATTER OF MOTION

AND

GALVANI'S FROGS

B. Innes Williams

Foreword by A. Rupert Hall

Rana

2000

First published in Great Britain 2000 by
Rana, Courtyard House, Church End, Bletchingdon, Oxfordshire OX5 3DL, UK

Designed and typeset by Judith Bastin on an Apple Macintosh in Quark Xpress
Printed and bound in Great Britain by Biddles Ltd, Guildford and King's Lynn

ISBN 0-9538092-0-X

Contents

Foreword

On opening the covers of this book and examining the contents page, some readers may experience some surprise. This is not a book about the early history of physics, still less a biography of the Italian physiologist Luigi Galvani – although his researches form a large part of its subject. To understand Galvani's thinking when he came to a new world of experience, neither quite organic or inorganic as then understood, was certainly the author's objective; to achieve this she thought it necessary to discover the background history of ideas concerning the origins of motion in the world from the time of the Greek founders of our science onwards.

Such ideas were of course in early times found in philosophy rather than in any science called (say) 'dynamics' which would not exist for two thousand years. Philosophers addressed themselves to such questions as 'How is a body moved?' Distinguishing the case of living bodies from that of inert bodies, the mover from the moved. Anything truly self moving was alive, it seemed, while the moved was inert and lifeless. As Dr Williams shows, the ramifications of these discussions were voluminous and subtle in the Middle Ages (and in some cases not without mathematical interest). They were to play an important role in the nascence of modern physical science, when questions were asked about the nature of local terrestrial motion (not for the first time) and were answered geometrically by Galileo.

Geometry, however, could not answer questions about the sources of motion or, to express the point in another way, about the origin of the forces which, when applied to naturally inert bodies, caused them to move. Because he could not geometrise force, Descartes denied its existence, arguing that no new motion is ever created in the universe but only transferred from body to body, there being a fixed quantity in the universe partitioned by the incessant impacts occurring between all the particles that constitute matter. After Descartes, Isaac Newton in time succeeded in making the concept of force respectable again, conjecturing in *Optics* that the "solid, massy, hard, impenetrable Particles" of which in the last analysis all matter is composed were each endowed with "certain Powers, Virtues or Forces" that cause the particles on which they act to move and their aggregates to bring about all the phenomena of nature. In Galvani's time the implications of these and other ideas for the explanation of motion and change in the universe were widely understood among learned men.

Galvani has often been treated as though he followed a purely empirical path of investigation frequently assisted by chance events, until inspired to pronounce that animal tissues contained electricity. The second part of Dr Williams' work shows how simplistic such an account is; her book describes the deep and rich intellectual context to which Galvani's investigations belonged, and on which he drew to account for his puzzling observations. It is true that Galvani was trained as an anatomist rather than as a philosopher but he was a product of the University of Bologna through which all the currents of European thought were flowing. Galvani was aware of the paradoxes that followed from his work: that dead animal tissue could seemingly create motion, that electricity could reside in living matter (as he believed). He was aware too of centuries of discussion lying behind his own approach to such ancient questions as What is matter? What is motion?

To all the philosophic discussions already in being at the opening of the eighteenth century there was added the new experimental science of electricity. It grew by the discovery of new effects, long lacking any accepted framework of ideas or a fixed language for discussion. The first theoretical ideas developed in Galvani's lifetime. Machines for the generation of electric charges were so fascinating that the presence of one in Galvani's laboratory is not surprising: given the character of his first new observations he could not fail to perceive some link between electricity and physiology.

As a successful thesis, this work was completed more than 20 years ago. Its topic has been little canvassed since and it has seemed worthwhile to issue a small private edition in order that it may be more generally available, without any attempt at revision or additions to the notes and bibliography. Attempts to take a long, coherent view of the history of science are not very numerous; as one such attempt this thesis, always highly original, deserves a wider circulation.

A. RUPERT HALL FBA

Tackley, Oxfordshire, 1999

Preface

This book has been prepared from the writings of my wife Billie because I found them so interesting and felt that they should be made available in a readable form. The first part on the Greeks and Middle Ages was in manuscript and there was more she had researched and written on the Medieval Period, the 17th century, René Descartes and electricity but this was less well digested and so was not in a state to be reproduced. Leaving out certain chapters inevitably created some gap in continuity. The second part from chapter 9 onwards is a slight rearrangement of her PhD thesis which she was encouraged to publish.

All this material had been set aside after the PhD was awarded in 1976 while Billie returned to medicine in order to undertake research in ophthalmology and to pursue other endeavours. It therefore remained in store for 20 years. When we retired I set about typing it into a presentable form. Unfortunately Billie was no longer able to make any revisions.

The more I have worked on Billie's writings, in the course of preparing them for publication, the more my admiration has expanded for the breadth and depth of her study of such a wide range of literature in at least five languages. To have read, understood and selected quotations from so many sources and in so many subjects in the classics and science required a remarkable brain and application over many years and I think it will be a long time before anyone will tackle such a project again. A novel aspect of her study was the use of experiments using modern apparatus to elucidate some of Galvani's observations. The contents of this book has convinced me that her 'cosmic' approach has provided an important insight into the history of a very interesting topic that has taxed the minds of philosophers and scientists over many centuries.

Specialists in the subjects of any one field are bound to have criticisms but to quote Bertrand Russell in the preface to his *History of Western Philosophy* (1961):

> *If there is any unity in the movement of history, if there is any intimate relation between what goes before and what comes later, it is necessary for setting this forth, that earlier and later periods should be synthesised in a single mind.*

There cannot be many who will have the breadth of intellect and patience to complete such syntheses and I do not believe that any delay in publication makes it any less significant.

It is obvious that a book such as this with a small market is unlikely to be published commercially. The situation might have been different if Billie had produced it 20 years earlier. In the circumstances I have decided to have a limited number of copies published privately for deposit in appropriate libraries in case it might be found useful for future scholars. Photocopies of many of the references as well as the unprinted chapters will be deposited in the Wellcome Library of the History of Medicine.

To get this book published, I enlisted the professional help of Judith Bastin. I would like to thank her for all she has done and especially for the meticulous and kind way in which she suggested improvements to the text and style of the book. Her resilience, in the face of what turned out to be a much more difficult task than I had anticipated, was a repeated source of admiration.

The production of this volume has been a labour of love in which I have been greatly encouraged and helped by Professor Rupert and Dr Marie Hall who were Billie's mentors for many years after she entered the history of science in her forties. Rupert and Marie have become close friends and neighbours in retirement in an adjacent village in Oxfordshire. I am very pleased to have been able to show my love and admiration for Billie's work over many years by producing this volume.

PETER WILLIAMS

Bletchingdon, 1999

ACKNOWLEDGEMENTS

In her thesis Billie thanked (the now late) Dr Edwin Clarke and Professor and Mrs Rupert Hall for their help. She acknowledged her indebtedness to Dr R. Gosling of the Department of Physics at Guy's Hospital Medical School for his advice and the provision of apparatus and facilities for the laboratory studies of Galvani's experiments. She also thanked the libraries of the Wellcome Institute of the History of Medicine, University College and The Senate House, University of London, The Royal Society and The Royal Society of Medicine. I should like to add my thanks to the Wellcome Institute Library for help with the references and for permission to publish the portrait of Galvani. Professor G. Tabarroni has kindly given permission to publish the pictures of the Bologna Institute and the drawing of Galvani's experiments.

Introduction

The philosophy of motion

Man's desire to find a common explanation for apparently similar phenomena has a long history. There seems to be an inherent intellectual satisfaction in the reduction of various effects to a single cause although the direction in which this reductionism has taken place has changed radically over the centuries. In the case of the phenomenon of motion or movement, this desire for a reduction of its various manifestations to a common cause has been of particular interest since the ability to move spontaneously is one of the more obvious and fundamental properties of living as opposed to non-living bodies. Motion has therefore been a subject for speculation and study from the earliest times since its explanation would seem to be the key to the mystery of life itself.

The tacit assumption, by man, of the fundamental association between life and movement has had an enormous influence on the ways in which he has considered it and investigated the problem of motion in general. It has linked the thoughts of men of widely different persuasions, interests and abilities over many centuries, for who can say whether the key to life is to be found in the understanding of the motion of non-living bodies or that the explanation of motion in non-living bodies is to be found in the unravelling of the mysteries of the motion of living bodies? At the moment we would seem to favour the former proposition, but in the past, the reverse has been true and in the future it may become true once more.

In the past, philosopher and physician, now physicist and physiologist, are linked by this apparent equation between life and motion, and both have a vested interest in each other's discoveries. When Galvani began his investigations he certainly hoped that physical explanations of motion would be applicable to this physiological problem of muscular activity and that the ultimate mechanism of movement in the living animal would be similar to that associated with motion *ex vivo*. The raw materials for his attempted physical model of muscular contraction were then, drawn from those very notions as to the nature of motion in general, developed by 'the philosophers' over the years prior to his investigations.

The purpose of this book, then, is to seek out the roots of those philosophical concepts of self movement which Galvani inherited and to which we might expect him to have turned for the physical basis of his ideas. His aim was to describe muscular motion as an example of self-movement in animals dependent on a series of events or material changes analogous to those he believed to be associated with the fundamental mechanism of motion outside the living animal. In order to understand these concepts we become involved with the problem of motion in general. To do otherwise is not only difficult, since historical ideas of motion and self-movement are inextricably associated, as we have suggested above, but inadequate, if we wish to approach our problem with Galvani's philosophical outlook. Much of this book will then of necessity be concerned with motion that is not organic.

To return to the problem facing Galvani, that of demonstrating that muscular motion is dependent on changes analogous to those occurring in association with motion *ex vivo* we shall see that for him, this meant demonstration that self-movement in the living animal is dependent on a material, associated specifically with the capacity for motion.

The material which history has decreed shall be linked with his name is electricity but as we shall discover later, Galvani's ideas about the general nature of motion in animals were established long before electricity came to occupy its motive rôle in his theories. He had been searching for "the material of motion" in his frogs long before the imponderable electrical fluid appeared to be the material he sought. It was as though electricity had for him, the exact configurations of the missing piece in a mental jig-saw puzzle the background of which he had already completed.

The background is what we must discover if we are to see the whole picture of the jig-saw, and the stuff of the background is, literally the stuff of motion. What we need to know is what was thought about this stuff of motion when Galvani began to have his thoughts about muscles and their mechanism of contraction. In order to discover this we must understand the establishment and development of the various traditions associated with the physical notions of movement and consider man's earliest attempts to rationalise natural phenomena.

B.I. WILLIAMS

Epsom, 1974

1

Early Greek ideas about motion

But because they believe that nothing can produce movement, which does not itself move, they have supposed that the soul is one of the things which move.[1]

Aristotle

The association of the capacity for self movement and change with living animals and plants, is obvious to the most primitive mind and an animistic explanation for motion in general is a natural starting point for the rationalisation of its origin and nature. As Kirk and Raven point out:

> It is a common primitive tendency to regard rivers, trees and so on as somehow animated or inhabited by spirits: this is partly, though not wholly, because they seem to possess the faculty of self-movement and change, they differ from mere sticks and stones.[2]

This recognition of one of the most striking properties of living things is woven into the fabric of all early attempts by Greek philosophy to understand the nature of motion and the concepts, first developed in the sixth century before Christ, have had a remarkably tenacious hold on man's ideas as to the nature of motion through the centuries. The development of these early ideas established certain precepts which, although modified with time, can be recognised in the physical and physiological theories held two thousand years or more later.

The early Greek philosophers were concerned with the fundamental problems of the nature of matter and the changes it underwent to produce the natural phenomena of the world about them. The desire to rationalise their thoughts, within a unitarian concept, grafted on to a primitive animism inherited from their ancestors, led to their having a comprehensive view of the nature of motion which included all types of change: those of apparent self-movement as well as what we should term secondarily induced movement. The revolutions of the heavenly bodies, the movements of animals and plants, meteorological changes as well as the movement of inanimate objects brought about by human and animal agencies were all rationalised from the same starting point. But the animistic orientation of their thought made the unifying basis for any general theory of motion, life. The origin of all movement in the universe was sought in the nature of life since its essential property was apparently, the capacity for self-movement. By deduction therefore the origin of all motion was sought in the nature of self-movement.

The first concept adopted by the Greeks was then the outcome of a basically animistic view of the world, inherited from their primitive ancestors.

Closely linked with it and a logical outcome of it, was the association of motion with divinity. Since the Homeric Gods were conceived of as enjoying everlasting life and as capable of undergoing infinite change and motion, they were associated with an infinite degree of self-movement.

Now the early Greek thinkers of Ionia were materialists. They did not conceive of reality apart from its corporeal extension in space, so that an infinite degree of self-movement was synonymous for them, with an infinite quantity of the material of self-movement. This materialisation of self-movement, so necessary within the framework of thought at this time, is the key to the understanding of the development of ideas during succeeding centuries. But to return to the Gods: this view of self-movement required that they must consist of a material, the very nature of which was 'pure' self-movement or 'pure' motion – a unique, divine, matter.

This identification of motion as a material had interesting consequences. Firstly, it led to the assumption that the capacity for self-movement demanded a quantity of this material in the moving body and presumably the greater the quantity present, the greater the potential for self-movement. Thus the Gods were 100% pure material of motion, while the material substance of lesser bodies contained or was permeated by this divine matter to a greater or lesser degree, inanimate objects having none. Secondly, it required that the attributes of self-moving matter were suitable to its role in the universe. Self-movement became associated therefore with the properties of a body capable of moving with the greatest facility and speed, and at the same time worthy of divinity. Hence it was required to be the essence of purity, rarity and pervasiveness – highly subtle and quite invisible.

Since the origin of all motion was referred to the power of self-movement, how then was this subtle, divine matter of self-movement associated with the movement of inanimate objects? How did the Ionian Greeks consider the problem of the motion of a stone, thrown from a hand or a leaf blown by the wind?

Aristotle* refers to this problem when he is analysing past views as to the nature of the soul, in particular the question of whether the soul itself must be self-moving since it produces motion in other bodies, for example, animals:

> But because they believe that nothing can produce movement which does not itself move they [earlier Greek philosophers] have supposed that the soul is one of the things which move.[1]

Aristotle is intent on proving just what the early Greeks did not believe: that is, that the soul being divine matter cannot be capable of self-movement, a concept which he goes on to develop as the keystone of his theory of motion, and which we will discuss later. What is important here, is the fact that he has put his finger on the essential idea of these earlier philosophers, the view that in order to cause motion, a body must be capable of self-movement. Now implicit in this concept is the idea that self-moving matter imparts motion because it is itself in motion. It is divine, it is self-moving, and therefore it is motive.

How the earliest Ionians conceived of this divine matter as acting is open to speculation. We have very fragmentary knowledge of how the earlier writers such as Thales*, Anaximander* or Anaximenes* thought about motion, if indeed they did think specifically about it, beyond the fact that it was originated by a divine matter capable of self-movement, for example, the 'soul' of Thales, the 'indefinite' of Anaximander and the 'primal air' of Anaximenes. What we can be sure of is that of the three qualities of divinity, self-movement and motive power were supposed to be present in this highly rarefied matter. Thales certainly attributed this matter (soul) to the Magnesian stone because it attracted iron.

> *Thales, too, . . . seems to suppose that the soul is in a sense the cause of movement since he says that a stone* [Magnesian] *has a soul because it causes movement to iron.*[3]

A magnet possessed soul because it was motive. We have no reference to self-movement in the magnet. Indeed if Thales had recognised the orientation of a magnet in the earth's field it would doubtless have reinforced his attribution of soul to it. It would be interesting to speculate on how Thales did indeed envisage the activation of the iron and his problem here may well be expressed in his view that somehow or other, soul permeated the world. As Kirk and Raven say:

> *Some think that the soul pervades the whole universe, whence perhaps came Thales' view that everything is full of Gods. And some say that it* [soul] *is intermingled in the universe, for which reason perhaps Thales also thought that all things are full of Gods.*

And:

> *Thales said that the mind of the world is God, and that the sum of things is besouled, and full of daimons; right through the elemental moisture there penetrates a divine power that moves it.*[4]

Thales, unlike other thinkers of his time had not identified soul with his elemental formative matter (water), and the reference to divine power permeating elemental moisture suggests that the matter of self movement was present not only in living things but also, in a general sort of way, in the atmosphere, and capable of entering both living and non-living bodies. If he thought this he may well have imagined some sort of flow of soul from the Magnesian stone to the iron to which it imparted movement. However, this is mere conjecture and we have no idea how soul was believed to bring about this activation, although, as we shall see later, Galen's reference to the views of Epicurus suggest a mechanistic development of such a view.[5]

So far then we can recognise the Ionian concept of motion as represented by a corporeally extended, material substance embodying the properties of divinity, motive power, self-movement – and the physical attributes considered requisite in a self-moving body. Subsequent developments in Greek philosophical thought were to destroy the comprehensive simplicity of this view, robbing the basic idea of a material of motion, of its divinity and motive power or, looked at from the opposite point of view, creating the concept of divine and motive power as separate abstract qualities. The net result of these trends was to leave the concept of a material of motion, with its special physical properties, intact and ready for further sophistication in terms of the nature of such properties. The two major influences responsible for such a development were: 1, the growth of a theological element which tended to separate off divinity from the other members of the original complex and 2, the postulation of an atomic theory which allowed the more specific development of the physical properties ascribed to the material matter of motion as it became robbed of its divinity. Probably the first trend in this direction occurred when Xenophanes* attacked the belief in multiple Gods by postulating the existence of one God only. Instead of the many Homeric Gods, capable of infinite self-movement, he envisaged one God, who was both material and motive, but not motionless. This God's motive activity was brought about by the power of his will, movement on his part being both unseemly and unnecessary, for, it was thought that he "shakes all things by the active will proceeding from his insight"[6]

Here we have the beginning of the association of divinity with the thinking, willing mind, although Xenophanes claims God was still considered by him as a material space-occupying object. This idea of divinity as an arranging or controlling force was also proposed by Heraclitus* but he did not rob his arranging force or 'logos' of either mobility or extension in space. For Heraclitus divinity was identified with the most rare form of fire found in the heavens the activity of which controlled all changes in the universe – and further, man's intelligence or willing mind was supposed to be dependent on breathing in this aether or logos from the air:

> Heraclitus said that the soul is a spark of the essential substance of the stars (scintillam stellaris essentiae).[7]

> According to Heraclitus we become intelligent by drawing in this divine reason [logos].[8]

Both these ideas of Heraclitus are important as factors in the development of concepts of motion. His identification of the matter of self-movement with a pure heavenly fire, produced the most suitable analogy man was to find for centuries when he considered the physical nature of motion: the power of self-movement and fire were to become firmly associated in his mind, although the type of 'fire' was to undergo considerable sophistication. The second idea, that man's intelligence or willing mind was dependent on his breathing in this divine logos from the air, is also interesting. It is presumably a development of Anaximander's concept of an all enfolding 'primal air', as the life principle. Since the life principle or divine material of self-movement had become identified with pure fire, this now had to be considered as pervading the atmosphere and entering living animals during the act of breathing.

Whereas we cannot be sure of the locality of the soul of Thales, and can only conjecture its presence in the atmosphere, Heraclitus quite definitely indicates it as a constituent of the air and further reinforces the belief that vital movements depend on its activity, just as do the movements of non-living bodies burning in the air (thunderbolts) or meteorological happenings in the sky.

Without becoming deeply involved in the logical arguments offered by the Eleatic Greeks in defence of their view that reality was not indeed the changing moving, material world man perceives with his sense organs but a motionless timeless abstract concept, we can appreciate the general nature of their thought and the influence it had on the development of our main interest, the interpretation of the cause of movement. The dissociation of the triad of divinity, motive power and self moving matter begun when Xenophanes made divinity a non-moving material, was extended by later thinkers who were groping towards a non-material concept of divinity. The 'dematerialisation' of divinity and consequently of motive power was to leave self-moving matter, with all the physical attributes it had acquired, as the ultimate instrument of motion but in the role of an intermediary body acting somewhere between an abstract divine non-moving, motive power and the object to be set in motion. Because of its relationship to the development of ideas of divinity this process of abstraction was associated specifically with motive power: the tacit assumption of the role of self moving matter as an adjunct never seems to have been destroyed.

The slow and fitful process by which the motive power lost its material identity is reflected in the views of such Eleatic thinkers as Empedocles* and Anaxagoras*. In the single spherical world postulated by Empedocles, there were six elements, earth, air, fire, water, love and strife. The first four of these were set in motion and rearranged to produce the diversity of matter recognisable around us by the motive power of the other two elements, love and strife. Now, here there is the beginning of the confusion as to the nature of these two elements. Empedocles certainly sees them as spatially extended but at the same time treats them as abstract forces, a point which Aristotle recognises:

> Empedocles also has a paradoxical view: for he identifies the good with Love. But this is a principle both as mover (for it brings things together) and as matter (for it is part of the mixture).[9]

And:

> He makes the material elements four in number, fire, air, water and earth, all eternal, but changing in bulk and scarcity through mixture and separation; but his real first principles, which impart motion to these are Love and Strife . . .[10]

Anaxagoras takes a more definite step in the separation of matter and motive power, by identifying the single, intellectual motive force of the 'Mind' as the quality ultimately responsible for motion, but he is still bound to a view that gives it a corporeal identity. He strives to give it qualities of purity and rarity and in fact, as Kirk and Raven point out, to describe "a true incorporeal entity", but does not in fact take the final step of dematerialising motive power.

While the abstract trend in Greek thought was giving rise to the idea of a non-material, non-mobile motive power in the world, the identification of self-moving matter with the material of fire was being reinforced by the atomic view of the world, put forward by Leucippus* and Democritus*. This theory solved the problem of the diversity of matter and motion by postulating that all matter is composed of an infinite number of atoms or irreducibly small, indestructible particles moving in a void. Two points in their theory are of special interest for us the shapes of these atoms and the origin of their motion. The atoms were conceived of as having an infinite number of shapes and by an infinitely possible number of jointures, between these, the various material bodies of the earth were supposed to be formed. The shapes of the atoms allowed for two main types of association or linkage between atoms: the approximation of like atoms leading to pure substances, the approximation and interlocking of unlike but reciprocally shaped atoms resulting in complex bodies. In the case of spherical atoms, the only jointure possible between these would not allow of the rigid form possible with the interlocking process available to atoms with complicated appendages. The spherical atom therefore was the obvious choice for the material of fire and self-movement and this is in fact the choice the Atomists made. Furthermore, the smallness of these round atoms gave them added powers of pervasiveness and mobility:

> For forms and atoms being countless, he [Democritus] calls the spherical ones fire and soul, and likens them to the (so-called) motes in the air, which can be seen in the sunbeams passing through our windows; . . . And Leucippus adopts a similar position. It is the spherical atoms which they call the soul, because such shapes can most readily pass through anything and can move other things by virtue of their own motion; for they suppose that the soul is that which imparts motion to living things.[11]

The Atomists then according to Aristotle identified self-moving matter with small round atoms, which were the atoms of fire. There doesn't seem to be great stress on this being a specifically rare type of fire or aether as postulated by Heraclitus: the Atomists appear to make the analogy between ordinary fire and self movement, stressing the essential identity of fire or heat with motion, on a mechanical basis. Furthermore, it is stated quite definitely that these fire atoms can "move other things by virtue of their own motion". The concept we suggested was implicit in the physical attributes of self-moving matter in much earlier times.

Adherents of the atomic view, then, attributed a definite physical nature to self-movement and identified it with the fast moving, and invasive, round atoms of fire and further since soul or divinity was also identified with these spherical atoms the problem of the origin of motion was avoided, since motive power and the mechanical instrument of motion were united in one substance. Aristotle however was not very happy with this theory and pursued the cause of the origin of motion, in his criticism of the Atomists:

> When therefore Leucippus and Democritus speak of the primary bodies as always moving in the infinite void they ought to say with what motion they move . . .[12]

It would seem to me that the Atomists were quite clear, really, about the cause of motion in their atoms. The origin of all motion was eternal and divine and rested in the round fire atoms. There always had been atoms in

the infinite void and they always had been in motion since the round particles were capable of imparting motion to all other particles by means of
collisions. Kirk and Raven suggest the Atomist's are vague about the origin
of movement but there seems little doubt that this is what they meant.[13]
Aristotle is quite happy about the derived motion of collision, but not happy
with the Atomists identification of the true origin of motion with the body
which is the instrument of self-movement by means of its physical attributes
and activities. In fact, Aristotle's own theory of motion was a development
of the trends we have already discussed, trends by which motive power became separated from self moving material in the chain of events responsible
for setting a body in motion. He was a pupil of Plato* in this respect and it is
to Plato's and Aristotle's development of the Ionian concept of motion that
we turn in the next chapter.

Notes

1 Aristotle (1957) *De Anima (On The Soul)*, Bk I, ii 403b 29, London, William Heinemann
   Ltd
2 Kirk G.S. and Raven J.E. (1964) *The Presocratic Philosophers*, Cambridge, Cambridge
   University Press, p. 95
3 Loc. cit., Note 1, 21, p. 27
4 Loc. cit., Note 2, pp 94–95
5 Galen (1952) *Natural Faculties*, I XIV 45. London, William Heinemann Ltd
6 Loc. cit., Note 2, p. 169, Note 174
7 *Macrobius S. Scip.* 14, 19 quoted in K and R, loc. cit., Note 2, p. 207
8 Sextus adv. math. VII 129, quoted in K and R, loc. cit., Note 2, p. 207
9 Aristotle *Met* A9 1075 b1 quoted in K and R, loc. cit., Note 2, p. 330, Note 428
10 *Simplicus Phys.* 25 21, loc. cit., Note 2, p. 329
11 Loc. cit., Note 1, 403 b 34, pp 19–20
12 Loc. cit., Note 2 quote from Aristotle *De Caelo 2*, 300b 8, p. 416
13 Ibid., p. 417

* See Biographical Index

2

The views of Plato and Aristotle

We must then start afresh and examine the question: if there is any self-moving agent of motion how does it move itself and with what sort of motion.[1]

Aristotle

In the previous chapter we have seen how the materialistic outlook of the Ionian Greeks identified the three elements motive power, self-movement and divinity as residing in one substance which I have referred to as the material of motion and furthermore, how the development of a striving after an abstract view of divinity and motive power was beginning to disrupt this originally simple concept. This trend was developed further by Plato who continued the process started by Xenophanes, Parmenides* and others who were concerned with divinity as a force of creation and intelligence, rather than an instrument of motion. For Plato the universe was a reasonable ordered entity and must therefore be created by a rational intelligent being or force. This force which he refers to as God the Creator or Demiurge was motive and divine but not involved directly in the mechanics of motion, that is, not self-moving.

Now, starting from the original concept, the removal of the essential physical property of self-motion from the divine, originator of motion should logically lead to the need of three factors in any system producing motion, the ultimate divine, intelligent motive power (A), a self-moving material, originally set in motion by A (B) and the matter set in motion by contact with B (C). The relative importance given by any thinker to any one or more of these three factors tends to blur the basic pattern and at times it seems almost lost but by using it as a basis for analysing their thoughts, the scheme helps us to appreciate the difficulties they encountered when dealing with the causes of motion and to understand the confusion and contradicting statements that they sometimes made.

Applying this scheme to Plato's universe how do we identify A, B and C – and most important, from our point of view, what was the role of B as the immediate cause of animal movement? Our source for Plato's idea is the *Timaeus*, where he describes his world picture and its origin. The metaphorical way in which he represents his ideas make these sometimes difficult to identify but certain essential features appear. In terms of the Macrocosm or universe, we can identify three elements of our schema as follows:

A = Creator = Demiurge = Intelligence = Divinity.[2]
A + B = World-Soul.[3]
C = 4 Elements (Air, Fire, Water, Earth) created from the initial chaos.[4]

A does not present any conceptual difficulty for us. It is the single, ultimate abstraction of motive power and is non-mobile. Similarly C, the objects in the universe set in motion can be seen as the form of Empedocles' material substances remaining, if love and strife lose their material identity and become translated into abstract motive powers. The view that the material substance of the world was derived from these four elements was that most readily accepted by Greeks and later generations and was of course in contradistinction to the atomic view. It held the field through the Middle Ages until the revival and sophistication of its rival in the mechanistic philosophy of the 17th century.

This leaves us with the identity of (B) which according to our scheme is material and self moving, set in motion by the Creator (A) and imparting movement to the four material elements (C), that is, the 'world-soul' should be material, not abstract which makes the choice of the word 'soul' unfortunate for us. Where Plato describes the complicated procedure by which the 'world-soul' is cut into strips and mixed in with the material elements (somewhat as a cook popping ingredients into a mixing bowl) he makes it clear that it is at least part material (hence world-soul = A+B):

> From the indivisible, eternally unchanging Existence and the divisible changing Existence of the physical world he mixed a third kind of Existence . . .[5]

So the 'world-soul' is part abstract and part the material of the physical world but it is in eternal self-movement, abstract movement in that it is continually thinking about the world and actual movement in that it forms the material orbits of the heavenly bodies which it moves by virtue of its own perpetual self-motion. But what was the material constituent of the 'world-soul'? Plato is not specific about this in the *Timaeus*.[6] It could even be a harmonious blend of all the elements. He certainly describes the heavenly bodies as "made mostly of fire" but this doesn't necessitate that the 'world-soul' which is responsible for their eternal movements is likewise made of fire, so we must admit that we cannot identify the material nature of Plato's 'world-soul' specifically with any one element or combination of elements.

In the microcosm of man there is again evidence of the dichotomy of Plato's view as to the nature of his intermediary mobile (B). The ultimate origin of motion in man is again the Creator who is abstract and external and acts independently *via* man's soul which is a part of the 'world-soul' contained in his body. Our identification of A, B and C, is therefore analogous to that in the macrocosm B being identified with man's personal bit of the 'world-soul', as it were. And again the part material, part abstract nature of the soul is reflected in Plato's description of this. In the famous Platonic division of the soul into three parts, one is apparently immortal and divine while the other two are mortal and definitely not divine. The divine immortal soul is according to Plato situated in the head (=brain) where it is safe from contamination by the mortal parts (of the soul), separated from them by the neck:

> And since they shrank from polluting the divine element with these mortal feelings more than was absolutely necessary, they located the mortal element in a separate part

of the body, and constructed the neck as a kind of isthmus and boundary between head and breast to keep them apart.[7]

When we come to consider how Plato actually envisaged the mortal parts of the soul we are in difficulties because of the metaphorical nature of his language. The two mortal parts are separated, we are told by the midriff, the better part above, the lesser below, "rather as a house is divided into men's and women's quarters".[7] But where exactly was the former part of the moral soul situated?

> *The part of the soul which is the seat of courage, passion, and ambition they located nearer the head between midriff and neck; there it would be well placed to listen to the commands of reason and combine with it in forcibly restraining the appetites when they refused to obey the word of command from the citadel. They stationed the heart, which links the veins and is the source of the blood which circulates through the body's members, in the guard-room, in order that when passion was roused to boiling point, . . . whether by external action or internally by the appetites, commands and threats should circulate quickly . . . And because they knew that the swelling of the heart which makes it throb with suspense or anger, was due to fire, . . .*[7]

Certain things seem to be implied in this quotation. Firstly, that the superior part of the mortal soul was in or near the heart, and that it was activated by the divine, immortal part of the soul in the head. (A activating B). Secondly, that its activity was associated with the production of heat which could be dispersed through the body *via* the vascular system. And furthermore, the swelling of the heart was due to fire. Here the material agent of motion (B) seems to be definitely identified with fire. Similarly the lesser part of the mortal soul, situated near the liver and likened, poetically to a wild beast at a manger, brings about the movement of food, its penetration and breaking up – the rôle Plato assigns to the smallest of his elemental particles, fire.[8] Plato never actually identifies his mortal souls with the material fire, but the suggestion is there, despite the confusing references to appetites and emotions as the cause of motion. This confusion recurs, as we shall see with Aristotle, but when the tripartite division of the soul is adapted to the Stoic philosophy – particularly in the views of Galen* and sophisticated into a theory of spirits the implication becomes definite.

Mechanistic explanations for the immediate cause of physiological phenomena were certainly not foreign to Plato's thought. When dealing with the problem of the nature of sense-perception specifically pleasure and pain he says:

> *In any account of qualities sensible or non-sensible we must remember the distinction we have already made between substances of a mobile and of an immobile structure; this is the clue which our investigations should follow. For what is naturally mobile, when affected by even a slight impulse, spreads it round, one particle passing it on to another until it reaches the consciousness and reports the quality of the agent.*[9]

By analogy it is reasonable to assume a similar activity of a 'naturally mobile structure' as the immediate agent in animal movement.

Despite the emphasis given by Plato to the importance of the Creator as the ultimate source of motion in both the macrocosm and microcosm, it seems justifiable to accept that he still retained the concept of an intermediary, 'naturally mobile structure' as the immediate cause of motion, and that we can identify it with B in our scheme. The fact that he chose to designate it as 'soul' is confusing for us particularly as he visualised only part of this soul as being material, and therefore mobile, the other abstract or divine part being identifiable with A in our terms of reference.

When we come to consider the development in theory made by Plato's pupil, Aristotle, we see the continued effects of his inheritance from Plato and from the earlier Greek philosophers. Aristotle is much more explicit, and much more easily understood than Plato, on the question of motion in general.

Aristotle's burning problem was with the true and ultimate origin of motion. In *The Physics* he sets out, among other things, to prove that this ultimate origin of motion is not as the Ionian thinkers had believed, motile by means of its own self-motion, but immovable:

And so it happens that every physical body which causes motion must be capable of being moved; for whenever it causes motion it is itself under the action of some other body which is keeping it in motion. But the inference that has sometimes been drawn, that there is no cause of a thing being in motion, which cause is not itself in motion, is false.[10]

By deduction he comes to the conclusion that the ultimate source of all and any motion, is unmoved. In a general way he then proceeds to consider the nature of self-movement:

We must, then, start afresh and examine the question: If there is any self-moving agent of motion, how does it move itself and with what kind of motion?[11]

This investigation leads him to the conclusion that in any apparently self-moved body there must be at least two factors involved in its activity: an unmoved, motive agent and a mobile moved by it:

All the other alternatives being exhausted, then, we conclude that one factor of whatever is self-moved causes motion without being in motion and the other is moved, for only so is self-movement possible.[12]

He proceeds from this basic assumption to describe the elements in his 'model of motion' and since it is so relevant to our theme of the part played by a self-moving material, I quote it in full:

Again, if the whole moves itself, it must (as we have just seen) include a factor that causes motion and another that is moved; so if the whole AB is to be described as 'moving itself,' we may also say that it is moved by the moving factor A. Now since the motor may either be in motion itself (under the action of another motor) or may not be in motion at all, and since the thing moved may in its turn either be moving something else or moving nothing, the self-mover must embrace a factor that causes motion but is itself unmoved and also a factor that is in motion and that may or may not, as the case may be, convey motion to something else. Let A then be the unmoved mover, B what is moved by A and in its turn moves C, which is moved by B but itself moves nothing. (There may of course be any number of links between B and C, but, as it makes no difference, we suppose one only). Then ABC taken as a whole group moves itself. But if I take away C out of the group, AB will still move itself, A being the mover and B the moved; but C will neither move itself nor be moved at all. And neither will BC move itself without A, for B can only move anything at all in virtue of being moved by something else, not by any factor it contains in itself. It is then only AB that really moves itself.[12]

Here we have the clear statement of the three factors involved in movement according to our previously adopted scheme and Aristotle makes it clear at the end of his chapter that this pattern applies to the organic as well as the inorganic situation, macrocosm as well as microcosm:

. . . for in the three links of mover, instrument of motion, object moved, the last must experience motion but need not cause it; the middle term must be in motion itself as well as causing motion in something else (for it accompanies the changes of the thing it moves and keeps pace with it . . . And since we find as the last term of the series entities, (inanimate objects, to wit) capable of being moved but not of initiating motion, and other entities (living organisms, to wit) including in themselves a factor capable of initiating motion and also one capable of being moved, . . .[13]

If we pursue this general pattern of A, B and C in the macro and microcosm what evidence have we for the identification of B with a specific matter, such as fire? Aristotle having adopted the four elements of Empedocles and arranged his universe in a spherical continuum like Plato with concentric regions of Earth, Air, Fire and Water, postulated a fifth element the Quintessence which was the divine material of the heavens and their contents, sharply separated from the base material elements of the sub-lunar world. (that is, earth, air, fire and water). The motion of the Quintessence was eternal and circular and its eternal self-movement was originated by the ultimate eternal, non-moving motive power equated with 'pure desire,' 'intelligence' or 'God'. Hence in Aristotle's language we can identify our scheme thus:

A = The unmoved mover = Intelligence
B = Quintessence
C = Four elements (Earth, Air, Fire and Water)

When we come to look at the properties Aristotle bestows on his Quintessence, we find a remarkable resemblance to those that former generations had bestowed on their 'matter of motion'. It was a rarefied form of fire, invisible, pervasive, light and self-moving. Unlike Plato, Aristotle's intermediary agent of motion is entirely material, if of a somewhat unique nature. He makes it quite clear that his Quintessence is not fire, an element of the sublunar world although one can imagine he envisaged it as a special type of fiery vapour much as Heraclitus had. It was certainly closely akin to heat.

Now considering the microcosm and the identity of A, B and C it is much more difficult to be sure what Aristotle means. Following his clear-cut analysis of the factors involved in movement, given in *The Physics*, we are led to expect animal movement to result from the activity of the divine, non-moving motor (= the soul (A)) setting in motion a material substance capable of eternal self-movement (B) and acting as the immediate activator of the animal or parts of it (C). Again, as with Plato care must be taken in the interpretation one gives to Aristotle's use of the word, soul. In fact, in the strictest sense he uses it for his abstract divine unmoved mover (A) and when he talks of the 'faculty of the soul' he is referring to our factor (B), which is the self-moving eternally-moved material analogous to Plato's mortal soul. The task of identifying A and B is not easy for the reader.[14] It is only by following up hints thrown out in widely scattered parts of his writings, piecing them together and deducing their logical content, that one can pin down his system.

In *De Anima* the locomotion of animals is discussed at length.[17] We are told that this is caused by desire of the 'appetitive faculty' roused to action by the contemplation of objects of desire the pursuit of which will be of benefit to the animal. In the case of man, who has a mind, this can replace the objects of desire as an initial motive power. We are thus led to the position where A is equated with the abstract force of the mind or unmoving external objects of desire and B, apparently with the faculty of desire or appetite. There is no mention of any material substance acting as an eternally moved, self-mover, and identifiable with appetite: an omission W.S. Hett notes in his introduction to the Loeb Classics edition of *De Anima*.[15]

In *Movement of Animals*, the subject is pursued once more and the unmoved mover identified again.[16] "So the objects of desire and intellect first set up movement . . ."[17] and,

> The prime mover then moves without itself being moved, but desire and the desiderative faculty set up movement while being themselves moved.[18]

"Desire and the desiderative faculties" are certainly equated with B and therefore we must believe one of three things: 1. Aristotle has abandoned the concept of B as a material substance acting mechanically; 2. Desire = Appetite is materialised; 3. The chain of factors in his basic model has been lengthened to include two abstract factors prior to a material activation as yet unidentified. Leaving aside the possibility of 1 being true, we can look for evidence of 2 or 3 above, representing the true picture.

Talking of animal movement Aristotle says:

> The moving cause is of two kinds; one is unmoved and the other both moves and is moved. The former is the practical good, while that which both moves and is moved is the appetite (for that which is moved is moved qua *influenced by appetite, and* appetite qua *actual is a kind of movement) and the thing moved is the animal.*[19]

He then continues:

> The instrument by which appetite causes movement belongs already to the physical sphere; so it must be considered among the functions common to body and soul.[20]

However, Aristotle proceeds to identify the physical instrument with such structures as a ball and socket joint, that is, C, so we are still left without reference to any material identifiable with B and must assume desire or appetite are abstract, although we have had the hint that "appetite . . . is a kind of movement".[20]

When we look at what Aristotle has to say in his *Generation of Animals*, we are supplied with just the material we have been looking for, although here the reference is not specifically to animal locomotion:

> *Now so far as we can see, the faculty of Soul of every kind has to do with some phys-ical substance which is different from the so called "elements" and more divine than they are; and as the varieties of Soul differ from one another in the scale of value, so do the various substances concerned with them differ in their nature. In all cases the semen contains within itself that which causes it to be fertile – what is known as "hot" substance, which is not fire nor any similar substance, but the pneuma which is enclosed within the semen or foam-like stuff, and the natural substance which is in the pneuma; and this substance is analogous to the element which belongs to the stars.[21]*

So the faculties of the soul and therefore the faculty of appetite "has to do with" a physical substance analogous to the Quintessence and called pneuma. Again Aristotle fails to equate appetite precisely with a material substance and suggests that appetite uses pneuma as its tool, so that it seems likely that the third of the possibilities suggested above is the most likely, that is, B, represented by the pneuma has been relegated one place in his system to allow two prior motive powers. But this is impossible in his own terms. There can only be one unmoved mover and he has himself said that appetite is the moving mover. We are therefore forced to the view that Aristotle's ideas are not wholly consistent with his originally laid down scheme in as much as he has introduced a non-material self-moving element into category B which also contains the material element, pneuma, the latter retaining all the physical qualities we have seen established for a material of self-motion. Perhaps Aristotle's lack of precision is reflected also in his ten-tative suggestion above that pneuma is not altogether a straight-forward material element but is more divine than they are.

This divinity ascribed to pneuma stems from its analogy with the heavenly bodies, the sun in particular which is composed of the Quintessence and contains heat of a special type not like fire but of the nature of a biological warmth. The pneuma then is not homogeneous in as much as it likewise contains this special form of heat ". . . and in all pneuma soul-heat is present, so that in a way all things are full of Soul".[22] And:

> *And that portion of the soul-principle which gets enclosed or separated off within the pneuma makes a fetation and implants movement in it.[23]*

Here again there is some ambiguity in that the soul, which Aristotle was at such pains to disassociate from self movement is identified as the movement producing element in pneuma. As for the pneuma itself it is not made abun-dantly clear whether the 'innate heat' element is the truly self-moving mover or whether the rest of the pneuma performs this function. The suggestion is always there that the essentially 'vital force' bringing about movement whether generation or locomotion is indeed the innate heat and this is prob-ably a modification of earlier views of fire as the material of motion. If this is so, then perhaps Aristotle thought of the innate heat, causing movement in the fine aether substance of the pneuma in much the same way as fire produces the expansive movement of steam or air. A.L. Peck in his summary to *Generation of Animals* cites a reference to the action of air which may be suggestive as an analogy in Aristotle's mind:

> Were it not for a body of the nature of air, there could be no such thing as enforced motion. By the same action it assists the motion of anything moving naturally.[24]

If we take the final movement of the animal as representing 'enforced motion' and the action of the innate heat as that body 'moving naturally' air becomes the analogue of the aether-like pneuma, which by its movements assist this naturally moving heat. In fact Aristotle seems to have extended his original concept of the links involved in the chain of motion from three to five, by replacing the originally unitary concept of an intermediate self to moving matter (B) with three elements:

1. The appetitive faculty.

2. The innate heat.

3. The pneuma (apart from the heat element).

If indeed, this is so, how did he envisage movement is brought about in animals? Towards the end of *Movement of Animals* he gives us some idea of his final scheme for animal movement and makes it obvious that a mechanical self-moving material must exist in animal bodies:

> In accordance with the definition which defines the cause of motion, desire is the central origin, which moves by being itself moved; but in animate bodies there must be some bodily substance which has these characteristics. That, then, which is moved but does not possess the natural quality of setting up movement may be affected by a power external to it, and that which causes movement must possess some power and strength. Now all animals clearly both possess an innate spirit and exercise their strength in virtue of it. This spirit seems to bear the same relation to the origin in the soul as the point in the joints, which moves and is moved, bears to that which is unmoved. Now since the origin is in some animals situated in the heart, in others what corresponds to the heart, it is therefore clear that the innate spirit [= pneuma] also is situated there. Whether the spirit is always the same . . . ; at any rate it is clearly well adapted by nature to be a motive power and to exercise strength. Now the functions of movement are thrusting and pulling so that the organ of movement must be able to increase and contract. And the nature of spirit has these qualities; . . .[25]

Aristotle goes on to liken the animal body to a well governed city state with its one centre of control (the heart), seat of the soul, so that both A and B are in Aristotle's scheme, situated in the heart which is logical in view of their inextricably involved relationship in his mind. Elsewhere we are told that the heart is the centre also of sense perception. The physical accompaniments of mental activity are always appreciated by Aristotle and by making the heart the mental as well as the mechanical or instrumental centre of control he is able to develop an integrated system of explanation for animal movement (by the way depriving the brain of a functional role and relegating it to that of a cooling mechanism).

The fully developed Aristotelian scheme for animal movement was then as follows: The unmoved mover, equated with mind, intelligence (rational man) or "objects of desire in the sphere of action" (man and animals) brings about movement in the appetitive or desiderative faculty. This movement is communicated to the pneuma (almost certainly to the innate heat which in turn moves the pneuma) and the movement of the pneuma stimulates the animal or its parts mechanically. Incoming stimuli from the sense organs affect the imagination (also located in the heart) and seem to be represented by movements of the pneuma in 'vessels' passing to the heart. The 'alterations' of these movements of pneuma in the heart stimulate the imagination (in abstract terms) and cause an increase or decrease in the heat of the blood (in mechanistic terms). This in turn produces expansions and contractions of the pneuma which eventually bring about movement of the animal, for example, its limbs:

> The origin, then, of movement . . . is the object of pursuit or avoidance in the sphere of action and heat and cold necessarily follow the thought and imagination of these objects[26]

So the activity of the pneuma causing expansion and contraction by means of its thrusting and pulling not only acts as the intermediary of movement but is stimulated to action by processes which bring about temperature changes too (by movements of the heart?). In this way Aristotle equates movement with heat production in as much as they both have a common cause.

We have had to search at length for the model of motion in the microcosm, especially with regard to B. Aristotle is also guilty of failing to specify whether the soul of man is part of his cosmic unmoved mover or merely analogous to it. From the point of view of animal movement we have seen that the need for a material self-moving body acting as an immediate cause of animal movement was still evident in Aristotle's scheme. The role of an eternally self-moving body as responsible for spontaneous animal movement was still vital to his concepts although other factors were interpolated in his schema so as to obscure the basic pattern.

Notes

1   Aristotle (1960) *The Physics*, VIII v 257a, London, William Heinemann Ltd
2   Plato (1965) *Timaeus*, 4. 30, H.D.P. Lee (transl.), London, Penguin Books Ltd
3   Ibid., 6
4   Ibid., 3. 5
5   Ibid., 6. 35
6   Ibid., 8. 40
7   Ibid., 38.70
8   Ibid., 26. 58
9   Ibid., 32
10 Loc. cit., Note 1, *The Physics*, III I 201a 26
11 Ibid., VIII v 257a, 33

12 Ibid., VIII v 258a
13 Ibid., VIII v 258b
14 Aristotle (1963) *Generation of Animals*, II III 736b, A.L. Peck (transl.), London, William Heinemann Ltd
15 Aristotle (1957) *De Anima (On The Soul)*, III X, W.S. Hett (transl.), London, William Heinemann Ltd
16 Aristotle (1961) *Movement of Animals*, IV 700a, A.L. Peck (transl.), London, William Heinemann Ltd
17 Ibid., 700b 23
18 Ibid., 701a 36
19 Loc. cit., Note 15, III X 433b 14
20 Ibid., 433b 18–20
21 Loc. cit., Note 14, II III 736a
22 Ibid., 762a 20
23 Ibid., 762b 18
24 Aristotle (1960) *On the Heavens*, III II 301b 30, W.K.C. Guthrie (transl.), London, William Heinemann Ltd
25 Loc. cit., Note 16, 703a X 4
26 Ibid., 701b VIII

* See Biographical Index

3

Epicurean ideas

First I say that the mind, which we often call the intelligence, in which is situated the understanding and the government of life, is a part of man, no less than hands and feet and eyes are parts of the whole living being.[1]

Lucretius

The philosophy of life, developed by Epicurus* and publicised so elegantly by Lucretius* in the Roman world of the 1st century BC is important in our story of the development of concepts of animal movement because it embodies the ultimate in the materialist interpretation of the factors we have been considering to date. The other schools of philosophy to be considered differed in that they developed the essentially abstract elements (Neoplatonism) or used both materialist and abstract elements (Stoics) although in the case of the latter too, the general emphasis was a less rigidly mechanistic interpretation.

Epicurus adopted the basic features of the atomic system of Leucippus and Democritus, solving the problem of matter, its diversity and motion by envisaging all the material substance of the world as composed of irreducibly small, discrete atoms moving with a perpetual motion in the void.[1] All reality or being was represented by the atoms: all non-reality or non-being by the void (the minor modifications to the original theory made by Epicureans need not trouble us here). However, living as he did after the time of both Plato and Aristotle, we might expect him to interpret the processes involved in animal movement not only in terms of atomism but also by the adoption of some of the features of these other earlier philosophers.

Our source for these ideas is the poem 'De Rerum Natura' of Lucretius the Roman poet who so avidly adopted the Epicurean philosophy and preached it so ardently to his fellow Romans. Book III, *Life and Mind* contains much that is relevant to our particular interests. After initial introductory passages, Lucretius states the essential tenet of the Epicurean view that the mind is a corporeally extended reality and as such must have a locality in man's body. All previous ideas as to mind being a harmony or arrangement are dismissed as inherited from the myths of the past. He adjures his readers to ". . . give back the name of harmony, brought down to musicians from high Helicon, . . ."[2] His evidence for this belief is reasonable.

How can the harmony of the mind be likened to the harmony of a healthy body, he argues, for the visible body may appear ill while:

> *For indeed the body which we can see plain before us is often sick, although we are yet happy in the other part which lies hidden; and again it often happens that the contrary is true in its turn, when one wretched in mind is happy in all his body, not otherwise*

than if the sick man's foot gives him pain when there is no pain meanwhile in the head.[3]

Furthermore, while we are asleep, something in us is awake to all sorts of stimuli.

So much for the mind or intelligence which previous generations of Greeks had been at pains to dematerialise: Epicurus at once re-establishes it as a material space-occupying entity (A in our scheme). But what of B and the proliferation of B created by Aristotle? This is represented by the 'vital spirit' which according to Epicurus is certainly in our limbs because after a limb has been severed from its body, a degree of 'life often lingers'. The nature of this vital spirit is then further described. It is a mixture of two types of atom; wind and heat:

> *. . . firstly it happens that if a great part of the body be taken away, yet life often remains in our frame; and again when a few particles of heat have dispersed abroad and air is driven out through the mouth the same life in a moment deserts the veins and leaves the bones; so that from this you may recognize that not all particles have a like function or support life equally, but rather that those which are seeds of wind and warming heat see to it that lingers in the frame. There is therefore within the body itself a heat and a vital wind which deserts our frame on the point of death.*[4]

Here we can recognise at once the two material constituents of Aristotle's intermediary mobile innate heat and pneuma represented by heat and wind atoms. For Epicurus, B is represented by the vital spirit = heat + wind.

Having materialised A + B, Epicurus then joins them together into a single substance. But this 'mind-spirits' complex is arranged so that the 'mind element' occupies the heart while the 'spirit element' is distributed throughout the body (by way of the blood vessels). Why, if this is a homogenous mixture, it should be thus located, he does not venture – certainly not on mechanical grounds. It is enough for him that mind must occupy the breast, "For in this place throbs terror and fear, hereabouts is melting joy."[5] He has simply developed the psychosomatic notions of Plato, Aristotle and others concerning the relationship of abstract passions to physical correlatives and espoused a purely somatic view of their nature. Furthermore he has followed Aristotle in siting both A and B in the heart and its extensions, the blood vessels.

This idea of the 'mind' part of the vital spirit remaining as a sort of reservoir in the heart and the rest of the vital spirit diffusing through the body to bring about movement, is given a completely mechanical interpretation. Certainly, we are told that the diffused part of the vital spirit ". . . obeys and is moved according to the will and working of the intelligence",[6] but this is a process conceived in terms of matter and movement. "Obeying" must be interpreted as moving in response to the mechanical stimulus of contact. If, every movement of mind is not transferred to the rest of the vital spirit, in the same way as when a part of our body suffers pain, this can remain a purely local effect. However:

> *. . . when the intelligence is moved by more vehement fear, we see the whole spirit throughout the frame share in the feeling . . .*[7]

The mechanical effects of this, produced in the body, are described, and a better picture of the body's response to stimulation of the sympathetic nervous system would be hard to find:

> . . . sweatings and pallor hence arise over the whole body, the speech falters, the voice dies away, blackness comes before the eyes, a sounding is in the ears, the limbs give way beneath; in a word we often see men fall to the ground for mental terror.[8]

Pursuing this line of argument, Lucretius reiterates his belief in the material nature of mind and spirit. The activities of the mind and spirit all involve touch and touch in turn involves matter. Citing the case of a deep wound, he concludes that the "nature of the mind must be bodily, since it suffers by bodily weapons and blows". This idea echoes the Greek concept 'like recognising like' or 'like affecting like' which seems to have held such an important place in philosophy well into the Middle Ages. Only the mind or spirit can comprehend spiritual things and by the same token only material things can be affected by material things.

Having established the material nature of mind and spirit and identified them in one substance, we can expect to recognise all the physical properties of an old friend the matter of motion donated to mind (as well as, of course, to spirit). Thus we find Lucretius telling us that ". . . it is exceedingly delicate and formed of exceedingly minute particles".[9] The mind must be exceptionally mobile because its response to stimuli is so rapid:

> But that which is so readily moved must consist of seeds exceedingly rounded and exceedingly minute, that they may be moved when touched by a small moving power.[10]

Here we arrive back at square one with Aristotle. If there is no abstract, nonmoving mover, what provides the "small moving power"? This question is answered by a more detailed description of mind [= spirit].

Referring to the apparent loss of heat and breath associated with death, Lucretius describes this as:

> For a kind of thin breath mixed with heat leaves the dying, and the heat, moreover, draws air with it.[11]

Heat always contains air because being sparse, that is with its atoms relatively widely separated, it must have many atoms of air between these. Therefore, mind must be at least threefold in composition, rarefied wind + heat + air, the air being contained within the heat, by necessity. But apparently this composition is not adequate to create sentience:

> . . . since the mind cannot admit that any of these can produce sense bringing motions and the thoughts which it itself revolves[12]

Therefore, Lucretius continues, a fourth component must be added to these, this being "without name". This nameless component is then the factor supplying the slight push that sets the matter of mind in motion. So we have taken the source of movement back one stage further.

Lucretius, in his earlier more general description of mind and spirit has referred to the need for the particles or atoms composing it to be easily moved, but this we must presume to refer to the atoms of rare wind, heat and air as well as this nameless fourth component. Now we are told that it is this fourth component that is the most exquisitely mobile, the lightest conceivable type of atom the movement of which represents the sensory stimulus to mind and spirit and thence to the limbs.

> *A fourth nature must therefore be added to these; this is entirely without name; nothing exists more easily moved and more thin than this, or made of elements smaller and smoother; and this first distributes the sense giving motions through the limbs. For this is first set in motion, being composed of small shapes; after that, heat takes on the movement, and the unseen power of wind, then the air; after which all is set in movement, the blood is agitated, the flesh is all thrilled through with feeling, [the] last is communicated to bone and marrow it maybe the pleasure, it may be the opposite excitement.*[13]

By creating this sequence of mechanical events to account for movement, the Epicureans have as it were, identified the fourth component with B and multiplied the number of recognised elements corresponding to C (heat, air, rarefied wind) and these go to the limbs.

Now if this fourth component is self-moving, why is the mind not constantly stimulated in turn stimulating the body? Indeed according to the Atomists all atoms are constantly in motion so how is the apparent intermittency of vital movement to be accounted for? This isn't made clear. Presumably it is a question of degree of agitation of the atoms. The various sensory stimuli, represented by the impact on the animal body of moving atoms of matter in the outside world, increase the mobility initially and predominantly in the atoms of the fourth component and this mechanical agitation, if of sufficient amplitude, sets the mind in motion and in turn the limbs, *via* the intermediary mobiles discussed. In fact one can consider the Epicureans as viewing all matter as self-moving and therefore equated on our scheme. Having adopted this view however they then had to impose a scale of mobility in order to account for the apparent intermittence of animal movement.

One last point is of interest, the origin of the various mobiles described. Epicurus almost certainly regards air as being drawn into the heart from the outside, that is, it is the ordinary air of the atmosphere. Heat and the rarefied wind, the analogues of Aristotle's pneuma + innate heat, are acquired at birth from the animal's parents as presumably this most vital and essential fourth element.

Notes

1 Lucretius (1966) *De Rerum Natura*, 2, 55, W.H.D. Rouse (transl.), Cambridge Mass., Harvard University Press
2 Ibid., 3, 133
3 Ibid., 3, 106–114
4 Ibid., 3, 121–129
5 Ibid., 3, 145–146
6 Ibid., 3, 147
7 Ibid., 3, 153

8   Ibid., 3, 154–158
9   Ibid., 3, 180
10 Ibid., 3, 185
11 Ibid., 3, 235
12 Ibid., 3, 240
13 Ibid., 3, 242

* See Biographical Index

4

Stoic ideas

Zeno gives this definition of nature: nature (he says) is a craftsmanlike fire, proceeding methodically to the work of generation.[7]

Cicero

We have considered the Epicurean view of movement and seen how rigidly mechanistic it was in terms of atoms moving in the void. Contemporary with this philosophical outlook was that of the Stoics, the two Greek schools coming into being in the early 3rd century BC and growing in strength to become the dominant philosophical schools in the Roman world, well into the 2nd century AD. It was the Stoic view of the universe however, which seemed to find the Roman temperament more fertile for its reception and development and the derivative elements of Stoicism, moral rectitude, self-denial etc, are what we tend to associate with the Roman character in its noblest guise.

It is with the essential conceptual background of Stoicism however, that we are concerned as a basis for the physical interpretation of motion in general and animal movement in particular. By adopting an atomic hypothesis and endowing all atoms with motion (either primarily in the case of the fourth element or secondarily as a result of collisions, in the case of others) the Epicureans simply avoid the need to deal with the origin of movement. Their mechanistic explanation of movement is therefore relatively easy to analyse in terms of the scheme we have adopted. The Stoic view is less easy to analyse since it involves considering how movement is caused and the Stoic attempt to relate this to physical events is not always consistent or clearly expressed.

The essential difference between the two philosophies stemmed from two basically different concepts of the arrangement of matter in the cosmos and the forces affecting this. The Stoics denied the existence of void and in the tradition of Plato and Aristotle viewed the world as a continuum of matter. Everything in existence, capable of being acted upon and changed or capable of bringing about change was material and only from four different types of material at that – earth, water, air and fire. Starting from this concept of a world filled entirely by their four elements, the Stoics had to account for the motion of these elements if any of the changes we see occurring in life were to be explicable.

In other words they had the same problem as Empedocles but they did not have 'love' and 'strife' as two extra elements endowed with the ability to cause movement in them or their co-elements. The role of motor had therefore to be given to one, or more, of these four, or to an outside power (equivalent to Aristotle's unmoved mover), or to both. The Stoic solution to this problem was a grand compromise and as a compromise showed contradictions which caused difficulties for their commentators and provoked criticism from their contemporaries.[1]

A useful description of the Stoic philosophy of nature is that given by Cicero*, through the lips of Balbus in his treatise, *De Natura Deorum et Academica*. Lucilius Balbus, an imaginary character who is defending the Stoic view against protagonists of opposing philosophical schools, develops his argument in Book II. The basis of his philosophy, which he is at great pains to establish in his opening remarks, is the belief in the existence of a divine power, and the first (and most reasonable) evidence he puts forward for this belief is the regular motions of the heavenly bodies. Referring to these he says:

> ... *what can be so obvious and so manifest as that there must exist some power possessing transcendent intelligence by whom these things are ruled? Were it not so, how comes it that the words of Ennius carry conviction to all readers "Behold this dazzling vault of heaven, which all mankind as Jove invoke", and not only as Jove but as sovereign of the world, ruling all things with his nod and as Ennius likewise says – "father of gods and men", a deity omnipresent and omnipotent?*[2]

Reference to Jove, "ruling all things with his nod" is certainly reminiscent of the God of Xenophanes, the Creator of Plato, and the non-moving mover of Aristotle, in his relation to the heavenly bodies regarded as second order deities. One might then tentatively identify Jove with A. This view is given support by the further statement that the heavenly bodies are controlled by an intelligent force:

> *Far more therefore, with the vast movements and phases of the heavenly bodies, ... is he (man) compelled to infer that these mighty world-motions are regulated by some Mind.*[3]

This would seem to identify Mind with Jove = divinity, an abstract, all powerful originator of movement, setting the heavenly bodies in perpetual self movement in a way completely analogous to the schemes of Plato and Aristotle. We should expect the heavenly bodies, therefore, to be composed of a material capable of self-movement and identifiable with B on our adopted scheme.

Leaving aside for the moment the obvious difficulty already apparent, that is, how Jove exists as a divine power in the completely material continuum of the Stoics, the next point of interest concerns the nature of the substance of the stars and planets and its relationship to the movement of earthly bodies, particularly that of animals. Now, Lucilius is quite clear in his identification of this with pure fire or heat, so as in previous concepts this element retains its role as self-moving matter. It is the presence of fire which causes movement = life in organic beings. If then fire, by its capacity for self movement causes motion in inanimate objects and vital movements in living animals, the Stoic had to consider all matter, that is, the whole universe, as living, in as much as heat is universally distributed, or else consider all movement including that of living animals as the result of physical changes brought about by heat. The Stoic adopted the former view and saw the whole world as animated and divine by virtue of the presence of heat, the degree of life or movement depending firstly on the quantity of heat a body contains and secondly on its dilution by the three other elements.

The importance of this dilution of fire is made very clear by Lucilius who refers to the three possible ways in which it can occur in the world. As an example of fire diluted by earth he refers to the fire produced by rubbing stones, fire he saw as released by this manoeuvre from its hiding place inside the stone-matter. Similarly, the warmth of hot springs results from the fire contained in water. Even air, which is cold contains some heat or fire (c.f. Epicurean view of heat containing air, in this book, Chap. 3, Ref. 13):

> Indeed the air itself, though by nature the coldest of the elements, is by no means entirely devoid of heat; indeed it contains even a considerable admixture of heat . . .[4]

Having dealt with the three elements, earth, water and air and their contained heat, Lucilius then refers to the latter itself:

> There remains the fourth element; this is itself by nature glowing hot throughout and also imparts the warmth of health and life to all other substances.[5]

And later we are told:

> Moreover that glowing heat of the world is far purer and more brilliant and far more mobile, and therefore more stimulating to the senses, than this warmth of ours by which the things that we know are preserved and vitalised. As therefore man and the animals are possessed by this warmth and owe to this their motion and sensation, . . . considering that it is possessed by an intense heat that is stainless, free and pure, and also penetrating and mobile in the extreme; especially as this intense world-heat does not derive its motion from the operation of some other force from outside, but is self-moved and spontaneous in its activity; for how can there be anything more powerful than the world, to impart motion and activity to the warmth by which the world is held together?[6]

The above quotation contains many points of interest. Firstly, it reasserts the role of fire as an all-permeating element which is self-moving and life giving. The apparently double nature of heat suggested by reference to "this warmth of ours" as well as this "glowing heat" has already been explained. There is only one element, fire. In its pure unadulterated form it is the glowing heat of which the stars and planets are composed; on earth by nature of its dilution it becomes "this warmth of ours".

Secondly we are told that this highly mobile and penetrating heat does not derive its motion from an outside force, for nothing can be more powerful than the world. This may be interpreted in two different ways: either the reference to an outside power refers to an earthly substance giving it a push or, and I think this more likely, it refers to any abstract prime mover. In other words A + B are merged together in the Stoic analysis of motion and Jove is identified absolutely with B, the stars, the planets and the glowing heat. Interpreted in this way, Jove was omnipresent and omnipotent quite literally, since the mind of Jove or the world was quite simply one of the elements, fire. Hence the presence of divinity or an animation in all things, views the world as a rational, sentient being and retains an all powerful God or prime-mover in a purely material universe. The inevitable reductions of Stoicism, that is, the identification of divinity with self-moving matter (A with B) and the dual role of fire both as matter and a force capable of moving matter is, not unnaturally, sometimes obscured in Stoic writings and indeed was not always accepted or understood by many adherents of a continuum theory of the universe. Hence the difficulty of analysing what different writers mean by divinity, soul, nature or divine fire. Many including Galen, whose work we shall be considering, write as though nature or soul is a force anterior to fire, that is, identifiable with A and in this respect are not truly Stoic:

> . . . on the other hand, Nature is not posterior to the corpuscles, but is a long way prior to them and older than they; and therefore in their view it is Nature which puts together the bodies both of plants and animals; and this she does by virtue of certain faculties which she possesses . . .[8]

What is certain is that fire = self moving matter = B. The role of fire in the Stoic analysis of motion has been discussed so far without reference to the 'pneuma' a term which is constantly encountered in Stoic writings. Referring to the Stoic view of the continuum, Sambursky says that whereas the continuum of Aristotle was passive:

> . . . the Stoics transformed it into an active quality and made it the governing principle in all the physical phenomena of the cosmos.[9]

He continues:

> The active substance in the Cosmos which binds it firmly together into a single dynamic whole is "pneuma" the Greek word for "spirit" or "breath".[9]

The particular part of the continuum which was transformed into this governing principle was composed of the elements fire and air. We have seen already how one of the elements, fire, differed from the other three in that it was divine, self-moving and thereby the cause of movement. The secondary role, assigned to air, was apparently that of a binding agent:

> Those who have most expounded the concept of the binding force, like the Stoics, distinguish this binding force from what is bound together by it. The substance of the pneuma is the binding agent, while the material substance is what is bound together by it. They therefore say that air and fire bind together, whereas earth and water are bound together.[10]

Two elements fire and air therefore had a dual role to play in natural events, being both matter and architect – a difficult concept for commentators. The clue to the understanding of how "air and fire bind together" lies in the Stoic view of air, as cold and non-mobile – the direct antithesis of fire. This idea, a development of the concept of opposing qualities expounded by Pythagoras, is in direct contradistinction to the views of Epicureans or indeed Plato or Aristotle who saw air as a rare, highly mobile form of matter most easily set in motion by the appropriate motor. There are therefore, most important differences between the pneuma of Aristotle and that of the Stoics.

Apart from the Aristotelian need to differentiate between Quintessence and pneuma – a differentiation unnecessary for the Stoics – there is the fundamental difference in the view of the nature and rôle of air. The significance of air is that it is partly opposite in nature to fire – pervasive but cold and that it acts as a damper on the mobility of fire. Indeed, air, fire and water all act in this antagonistic way, but air, by nature of its rarity and powers of penetration as well as its maximum 'coldness' is the true and most efficient damper. We have then the concept of a divine, infinitely mobile element, fire, constantly counterbalanced in its activity on earth by the other elements but *par excellence* by air. Air therefore, by virtue of its non-motility, tends to contain, limit or bind matter, while heat tends to expand and activate and the two forces are in constant opposition, the activity or quality of any material object (shape, size, colour) depending on the resultant of these two forces.

This fundamental difference in the view Stoics took of air was not easily recognised by contemporary critics. The quotation above alludes to both air and fire as binding agents, and Lucilius refers to fire as the element "by which the world is held together,"[6] although this is in the sense of "life giving" rather than limiting. The difficulty over the nature of air is expressed by Plutarch*, in his analysis of the contradictions existing in the Stoic philosophy. Not only does he have difficulty seeing how an element can also be a force – that is, how fire and air can act on earth and water and also be acted upon, but also how air can be light and tend upwards like fire, but also be cold and dark and oppose fire in its action. The Stoics by retaining the pervasiveness of air while substituting non-mobility for mobility produced a concept capable of explaining motion, and its absence. The rôle of air as a non-mobile is also obscured by its association with breath and life, so that it tended to become identified with vital movements. Logically this is in fact the reverse of the Stoic view; air was merely the diluent and antagonist necessary in animals by virtue of its ability to oppose or damp the intense mobility of fire, the true mobile. With these points in mind, the Stoic concept of animal movement becomes logical. The tension of the pneuma (pneumatic tonus) or resultant of the opposing activities of the two architectural elements, air and fire, is the basis for the balance of nature so fundamental to the Galenic view of physiological function, the physical concept behind the teleological explanation of the natural faculties which he offers. For while Galen regarded Nature as "prior to the corpuscles", the sublime artist who did all for the best, his reason for regarding Nature as inherently incapable of bringing about what was not for the best, was based on the sub-conscious association of Nature's activity with the balanced activities of fire and air, heat and cold. The mutual antagonism of these factors in the living body is the concept behind his view of physiological activities: the ebb and flow of blood, the attractive and excretory function of the kidney, the retentive and expulsive activity of the uterus and so on. Only when this balance is upset does malfunction occur.

Galen's writings are our most useful guide to the Stoic interpretations of movement in animals, and certainly the most comprehensive. While he was not strictly a disciple of the School, his explanations of physiological activity in animals and man and the concept of disease processes which he developed from this starting point are based essentially on the ideas we have been discussing. Among his many writings are two major works devoted to physiology and functional anatomy. *The Natural Faculties* and *The Use of Parts* may be taken as expositions of this view as a general theory and the smaller treatise *On the Motion of Muscles* as its application to the specific subject of muscle function.

It is important to recognise that Galen was above all an anatomist. His approach to problems of human function was firstly to discover as much as possible about the structure of the human body, by direct study where possible, by comparative study of animals where not, and then to look for a philosophical explanation which could be adapted to the disposition and character of the structures as he saw them. He was not primarily a philosopher and shows a great reluctance to become embroiled in philosophical arguments concerning the nature of the soul, etc:

> ... and yet it is impossible to avoid altogether saying something about the substance of the soul if one is explaining the structure of the body that contains it, but though this is impossible, we can nevertheless turn back quietly when it is unnecessary to linger.[11]

His opening remarks in Book I of *The Natural Faculties* appear to shatter the unitarian Stoic philosophy by his differentiation between 'soul' and 'nature':

> Since feeling and voluntary motion are peculiar to animals, whilst growth and nutrition are common to plants as well, we may look on the former as effects of the soul and the latter as effects of the nature.[12]

However, he adds:

> And if there be anyone who allows a share in soul to plants as well, and separates the two kinds of soul, naming the kind in question vegetative and the other sensory, this person is not saying anything else, although his language is somewhat unusual.[12]

In other words, nature or soul is responsible for animal and plant activity. There is no attempt to define or describe the difference between animal and vegetative soul in terms of their substance, and while frequent reference to Zeus throughout his writings make us aware of Galen's belief in divinity, the role this played in relation to nature is never discussed. Galen doesn't attempt to distinguish between divinity, soul and nature. We can only assume that he left the problem in abeyance or else postulated their identity, in accordance with Stoic theory. However, this is not really material to the development of his theme. He simply starts from a more anterior point, as it were, and discusses the way in which nature works. His book is to be concerned with the origin of the effects of nature:

> Thus we shall enquire, . . . from what faculties these effects themselves, as well as any other effects of nature which there may be, take their origin.[13]

Galen then proceeds to say that animal functions are concerned with motion or change of various kinds, and that such motion is brought about by these faculties:

And activity *is the name I give to the active change or* motion, *and the* cause *of this I call a* faculty. *Thus, when food turns into blood, the motion of the food is passive, and that of the vein active. Similarly, when the limbs have their position altered, it is the muscle which produces, and the bones which undergo the motion. In these cases I call the motion of the vein and of the muscle an* activity . . .[13]

So, the veins, and the muscles, as all living tissues, are endowed with a faculty which can be described as the ability to cause motion in contiguous parts and thereby bring about the dynamic changes of living organisms. Galen then tells us how this motion is brought about:

It appears to me, then, that the vein, as well as each of the other parts, functions in such and such a way according to the manner in which the four qualities *are mixed. There are, however, a considerable number of not undistinguished men . . . who refer action to the Warm and the Cold, and who, subordinate to these, as passive, the Dry and the Moist; . . .*[14]

Galen then refers to the Aristotelian view of all four qualities as responsible for change and chooses to adopt it in preference to the view of Warm and Cold as exclusively active. It will be noted that Galen is referring to four qualities or differences recognisable by sense perception, whereas Zeno, the founder of the Stoic school, attributed motor power primarily to the material element, fire, which was antagonised by three other elements. Galen notes this difference and characteristically avoids getting involved in a discussion of the problem:

As to whether we are to suppose that the substances *as well as their* qualities *undergo this intimate mingling, as Zeno of Citium afterwards declared, I do not think it necessary to go further into this question in the present treatise.*[13]

The fact that Galen is aware that he has shelved the fundamental question of the prime origin of all movement is apparent from his reference in Book I, Chapter IV:

The so-called blood making *faculty in the veins, then, as well as all the other faculties, fall within the category of relative concepts; . . . and so long as we are ignorant of the true essence of the cause which is operating, we call it a* faculty.[15]

So, motion is concerned with the various faculties with which the body is endowed, and these faculties operate through the warm, cold, dry and moist qualities or elements. Without ever suggesting directly that fire, or the warm, the 'innate heat' of animals, is a self-mobile, acting mechanically as envisaged by the Stoics, Galen indicates that this is probably the view he would give if questioned specifically. The fact that he involves all four qualities or elements with motion is no more than an acceptance of the Stoic view that fire is antagonised by all three other elements to a degree and his stress on the activity of an animal being dependent on the harmony or balance of these elements is an extension of this view. He certainly thinks that the predominant balance at work in the production of a physiological activity is that between warm and cold or fire and air:

*Of course, if anyone were to maintain that in the case of animals and plants the Warm
and Cold are* more *active, the Dry and Moist less so, he might perhaps have even
Hippocrates on his side.*[14]

Furthermore, Galen's view of cardio-respiratory function depends on this
basis. Bearing in mind the essentially non-mobile nature of air = the Cold,
the description given in *The Use of Parts*[16] must be interpreted not as a series
of elaborations of the air by the innate heat of the body, but rather the
reverse, the modifications made by air (and to a lesser degree of the other
elements) on the infinitely hot, infinitely mobile, innate heat:

The outer air drawn in by the rough arteries [trachea and bronchial tubes] *receives
its first elaboration in the flesh of the lungs, its second thereafter in the heart and arteries particularly those of the retiform plexus and a final one in the ventricles of the
encephalon, where its transformation into psychic pneuma is complete. This is not
the proper time to explain the usefulness of this psychic pneuma or to tell how it is
that we who confess that we are still completely ignorant of the nature of the soul
(psyche), nevertheless venture to call this pneuma, psychic.*[16]

The elaboration, or interplay between the innate heat and air produces substances with distinct qualities, particularly as regards rarity and mobility. The
final reaction taking place in the brain and producing psychic pneuma, which
is the rarest and most mobile derivative, must be considered as having the
greatest quantity of fire substance in proportion to air substance, a reasonable
view as air could be considered as dissipated in its journey through the body
to the brain (and require renewal by breathing). Looked at from our point of
view pneuma is the substance nearest to pure fire existing in the animal body
and this is the substance necessary for muscular movement, the 'animal
spirits'. These spirits have to pass along the cavity of the nerves to any muscle
involved in activity, so presumably their material presence is necessary in the
muscle before contraction takes place. This process is not action at a distance,
nor is it abstract or vital in concept. If the 'animal spirits' or modified innate
heat is required in the muscle, surely the deduction must be that its action is
mechanistic – that it in fact acts to cause movement because it is mobile itself,
and by contact causes the muscle to move? Presumably the 'animal spirits'
are the matter of motion B, and their presence sets muscle tissue in action.

This brings us to the really fundamental problems of animal movement,
the difference between voluntary and involuntary contraction, the question
of the difference in the physical state existing when contraction is excited
and when it is not. The question of voluntary movement was presumably
answered by the presence or absence of 'animal spirits', directed to the
muscles by some unexplained activity of the brain:

*Thus in the nerves, some great power resides flowing to them from the great source
ARCHE . . . The nerves, being analogous to conduits, carry power to the muscles
from some fount in the brain.*[17]

Why, how or when this occurs is not discussed. All we can surmise is that
for some unknown reason, 'animal spirits' pass into the muscles, and agitate
the fibres mechanically during the course of the contraction. But what was

envisaged as occurring when the contraction ceased? Since the activity of innate heat is divine, perpetual and not dependent on an outside force, why should the contraction end, the movement cease?

There are three possible ways in which this might have been envisaged: 1. The spirits returned to the brain along the sensory or motor nerves at the end of a movement; 2. They passed into the blood, or 3. They were antagonised by the action of the earth, water and air in the muscles. Whichever was taken as the explanation, no reference is made to it by Galen.

He refers to the difference between voluntary and involuntary motion, with reference to the heart:

> The motion of the heart, being compounded of the double and complex perpetual motion of diastole and systole, does not require voluntary impulse for its initiation. The motions of the muscles [that is, voluntary] are not the same and would not arise without voluntary impulse.[18]

But what is the difference if the motions of the heart are due to innate heat and voluntary movement depends on the presence of 'animal spirits' which we have seen are also essentially innate heat? The difference cannot be one of immediate mechanism but only of control.

Nature, by virtue of the balanced antagonism of heat and air, maintains involuntary movement at a mechanical level: it must therefore be assumed that the spirits were withdrawn from the muscle at the end of the voluntary movement (that is, 1 or 2 above), presumably to be redirected elsewhere (other muscles) as required. This view would allow for the maintenance of a constant level of innate heat in a body from birth to death, which is consistent with Stoic belief.

In his excellent treatise on the surgical anatomy of muscles[17] Galen discusses the various types of movement any muscle can undergo and differentiates carefully between the shortening that takes place when a muscle is cut across and the contraction which takes place in response to the arrival of 'animal spirits'. The muscle has therefore "shortening apparent in its substance" as well as the ability to shorten in response to the brain's command. He says therefore:

> . . . it is necessary to find the difference between the motion of the substance of the muscles and the power making use of it.[19]

To what then does Galen attribute this intrinsic ability of the muscle to contract in the absence of 'animal spirits'? And what is the complete explanation of the process? What is responsible for the retraction of the cut ends of a muscle belly? Since this retraction occurs in a denervated muscle, it is independent of 'animal spirits' coming from the brain. But movement is the prerogative of heat – in this case 'innate heat' – so logically the muscle must have a basic store of 'innate heat' so processed as to bring about this intrinsic contraction. If we accept this as the concept, we can envisage a comprehensive scheme whereby all muscles, voluntary and involuntary have a store of 'innate heat' or 'animal spirits', adequate to bring about retraction or the involuntary, contraction of the heart, gut etc. The addition of 'animal spirits' modifies this by literally increasing the quantity of mobile matter for as long as the brain or will demands. In this way, for example, both types of breathing, voluntary and involuntary, can be explained at muscle level in quantitative terms. In the case of movements of voluntary muscles for example, those involved in flexion and extension of the forearm, a similar situation exists, for the store of spirits results in the natural tonus of the muscles and to this is added the spirits arriving from the brain and being essential for complete flexion or extension:

> From these phenomena, obviously, it is to be learned that the body of the muscle would never arrive by itself at exact and complete flexion if not urged by the power from the brain.[19]

All this may seem to be somewhat conjectural, but the idea of a store of 'animal spirits' in any muscle needing a boost or activation in the form of added spirits sent *via* the nerves from the brain seems a likely answer to the problem, and certainly fulfils the requisites of the scheme Galen had in mind.

Notes

1   Bétoland V. (1870) *Oeuvres Completès de Plutarque*, 43, Tom. 4, Paris, Libraire Hachette et Cie, p. 457
2   Cicero (1994) *De Natura Deorum*, II ii 4, H. Rackham (transl.), Cambridge, Mass., Harvard University Press, Loeb Classical Library
3   Ibid., II v 15
4   Ibid., II x 26
5   Ibid., II x 27
6   Ibid., II xi 30–31
7   Ibid., II xxii 57
8   Galen (1952) *The Natural Faculties*, I xii 28, London, William Heinemann Ltd
9   Sambursky S. (1963) *The Physical World of Greeks*, London, Routledge and Kegan Paul, p. 132
10 Ibid., p. 135.
11 Galen, *The Use of Parts*, p. 418
12 Loc. cit., Note 8, I I
13 Ibid., I II
14 Ibid., I III
15 Ibid., I IV
16 Loc. cit., Note 11, p. 347
17 Galen (1968) *On the Motion of Muscles*, Bk I, Chap. I, C.M. Goss (transl.), *American Journal of Anatomy*, Vol. 123
18 Ibid., Bk I, Chap. III
19 Ibid., Bk I, Chap. VIII

* See Biographical Index

5

The Neoplatonists

Scientifically, they incorporated elements of every doctrine with the exception of Epicureanism; going back with studious interest to the Presocratics many fragments of whom the latest Neoplatonist commentators rescued just as they were on the point of being lost. On the subjective side, they carried thought to the highest point reached in antiquity.[16]

Thomas Whittaker

In previous chapters, we have seen how the materialistic interpretation of nature and motion adopted by the Presocratic philosophers became modified in two main directions to produce the Stoic and Epicurean theories of matter. Despite the fundamental differences in these two philosophies, they evidenced their common ancestry by their retention of the need for a materialistic explanation of the universe and of motion. We have noted how the problem arose with Empedocles and his elements, love and strife, how Aristotle remarked on the problem of whether they were forces acting on elements or elements being acted upon or both. In the case of the Stoics the problem was still there for air and fire which were envisaged as both force acting and at the same time, element acted upon – a paradox attacked by Plutarch among others. The identity of motion with a material was always present and in the case of animal movement we have seen how this material came to be represented by the 'animal spirits', the essential component of which was the 'innate heat' of the individual animal. We have also seen how this 'innate heat' was considered as a part of the 'innate heat' of the cosmos, materially identical with the heat of the sun and stars, a portion of which entered the animal body at birth. It is in this identity that the Macro-Micro cosmic philosophy had at its roots. The unitarian views of the cosmos as an organic being was certainly the general expression of this outlook but the essential feature was the absolute identity of the material of motion in the individual animal body with that of the stars and planets which had been endowed with this faculty for eternal self-movement by some external force such as Plato's 'creative demiurge' or Aristotle's 'prime mover'. Herein lies as a natural sequel the rationale for astrology as a genuine philosophical study. It was based on a concept resulting from rational deductions in no way dependent on magic, myth or mysticism.

The quotation at the top of this chapter refers to the direction in which Neoplatonic philosophers developed the beliefs of earlier thinkers. The striving after an abstract concept of 'being' reached its ultimate development in their hands. The 'abstraction' of motion by Stoics and Epicureans remained at the stage of a material with spirit-like properties of lightness and rarity – as near to a lack of material character as they could get, having as they did a thoroughly materialistic outlook. What the Neoplatonists did, in theory anyway, was to carry this trend towards abstraction to its ultimate limits, abandoning the material basis of all modes of being. This involved a dematerialisation, not only of motion – a development we might consider reasonable – but the denial of the material reality of matter itself. Now such a development presents obvious difficulties for us in our search for a concept of the material of motion in animal bodies! If there is no material basis to matter or motion, we might expect this phase of thought to present us with an isolated development which does not fit into the general trend of historical events as we have seen them so far. This however is not the case for two main reasons. In the first place, any absolutely abstract concept of nature is extremely difficult to describe and precludes any progressive thinking about why or how things happen, for, in essence, nothing is happening – that is, not in the sense we know it. Secondly, the Neoplatonists were the inheritors of all that had gone before, all the previous notions of earlier Greeks as to the nature of matter and motion and despite avowals of a non-materialistic philosophy we find materialistic and mechanical ideas woven through the fabric of their concepts. These mechanical ideas are important to us, since they provide the link which carries forward earlier ideas and provides the material for medieval theories.

The Neoplatonic philosophy is probably most comprehensively expressed in the writing of Plotinus*, who is generally regarded as the founder of the school. His works were produced as lecture notes written specifically for the many students whom he taught in Rome. These notes, were collected by his pupil Porphyry and arranged in a series of six volumes, *The Enneads*, each of these containing a number of chapters dealing with topics he had argued out with his students.

The Cosmogony of Plotinus depended on the belief that the only true reality or form of being is immaterial, yet responsible for all other modes of being, whether material, mental, temporal or eternal. This immaterial concept he named "The One" since he identified it with absolute unity and goodness.

Now, even allowing for any inadequacy of language, the problem of describing such an abstract system is extremely difficult and Plotinus was compelled to use metaphors or models based on human experience in order to convey his ideas. It is in the nature of these metaphors that we see the development of previously held views of matter and motion.

The most constantly recurring metaphor Plotinus uses in his attempt to describe "The One" is that of a point of light radiating its energy in all directions, equally.[1] By means of this radiation or emanation, which is described as occurring through darkness, succeedingly greater spheres of being or hypostases are formed. In this way, the first sphere formed is that of the intellectual soul, the second that of the 'world-soul', the third individual soul, the fourth nature, and finally that of shapeless undefined matter. All of these depend on the activity of "The One," but each is also the result of the activity of its predecessor. Now Plotinus stresses again the inadequacy of his analogy:

there is no spatial or temporal concept in his mind. All these modes of being proceed from one another in a timeless way and all are abstract in origin.

Pursuing this model further, we find that Plotinus tells us that the first derivative of "The One", that is, Intellectual Soul or the World of Intellectual ideas, is the result of the activity of "The One" on darkness. From Unity, two types of 'otherness' are produced, one of which is 'movement', the other, 'the mode of being' identified with intellect:

> For this reason Movement, too, was called Otherness, because Movement and Otherness sprang forth together. The Movement and Otherness which came from the First [The One] are undefined and need the First to define them; and they are defined when they turn to it. But before the turning, matter, too, was undefined and the Other and not yet good, but unilluminated from the First. For if light comes from the First, then that which receives the light, before it receives it has everlastingly no light; but it has light as other than itself, since the light comes to it from something else. And now we have disclosed about the intelligible matter more than the occasion demanded.[2]

Believing that many would disagree with the final sentence of Plotinus let us explore this model further. What he seems to be saying is that "The One" gives rise to a movement which in the first place produces intelligible matter by its action on darkness, but the intelligible matter and movement are not demarcated or given form unless a second movement occurs, ("the turning of movement" [note the presumption of movement as a substance] and 'Intelligent Matter' into "the First.")[3] Now Plotinus considered light as incorporeal and therefore, presumably, without a finite speed of movement so what better analogy could there be for him when he came to describe a situation apparently requiring motion, but to which he had denied motion by virtue of his abstract concept. To gild the lily, or enhance the status of his chosen analogy, he was led to describe this light as "light above light",[4] a device reminiscent of the way in which Aristotle was led to postulate the existence of a Quintessence (a substance denied by Plotinus) or the Stoics a specially rare heavenly fire. This "light" was also unique in its ability to radiate itself without losing any of its power. If we return to the analogy, how can we interpret this "turning back" activity necessary for the delimitation of "Intelligent Matter"? Pursuing the model of a source of light radiating centrifugally to the boundary formed by indeterminate matter, the whole concept becomes logical if all the light radiated is considered as reflected back at the various hypostases, including the limiting boundary, so as never to leave the system. In other words the analogy of a series of progressively larger reflecting yet translucent surfaces centred round a source provides a very good model for someone looking for movement without apparent movement, force without apparent loss of force, matter without matter, if we consider the various hypostases as images produced by reflection. It is only when light is reflected back from a surface of darkness (= unformed matter) that that matter gains delineation:

> And the depth of each individual thing is matter: so all matter is dark, because the light [in each thing] is the rational forming principle.[5]

and the simple beauty of colour comes about by shape and the mastery of the darkness
in matter by the presence of light which is incorporeal and formative power and form.[3]

Thus by a series of situations in which light enters and is reflected back the various Plotinian hypostases are given shape, size and 'being', although each subsidiary level of being is illusory in as much as it is only a reflection of a reflection of "The One". Thus, the world of intellectual ideas is the result of darkness informed by "The One"; the 'world-soul' in turn by light radiated from the world of intellectual ideas and so on down the scale. Eventually matter as we know it, the bodies of earthly existence, results from the action of Nature on darkness. Here then is a model based on the current knowledge of the laws of reflection, established originally by Euclid*, but investigated, as was the field of optics generally, by Ptolemy more or less contemporaneously with the Neoplatonic school.

It would appear then that light, if only in a metaphorical sense, has taken over the shaping or delimiting function which the pneuma performed for the Stoics. Heat has given way to light. But the general development of thought to date has conceived of the shaping, or form giving, which the shapeless substratum of matter requires, in order to produce discrete bodies, as due to the same entity as that responsible for the motion or activity of these bodies, once formed. Hence we might expect the 'material of motion' to be identified with 'incorporeal light'. What evidence have we then for the view that movement in general and in animals in particular requires the presence of this 'incorporeal light'? Is the reference to the 'animal spirits' conceived as light?

It has been stressed that Plotinus was at pains to make it clear that his models were purely metaphorical so what we are analysing is a model and not what he conceived of as an appropriate explanation. Its interest for us is in the nature of the model and its relationship to our mechanical analysis of motion, in terms of the components A, B and C.

From what has been said already, it will be realised that the Plotinian system represents a return to the pre-Socratic unitarian view which unites the divine cause of all motion, the moving matter and matter moved within one entity. It shows links with the components of the Platonic, Aristotelian and Stoic systems of motion. Thus we find the creative and moral qualities of Plato's 'demiurge' taken over by "The One", while Aristotle's unmoved 'intelligence' has similarities to both "The One", in its role as source of all movement, and to the Plotinian world of 'intellectual ideas' as self-thinking, pure thought. From our point of view it is not profitable to try to analyse the various Plotinian levels of being in terms of unmoved mover and self-moving matter, beyond the recognition of 'incorporeal light' as the concept which was associated with the attributes of motive power and self-mobility, and to recognise that each level of soul down to nature depended for these qualities on the light it contained as a result of emanation, originally from "The One". All we can do is to recognise points at which Plotinus implies inheritance of earlier, mechanistic ideas.[6] Thus, talking of the 'mortal soul', he says:

> *This is the starting point of all motion, and becomes the leader and provider of motion to all else: it moves by its own quality and every living material form owes life to this principle, which of itself lives in a life that, being essentially innate, can never fail.[7]*

Clearly, here is a statement of the Presocratic creed of the motive, self-moving soul. We have references to 'soul' moving by its own quality and providing motion to all else. We get a glimpse of the ultimate action of the motive force in terms of Plotinus's description of how nature acts on earthly bodies, 'nature' being the most peripheral or distant emanation of the motive power of "The One", shaping and giving body to the material objects we recognise, both organic and inorganic (in our terms):

> *But what is the difference between the Wisdom thus conducting the universe and the principle known as nature?[8]*

> *This Wisdom is a first (within the All-Soul) while nature is a last . . . Nature thus, does not know, it merely passes,* automatically, *to its next; and this transmission to the corporeal and material constituents its* making power: *it acts as a thing warmed communicating to what lies in next contact to it the principle of which it is the vehicle so as to make that also warm in some less degree . . . Nature being thus a mere communicator . . . For Nature has no perception or consciousness of anything . . . while Nature's function is to engender – of itself through an act derived from the active principle (of the soul).[9]*

Perhaps it is not unjustifiable to see light, in the guise of 'nature' as the analogue of our material of motion B, in the above context. That this is in fact so, is reinforced by Plotinus's reference to fire. Despite his repeated arguments against the materialistic view of the Stoics and his denial of 'pneuma' as a life and movement giving substance he refers on one occasion specifically to fire in this way. Having described light as the form-giving substance, he goes on:

> *This is why fire itself is more beautiful than all other bodies, because it has the rank of form in relation to the other elements; it is above them in place and is the finest and subtlest of all the bodies, being close to the incorporeal.[3]*

A.H. Armstrong refers to this passage and suggests these are surprising statements from Plotinus. He says:

> *This would fit well enough in a Stoic but it is startling to find it in Plotinus even in an early treatise. The whole passage is on the borderline between Neoplatonism and Stoicism. It combines the doctrine that there is no clear frontier between material and spiritual because the principle of reality even in material things is spiritual with the doctrine that there is no clear frontier because "spirit" is only the finest subtlest form of matter.[10]*

In the same chapter Armstrong deals with the way in which Plotinus developed his ideas of the association between incorporeal life as an emanation and the life-force, the association which we too have noted.

Direct references, to the precise cause of movement in the animal body are, not unsurprisingly, difficult to find in Plotinian writings and we have to piece them together in an attempt to understand how he envisaged this as taking place. What we are interested in is the relation of the mortal soul (and through it all higher modes of being (A)), Nature (B) and the animal body (C). Now like all philosophers, Plotinus was concerned with the way in which his abstract concept of soul inter-reacted with matter in the human body and a great part of his writing is concerned with this. He tackles this however, not from the motor side, as we perhaps would have liked, but from the sensory, his main concern being with sensory perception and psychology. This for the most part is where we have to look for clues as to his probable view of motor function.

In his section entitled, *What is the living being?*, he refers to this problem of soul-matter relationships and the difficulties inherent in the interaction of two unlike qualities, a problem he aptly likens to "Talking about a line being mixed with white."[11] If these two qualities are fundamentally different, "How then are affections common to body and soul?"[12] Here we are back with the problem Aristotle presented us with when we tried to analyse his views of the 'appetitive faculty' and its relation to 'pneuma'. Plotinus does not know whether affections are purely the province of the soul or the body:

> Or do they belong to the body too, because blood and bile must boil and the body be in a certain state to stir appetite as in the case of sexual passion . . . But how could the man manage to desire at all if the desiring part was not moved.[12]

He reverts to the basic concept of an unmoved mover acting on a self-mobile, which passes on its motion:

> But perhaps it is better to say in general, as a result of the presence of the powers of the soul [A] it is their possessors which act by them and the powers themselves are unmoved and only impart the power to act to their possessors. But if this is so, when the living being is affected, the cause of its life which gave itself to the compound, can remain unaffected, and the affections and activities belong to the possessor. But if this is so, life will belong altogether, not to the soul, but to the compound. Certainly the life of the compound will not be that of the soul: and the power of sense perception will not perceive, but that which has the power. But if sense perception is a movement through the body which ends in the soul, how will soul not perceive? When the power of sense and perception is present, the compound will perceive whatever it perceives by its presence.[13]

In other words, soul and body must come together in some way to form a compound which acts mechanically. Perception is a movement which must occur at the level of this compound since the 'powers' of perception resides in the soul which is non-mobile:

> Let us say that it is the compound which perceives and that the soul by its presence does not give itself qualified in a particular way either, to the Compound or to the other member of it, but makes, out of the qualified body and a sort of light which it gives of itself, the nature of the living creature, another different thing to which belong sense-perception and all other affections which are ascribed to the living body.[14]

The 'compound' then brings about life (= movement), in sensory terms and by deduction, in motor terms, since Plotinus refers to it as the cause of "activities". The unmoved mover soul (A), radiates light (B) which joins bodily matter (C) and B and C acting together represent the mechanism of perception and movement.

This B + C compound is active in all bodily function, each bodily organ being specially fitted to receive this 'faculty' of the soul:

> *A living body is illuminated by soul: each organ and member participates in soul after some manner peculiar to itself; the organ is adapted to a certain function, and this fitness is the* Vehicle *of the soul faculty under which the function is performed.*[15]

Plotinus is virtually identifying 'faculty' with an agent which brings about activity in an organ through its presence there. He continues in this vein:

> *The vehicles of touch are mainly centred in the nerves – which moreover are vehicles of the faculty by which the movements of the living being are affected – in them the soul-faculty concerned makes itself present; the nerves start from the brain. The brain therefore has been considered as the centre and seat of the principle which determines feeling and impulse and the entire act of the organism as a living thing; where the instruments are found to be linked, where the operating faculty is assumed to be situated. But it would be wiser to say only that there is situated the first activity of the operating faculty; the power to be exercised by the operator – in keeping with the particular instrument – must be considered as concentrated at that point at which the instrument is to be first applied; or since the soul's faculty is of universal scope the sounder statement is that the point of origin of the instrument is the point of origin of the act.*[15]

Plotinus's reference to the first activity of the operating faculty is interesting. In a later paragraph he refers to the fact that this faculty is in contact with, and "draws upon" the "Reason Principle" while "downward, it is in contact with an inferior of its own". So, this faculty (B = light = our matter of motion) has to be in contact with the 'store of soul' in the brain and also be concentrated in the instrument of motion.

At the conclusion of the previous chapter we postulated a content of 'animal spirits' in the muscle (at all times) as the cause of the inherent ability of cut muscle to retract while an extra supply of spirits from the brain *via* the nerves was necessary for the bringing about of movement. This situation would also account for the intermittancy of animal movement in a muscle at all times containing some matter of motion. If we consider the development of the dual view of heat, pneuma and now light as both a shaping medium as well as a medium causing movement the need is obvious for every body with shape, that is, every "formed piece of matter" on earth to have a certain content of this matter of motion. That is a muscle must have a store of heat, pneuma or light in its resting state. If now, we wish to explain its movement, we have to bring an added quantity of this material of motion to it, *via* the nerves from the brain. This may well be what Plotinus is referring to when he talks of the first activity of the operating faculty. Muscles have their store of light or they would have no form; in order to move, light must be supplied *via* the nerves from the brain where the universal soul comes into contact with the body compound, B + C.

Notes

1   Plotinus, *Enneads*, V, 1.6‡
2   Ibid., II, 4.5
3   Ibid., I.6
4   Ibid., V 3.12
5   Ibid., II 4
6   Armstrong, Chap. I†
7   Loc. cit., Note 1, IV 9.14
8   Ibid., IV 4.13
9   Ibid., IV 13
10 Loc. cit., Note 6, p. 55†
11 Loc. cit., Note 1, I.4
12 Ibid., I.5
13 Ibid., I. 1.6
14 Ibid., I.7
15 Ibid., IV 3.23
16 Whittaker T. (1928) *The Neoplatonists*, 2nd edn, Cambridge, Cambridge University Press

* See Biographical Index
† This is a manuscript reference, but the source has not been traced. Ed.
‡ This is almost certainly the Loeb Classics edition edited by A.H. Armstrong. Ed.

6

The Middle Ages and 17th century

(A note abstracted from the 1975 PhD thesis on some of the changes during this era)

The complete materialism of the early Greeks led to the view that any body capable of self-movement had this power as a result of its content of a unique, universally distributed self-moving matter.[1] This matter later became identified as the 'breath of life' or pneuma. Aristotle's concept of a universal, non-moving 'prime-mover' led to the adoption of the fundamental idea that the prime-mover (A) activates the self-moving matter (B) which by direct contact activates 'ordinary' matter, incapable of moving itself (C).[2] This model survived the Middle Ages although its mechanical basis tended to become obscured by the medieval development of the Doctrine of Forms. In terms of muscle activation, the medieval philosophers interpreted our model as follows:

A: God, or Man's will *via* God
B: The subtle spirits conveyed along nerves = the 'animal spirits'
C: The formal cause that makes a muscle 'muscle-like' or capable of responding to B.[3-5]

The 17th century development of the microscope together with progress in experimental chemistry, led to a search for a more useful interpretation of C. The classical Greek elements, earth, air, fire and water became replaced by new elemental concepts, mercury, sulphur and salt and these came to be conceived of as particles obeying the laws of Newton*. The model for the 17th century, as applied to muscular motion, was therefore essentially the same as that proposed by the Greeks, but the chemical notion of the element sulphur as composed of subtle particles, capable of a coarse vibration when set in motion by the subtler particles of the aether, led to the sophistication of the original idea of a C as being composed of only one type of matter. The model now had the following components:

A: The will
B: The 'animal spirits' = aether (in the nerve)
C: The sulphureous or sulphur type particle (in the muscle)
D: The muscle particle proper

Various authors adopted this model, which is particularly associated with theories of philosophers such as Thomas Willis*, and John Mayow*, which are developed in the following two chapters of this book. Willis considered that an elastic particle in the nerves interacted in an explosive manner with a sulphureous or nitrous particle brought to the muscle in the blood, the reaction resulting in a ballooning up of the muscle (that is, an increase in volume).[6] Mayow disagreed with Willis as regards the increase in volume but he also viewed muscle activation as the result of the interaction of 'nitro-aerial particles' brought to the muscle in the nerve and 'saline-sulphureous particles' brought by the blood.[7] The assumption that a muscle increases in volume during activity originated in Alexandria, Erasistratus* believing that:

> . . . muscle becomes filled with pneuma and increases in thickness while decreasing in length.[8]

17th century vesicular theories such as that of René Descartes*, retained the Greek concept and considered the distension as a general ballooning up of the whole supposed 'cavity' of the muscle[9] but later theories attempted to explain it as a summation of the inflation of a number of 'vesicles' or 'cells' of which they supposed the individual muscle fibres to be composed. This development arose as a result of the need to explain the obvious lack of any significant increase in the overall dimension of an active muscle.

Notes

1 Kirk G.S. and Raven J.E. (1964) *The Presocratic Philosophers*, Cambridge, Cambridge University Press. See Chaps I, II, III, V and VI

2 Aristotle (1963) *The Physics*, Vol. 2, P.H. Wicksteed and F.M. Cornford (transl.), London, William Heinemann (Loeb Classical Library), pp 335–339

3 Michaud Quantin P. (1966) *La Psychologie de l'Activité chez Albert le Grand*, Paris, Librarie Philosophique J. Vrin. See also Magnus Saint Albertus*

4 Crombie A.C. (1953) *Robert Grosseteste and the origins of experimental Science, 1100–1700*, Oxford, Clarendon Press. See also Robert Grosseteste*

5 Sharpe D.E. (1930) *Franciscan Philosophy at Oxford in the 13th Century*, London, Oxford University Press

6 Willis T. (1684) *Dr Willis's Practice of Physik, being the whole works of that renowned and famous physician Containing These eleven Several Treatises*, Vol. V, London, printed for T. Drign, C. Harper and J. Leigh. 'Of muscular motion', pp 34–50, especially p. 42

7 Mayow J. (1957) *Medico-physical Works . . .*, reissue edn published for the Alembic Club, Edinburgh and London, E. and S. Livingstone Ltd, pp 244–255

8 Bastholm E. (1950) *The history of physiology from the natural philosophers to Albrecht von Haller . . .*, Copenhagen, Ejnar Munksgaard, p. 64

9 Descartes R. (1972) *Treatise of Man*, French text with translation and commentary by T.S. Hall, Harvard Monographs in the history of Science, Cambridge, Mass., Harvard University Press, pp 22–29. See also, Fulton J.F. and Wilson L.G. (1966) *Selected Readings in the History of Physiology*, Springfield, IL, Charles C. Thomas, pp 202–204

* See Biographical Index

7

The Anatomist and muscular motion:
Thomas Willis (1621–1675)

The works of Thomas Willis have been selected for discussion because his approach to the problem is above all that of a practical anatomist. The mechanical interpretations of the model we have established are based on his researches, supplemented by the results of other workers. Granted that he based his theories on this model – and we shall see that he did – his work adds a new dimension to that of Descartes in as much as it illustrates the experimentalist's attempt to define the conditions under which any such model functions. Willis has the caution typical of the best 17th century philosophers: he tries to differentiate between what is mere conjecture and what he believes he has demonstrated as fact and he always tries to justify his conjecture on what he considers sound mechanistic principles. Willis was a practical chemist of some experience and this caution is reflected in his adoption of the "new chemical principles". We should therefore expect his interpretation of muscular motion to be based on this background of chemical and anatomical experience. The key to the rationale of his ideas is to be found in the opening discourse in *The Medical Works of Willis* (1659), which he entitles 'Of Fermentation, or the Inorganical Motion of Natural Bodies'. Here, at the very beginning of his treatise, the reader's attention is directed to the process which Willis sees as responsible for all the change we recognise in Natural Bodies and it is due to an "Inorganical Motion". In the opening paragraph of the discourse Willis tells us what this fermentation is. Referring to the fact that the use of the word is rare:

> . . . in the Vulgar Philosophy, where Natural things are unfolded, with the vain figments of Forms and Qualities,[1]

he says its use is quite usual:

> . . . among the more sound (especially of later years) who respect the Matter and Motion chiefly in Bodies . . . Fermentation . . . is well known in making of Bread and in the purgings of new Wine, Beer, and other potable Liquors; thence it is also applyed to the other things, which are wont to swell or grow turgid, after the same manner: that at length it signifies, whatsoever Effervency or Turgency, that is raised up in a Natural Body, by particles of that Body variously agitated.[1]

Willis then proceeds to introduce the idea that fermentation occurs in bodies consisting of heterogeneous particles. It is a widely spread phenomenon of nature, occurring in all sorts of situations, organic and non-organic but it seems to require the presence of "unlike particles of matter":

> Bodies of a divers Consistency and Habitude are apt to a Fermenting, viz. either Thin or Thick Liquid or Solid, Animate or Inanimate, Natural or Artificial; in all which is

found an Heterogeneity of parts or particles, to wit, there are in them some substances
light, and always endeavouring to fly away: and also there are others thick, earthy and
more fix'd, which entangle the subtil Particles, and detain them in their Embraces,
whilst they endeavour to fly away; from the strivings and wrestlings of these two
twins, in one Womb the motion of Fermentation chiefly proceeds; but on the contrary,
what things do not ferment for the most part, consist of like Particles, and are of the
same Figure and Conformation, which indeed consociat[e] among themselves, without
any Tumult or Turgescency . . .[1]

This notion as to the different behaviour of bodies as a result of their content
of homogeneous or heterogeneous particles rested on the practical evidence
that bottling up new wines and beers results in fermentation, heat production and explosive properties while distillation of such wines and beers
followed by bottling up of the separated parts results in no fermentation.

Having described what he envisages as fermentation, Willis proceeds to
describe the nature of the particles which he considers play a part in the
process. It is at this juncture that he describes briefly the various theories of
matter inherited by the 17th century and gives his reasons for adopting the
then new principles of Spirit, Salt, Sulphur, Water and Earth. These principles are not regarded by him as elemental particles but rather as the
various states of matter in which the true, imperceptible elements reveal
themselves in natural phenomena and chemical experiments. Willis, like
Boyle*, does not commit himself to describing the ultimate elements – indeed
how could he? – but he does feel able to describe the properties of certain
types of matter as a result of his chemical work:

I mean by the name of Principles, not simple and wholly uncompounded Entities, but
such kind of Substances only, into which Physical things are resolved, as it were into
parts, lastly sensible. By the intestine motion, and combination of these Bodies are begot,
and increase: by the mutual departure and dissolution of these, one from another, they
are altered and perish. In the meantime, what Particles are gathered together in the
subjects, or depart away from them, will appear under the form of Spirit, Sulphur,
Salt, or of one of the rest.[2]

In his second chapter Willis naturally proceeds to a description of these
principles, "the properties and affections" and the first principles he deals
with are the spirits. Spirits are the most subtle type of matter and his description of their properties fulfils all our criteria for a matter of motion:

Spirits are substances highly subtil and Aethereal Particles of a more Divine Breathing,
which our Parent Nature hath hid in this Sublunary World, as it were the Instruments of
Life and Soul, of Motion and Sense, of everything; whilst they of their own Nature, are
always enlarged, and endeavouring to fly away, lest they should too soon leave their sub-
jects, they are bound sometimes with more thick Particles, that by entering into them,
and by subtilising them, and Variously unfolding them, they dispose the substance to
maturity, as is to be observed in the Vegetation and Fermentation of Bodies; sometimes,
being restrained within some spaces, to wit, the Vessels or Bowel of living Creatures, they
are compelled more often to repeat the same measures of their motions for the performing
the works of Life, Sense and Motion. From the motion of these proceed the animation of
Bodies, the growth of Plants . . . they determinate the Form and Figure of everything . . .[3]

We are next told that:

> *In the Constitution of a living Creature, where there is greater Use of Spirits, for Sense and Motion, a far more plentiful quantity is found.*[3]

These two quotations show that Willis envisaged the 'spirits' as the principle of motion in all senses including that determining "the Form and Figure of everything". Yet, in his definition of fermentation he stresses the necessity for the presence of heterogeneous particles, if this intestine motion is to occur. In other words the subtle particle of the 'spirits' acting alone or as an auto-stimulus is not the situation he visualises as responsible for the motions of nature. Fermentation results from the action of 'spirits' on the second most subtle of spirits, 'sulphur'. It is as though 'sulphur' particles, which when set in motion seem to vibrate with a greater amplitude, are necessary as an added factor. Willis identifies 'sulphur' with what we should term the combustible parts of matter. The flame or fire leaving a burned body is composed of streams of 'sulphur' particles together with 'spirit' particles which were the origin of their motion. In other words, Willis has modified the original concept of a subtle particle of fire which is identified with self-movement so as to conceive two types of particles: The most exquisitely subtle 'spirits' and the next most subtle, 'sulphur' [= fire]:

> *Sulphur is a Principle of a little thicker consistency than Spirit, after that, the most active: for when the Spirits first break forth from the loosened substance of the mixture, presently the Sulphureous Particles endeavour to follow . . . The substance of Sulphur, though less subtle is yet of more fierceness and unruliness than the Spirits are . . .*[4]

The true quality of self-motion however belongs to the spirits:

> *For they abounding in any mixture, never lye idle, and always in motion, bring various alterations to the subject where they dwell . . . But Sulphur, although it abounds, doth not easily evaporate but have need of strong heat, or an actual fire, that may make a way for it.*[5]

This fermentive activity between 'spirits' and 'sulphur' is the basis of animate as well as other movements and Willis discusses this in his chapter entitled 'Of things to be Observed of Fermentation about Animals'. He says that, "It is so certain that the Bodies of Animals, consist of the aforesaid Principles that it wants no proof". Life begins in the embryo with the activity of "Spirit Fermenting in the Heart" and by its activity "makes hollow places for itself"[6] and thus shaping our blood vessels for the nourishment and sustenance of the animal. But this spirit, fermenting in the heart, is not the only ferment in Willis's scheme. The pluralistic concept suggested by the principle of Spirits allows him to postulate different ferments acting in different parts of the body and responsible for bringing about various physiological processes, that is, digestion would be brought about by a different type of spirit matter from that in the heart and so on – or at least Willis does not feel he has reason to suggest they are identical in nature although they have certain apparent properties in common, to wit self-motion and subtlety. However, when he describes the process whereby the 'animal spirits' are produced in the brain by a straining off of coarser less mobile particles, we are dealing again with the Galenic concept. However, Willis postulates a ferment in the brain which acts further on the strained vital spirits (= 'animal spirits') to make them "more fit for the performing of the offices of sense and motion".[7] Willis describes various ferments responsible for various processes in the body and the fact that they are postulated as multiple rather than single is probably only a reflection of his caution as to the essential nature of Spirits. Our problem is to analyse how he visualised muscular motion was brought about by the activity of such spirit and sulphur particles.

Willis's *The second Medical and Physical Discourse of Muscular Motion* (1684)[8] has all the attraction of an exposition by an author who is dealing with a topic in which he is not only interested but experienced. Willis was a professional anatomist, at home with animal and human organs, interested in their structure, skilled in displaying this and trying to relate it to functions. The whole discourse is based on the results of his own researches and we are able to understand the reasons for his views because he describes his experiments and shows us why he was led to such and such an opinion.

Having divided the faculties of the soul into the Sensitive and Motive, Willis says:

> *The motive Faculty of the bodily Soul is wont to be exercised with another kind of Action than the sensitive, viz. with a diverse aspect and tendency of animal Spirits.*[8]

This "diverse aspect and tendency" consists of:

> *an heap of animal spirits being everywhere disposed in the motive parts, sometimes one, sometimes more are raised up by the Soul, which by that means being expanded with a certain force, and as it were exploded, they blow up the containing bodies, and so the same, being increased as to their thickness, and made short as to their length, are made to attract the adjoyning member, and stir up local motion.*[8]

Willis says that in motion, three things ought to be considered:

> *First, the original of the Action . . . which is always in the Brain or Cerebel. Secondly its instinct or transmission of the thing begun to the motive parts, which is performed by the commerce of the Spirits lying within the Nerves. Thirdly, the motive force itself, or exertion of the Spirits implanted in the moving parts, either into a contractive or elastik force.*[8]

Here we have Willis's clear definition of the various parts of our model and again we can see the emphasis on the "exertions of the spirits implanted in the moving parts" as the "motive force itself" stressing the 17th century view of the muscle component as not only of equal but prime importance as the factor responsible for motion. That it is the peripheral end of the model that interests Willis is again made clear when he elaborates the third factor in the above quotation. The part played by the brain and nerves does not seem to present a major problem: what does, is the way in which a muscle carries out its "local motion":

> *As to what belongs to local motion . . . though it may be sufficiently understood, that the beginning of the motion to be performed is designed in the Brain or Cerebel, and*

that its instinct is conveyed wholly by the Nerves; yet by what means the muscles per-
form that work, far exceeding any mechanik virtue or operation, seems most hard to be
made plain.[9]

Muscular motion is seen by Willis as a mechanical problem to be understood as a result of understanding the mechanical function of the parts of the
machine. He dismisses the opinion held by various authors that the mere
presence of the soul is responsible for muscular motion:

. . . for what end are the motive Organs framed with wonderful artifice and manifold
difference, unless that after the manner of Machines, they might perform their oper-
ations by an orderly structure and, as it is were mechanical provision of parts? Truly
it will be no hard thing to apply the exercises of a Muscle and the whole nervous
Function, and to explicate them according to the Rules, Canons and Laws of our
Mechanick.[9]

Willis's first task then is to analyse the parts of his machine, to study their
structure. He therefore proceeds to a lengthy description of the gross anatomy
of muscles quoting the experimental work and theories of Stensen although
he had carried out a considerable number of dissections on muscles from the
leg of an ox. A great deal of this description deals with Stensen's theory
based on geometrical considerations, with which Willis agreed, but which is
not of direct concern to us. The essential points are Willis's recognition of
the muscular fleshy fibre as the true and only contractile matter (which he
acknowledges Stensen was the first to demonstrate) and his descriptions of
the distribution of nerves, tendons, connective tissue and blood vessels. That
only fleshy fibres contract is clearly seen in the automatic contraction and relaxation of the diaphragm of "dissected, living creatures" says Willis.[10]

Observation of diaphragmatic movements in vivisection experiments led
him to note:

Whilst you behold this to be so done, you will easily think, that something, to wit,
spirit or subtil matter doth flow from the Tendons into the flesh or fleshy fibres, which
entring upon them on either side, blows them up . . . then when that matter recedes from
the flesh or fleshy Fibres, into the Tendons, the Fibres being emptied and loosned
from their corrugation or wrinkling, are restored to their former longitude . . .[11]

Still presumably, referring to diaphragmatic contraction and relaxation Willis
now proceeds to demonstrate that the contractile ability resides in an individual muscle fibre:

if that the Membrane of the Muscle being drawn away, you shall separate some fleshy
Fibres from others by cutting the little fibrils, whereby they are joyned and loosen
them quite, you will see them so singular and free, to be wrinkled or drawn together in
every motion, like the others compacted together.[11]

The next stage in Willis's analysis of muscular activity is to separate the
muscle fibre in various ways from its tendon. Separating one end only does
not remove the fibres power of contraction, thus:

. . . these Fibres so loosned and freed, some cut off in one end, and separated from the
Tendon, did yet contract themselves to the motion of the muscle . . .[11]

And furthermore, total separation of the muscle fibres from the tendons still leaves the fibre with the ability to contract:

> *After this I divided with a pair of scissers, a certain fleshy portion of the thinner Muscle, in three or four pieces transverse, the bigness of an inch: which being done, the portions cut off in either end, only entred into, for a short space, some light and inordinate corrugations and presently became immoveable. The other extreme portions of the Muscle so cut, sticking to the Tendons, continued to be much more lively and longer contracted, but irregularly and convulsively, to wit, with a certain intortion of the Fibres.[11]*

These experiments confirm Willis in his view that co-ordinated muscular motion depends on the supply of spirits *via* the tendons acting upon responsive particles resident in the muscle fibre. These internal muscular particles are capable only of producing uncoordinated, transitory movements:

> *Truly in the Fibres so cut off, some small footsteps of contraction did remain for a little while, partly by reason of the Instinct of Motion delivered through the membranaceous fibrils . . . and partly because the animal Spirits, implanted in the fleshy Fibres, now divided from the rest and left without influence, did exert or put forth their utmost contractive endeavours after the usual manner.[11]*

It is due to the "implanted" 'animal spirits' that "footsteps" of activity remain in excised portions of muscle. Similarly, this is the reason for the contractions seen in a heart (or excised portion of it) after removal from the body. Just enough 'animal spirits' are left in the muscle to continue to "exert or put forth their utmost contractive endeavours after the usual manner."[11]

Willis now tackles the problem of the supply of these motive agencies to the muscles and to discuss the nature of the internal, muscular particle stirred up into activity by the implanted 'spirits'. He says there are two sources which require our attention: the blood vessels and the fibrils between the fleshy fibres. He deals with these fibrils first. These he sees as the structure which conveys the 'animal spirits' passing along the nerve, to the fleshy fibres. This in fact is a furtherance of the age-long failure to differentiate between nervous and connective tissue elements in muscle. Willis postulates a connection between the nerves and the tiny interstitial strands or terminal fibres of the tendons running between the fleshy fibres.

> *On every muscle, . . . there is stretched on every side a membranaceous covering; besides, other little Fibres transverse, to wit, membranaceous, are woven between the direct moving, fleshy fibres of every one, which clothe each of them, and keep or fasten them together, yea (as it seems probable) they both communicate to all the fleshy fibres the same instinct of obeying the motion and also carry to the Tendons, the troops of the inflowing Spirits, received from the Nerve.[10]*

The little fibrils thus have a dual purpose: they act mechanically binding individual fleshy fibres so that these act in unison and they distribute nerve spirits to the tendons.

The second distributive agent to be considered is the blood. By means of an injection experiment, Willis demonstrates the vascularity of the flesh and fleshy fibre and fibrils in contrast with the avascularity of the tendons. He says it is clear that blood "doth wash all the fleshy and membranaceous fibres which are interwoven with these", because:

> if the Spirit of Wine, tinctured with Ink, be put into an artery belonging to any Muscle, the vein in the mean time being tyed close, the superficies of all the fleshy fibres and transverse fibrils are dyed with blackness, the Tendons being then scarcely at all changed in their colour; it appears from hence, that the blood doth every where outwardly water all the flesh or fleshy fibres, and only those.[12]

Willis says he is not yet certain whether blood itself enters right into the fleshy fibres or only "a subtle liquor" which is the same as that which drips from fresh muscle. But he is certain that all the fibres:

> . . . fleshy, tendinous and membranaceous, are perpetually and plentifully activated by the implanted and inflowing animal Spirits.[13]

Having demonstrated that the fleshy fibres are endowed with many blood vessels he refers to a famous experiment of Stensen's which showed that this vascularity is essential for muscular contraction. Stensen had tied the descending aorta of a living dog and caused voluntary motion to cease:

> . . . that the continual afflux of the blood is nevertheless necessary, an Experiment cited by the Ingenious Steno [Stensen], and proved of late by others, plainly confirms. He hath observed that in a living Dog, the descending great Artery being tyed without any previous cutting off, the voluntary motion of all the posterior parts have ceased, as often as he tyed the string and as often returned again as he loosened the knot.[13]

It thus seems clear to Willis that something brought by the nerve and something brought by the blood are essential for contraction. He now returns to his mechanical principles and sees how he can relate his anatomical-physiological findings to a mechanical model.

The extraordinary thing about muscular motion is the great increase in motion between source and end point – a consideration we have touched upon. Mechanically the magnification of the original effort must surely have baffled philosophers from earliest times. How can a mere thought bring about the movements of our limbs? Where does the magnification occur? Willis was certainly aware of this difficulty and felt its explanation was the key to the understanding of the greater problem. "Further we notice that the motive force is far greater in the Muscle, or in the end, than in the beginning or middle."[13] Willis considers how this increase can be brought about mechanically and discusses such machines as levers, pulleys and windlasses as a means of so doing. This he feels covers the increase in power dependent on the particular anatomical arrangement of various muscles for example, point of insertion of tendon, length of fibre etc, but another method seems necessary to explain "that the motive power in the muscles doth so exceed the force transmitted from the Brain through the Nerves."[14] This second method of increasing motive power is by the addition of a second force, thus:

> Secondly, there is another way of multiplying the motive force to a great degree, and also at a great distance, which is performed with the addition of new forces or of fresh supplies, to wit, when the elastic Particles, or those making the force, being disposed

and shut up in private places, as it were little Cells, afterwards, as occasion serves, are sent forth by a light contact or blast of a remote Agent, into the liberty of motion . . .[14]

He then cites the various examples of such explosive motion; for example, "Air compacted and shut up," and gunpowder. In other words while you may be able to explain magnification of muscle motive power at the peripheral end in terms of gross anatomy (for example, lever principle):

But truly this doth not hold as to the other moving parts, to wit the Brain and Nerves . . . because it seems impossible, that a contraction so strongly performed by a Muscle, should be begun by the tender and immoveable Brain, and continued through the small and fragil nerves, but that it must necessarily be supposed some motive Particles are hid in the Muscle, which . . . are stirred up according to the Instinct, delivered by the nerves from the Brain; into motion as it were with a certain explosion. But what these Particles may be, by what means they are instigated into motion, and how they induce the contraction of a Muscle, seems most difficult to be unfolded.[14]

Since only the fleshy fibres contract, the 'animal spirits' or elastic particles "are only or chiefly agitated among the fleshy fibres."[15] This would lead one, says Willis, to suspect that there were no 'animal spirits' in the tendons, but this is not so. The first evidence he thinks he has for this belief is the relatively sharper sense of touch in tendons as compared with muscle, any lesion of a tendon bringing on "a very cruel pain" and accompanied by a swelling in the neighbouring fleshy parts. He produces more convincing evidence through his other experimental observations. Watching the contractions and relaxations of a living muscle made him sure that the "Spirits or certain elastik particles did rush into the fleshy fibres from either Tendon . . ."[15] and that "The same particles presently coming back from the flesh into the Tendons, the relaxation of the Muscle happened."[15] He therefore set about backing this hypothesis with experiment:

In a bare or naked Muscle, when I had separated every fleshy fibre or a company of them apart from the rest, in the whole passage by help of a Microscope, I most plainly perceived the Tumor begun at either end of the flesh, to be carried toward the middle, as it were by the Spirits entred here and there at once . . . Further (which I mentioned before) each fibre being tyed about the middle, being as it were as yet free and compacted with the others, was contracted or drawn together but a Ligature being put to both ends, it remained flaggy constantly above or beyond the bound place.[15]

To complete his investigation, Willis then put two ligatures "at equal distances from the middle and ends about the same bundle of fleshy fibres" and found that contraction and swelling occurred and arose "from either fleshy extreme to the places bound, but went no further; the middle part between in the mean time, being unmoved, remained flaccid."[15]

As a result of these experiments, Willis concludes that at each contraction Spirits leap out from the tendons into the fleshy muscle fibres and conversely at each relaxation, they return to the tendon.

It is at this point that Willis draws all the various ideas and information he has gathered together and proposes his theory to explain the whole process of muscle activity. So far we have had no reason to suppose the elastic particles in the muscle are not a type of spirit analogous to the 'animal spirits' and indeed, Descartes considered them identical in his theory. But Willis returns to his basic concept – the activity between heterogeneous particles – as being necessary to provide this increment in motive power. The subtle particle in the muscle cannot be identical with spirit or Willis's requirement of heterogeneity is not fulfilled. He therefore postulates that the muscle particle is sulphureous in nature or possibly nitrous. He will not however "pronounce anything rashly or positively" as to their nature. These particles are brought to the fleshy fibres in the blood: hence the vascular nature of muscle flesh and the cessation of muscular contraction on removing its blood supply. Hence also the avascular nature of tendon which if supplied with blood (and therefore its contained particles) would inevitably be contractile – which it isn't. Willis's complete model is described thus:

> . . . the animal Spirits being brought from the Head by the passage of the Nerves to every Muscle, and (as is very likely) received from the membranaceous fibrils, are carried by their passage into tendinous fibres, and there they are plentifully laid up as in fit Store-houses.; which Spirits . . . expanding themselves, . . . leap into the fleshy fibres; then the force being finished, presently sinking down, they slide back into the Tendons, and so viscissively. But, whilst the same animal Spirits, at the instinct given for the performing motion, do leap out of the tendinous fibres into the flesh, they meet there with active Particles of another nature, supplied from the blood, and presently they grow mutually hot.[16]

The resulting contraction being over, the "sincere or clear spirits" go back into the tendon, "the other particles being left within the flesh."

Willis's theory differs from our simple model in the postulation of heterogeneous rather than homogeneous particles as necessary for the production of activity. This is based on his primary hypothesis of fermentation as the basis of all motion but he does bring a considerable amount of evidence to try and justify it. Firstly, he remarks on the absence of any tumour or contraction in tendons, although, as he believes these contain Spirits. Further wounds in tendons result in tumours and spasm in muscle, that is, "where they [the Spirits] are violently driven among heterogene Particles."[17] Again why so good a vascular supply to muscle if the blood were not bringing an essential element to the fleshy fibre and "Muscles being fused or drenched with more plentiful blood, do perform the strongest endeavours . . ."[17] Certainly also, the replenishment of sufficient particles for repeated activity from the nerves does not seem likely: much more likely these are supplied from the copious vascular bed.

Willis's view that the nerve and muscle particles may be and, as he believes, are different in nature and derived from different sources is of significance for future workers as it opened up new possibilities in the search for the subtle particle in muscle and the belief that it was necessarily blood borne, and directed the search to a material normally present in blood as a promising line of enquiry. It also complicated matters by destroying the view that this particle was inevitably the same as that conveyed by the nerves. There might be two possible particles acting in two different situations or if Willis's hypothesis was false they might be identical. The only definite lead seemed to be that the one in the muscle was brought to it by the blood.

Notes

1   Willis T. (1659) *The Medical works of Willis*. Of the Fermentation or the Inorganical Motion of Natural bodies, I, p. 1
2   Ibid., I, p. 3
3   Ibid., II, p. 3
4   Ibid., II, p. 4
5   Ibid., II, p. 7
6   Ibid., V, p. 13
7   Ibid.,V, p. 15
8   Willis T. (1684) *The second Medical and Physical Discourse of Muscular Motion*, p. 34
9   Ibid., p. 35
10 Ibid., p. 37
11 Ibid., p. 38
12 Ibid., pp 38–39
13 Ibid., p. 39
14 Ibid., p. 40
15 Ibid., p. 41
16 Ibid., p. 42
17 Ibid., p. 43

* See Biographical Index

The biochemist and muscular motion: John Mayow (1641–1679)

When we come to analyse the model adopted by Mayow certain new developments are seen to occur. Mayow's theory of muscular contraction is described in his fourth treatise entitled, *On Muscular Motion and Animal Spirits, incidentally, on the motion of the brain and also on the use of the Spleen and of the Pancreas*,[1] published in 1674.

The physico-chemical principles on which he based his theory are put forward in his first treatise entitled *On Sal Nitrum and Nitro-aerial Spirit*,[1] which was published at the same time.

Mayow opens the first chapter of his first treatise with these words:

That this air surrounding us, which from its tenuity escapes the glance of the eye, and appears as a void to those who survey it, is impregnated with a universal salt of a nitro-saline nature, that is to say, with a vital, igneous, and highly fermentative spirit, will be obvious, I conceive, from what follows.[1]

It is with the nature and movement of this "universal, vital, igneous, and highly fermentive spirit" that Mayow is concerned and he sets out to justify his view of its existence as a component of the air and various bodies. In order to do this he discusses the nature of Nitre – a question which was receiving so much attention from authors at the time that it was as if:

it were ruled by fate that this wonderful salt should make no less noise in philosophy than in war, and fill the universe with its sound.[1]

Following the lead of Boyle*, Mayow considers that Nitre is composed of two salts, separable by distillation; a fiery acid salt which distils off and a fixed alkaline salt which remains behind. Similarly:

. . . if the acid spirit of nitre is poured upon any alkali, or, in place of the alkali, upon purely saline volatile salt, from the mutual strife of these two things coming together and the intense action, sal nitrum is generated, which will readily deflagrate when thrown into the fire. So that nitre would seem to be born fit for fights and hostile encounters, since it derives its origin from the mutual conflict of opposing elements and from enmity itself.[2]

By considering the formation of nitre in the soil, Mayow is led to the conclusion that since it is only in earth "impregnated with air" that nitre is formed naturally, the air must contribute one of its components and naturally it is assumed this must be its "more volatile and subtle part." It is inconceivable to Mayow that air contains common nitre:

> *Consequently, if that nitre were wholly derived from the air, then nitre of the more*
> *fixed sort, that is, common nitre, must reside in the air, but that such should fly about*
> *in the very rare air is not to be supposed.*[3]

So Nitre is derived partly from the earth and partly from the air. Mayow envisages "seeds" of alkaline salts lying buried in the earth which by a fermentive process develop into fixed alkaline salts – just as "metallic seeds" give rise to metals:

> *For certainly none of these salts can proceed from another source than the earth.*
> *Indeed, it is probable that earth, pure and simple, is nothing else than sulphur and*
> *fixed salt united together in the closest bonds . . . that it is only after a long period of*
> *fermentation, set up by the air and the weather, that they reach a state of activity.*[4]

After all says Mayow "if sulphur and fixed salt are melted by a gentle heat, there results from their union a mixture of a dark purple colour, very like a clod of earth."[4]

Mayow now turns his attention to the fiery acid salt, or acid spirit. He says that he initially considered that this nitrous spirit, itself, in a state of the finest sub-division, might be a constituent of the air and that when it met alkaline salts produced nitre. However, he decides against this view, "But when I had seriously considered the matter, the acid spirit of nitre seemed to be too ponderous and fixed to circulate as a whole through the very thin air"[5] and:

> *Besides, the nitro-aerial salt, whatever it may be, becomes food for fires, and also*
> *passes into the blood of animals by means of respiration, as will be shown below. But*
> *the acid spirit of nitre, being humid and extremely corrosive, is fitted rather for ex-*
> *tinguishing flame and the life of animals, than for sustaining them.*[5]

This then obviously leads Mayow to his concept of an active, vital and igneous component in his fiery acid salt, derived from the air. Referring to the experiments carried out by Boyle on the necessity of air for the maintenance of a candle flame and animal life he says that:

> *. . . there can be no doubt whatever that certain aerial particles are quite indispensable*
> *to the production of fire, and, indeed, it is our opinion that these are mainly instru-*
> *mental in the production of fire, and that the shape of the flame is mainly dependent*
> *upon these, thrown into extremely brisk motion . . .*[6]

In other words, nitrous spirit contains these nitro-aerial particles as their active component and nitrous spirit itself is in turn a component of nitre since the latter will deflagrate when mixed with sulphur in a glass which does not contain air, and also under water. For:

> *. . . let gunpowder, very finely ground, be made into a hardish mass with a little*
> *water, and let a small tube, closed at one end, be densely filled with it by forcibly ram-*
> *ming the stuff in with a stick. Next, let that gunpowder be set on fire at the open end*
> *of the tube, and the tube be inverted and plunged into water, and kept there. Then the*
> *gunpowder will deflagrate under water until it is all gone. Moreover, that powder . . .*
> *will burn in a glass containing no air, although other fires are presently extinguished*
> *because the aerial food is withdrawn – a sufficiently clear proof that sal nitrum con-*
> *tains in itself the igneo-aërial particles necessary to the production of flame; so that for*
> *its deflagration there is no need for a supply of igneous particles from the air.*[7]

Mayow now turns his attention to the role of sulphureous particles in combustion. These he considers essential to the production of a conflagration – nitre will only burn when thrown on to sulphureous matter. But the essential particle, he stresses, is the igneo-aerial particle supplied from nitre itself. In the case of the combustion of sulphureous matter in the air, the igneo-aerial particles are supplied by the air. It is due to its contained igneous particles that nitre unlike other bodies can burn independently of an air supply. He disagrees with the view of Willis that nitre contains sulphureous particles. Neither of the constituents of Nitre contains sulphureous matter so how can nitre itself do so?

> But, with all due respect to so eminent a man [Willis], I should have thought that nitre, pure and simple, is in no wise impregnated with sulphureous particles. For neither in the rectified spirit of nitre nor in pure sal alkali is any combustible sulphur to be found.[8]

How sulphureous matter reacts with the igneo-aerial particles is explained by Mayow in his description of the production of nitre in the earth. Mayow recognises five elements, nitro-aerial spirit, sulphur, salt, water and earth. Of these, Mayow sees nitro-aerial spirit and sulphur as the two "active" elements which by their motion fashion the other elements and bring about all the changes to things:[9]

> Nitro-aërial spirit and sulphur are engaged in perpetual hostilities with each other, and indeed from their mutual struggle when they meet and from their diverse state when they succumb by turns all the changes of things seem to arise.[9]

Thus Mayow is led to his description of the formation of nitre in the earth. In characteristically poetical terms, he describes the various interactions of his elements. Briefly, nitro-aerial spirit in the air passes into the earth, where it comes in contact with sulphureous matter which is combined with alkaline salt. The nitro-aerial spirit sets the sulphur in motion thus separating it from the alkaline salt and at the same time producing a considerable amount of heat, due to this fermentive activity. The nitro-aerial spirit then unites with the alkaline salt which, by the motion of the nitro-aerial spirit, has been brought to a liquid state. The heat engendered by the fermentive process is the natural heat of the earth which will bring about the generation of living things and thus initiates their living motion. The interaction of nitro-aerial spirit and sulphur is the basis of all living changes.

Mayow is constantly at pains to stress the prime role of his nitro-aerial particles in the processes in which they are involved. The production of the candle flame, and the fermentive changes we have described are initiated by this aerial particle. He makes very clear what we have deduced about the views of the 17th century on the initiation of motion. He does not adopt what he sees as the modern view of fire as the motion of any matter: he states categorically that it is dependent on a specific subtle particle:

> For I do not think we ought to agree with recent philosophers, who believe that fire can be produced by the subtle particles of any kind of matter if they are thrown into violent agitation. In fact, while the Peripatetics formerly assigned a distinct quality for almost every natural operation and multiplied entia unnecessarily, the Neoterics on the other hand

maintain that all natural effects result from the same matter, its form and its state of motion or of rest alone being changed, and that consequently anything whatever may be obtained from any thing. But in truth this new philosophy seems to depart too far from the doctrine of the ancients, and I have thought it better to take an intermediate path. It would certainly be a reasonable supposition that certain particles of matter which are unlike in no other respect than in the form and extremely solid and compact contexture of their parts, differ so much that by no natural power can they be changed one into another, and that the Elements *consist of primary, and in this way peculiar, particles. Hence, I conceive that fire can be produced only by particles of a certain kind, and this is obvious from the very fact that it cannot be kindled without nitro-aerial particles.*[10]

Similarly, nitro-aerial particles are the particles responsible for the initiation of vital movements. Thus far, Mayow's views seem to be analogous to those of Willis: the nitro-aerial particle seems to take on the role of an aether particle. He also envisages a highly subtle medium which is interspersed with the nitro-aerial particles and exists within the atmosphere and within the pores of bodies. His nitro-aerial particle originates in the sun which is a mass of such particles and is the matter of light. He therefore invokes three particles, the aether, nitro-aerial and sulphureous as interacting motion agents, thus pre-conceiving the basic pattern later hypothesised by Newton. Mayow's aether is subtler than the nitro-aerial particle and anterior to it as a motive agent. It is due to the aether in motion in the pores of bodies that they are elastic while aether in a resting state in bodies produces rigidity. Mayow developed the Greek concept of one matter of motion, the stuff of the heavenly bodies, into three, each of which retains some of the characteristics of its progenitor:

I may note here, by the way, that while I hold that nitro-aerial particles are the animal spirits, I do not wish to be so understood as if I thought nitro-aerial-spirit to be the sensitive soul itself: for we must suppose that the sensitive soul is something quite different from animal spirits, and that it consists of a special subtle and aethereal matter, but that the nitro-aerial particles, i.e., the animal spirits, are its chief instrument. For, indeed, as to the sensitive soul, I can form no other notion about it than that it is some more divine aura, *endowed with sense from the first creation and co-extensive with the whole world, and that a little portion of it, contained in a properly disposed subject, exercises functions of the kind which we observe and admire in the bodies of animals; but that that spiritual material, existing out of the bodies of living things, is not to be supposed either to perceive or to do anything but to lie quite dormant and inert being much as is the case with the sensitive soul when the animal is buried in sleep.*[11]

From our point of view the particle of interest is the nitro-aerial one. No purpose seems to be served in pursuing the role of Mayow's subtle aether since he declines to bring it into his biological theories. It has been mentioned merely to show how the original concept was sophisticated by the 17th century in an attempt to marry it to experimentally observed phenomena. Mayow applies his basic theory of motion to the problem of muscular contraction, setting out his ideas in his fourth treatise. In his opening paragraph he at once puts forward the fundamental and novel basis of his ideas regarding vital motion in general and muscular motion in particular: it is the result of the activity of a particle, that is, the nitro-aerial spirit which is respired by the animal and thus continually supplied from the atmosphere. Leaving aside the notion of an aether which he has referred to as implanted in animals at birth and which we may therefore truly identify with historic ideas of a resident, innate heat, Mayow is transferring importance from this to the air or rather to a constituent of the air which is necessary as the mechanical originator of motion. Air no longer has the role of a mere cooling agent, damping down the over-action of innate heat; it is now seen as the purveyor of an active constituent. This is an important new step which identifies respiration with the supply of what we should term the source of energy for all vital movements. He refers to his treatise *On Respiration* which he had published some years earlier and in which he put forward his ideas:

> That Nitro-aerial Spirit, is, by means of respiration, transmitted into the mass of the blood, and that the fermentation and heating of the blood are produced by it, has been elsewhere shown by us. But I shall now further add concerning the use of that inspired spirit, that it takes the chief part in the origination of animal motions, an opinion which I published now a good while ago, and still firmly hold; not that I have set myself to stick to it, as fixed to a preconceived hypothesis, but because I consider it most agreeable to reason.[12]

The cause of the production of motion of any kind is so obscure, he continues, that it is a problem exercising the minds of contemporary philosophers as much as the ancients. He continues:

> But . . . if there are such various difficulties as to motion in general, how much more obscure is that animal motion, in which we see to our astonishment enormous bodies execute quite stupendous movements of their own accord.[13]

Again we have a reference to the magnitude of animal movements. As with other philosophers, Mayow is aware of the problem of explaining what seems to be a great magnification in motive power between the willing of a movement and the contraction of a muscle.

Mayow begins his analysis of this movement with a discussion of muscular contraction since "No one doubts that the movements of animals are produced by the contraction of the muscles."[13] He says that such contraction is generally assumed to be due to the fact that the fibres are ". . . inflated with some elastic matter, so that while they swell as to breadth they contract as to length".[13] Mayow then gives a brief description of Willis' theory of muscular contraction which he criticises on several grounds.

Firstly, the volume of a muscle does not increase as a result of its activity. He quotes the experimental observation of Lower to this effect.

Secondly, if elastic matter inflates a muscle how is it that a muscle relaxes so quickly? How can such particles escape from the muscle, so quickly? If such an easy escape passage for the particles existed, there would be no reason for them to be trapped in the muscle during its contraction phase. Such particles would "pass through the fibres and not properly inflate them".[14]

Thirdly, Mayow does not envisage 'animal spirits' entering muscle fibres from the tendons and returning without some means of regulation. And fourthly if the spirits entering muscle effervesce with sulphureous particles, why don't they become worn out by this process and its effects? And if they do, how are they replenished?

*Besides as . . . the animal spirits springing forth into the fibres meet there particles of
another kind . . ., and at once, as a whole, mutually effervesce with them, it would
seem that these spirits would either be wholly dissipated, or be changed into something else quite different from what they were before; so that they would become
altogether unfit for again exciting effervescence.*[14]

And fifthly, Mayow considers that it is the fibrils inserted into muscle which
undergo contraction and not the true fleshy fibre – a consideration on which he
bases his theory as to the gross anatomical changes of contraction. The final
point on which Mayow disagrees with Willis is in the interpretation of the
latter's 'ligature experiments'. Mayow considers that the swelling of fleshy
fibres produced in the various modifications of these experiments is the
result of vascular engorgement and is not due to the damming back and retention of 'animal spirits' in their passage from tendon into muscle.

In fact the only point on which he seems to agree with Willis is in his belief that muscular contraction is:

*. . . produced by particles of different kinds mixed with one another in the structure of
the muscle, and mutually effervescing . . .*[15]

He discusses Stensen's geometrically based theory of contraction and agrees
with Willis in his idea that:

*. . . some new matter brought by the channel of the nerves is required for starting the
contraction of the muscle, inasmuch as, if the nerve distributed to a muscle be cut,
the contraction of that muscle becomes impossible.*[16]

Mayow then proceeds to discuss his idea that the actual, gross contraction
of a muscle is due to a corkscrew type of motion in the tiny fibrils of the tendons distributed between the fleshy fibres. The fleshy fibre he considers
purely as a means for transmitting blood to these fibrils. This theory is based
on anatomical and philosophical considerations.

Mayow like Willis, requires two sources of supply as necessary for muscular activity. In the first place, the integrity of the nerve is necessary, bringing 'animal spirits' to the fibrils and in the second place the vascular supply is
necessary. Evidence for the necessity of a vascular supply is seen in the continuous blood flow through the muscles, increased as a result of muscular
activity and the purpose of this is the deposition of particles from the blood
in the muscle fibres. Contraction of muscles squeezes more blood out of
them and allows a fresh supply to rush in. There is thus an automatic regulation of blood flow and thus of the supply of its contained particles. As final
evidence for the essential nature of the vascular supply, Mayow quotes
Stensen's experiment of ligaturing the descending aorta:

*Indeed, I think that the chief use of muscular flesh is that it may separate from the mass
of the blood certain particles necessary for the contraction of the muscles. Indeed, we
may point out that it is the function of all kinds of parenchyma to separate by way of
filtration some particles of a definite kind from the mass of the blood, as is manifest in the
parenchyma of the liver, the kidneys, and others of the kind. It is therefore probable that
the parenchyma of flesh which is associated with every muscle, has been constructed*

in order that by its means particles of a definite kind, necessary for setting up the con-traction of muscles, should be filtered out of the mass of the blood.[17]

The transit of blood through muscles is by way of a network of vessels which link the terminations of the incoming arteries and outgoing veins. The blood is not extravasated, *in toto*, into the muscle flesh but only certain particles are filtered through the walls of this network of fine vessels. Indeed, muscle flesh is conceived of by Mayow as made up of these fine vessels plus some thick sediment filtered through the vessel walls when the passage of the blood is slow. He thus does not accept that there exists any specific muscle flesh. On this basis, he explains the wasting of muscles in fever as due to the carrying away of the sediment by the quicker passage of the blood. Muscles are therefore, essentially, blood vessels and fibrils together with nerves.

Mayow now turns to the problem of the nature of these particles deposited by the blood. These he considers to be saline-sulphureous:

I think, namely, that sulphureous and saline particles brought to the highest volatility in the mass of the blood by its continuous fermentation in the manner elsewhere described, and most intimately joined together, are separated from the blood by the action of the muscular parenchyma and stored up in the motor parts for setting up their contraction.[18]

These sulphureous blood particles are formed from fat and hence the deposit of fat in non-active animals and its utilisation in active animals. In other words, the blood particle has been supplied by the animal's food intake.[18]

The other particle required for muscular contraction is supplied by the nerves in the 'animal spirits': it is the nitro-aerial particle which originates in the sun and passes into the atmosphere whence it is breathed in by the animal. Mayow dismisses the theories which explain the function of respiration as that of cooling the blood or of churning up the thick venous blood which the lungs receive – and thus turning it into arterial spirituous blood. If the lungs of a dog are inflated by a bellows:

. . . but in such a way that, through openings made here and there at their extremities, some of the air may pass out, the loss of which must be supplied by the bellows that the lungs may not collapse[19]

the animal will live although that sort of agitation of the blood cannot take place in fully inflated lungs. Again, if the movement of the lungs altogether ceases, the blood is still transmitted through them to the heart. However if the mouth and nose are closed after breath is taken and drawn into the lungs, death follows although the lungs remain inflated because expiration is prevented. In both cases the blood passes readily through the lungs and the breaking up of the blood in the lungs is also equal since the lungs are in both cases, equally distended. The reason the animal lives in one case and not the other is due to continual access of fresh air in the one and not the other. Mayow continues:

Let us now enquire what the aerial element is which is so necessary to life that we can-not live for even a moment without it. And indeed it is probable that certain particles

of a nitro-saline nature, and these very subtle, agile, and in the highest degree fermen-
tative, are separated from the air by the action of the lungs and conveyed into the mass
of the blood.[20]

The function of this particle cannot be only that of maintaining the blood in a
sufficiently fluid state (by its fermentive action) for circulation, since blood not
fully impregnated with air, "is sent readily enough from the right ventricle."[21]
Why then, does death follow when breathing is arrested? There must be
another more fundamental use for respiration. Mayow thinks this fundamental function is the activation of muscles, paramount among which is the heart:

> *Life, if I am not mistaken, consists in the distribution of the animal spirits, and their*
> *supply is most of all required for the beating of the heart and the flow of blood to the*
> *brain. And it appears that respiration chiefly conduces to the motion of the heart in*
> *the manner to be stated elsewhere. For it is probable that this aerial salt is altogether*
> *necessary for every movement of the muscles; so that without it there could be no*
> *pulsation of the heart.*[22]

Thus Mayow arrives at a comprehensive theory which makes all vital
motion depend on an aerial particle in continuous supply. But the effervescence between this particle and the sulphureous particle of the blood would
not occur if both were normal constituents of the blood. Therefore the nitro-
aerial particle which we have traced into the blood of the lungs to the heart
has to pass through the brain and enter the nerves whence it reaches any
muscle it is to activate. Since inspired nitro-aerial particles do exist in the
blood (on their way to the brain) Mayow must envisage their passage
through the brain as essential to their alteration in some way so as to render
them sufficiently heterogeneous with the sulphureous particles which are
also in the blood – otherwise why does a muscle require a nerve supply?
The blood does in fact contain both particles on Mayow's theory. Whether
he sees the cardiac muscle as unique in that the respired nitro-aerial particles, immediately on reaching the heart, effervesce with sulphureous
particles resident in this muscle while other voluntary muscles require the
spirits to be supplied *via* the brain and nerve is not altogether clear, although
his categorical statement that two particles together in the blood cannot
effervesce suggests that Mayow sees the cardiac nerves as the channel for
supply of 'animal spirits' to the heart – as with all other muscles:

> *For if it be allowed that the sudden contraction of the muscles results from the inter-*
> *mixture of particles of different kinds, mutually moving each other, then it is scarcely*
> *to be supposed that the particles of both kinds, by the effervescence of which the con-*
> *traction of the muscles is caused, proceed from the mass of the blood; for liquids de-*
> *rived from the same source reunite without any effervescence, so that it appears that*
> *something extraneous is required for the production of the motive fermentation.*[22]

Summing up Mayow's theory we see that the aerial particle is identified
with the active agent in the 'animal spirits'; the active particle in the muscle
is identified with something originating in the food and passing in the blood
to that muscle. The concept of an aerial particle as necessary for the mechanism of muscular movement not only makes this biological function the

fundamental vital process but serves to identify it more precisely with the mechanical events occurring outside the animal body and considered by the 17th century as the result of the interaction of particles in the atmosphere. The activation of muscle could be considered as a reaction between particles in motion analogous to a great many other vital and non-vital processes dependent on the same particles and Stensen's concept of the muscle fibre as the contractile unit was correct. Mayow's anatomical ideas as to the nature of muscle flesh and the role of the fibrils as contractile elements were as we know erroneous but this is a side issue which need not concern us.

Mayow's ideas as to an aerial constituent which was necessary to life and his famous experiments, which continued Boyle's investigation of its nature, proved that this constituent occupied a fourteenth part of the air we breathe. In Mayow's view it was this constituent, the nitro-aerial spirit, which was responsible for the gain in weight of antimony when calcined. His ideas however, became overshadowed by a different doctrine which we are going to discuss in relation to muscular motion in a later chapter.

The development during the 17th century of the idea of two heterogeneous particles responsible for muscle activation pointed to the food as a source of the muscular component and the air as that of the nervous. Unless these two particles should in fact be found to be similar there was not any suggestion that the one resident in the muscle was in fact derived from the air. The problem as to the source and nature of the muscle spirits was still wide open.

Notes

1   Mayow J. (1957) *Medico-Physical Works*, Edinburgh, E. and S. Livingstone Ltd, 1, I, p. 1
2   Ibid., 1, I, p. 3
3   Ibid., 1, I, p. 4
4   Ibid., 1, I, p. 6
5   Ibid., 1, II, p. 8
6   Ibid., 1, II, p. 9
7   Ibid., 1, II, pp 9–10
8   Ibid., 1, II, p. 10
9   Ibid., 1, V, p. 35
10 Ibid., 1, III, pp 16–17
11 Ibid., 4, IV, p. 259
12 Ibid., 4, I, p. 229
13 Ibid., 4, I, p. 230
14 Ibid., 4, I, p. 232
15 Ibid., 4, I, p. 233
16 Ibid., 4, I, p. 234
17 Ibid., 4, III, p. 240
18 Ibid., 4, III, p. 242
19 Ibid., 2, p. 204
20 Ibid., 2, p. 205
21 Ibid., 2, p. 207
22 Ibid., 2, p. 208

* See Biographical Index

The philosophical background to the biophysical concept: Newton's model for muscular motion

And now we might add something concerning a certain most subtle spirit which pervades and lies hid in all gross bodies; by the force and action of which spirit the particles of bodies attract one another at near distances, and cohere, if contiguous; and electric bodies operate to greater distances, as well repelling as attracting the neigbouring corpuscles; and light is emitted, reflected, refracted, inflected, and heats bodies; and all sensation is excited, and the members of animal bodies move at the command of the will, namely, by the migrations of the spirit, mutually propagated along the solid filaments of the nerves, from the outward organs of sense to the brain, and from the brain into the muscles. But these are things that cannot be explained in few words, nor are we furnished with that sufficency of experiments which is required to an accurate determination and demonstration of the laws by which this electric and elastic spirit operates.[1]

Isaac Newton

The purpose of this chapter is to consider the philosophical milieu in which Luigi Galvani (1737–1798) conceived and developed his fundamental ideas as to the nature of muscular motion. He forsook the technique of gross anatomy at an early stage, convinced that the contractile power of muscle depended essentially on its intimate composition. He saw his problem, right from the start, as a chemico-physical one and in order to understand the rationale of his approach we must examine the contemporary scientific scene for general chemico-physical explanations of motion and their application to the biological problem of muscular motion.

The immediate source of virtually all such explanations was the work of Sir Isaac Newton. The mathematical description of the forces of attraction and repulsion between bodies put forward in the epoch-making *Principia*[1] of 1687, was almost universally accepted although few were competent to understand the mathematical reasoning expounded in the text. But having accepted the mathematical deductions of the *Principia* the reader was not any nearer to an understanding of events responsible for any particular phenomenon. In fact, the *Principia* offered little (if anything) to the experimental investigator of Nature. Of much greater usefulness was Newton's later work, *Opticks*[2] published in 1704.

Coming as it did at the beginning of the 18th century, this book more than any other single work, provided the ideas on which succeeding generations of scientists based their theories and experiments. This is abundantly clear from a study of the scientific content of the writings of the first half of the 18th century as well as from the almost universal acknowledgement that *Opticks* receives from their authors. Written in simple clear English, its style is in complete contrast to the austere, mathematical, formal Latin text of the *Principia*. This alone assured it a wider audience but the influence it exerted was derived from the fact that it dealt with physical phenomena rather than mathematical abstractions and above all provided a comprehensive theory for the experimental investigation of diverse types of phenomena.[3]

Newton was well aware that the laws of motion he deduced in the *Principia* were "passive" in as much as they merely described the behaviour of particles of matter already in motion. The problem of what set matter in motion remained. It seemed necessary to postulate the presence of "active Principles" which, by virtue of their inherent property of self-movement, could initiate and recruit movement in other bodies, thus compensating for what he saw as the inevitable decrement of total movement in the universe, were this supplied solely from the collisions of particles obeying his laws of motion:

> *Seeing therefore the variety of Motion which we find in the World is always decreasing, there is a necessity of conserving and recruiting it by active Principles, such as are the cause of Gravity, by which Planets and Comets keep their motions in their Orbs, and Bodies acquire great Motion in falling; and the cause of Fermentation, by which the Heart and Blood of Animals are kept in perpetual Motion and Heat; the inward Parts of the Earth are constantly warm'd, and in some places grow very hot; Bodies burn and shine, Mountains take fire, the Caverns of the Earth are blown up, and the Sun continues violently hot and lucid, and warms all things by his Light. For we meet with very little Motion in the World besides what is owing to these active Principles.*[4]

And later, with reference to particles of matter he says:

> *It seems to me farther, that these particles have not only a* Vis inertiae, *accompanied with such Laws of Motion as naturally result from that Force, but also that they are moved by certain active Principles such as is that of Gravity and that which causes Fermentation and the Cohesion of Bodies.*[5]

Although he talks of "active Principles", Newton in fact supposed that there was only one universally distributed "active Principle", a material agent which he called the aether. He postulated that the aether was a fluid medium composed of extremely subtle mutually repulsive particles and, as we have seen, considered the activity of this fluid uniquely responsible for initiation and reinforcing the motion of other types of matter. His first reference to it by name occurs in the 18th Query appended to the later editions of *Opticks*, when he suggests that the heat loss from a thermometer *in vacuo* is as great as that from one in air, since in both cases the heat is conveyed away by the vibrations of the aether. He then proceeds to identify the aether with the medium responsible for reflection and refraction of light:

> *Is not the Heat of the warm Room convey'd through the* vacuum *by the Vibrations of a much subtiler Medium than Air, which after the Air was drawn out remained*

> *in the* Vacuum? *And is not this Medium the same with that Medium by which*
> *Light communicates Heat to Bodies, and is put into Fits of easy Reflexion and easy*
> *Transmission? And do not the Vibrations of this medium in hot Bodies contribute*
> *to the intenseness and duration of their Heat? And do not hot Bodies communicate*
> *their Heat to contiguous cold ones, by the Vibrations of this Medium propagated*
> *from them into the cold ones? And is not this Medium exceedingly more rare and*
> *subtile than the Air, and exceedingly more elastick and active? And doth it not readily*
> *pervade all Bodies? And is it not (by its elastick force) expanded through all the*
> *Heavens.*[6]

In succeeding queries, Newton postulated the activity of the aether as
responsible for phenomena of apparently diverse nature, reinforcing the
conjectures put forward in our earlier quotation.[7] In this way he gave
the 18th century a material agent of motion, of universal application, so that
all situations requiring the initiation or reinforcement of movement, whether
organic or non-organic, could be resolved into one involving the presence
and activity of the aether. The unifying effect of this concept on all branches
of scientific investigation was enormous; the aether became the key to the
problems of philosopher and physician, geographer and geologist, electrician and engineer – and it obeyed the Newtonian laws of motion.

In order to understand the way in which Newton considered that his
aethereal 'active Principle' brought about motion in such a universal fashion
it is necessary to remember that one of the major developments in the 17th
century had been the concept that the 'quality' of heat was merely a manifestation of the motion or vibration of particles of matter. Thus the heat of
any body was seen as depending on the number of corpuscles set in motion
and the rate of their vibration. When this vibration reached a certain critical
level the body burnt either gently with the production of smoke or violently
with the production of flame. Motion of particles was thus identified with
the phenomenon of combustion so that the model for the process of combustion could be applied to all situations where the motion of the parts of the
body was initiated or recruited.

The complete model for combustion – or the setting in motion of matter –
as envisaged by Newton, has to be deduced by reference to the ideas he puts
forward in the various Queries. As an advocate of the Mechanistic Philosophy,
he considered all matter to be particulate and he extended this to include
light "Are not the Rays of Light very small bodies emitted from shining
Substances?"[8] Furthermore, we are told that, in some way, bodies may receive their activity from light:

> *Are not gross Bodies and Light convertible into one another, and may not Bodies*
> *receive much of their Activity from the Particles of Light which enter their*
> *Composition?*[8]

How light activates bodies and how this is related to the activity of the
aether is first hinted at by Newton in one of his earliest Queries, when he
refers to the fact that rays of light are reflected or refracted in the neighbourhood of bodies rather than at their exact surfaces, suggesting that some
agent in the air, around them, is responsible:

Do not the Rays of Light which fall upon Bodies and are reflected or refracted, begin to bend before they arrive at the Bodies; and are they not reflected, refracted, and inflected, by one and the same Principle, acting variously in various Circumstances?[9]

The principle Newton has in mind is the aether "by whose Vibrations, Light communicates Heat to Bodies."[11] Increased vibration of aether particles seems to be the key event necessary in the combustion process and in the case of a body burning as a result of light falling upon it, this is brought about by the interaction of light and aether particles.

Combustion, however, occurs as a result of a great many agents other than light, according to Newton, and he lists these in Query 8. It must be presumed, therefore that these agencies act in a similar way by causing aether particles to increase their vibration which, in turn, increases the vibration of other particles in the body undergoing combustion. Newton, however, makes no reference to the aether in this interesting Query which otherwise goes a long way towards describing his complete model for combustion. He does however, specify another type of matter, as playing an essential rôle; The "sulphureous Bodies" (Query 7). The development of the concept of a sulphureous particle as one of the elemental types, will be discussed later:[12] it is sufficient here to note that this particle was considered to be somewhat larger than the aethereal one yet more subtle than other types of matter. Its essential characteristic was thought to be its ability to undergo a relatively rapid vibration as a result of contact with aethereal particles. This vibration, however, differed from that of the aether in its amplitude. The aether particles were characterised by a very rapid vibration of a small amplitude while the sulphureous particle was set into a violent activity of great amplitude, which in turn affected other particles. This resulted in a generalised motion of parts of any body resulting in sufficient heat production to lead to combustion, and the emission of light particles:

Do not all fix'd Bodies, when heated beyond a certain degree, emit Light and shine; and is not this Emission performed by the vibrating motions of their parts? And do not all Bodies which abound with terrestrial parts, and especially with sulphureous ones, emit light as often as those parts are sufficiently agitated; whether that agitation be made by Heat, or by Friction, or Percussion, or Putrefaction, or by any vital Motion, or any other Cause? As for instance: Sea-water in a raging Storm; Quick-silver agitated in vacuo; the Back of a Cat, or Neck of a Horse, obliquely struck or rubbed in a dark place; Wood, Flesh and Fish while they putrefy; vapours arising from putrefy'd Waters usually called Ignis Fatui; *Stacks of moist Hay or Corn growing hot by fermentation; Glow-worms and the Eyes of some Animals by vital Motions; the vulgar* Phosphorus *agitated by the attrition of any body or by the acid Particles of the Air; Amber and some Diamonds by striking, pressing or rubbing them . . . So also a Globe of Glass of about 8 or 10 Inches in diameter, being put into a Frame where it might be swiftly turn'd round its Axis, will in turning shine where it rubs against the palm of one's Hand apply'd to it: And if at the same time a piece of white Paper or white Cloth, or the end of ones finger be held at the distance of about a quarter of an Inch or half an Inch from that part of the Glass where it is most in motion the electrick Vapour which is excited by the friction of the Glass against the Hand, will by dashing against the white Paper, Cloth or Finger, be put into such an agitation as to emit Light, and make*

the white Paper, Cloth or Finger, appear lucid like a Glow-worm; and in rushing out
of the Glass will sometimes push against the Finger so as to be felt . . .[10]

This rather lengthy quotation has been included for a number of reasons: firstly because it is the most comprehensive statement Newton makes about the events involved in the combustion of matter; secondly because it is a statement of his reduction of a great number of widely diverse phenomena (many of them involving organic processes) to a uniform pattern of events, a reduction which suggests that the understanding of any one situation where combustion occurs will lead to an understanding of any other; and thirdly because by virtue of this reduction we are able to understand the rationale behind the experimental study of combustion during the first half of the 18th century with reference to the specific, physiological process involved in muscular excitation and contraction.

The essential elements in this model are then as follows. A primary and entirely external agent such as heat, friction, percussion, putrefaction, or a 'vital motion' when put in contact with aether particles increases their rate of vibration. These aether particles are both an external and internal agent in that they are universally distributed both in the air and within the interstices of bodies as one of their constituent types of matter. Once their vibration is sufficiently increased, they in turn set the sulphureous particles (which are entirely internal) into their coarse and violent vibration which in turn is communicated to the other, grosser particles of which the body is composed. This motion of particles results in the production of heat and if of sufficient intensity, the expulsion of any particles of light within the body.

Translated to the situation of muscular motion, 'the combustion' which takes place may then be considered as follows: A 'vital motion' (brain power, thought, the willing of an action) causes greater vibration of aether particles which in turn activate 'sulphureous particles' which in turn activate 'muscle particles'. The muscle contracts and theoretically there is a heat production and possibly light production. That this is what Newton had in mind as a model is evident from his own words, particularly in Query 24; so often quoted by 18th century authors:

Is not Animal Motion perform'd by the Vibrations of this Medium, [that is, the
aether] excited in the Brain by the power of the Will, and propagated from thence
through the solid, pellucid and uniform Capillamenta of the Nerves into the Muscles,
for contracting and dilating them? I suppose that the Capillamenta of the Nerves are
each of them solid and uniform, that the vibrating Motion of the Aethereal Medium
may be propagated along them from one end to the other uniformly, and without
interruption: For Obstructions in the Nerves create Palsies . . .[11]

The main site of action of the vibrating aether would seem to be in and around the solid nerves which act as a means of transmission, so that although Newton does not say so, the sulphureous particles which are to receive this transmitted vibration are presumably at the "end of the line", that is, in the muscle where the motor nerve terminates. So logically there have to be two intermediary material agents involved in muscular contraction;

the aether acting in and around the nerve and the sulphureous receptor which is a constituent of muscle.

The problem facing the biologist who adopted this Newtonian model as a basis for the mechanical explanation of muscular motion was, therefore, threefold:

1. The identification of an aether-like particle in nerve,
2. The identification of a sulphureous receptor-particle in muscle,
3. The demonstration of the interaction of these particles as a necessary accompaniment of the physiological process.

This was still the definitive problem which Galvani was to tackle half a century after the publication of *Opticks*, although the theories developed during the intervening years were to influence his ideas as to the possible identity of the motive agents involved in Newton's model.

Notes

1 Newton I. (1687) *Philosophiae Naturalis Principia Mathematica*, London, J. Streater for the Royal Society
2 Newton I. (1704) *Opticks: or A Treatise of the Reflections, Refractions, Inflections and Colours of Light*, London, Printed for S. Smith and B. Walford, printers to the Royal Society
3 Newton I. (1952) *Opticks . . .*, New York, Dover Publications Inc. Based on the 4th edn, 1730. See the preface and dedication
4 Ibid., Query No. 31, p. 399
5 Ibid., Query No. 31, p. 401
6 Ibid., Query No. 18, p. 349
7 Ibid., Query No. 29, p. 370
8 Ibid., Query No. 30, p. 374
9 Ibid., Query No. 4, p. 339
10 Ibid., Query No. 8, p. 340
11 Ibid., Query No. 24, p. 353

* See Biographical Index

10

The adoption and interpretation of Newton's model: aether to electricity

During the 18th century three developments occurred which were of importance in the theoretical approach to the problem of muscular motion: the Newtonian model became established as the basis for its investigation and the aethereal and sulphureous particles became identified in the minds of philosophers with electricity and phlogiston respectively.

The idea of the mechanical interaction of two heterogeneous particles as the necessary event in the activation of muscle evolved during the 17th century but it was believed that the process depended for its effect on its explosive nature. The key assumption was that a muscle increased its volume during activity. The truth of this was questioned towards the end of the 17th and beginning of the 18th century and a growing school of adherents to the 'non-vesicular' as opposed to 'vesicular' theory arose.[1] The critical experiment demonstrating that, in fact, no increase in volume occurs was carried out for the first time by Jan Swammerdam* while he was still a student at Leyden, during the years 1661–1665, although a description of this did not appear in print until it was included in his collected works, published under the title of *Bybel der Natuure* (1737–1738).[2] In one variant of his experiment he placed an isolated skeletal muscle of a frog in a little glass siphon, the upper part of which was elongated into a capillary tube containing water. The nerve of supply to the muscle passed through a small hole in the siphon just below the upper part. Taking pains to cement this hole around the issuing nerve (so as to prevent air leakage) Swammerdam stimulated the latter by squeezing its end with a pair of forceps. When the muscle contracted as a result of this, the level of the drop of water in the capillary tube did not rise but sank a little way, although Swammerdam admitted that this sinking was, "so inconsiderable, that it can scarce be perceived."[3]

In 1677 the English physician Francis Glisson* described an experiment which illustrated the same point *viz* the lack of increase of a muscle's volume during activity. This *in vivo* variant involved the total activity of the muscles in a "strong brawny man's" arm.[4] Glisson demonstrated that when the man contracted all these muscles, not only was there no increase in their total volume as compared with the relaxed state but that a slight diminution occurred. This experiment was performed at the Royal Society by Dr Jonathan Goddard* in 1669.[5] Goddard was a colleague of Glisson's who, according to the noted diarist Aubrey, was a skilful demonstrator and was often called upon to carry out experiments in front of his fellow members.[6] References to the *experimentum crucis* by Browne Langrish in his Croonean lectures published in 1747 suggest that he is ignorant of Swammerdam's experiments published in 1738.[7]

These experimental results demanded a new theory of muscular motion which would explain contraction either without any change or with a slight decrease in volume of the active muscle and the various hypotheses put forward at this time reflect the need to explain this situation. Their authors had in common a reverence for Newton and were more than ready to turn to the ideas put forward in *Opticks* as the source and justification for their own theories.

The problem of applying the Newtonian synthesis to the events taking place in the depth of a contracting muscle was a difficult one but the new generation of Newtonian scientists was supremely confident in the fundamental and comprehensive truth of its ideas. Muscular motion had to be explicable in terms of the laws of attraction and repulsion between ultimate particles of matter, as described by Newton. Now, as we have seen, Newton was at great pains to make it clear that these laws were merely the description of the 'passive' activity of particles of matter, incapable of altering their existing state of rest or motion unless by collision with other particles. Particles of ordinary matter are attracted to one another as the reciprocal of the square of the distance separating them but Newton did not believe that particles of ordinary matter exert any mutual attractive force of their own. Although he was able to describe the motion of bodies, mathematically, as if such intrinsic forces act at a distance, Newton invoked the model of aethereal particles acting as a 'contact agent' in order to explain the physical changes which he could describe in terms of the inverse square law of attraction. The aethereal matter was different from ordinary matter and an 'active principle' in that it could initiate motion due to its own inherent self motion. Newton does not offer any specific explanation as to how contact with mutually repulsive aether particles causes the mutual attraction of ordinary matter, although he hints that there is an attraction between the aether and ordinary matter. He certainly regards the aether as responsible for the cohesion of particles of matter in any body and the agent thereby which gives it definition, dimensions and shape.

In his famous letter to Boyle written in 1678, Newton discusses the rôle of the aether, with especial regard to this cohesive force. In his fifth supposition regarding its behaviour he discusses the case of two bodies approaching one another, the aether in the intervening space becoming thereby rarer, the closer they come together. He says that when this happens, "they [*the bodies*] will begin to have a reluctance from being brought nearer together"[8] this reluctance increases until the intervening aether becomes so rarefied that the excess of external pressure of the aether surrounding the bodies is sufficient to overcome the reluctance which exists as a result of this. In other words, the aether between bodies is acting as an agent of attraction for these bodies, although Newton does not specifically say that an aether particle attracts a particle of ordinary matter and hence the presence of aether particles brings together particles of ordinary matter.

Whatever Newton may have had in mind as the ultimate mechanism involved, the essential factor of which the 18th century was aware was that particles of ordinary matter were mutually attracted and held together in the presence of the aether and that presumably an increase in the amount of aether or in its activity, brought about an increase in this cohesive force. Here was a concept tailor-made for the situation of muscular stimulation and contraction as demonstrated by Glisson's experiment. Whereas the 17th century (and earlier) mechanical theories had depended on the concept of an elastic particle conveyed by the nerve to the muscle, where by its action it increased the mutual repulsion of muscle particles, Newton's suppositions provided the basis for explaining how an analogous elastic particle brought about mutual attraction of muscle particles. By applying the pattern of events at particulate level to what occurs when a single muscle fibre and hence a whole muscle is activated, Newton's successors believed they had the explanation, in general terms, of muscular contraction associated with no increase or with some decrease in total volume.

Reference to some theories of muscular motion put forward during the first half of the 18th century, is interesting as evidence of the different ways in which philosophers tried to adapt the basic Newtonian concept to their problem. One thing they all had in common, was an acceptance of the rôle of the aether as the mobile agent of the nerves. In fact, the Newtonians, of this time, were apparently so carried away with the importance of the aether particle that they seem to have overlooked the rôle of the other mobile agent in Newton's model, for there is a striking absence of interest in the sulphureous particle acting as a mobile intermediary between the aether and the muscle particle proper. During this period none of the theories put forward refer to the rôle of a sulphureous particle in muscle as of importance in the sequence of events leading to muscular contraction.[9] Up until about 1750, aether particles, which were believed to be normally occupying the pores of muscle, were seen as responsible for the cohesion of a muscle's particles during its inactive phase and contraction was viewed merely as the increase in the quantity or activity of aether conveyed by the nerve at certain times.

Reference may be made here to two anatomical points concerning the nerves and muscles. At this time, opinion was divided as to whether the nerves were solid or hollow. The classical view, held since antiquity, was that nerves were hollow tubes along the central canal of which there flowed a fine fluid of subtle spirit, designated the 'animal spirits' which, on reaching the muscle supplied by the nerve, brought about contraction.[10] By the 18th century this view was firmly held by many, the brain being considered to be a gland which secreted the nervous juice.[11]

Newton on the other hand, viewed the nerves as solid cords set in vibratory motion by the aether particles in and around their central connections in the brain and transmitting this vibration to their peripheral endings in muscle.[12] Many philosophers followed him in this view so that both opinions are encountered with about equal frequency in the writings of this time. From our point of view this is not of great significance since the 'animal spirits' became identified with the aether and the method by which the nerve agent reaches the muscle does not materially alter the way in which its action is considered as taking place.

The second anatomical point of interest concerns the muscles. The commonly used term 'fibre' denotes what the writers of this time thought of as the ultimate anatomical unit of which the muscle is composed. Their view of what occurs to a fibre is generally translated to the gross activity of a whole muscle and also is accepted as reflecting the activity of the ultimate particles of ordinary muscle matter, as opposed to other particles present.[13]

In 1694 William Cowper*, the English anatomist, published his book *Myotomia Reformata . . .*[14] and 30 years later a revised edition appeared as a posthumous publication.[15] This later volume became a standard textbook of regional anatomy running to a number of editions and being widely respected. It has an interesting introduction by Dr Henry Pemberton*, whose *A View of Sir Isaac Newton's Philosophy*,[16] published four years later was one of the outstandingly popular introductions to Newtonian science to appear in the 18th century.

In his introduction to this anatomical work, Pemberton investigates the supposition that the muscular fibres are composed of vesicles or cells, the inflation of which is responsible for muscular contraction. Referring to the views of such workers as Borelli*, he has the following to say:

> *Accordingly most of the late writers upon this Subject have supposed these Fibres to be formed into Vesicles or Cells whose inflation or distension by some fluid within them they conclude to be the cause, that contracts these Fibres and the Muscle.*[17]

The opening pages are devoted to geometrical propositions concerning "the size of the cavity of muscular cells" in the relaxed and contracted state and calculations as to how much any single fibre and hence any whole muscle might be expected to enlarge on the basis of a vesicular theory. Reference is made to the works of Nicolaus Stensen and Giovanni Borelli and the latter's ideas rejected since Pemberton feels that he offers no experimental evidence in support of his theories. The microscopic work of Antonj van Leeuwenhoek* and Jean Bernoulli* is considered since both had suggested the existence of anatomical structures responsible for dividing a muscle fibre into small vesicles but since such structures are called into question as a result of Cowper's observations, the evidence for a vesicular theory is found wanting.[18]

Pemberton stresses the fact that no experimental evidence has been produced for any postulated increase in a muscle's volume during activity and that "writers upon the subject" have been forced to accept that there is little if any. He refers to the views of Stensen,[19] who agreed that this is so (as did Borelli)[20] although Borelli was convinced that while the external contour of a muscle is not enlarged during activity,[21] its total bulk of actual muscular tissue is increased by pushing out blood. He was led to this erroneous view as a result of his mistaken conclusion from his studies of the heart. Borelli believed that the external surface of the contracting heart does not decrease during systole although its chambers become closed up.[22] Hence he concluded a similar event takes place in skeletal muscle.[23]

Borelli considered that the ultimate anatomical unit of the muscle, the muscle fibre, as made up of a chain of rhomboid-shaped vesicles the inflation of which results in the shortening of the fibre when a muscle is active.[24]

Jean Bernoulli sought anatomical evidence for the presence of vesicles in a fibre by postulating that the slender filaments (of connective tissue) which bind fibres together, might be twisted spirally around individual fibres thus dividing each one into a number of vesicles.[25]

Leeuwenhoek, as a result of his microscope studies eventually concluded that the ultimate anatomical unit in a muscle is a single hollow tube, the muscle fibre. Earlier studies however had led him to the erroneous view that the fibre is composed of a string of globular vesicles.[26] Referring to the various theories of the 17th century, based on the concept of a fermentive or explosive reaction between two heterogeneous particles, one brought to the muscle by the nerve, the other by the blood,[27] Pemberton describes in some detail that put forward by James Keill* in 1718. Keill was a Newtonian and based his ideas, ". . . on the Principle of Attraction that has been discovered by numerous experiments to belong to the small parts of matter."[28]

His theory supposed that the nerves opened by numerous orifices into each 'cell'. The 'animal spirits' thus brought to the muscle cell were believed to be attracted and accelerated towards the red blood globules which will resist the attraction to a degree, that is, they will not move towards the drops of 'animal spirits' exuded from the nerves, but will exhibit a decrease in the cohesion of their enveloping membrane. This expansion of the membrane of the red globules, was believed to allow the subtle particles (which, Keill postulated, existed inside the globules) under pressure to expand, and this expansion of a fibre was seen as the cause of muscle contraction.[29] Yet this theory is essentially vesicular and Pemberton's discussion and criticism reveal it as such despite the author's acquaintance with Newtonian principles. Pemberton will not admit of any increase in a muscle's volume during activity nor will he countenance the need for two heterogeneous mobile particles. All that is required is the ubiquitous activity of the aether:

> For we need not have recourse to any imaginary Elasticity in a Fluid, flowing in the Fibres if we assume with him (Newton) that the Fluid contained in the Nerves is probably no other than part of that subtle rare and elastic Spirit, he concludes to be diffused through the Universe, as the most likely cause of Reflection, Refraction . . . The same Spirit he supposes to communicate Heat to Bodies and to produce all those appearances in which the small Particles of Matter appear to attract and repel each other.[30]

Pemberton continues by likening the process of muscular motion to combustion:

> Allowing, I say, the Fluid of the Nerves to be a part of this Spirit [i.e. the Aether] the Intumescence of the Juices in the Cells of the Muscle fibres may in some degree be illustrated by a very similar Operation in Nature the forementioned Expansion of Bodies by Heat. For if we ascribe this Expansion to the vibratory motion of the subtle fluid within the Body, there will be nothing required for the present Purpose than to say, that the mind when it wills a part to be moved acts upon this Spirit at the

Extremity to which it is present in the Nerve so as to communicate a proper pulsation and vibratory Motion of the spirit through the whole Nerve composed of so uniform a substance that the excited Pulses may be propagated through it without interruption 'til they arrive at the Cells of the muscular Fibres, where they may cause such an Agitation in this same elastic Spirit within the Juices wherewith the Cells are filled, as may rarefy and dilate those Juices.[31]

Although Pemberton sees the vibratory activity of aether as the common cause of both heat production in bodies and muscular motion, he is concerned that there is no considerable heat produced by an active muscle. This reference to an expected production of heat by an active muscle, illustrates the way in which the model for combustion was being adopted as applicable to the situation of muscular motion. In order to account for this, he supposes that, just as the variations in rate of vibration of the air which are responsible for producing different sounds does not account for the different qualities of musical notes, similarly there may be variations, other than in rate, which occur in the aether responsible for bringing about muscular motion.

However, Pemberton admits that contemporary knowledge does not go very far towards a true understanding of why this aethereal motion causes muscles to contract. Philosophers have been too ready, he says, to deal with such grand principles of nature as to ". . . how a World or an Animal might be formed" although ". . . they have shown themselves not really able to discover the obvious Laws of Motion."[32] He sums up his ideas by saying:

If I am not mistaken, we must have made a much greater Progress in Knowledge of Nature, before any Light can be got in so recluse a Subject with the least Degree of Certainty. While we are wholly strangers to the Principle that causes the parts of matter to adhere together, and how it comes to pass that this principle should operate with so much strength while the Parts of the solid Body are yet kept from the most intimate Contact they are capable of; how a Body should be increased in all its Dimensions by Heat and yet retain in great measure its solidity; how can we know that there is some power in Animals, that can operate upon this Principle, which keeps the parts of their Fibres together and can strengthen the Effects thereof upon proper Occasions, so that the Particles of those Fibres shall be made to approach each other with great Force. And if the cause of Muscular Motion should be so remote as this Principle, which I see no absurdity in supposing, it is impossible for us in the present Infancy of Natural Philosophy to discover anything concerning it.[33]

That Pemberton, a leading Newtonian, should have been asked to write the introduction to Cowper's book is indicative of the direction in which ideas were turned in the search for the understanding of the fundamental evidence responsible for muscular contraction. Ten years later we find a similar reference to Newtonian principles in the first of two works relevant to the subject published by the Irish physician Bryan Robinson*. *A Treatise of the Animal Oeconomy*[34] appeared in Dublin in 1734. Section II deals with muscular motion and the author bases his theories on those in *Opticks*, taking every opportunity to quote Newton's view at length. Adopting the Newtonian concept of the nerve as a solid cord, Robinson adapts the model of combustion to muscular motion thus:

Muscular Motion is performed by the Vibrations of a very Elastic Aether, lodged in the Nerves and Membranes investing the Minute Fibres of the Muscles, excited by Heat, the Power of the Will, Wounds, the Subtile and active Particles of Bodies, and other Causes.[35]

Robinson has extended Newton's group of external agents, capable of setting in motion the combustion process. This has an experimental basis since he demonstrates that not only heat and the power of the will, but also traumatic agents such as wounds, drugs and poisons can bring about muscular contraction.[36] Like many others he justifies his adoption of the aether as a suitable nerve agent in terms of the character of the nerve-stimulus. The rapidity with which this begins, passes along the nerve and subsequently ceases can, he feels, only be explained in terms of a rapidly vibrating particle – and like so many of his contemporaries he makes the analogy of the passage of a sound wave resulting from the vibration of air particles.[37] After some lengthy quotations from *Opticks*, regarding the properties of the aether, Robinson describes how this is involved in bringing about muscular motion:

When by the Power of the Will, a vibrating motion is excited in the Aether in those Ends of the Nerves which terminate in the Brain; that Motion is in an Instant propagated thro' their solid and uniform Capillamenta to the Membranes of the Muscles, and excites a like Motion in the Aether lodged within those Membranes; and a vibrating motion raised in the Aether within the Membranes increases its expansive Force; an Increase in that Force swells the Membranes; a Swelling of the Membranes causes a Contraction of the fleshy Fibres, and Motion in the Part to which the Extremities of Muscles are fastened.[38]

This is not much more than a general statement. There is the suggestion of a compensatory squashing together of muscle tissue proper as the result of the expansive action of the aether within the membranes: if the volume of the whole muscle is not going to increase, Robinson has to reduce the volume occupied by the muscle tissue proper. There is no attempt at any deeper analysis of events.

The opening paragraph of Robinson's second work entitled *A Dissertation on the aether of Sir Isaac Newton*[39] promises further elucidation of his ideas:

From the Account I have given of Muscular Motion in my Animal Oeconomy, it is evident that Motion is caused by the Aether. But it is not so clear from that Account, how a Swelling of the Membranes, causes a Contraction of the fleshy Fibres. This I shall now explain, from some further Experiments made on Animal Fibres.[40]

Robinson starts with the proposition that:

If an animal Fibre, by a Force acting upon it be increased or lessened, either in length or thickness; its Length will be reciprocally proportional to its diameter . . .[41]

He arrived at this proposition as a result of experiments carried out on a single hair (which, like muscle, he considered as an "animal fibre"). He wound an unextended hair in contiguous rings around a cylinder until the rings covered a certain, fixed length (about ¼ inch). He then extended the hair by attaching a weight to it and repeated the experiment, winding the stretched hair around the cylinder until the same length as before was covered. He found that the number of rings was greater when the hair was stretched, the product of the number of rings and the diameter of the hair being a constant, equal to the length of the cylinder covered. It follows that, since the number of rings was a measure of the length of the hair, this length was varying as the reciprocal of the diameter of the hair.

Robinson then removed the extending force and found the hair returned to its original dimensions, decreasing in length and swelling in thickness. This return to its former state occurred, according to Robinson, because ". . . the elastic Force of the Aether lodged within the pores of the hair, is greater when the hair is extended, than when it is in a natural State."[42] This is proved by the fact that, the quantity of matter in the hair remaining constant, the density will increase as its diameter lessens or its length increases. And, continues Robinson, referring to one of his earlier propositions, "an increasing density is associated with an increase of the elastic force of the aether contained within the pores of the hair."[43]

Having used the situation of an extended fibre to the unextended state as his model for showing what he considers to be the effect of an increased elasticity of the aether, Robinson proceeds to demonstrate:

> . . . a Vibrating Motion of the Aether within the Pores of an animal Fibre, raised by Heat or any other Cause, will increase the Diameter and lessen the Length of the Fibre; so shall be as 1/D.[43]

Robinson applied heat to an extended, but not stretched, hair and found that its length was lessened and further that a crooked hair became straight when heated (that is, shorter). From this he deduced that heat, by causing a vibrating motion of the aether within the hair, lessened its length, and therefore necessarily caused a proportional increase in its diameter. On allowing the hair to cool, he observed a reversal in the dimensions, since:

> . . . an Abatement of the vibrating Motion, on which the length of the Fibre increases will give an Opportunity to the Parts of the Fibre to be brought nearer together by their Attraction and so will lessen the Diameter in the same Proportion as the Length is increased . . .[44]

The final step in Robinson's argument is obvious. By translating his conclusions to the case of a single muscle fibre, he is led to the view that muscle contraction results from the same vibration of the aether.

Robinson's ideas are of some interest as an indication of one of the ways in which Newton's concept of the activity of aethereal fluid was adopted as an explanation of muscular motion. Robinson, however, despite his avowed indebtedness to Newton, was not using Newton's concept of an aether causing an increased cohesion of particles of matter, as his statement above shows. For him the activity of the aether must be seen as causing an increased repulsion of the parts of a muscle fibre. In other words, having accepted the fact that the volume of a muscle remains constant, he merely applied the 17th century theory to a non-expandable muscle, producing a vesicular theory *sans vésicule*.

The noted philosopher, John Desaguliers* refers to the problem of muscular motion in his *A Course of Experimental Philosophy*.[45] He criticises Alexander Stuart*, one of the last defenders of a vesicular theory, quoting the Glisson experiment and saying that he finds what Dr Browne Langrish wrote upon the subject the most satisfactory to him.[46]

Browne Langrish, MD, FRS*, was a Hampshire surgeon who produced two treatises concerned with muscular motion. The first, entitled *A New Essay on Muscular Motion, founded on Experiments, Observations and the Newtonian Philosophy*.[47] The second, *On Muscular Motion*, formed the content of the Croonean Lectures, read before the Royal Society in 1747.[48] Presumably the invitation to deliver these lectures can be taken as evidence of the acceptability of the views of the lecturer.

As the title of his first work suggests, Browne Langrish also looks to Newton for the answer to the problem of muscular motion. In the advertisement to this treatise, he says:

> *I have accounted for Muscular Motion after a Manner intirely agreeable (at least I think so) to the Principles of that most illustrious Philosopher Sir ISAAC NEWTON; and in doing of this I have made it appear very probable, if not certain, that every individual Corpuscle of Matter is endued with its determinate Poles, and does attract or repel every other similar corpuscle, which comes within its Sphere of Activity by the same Laws, and after the same Manner that two lodestones influence each other.*[49]

The idea that every corpuscle of ordinary matter is bipolar is the essence of Browne Langrish's theory, which he develops further in his Croonean Lectures. It is his attempt to explain the fundamental problem of how a fluid compound of mutually repulsive particles can bring about an increased cohesion rather than repulsion of particles of ordinary matter. As we have seen, Pemberton had no detailed theory to offer and Robinson did not in fact consider that this was what was happening.

Opening his account, Browne Langrish dismisses the blood as a direct cause of muscular motion, considering it merely as a fluid which warms muscle, making it responsive to the stimulus brought by the nerve in the 'animal spirits' and perhaps by its motion, "encouraging the motion of the animal Spirits through the Nerves".[50] He considered a muscle to be reduced in all its dimensions during activity and hence contain less blood at this time when in a relatively relaxed state. He therefore reasons that:

> *Action and Reaction being always equal, it appears from hence, that the Blood acts as an Antagonist against the contractile Power of the Fibres by extending and distending them, rather than having any Share in their Contraction.*[50]

In fact Browne Langrish sees the distending force of the blood as that which counterbalances the elasticity of muscle, and therefore as a force which acts against the natural tendency of the muscle elements to come together, that is, the retractive power exhibited by a cut muscle. And so by deduction he considers that active muscular contraction is produced by some force (physiologically, the 'animal spirits') increasing this natural tendency. In this respect, he approaches the cause of active contraction in the same way as

Robinson. But he then goes on to consider the nature of elasticity, inherent in muscle and says:

> *Now in order to understand the Nature of this rightly, it will be proper to consider that*
> *there is in all Matter a peculiar Power of Attraction and Repulsion; which Properties*
> *manifestly discover themselves in many things, and according to their particular Dis-*
> *positions they are called by the Names of Magnetism, Electricity, or Gravity.*[51]

Now Newton had hinted that magnetism, electricity and gravity were all manifestations of the activity of the aether but Browne Langrish elaborates this by postulating that the ability of a body to manifest specifically electrical, magnetic or gravitational forces is no more than the result of the size, shape or arrangement of its constituent particles. The agent causing the particles to behave in any of these ways is always the same and is, presumably the aether:

> *. . . 'tis very probable . . . that all the different Degrees of Attraction and Repulsion,*
> *which we now find in several Sorts of Bodies, proceed only from the various Shapes,*
> *associations and Combinations of their constituent Particles; so that it is entirely*
> *owing to such and such particular Structures and Dispositions of the component*
> *Particles, that some Bodies are naturally receptive and retentive of Magnetism, others*
> *of Electricity and others, neither of them, at least not within the Reach of our Senses.*[52]

And:

> *But notwithstanding these seeming Differences in the Tendency of some Bodies to-*
> *wards others, we have many Reasons to believe that the real Cause of Attraction and*
> *Repulsion is the same in all Bodies, and that all these different Phenomena, as well as*
> *the various Degrees of Cohesion, Hardness, Elasticity, etc., arise only from so many*
> *different Degrees of Attraction and Repulsion between component Particles and not*
> *from any material, essential Difference in the Cause.*[53]

What Browne Langrish is suggesting is that any body manifesting magnetic, electrical or elastic properties is in a state of tension as a result of the activity of the aether within its pores. Depending on the 'degree' of this vibration, there will be a disorientation of the constituent particles (of a bar of steel or a muscle for example) so that their normally adjacent and therefore neutralised poles are separated. Whether the 'inherent' polarity of material particles depends ultimately, as Newton postulated, on the presence of a resident minimal quantity of aether, Browne Langrish does not say, although, logically, this is what one would expect. (that is, in a non-magnetised bar of steel, a non-electric body, or a muscle which has been severed from its attachments and is flaccid). What he does believe is that an increase in the quantity or vibration of the aether present in these structures brings about the disorientation of particles responsible for the magnetic, electrical or elastic properties they exhibit in their active state.

In terms of a muscle then, there are three states to be considered. When it is flaccid the activity of the aether in its pores is merely responsible for bringing about the cohesion of the muscle particles giving it the structure and properties of flaccid muscle. These particles, are envisaged as lying in regular order so that their attracting and repelling surfaces are adjacent and therefore not producing a state of tension or elasticity. In the physiological state of tension (but not active contraction) there is an increased activity of this aether; the "reaction" to the distending force of the blood and the stretch produced by the attachment of the muscle to its point of origin and insertion. A further increase in this vibratory activity of the aether or an increase in the quantity present, further increases this elasticity which is manifested as muscular motion or contraction:

> And there is no doubt that if the same Cause which makes all the Fibres of a Muscle elastic, was to be suddenly increased, it would contract the Muscle still shorter, and be the Cause of Muscular Motion as long as such additional attractive Powers continued in the Fibres.[54]

The "additional attractive Powers" brought to the muscle are identified as the 'animal spirits'. Browne Langrish sees the action of the subtle aethereal 'animal spirits' on the muscle fibre as a particular example of the generally stimulating action of other subtle particles on animal fibres, quoting:

> . . . the immediate and wonderful Efficacy that Spirits of Sal Armoniac, Hartshorn or human Skulls have on the Body . . .[55]

The Croonean Lectures of 1747 are essentially a re-presentation of these ideas. The author stresses the error of a vesicular theory, referring to Goddard's experiment and states clearly that he believes muscular attraction results from an increased attraction between muscle particles, proceeding to use the arguments discussed above to explain how he thinks this is brought about.

The importance of these ideas lies in their concept of a state of tension or elasticity akin to electricity or magnetism, existing in a muscle fibre, quite apart from any effect resulting from an agent brought by the nerve. The similarities between the hypothetical aether of Newton and the mysterious electrical fluid so ardently pursued by electricians were at this time becoming increasingly obvious but in the field of nerve-muscle action analogies were nearly always made with reference to the 'animal spirits' conveyed by the nerve. In some respects, the most influential experiments relative to this were those carried out by Stephen Gray* whereby he demonstrated that the electrical virtue could be carried at great speed along various wires of great length.[56]

The similarity between the speed of passage of electricity along these conductors with that of the aethereal fluid along nerves is frequently referred to at this time and the possibility that the 'animal spirits' are electrical in nature was very much in mind.[57] Browne Langrish refers to this in his Croonean Lectures, saying that he has been informed by Mr William Watson*:

> . . . that the swiftness of the electrical Effluvia is prodigious; that one Stroke of his Hand down the Tube, when well electrified, was felt as soon as his Hand could be at the bottom of the Tube, through five Men standing upon electrical Cakes, and communicating with each other by a Cane, Sword or any other Non-electric.[58]

Browne Langrish goes on to make an analogy between this situation and the physiological one of muscular motion. He says:

Hence it follows, that if a Tube could be always excited, and was always applied to the End of a proper Cord or String the electric Matter, which is excited by Friction between the Hand and Tube, would ever be ready to exert its attractive Influence on Leaf-Gold, and such-like Things, when placed within a due Distance of the End of the String; and perhaps this may be very similar to the Motion and action of the Nervous Aether.[59]

In his *Observations on Man . . .*[60] published in 1749, David Hartley* takes up the problem of muscular motion and develops the idea of Browne Langrish further. In Proposition 16, he proposes that, "The Phenomena of muscular Contraction appear to be sufficiently agreeable to the Doctrine of Vibrations."[61] and makes certain suppositions:

First, That Vibrations descend along the motory Nerves, i.e. Nerves which go to the Muscles, in some such manner as Sound runs along the Surfaces of Rivers, or an electrical Virtue along hempen Strings. Secondly, That these Vibrations, when they arrive at the muscular Fibre, are communicated to them, so that the small Particles of these Fibres shall be agitated with like Vibrations. Thirdly, That the Vibrations, thus excited in the Fibres, put into Action an attractive Virtue, perhaps of the electrical Kind, which lies concealed in the Particles of the Fibres or the Blood-globules, or both . . .[61]

Hartley refers to the fact that Dr Pemberton considers the cause of contraction no other than an increase of the common cause of cohesion of muscle fibres and says that this is not contrary to his own views:

Neither is this Conjecture at all repugnant to the Supposition of an electrical Attraction above made, or to the Doctrine of Vibrations; for Electricity may reach to small Distances, without being excited by Friction and flow from the same Principle as the Cohesion of Bodies, as Sir Isaac Newton *has observed. It may therefore be the general Cause of Cohesion, and may be excited in the muscular Fibres in an extraordinary Degree, whenever extraordinary Vibrations are communicated to them. Or, if we suppose the Cause of Cohesion to be something distinct from Electricity, it may however be increased by the Vibrations of the small, cohering Particles.*[62]

Hartley's statement reveals the way in which the invisible and ubiquitous electrical fluid was beginning to take over the rôle of the equally invisible and ubiquitous aether. If the cause of cohesion in bodies were electrical, then the cause of muscular contraction had to be electrical, since in contemporary terms, muscular motion was considered as an exaggerated state of cohesion of the muscle particles. In terms of this model therefore, there had to be a basic store of electrical fluid within any muscle, and in order for it to become activated an added quantity of electrical fluid had to reach it *via* its nerve supply.

The possibility that Newton's hypothetical aether had a real existence as the electrical fluid was of course in the minds of electricians at this time, although, on the whole, before the Franklinian era they were inclined to base their theories on the assumption that electrical phenomena were due to a fluid *sui generis*. Joseph Priestley* refers to this in his discussion of the electrical theories advanced before that of Dr Franklin:

But far the greater number of philosophers suppose, and with the greatest probability that there is a fluid sui generis, *principally concerned in the business of electricity.*

They seem however, though perhaps without reason, entirely to overlook Sir Isaac Newton's aether . . .[63]

Nevertheless, when Benjamin Franklin* put forward his theory of electricity in 1749, it was clearly derived from the Newtonian concept of the aether and in many ways represented the ultimate development of the simple hypothesis. Writing to Peter Collinson* he set out his ideas as to the nature of the 'electrical matter'; the main points of which were:

1. The electrical matter consists of extremely subtle particles
2. These electrical particles permeate the pores of common matter
3. The electrical particles are mutually repulsive
4. The particles of ordinary matter are mutually attractive
5. The electrical particles are attracted by all particles of common matter[64]

By substituting the particle of electrical matter for the aether and the term 'common matter' for 'ordinary matter', Franklin has restated the suppositions Newton expressed in his letter to Boyle making explicit Newton's hint that aethereal (electrical) particles are attracted to particles of ordinary matter. Franklin's theory, which we shall return to later, was readily adopted on both sides of the Atlantic: there was a rationale it seemed for seeking the elusive yet worldly electrical particle where previously its aethereal counterpart had existed. Whether electricians in the mid 18th century thought of electricity as a fluid *sui generis* or not, its genesis was in fact from the aether and for this reason it became a logical contender for the role of mobile in models of muscular contraction.

Notes

1 See Chap. 6 for a brief resumé of the historical background to the model for muscular motion adopted by the mechanistic philosophers of the 17th century
2 Swammerdam J. (1737–1738) *Bybel der Natuure*, Leyden, Isaak Severinus Boudwyn Van der Aa, Pieter Van der Aa. The Latin translation was carried out by Heironymous D. Gaubius and was published as the *Biblia Naturae . . .*, Leyden, Isaacus Severinum Baldvinum Van der Aa, Petrum Van der Aa, 1737–1738, published by H. Boerhaave
3 Swammerdam J. (1758) *The Book of Nature or the History of Insects*, T. Flloyd (transl.), revised and improved by notes from Réaumur and John Hill, London, C.G. Seyffert, Part II, p. 127
4 (i) Glisson F. (1677) *Tractatus de Ventriculo et Intestinis*, London, E. F. for H. Brome, Chap. 8, paras 9–10, pp 166–168
    (ii) Fulton J.F. and Wilson L.G. (1966) *Selected readings in the History of Physiology*, Springfield, Illinois, Charles C. Thomas, pp 218–220, for an English translation
5 Ward C.J. (1967) *Lives of the Professors of Gresham College . . .*, The Sources of Science, No. 71, London, Johnson Reprint Corporation, p. 273, where reference is made to the experiment. Goddard read his 'An experiment to shew whether the muscles of an animal in their action are bigger or less in their total dimensions,' on 10 June 1669. This is referred to in the *Registers of the Royal Society*, Vol. IV, p. 95, read on 16 December 1669
6 See Sir H. Lyons, *The Royal Society, 1660–1940*, Cambridge, Cambridge University Press, 1944, p. 11
7 Langrish B. (1748) 'On Muscular Motion, The Croonean Lectures read before the Royal Society in the year 1747', suppl., *Philosophical Transactions*, Vol. 44, Lecture II, para. LXI, p. 27

8   Trenchard More L. (1962) *Isaac Newton, A Biography*, New York, Dover Publications Inc., pp 211–215. See p. 213

9   See this book, Chap. 11. For example, *The Philosophical Transactions of The Royal Society*, London, *L'Histoire de l'Academie Royale des Sciences*, Paris, contain no reference to the sulphur particle in this rôle during the years 1700–1750

10 Galen (1952) *On the Natural Faculties*, London, William Heinemann Ltd (Loeb Classical Library), p. 153 (II, vi. 80). Here Galen refers to the view of Erasistratus that nerves are hollow and contain the psychic pneuma

11 The concept of a brain as a gland-like structure had been considered since antiquity. See Littré E. (1853) *Oeuvres Completes d'Hippocrates . . .*, J.B. Bailliere et fils, Librarie de l'Academie Imperiale de Medicine, Tom. 8, pp 564–565 where the Hippocratic author of *On Glands* puts forward this view. See also Clarke E. and Bearn J.G., 'The Brain Glands of Malpighi Elucidated by Practical History', *Journal of the History of Medicine*, 1968, Vol. 23, pp 309–330, for a contemporary approach to the problem

12 See this book, Chap. 9

13 See loc. cit., Note 4 (i), pp 138–143, where this concept of the animal fibre as the fundamental unit of the animal body is discussed at length. In general, before the work of Nicolaus Stensen, a muscle was believed to consist of two main structures; the 'fibre' which passed into and was continuous with the fibres of the tendons at each end of the muscle and the flesh or 'caro' which filled up the spaces between them. This idea originated with the Alexandrian Greeks and was adopted by Galen who considered the 'flesh' of muscle is formed of condensed blood. The essential contractile element he believed to be formed by the nerves which on entering the bulk of the muscle, divided into increasingly fine branches and then joined again to leave the muscle as the tendon. The greater bulk of the tendon as compared with the nerve was, he considered, due to the joining of the emerging nerve with various supporting ligaments and bands. He was led to this view as a result of experiments which showed that cutting the nerve supply to any muscle rendered it incapable of contracting. This view was held until Stensen's publication *De Musculis et Glandulis Observationum Specimen* (1664) Amsterdam, P. Werner for P. Le Grand, appeared, although Vesalius noted that the muscle flesh actually became shorter and thicker during activity. Stensen's experiments convinced him that, in fact, it is the fleshy part of a muscle which is active and the tendonous part passive during contraction and his view came to be adopted during the 17th century. Stensen saw muscle as a collection of "muscle fibres", each fibre being in turn composed of a number of minute fibrils arranged longitudinally and bound together by the fibrillae of the muscle membranes. The central part of the fibre constituted the flesh, while at each end the fibre had the structure which passed into tendon. Strictly speaking then the essential contractile unit should have been referred to as the "fibre" but most authors who adopted Stensen's view used the term "muscle fibre" when wishing to convey the idea of the fundamental unit, thus compromising with Glisson's terminology for the fundamental unit in any part of an animal. See also Berg A., 'Die Lehre von der Faser . . .', *Virchow's Archives*, 1942, Vol. 309, pp 333–460

14 Cowper W. (1694) *Myotomia Reformata or a New administration of all in muscles of the humane bodies – to which are subjoin'd a Graphical Description of the Bones; and other anatomical observations*. Illustrated with figures after the life, London, Sam Smith and Ben Walford

15 Cowper W. (1724) *Myotomia Reformata or an Anatomical Treatise on the Muscles of the Human Body, illustrated with figures after Life, to which is prefixed an Introduction concerning Muscular Motion*, Richard Mead (ed.), assisted by Joseph Tanner, James Jurin and Henry Pemberton, London, R. Knaplock, W and J. Innys, J. Jonson

16 Henry Pemberton (1728) *A View of Sir Isaac Newton's Philosophy*, London, Printed by S. Palmer

17 Loc. cit., Note 15, p. xxxiv

18 Ibid., pp lxvi–lxx

19 Stensen N. (1667) *Elementorum myologiae specimen seu musculi descriptio Geometrica*, Florence, Ex tip. sub signo Stellae

20 Borelli G.A. (1680–1681) *De Motu Animalium . . . Opus posthumum*, Carolus Joannes a Jesu (ed.), Rome, Ex tip. Bernabo, Part II, Prop. 14

21 Ibid., Prop. 49

22 Ibid., Prop. 14 and 42

23 Ibid., Prop. 14

24 Ibid., Tabula IX

25 Bernoulli J. (1721) *Dissertatio Inauguralis Physico–Anatomica de Motu Musculorum*, Section II, Venice, tipis penellorum fratrum, pp 3 and 4

26 (i) See Leeuwenhoek A.V. (1720–1721) 'Observations upon the Membranes enclosing Fasiculi of Fibres with which a Muscle is divided' By Mr Leeuwenhoek FRS, Dr Sprengel, FRS (transl.), *Philosophical Transactions*, Vol. 31, No. 367, pp 129–134. See also, A.V.L, 'Observations upon the Vessels in Several Sorts of Wood and upon the Muscular Fibres of different Animals. By the same curious and inquisitive person'. Ibid., pp 134–141, especially, pp 139–140
(ii) A.V.L. (1685) *Anatomica et contemplation nonnullorum naturae invisibilum secretorium comprehensorum epistolis quibusdam scriptis ad illustre inclytae Societatis Regiae Londonensis Collegium; ab Antonio de L*, Leyden, Apud Cornelium Butesteyn, p. 43
(iii) A.V.L. (1719) *Epistolae physiologicae super compluribus naturae arcanis; ubi variorum animalium atque plantarum fabrica . . . novis experimentis illustrantur . . . hactenus numquam editae.* Delft, A. Beman, Epistolae 16 and 33

27 See Chap. 6 of this book

28 Loc. cit., Note 15, p. lxii

29 Keill J. (1718) *Tentamina Medico-Physica, ad quasdam quaestiones quae oeconomiam animalum spectant, accomodata, Quibus accesit Medicina statica Britannica*, London, G. Strahan, W. and J. Innys, pp 134–138

30 Loc. cit., Note 15, p. lxxiii

31 Ibid., p. lxxiv

32 Ibid., p. lxxvi

33 Ibid., p. lxxvii

34 Robinson B. (1734) *A Treatise of the Animal Oeconomy*, Dublin, G. Ewing

35 Ibid., p. 87

36 Ibid., pp 99–100

37 Ibid., p. 93

38 Ibid., p. 97

39 Robinson B. (1747) *A Dissertation on the Aether of Sir Isaac Newton*, London, C. Hirch

40 Ibid., pp 102–103

41 Ibid., p. 103

42 Ibid., p. 105

43 Ibid., p. 106

44 Ibid., p. 109

45 Desaguliers J. (1734) *A Course of Experimental Philosophy*, London, W. Innys

46 Ibid., pp 392–393

47 Langrish B. (1733) *A New Essay on Muscular Motion founded on Experiments Observations and Newtonian Philosophy*, London, Printed for A. Bettlesworth and C. Hitch

48 Loc. cit., Note 7

49 Loc. cit., Note 47, p. 1.

50 Ibid., p. 20

51 Ibid., p. 24

52 Ibid., pp 25–26

53 Ibid., p. 25

54 Ibid., p. 47

55 Ibid., p. 55

56 (i) Gray S. (1733) 'A Letter to Cromwell Mortimer, M.D., Sec. R.S. containing several Experiments concerning Electricity', *Philosophical Transactions*, Vol. 37, pp 18–44
(ii) Gray S. 'A Letter concerning the Electricity of Water to Cromwell Mortimer, M.D., Sec. R.S.' Ibid., pp 285–291

57 For example, see: Hales S. (1964) *Statical Essays: Containing Haemastaticks . . .*, The History of Medicine Series issued under the auspices of the Library of the New York Academy of Medicine, London, Hafner Publishing Company, Vol. II, pp 58–59. [A reprint of the first edition, London, W. Innys, R. Manby and T. Woodward, 1733]

58 Loc. cit., Note 7, p. 31

59 Ibid., pp 31–32

60 Hartley D. (1749) *Observations on Man, his frame, his duty and his expectations*, London, J. Leake and W. Frederick

61 Ibid., p. 88

62 Ibid., p. 89–90

63 Priestley J. (1966) *The History and Present state of Electricity with Original Experiments*, Reprinted from the Third Edition, London, 1775. The Sources of Science No. 18, New York, Johnson Reprint Corporation

64 See *Benjamin Franklin's Experiments: A new edition of Franklin's Experiments and Observations on Electricity*, With a critical and Historical introduction by I. Bernard Cohen (ed.), Cambridge, Massachusetts, Harvard University Press, 1941, pp 213–214

* See Biographical Index

The adoption and interpretation of Newton's model: sulphur to phlogiston to electricity

Newton's concept of an elastic, aethereal particle was readily adopted and developed during the first half of the 18th century as the basis for a physical explanation of muscular motion. What is perhaps surprising, in view of the repeated references authors give to Newton's 'Queries' as the rationale for their theories, is the almost complete disregard these authors show for the sulphureous particle and its possible role as a mobile agent resident in muscles. Although Newton's complete model for combustion has to be deduced from the various ideas he puts forward in different Queries there is little doubt that he is equating this with a general model for the production or increment of total motion in any system of particles, and the 'combustible particle', is therefore an essential and unique element in any such system. This lack of interest in the concept of a second receptor particle in muscle, capable of having its vibration augmented by a primary agent brought to it by way of the nerves, is particularly surprising in view of the historical development of such a concept during the latter part of the 18th century.[1] Theories based on the concept of an aethereal particle abounded between 1700 and 1750 and yet it is difficult to find more than a passing reference, let alone a comprehensive theory, based on the idea of a combustible particle as the mobile agent in muscle – although from the ideas put forward by Newton, a pair of particles were logical contenders for such a rôle.

However, despite its apparent failure to attract the interest of those who were seeking a bio-physical model for muscular motion at this time, the concept of a combustible particle, in the sense Newton envisaged, survived and was developed as the essential feature of the comprehensive theory of combustion which dominated chemical thinking in Europe until well into the seventh decade of the 18th century. The sulphureous particle was the ancestor of the "inflammable principle" of Ernst Stahl*, phlogiston, but it seems that it was only as ideas concerning the properties of phlogiston developed that its possible rôle in the process of muscular motion came up for consideration.

When Johann Becher* published his book, *Actorum laboratorii chymici monacencis, seu physicae subterraneae* in 1667,[2] he stressed his belief that the true elements of bodies can only be determined by chemical analysis. The three substances, salt, sulphur and mercury, which previous generations of chemists had believed to be elemental, he considered to be compounds each containing a truly elemental earth combined with another substance. Thus, 'sulphur' which had previously been associated with the property of combustibility, was considered by Becher to be a compound of an acid salt with an elemental earth to which he gave the name *terra pinguis*. This "true element" was so named by Becher because he considered it as that which was responsible for odour, colour, taste and combustibility – all properties commonly associated with oily substances. He was led to this idea from experiments in which he burned crude sulphur producing spirit of sulphur (= acid salt = sulphuric acid) and, as he thought, *terra pinguis* or the truly inflammable element which passed into the air with the flame.[3] This idea of an element or principle of combustibility existing in a bound state in naturally occurring compounds such as sulphur, was taken up by Becher's fellow-countryman Stahl who re-named it "phlogiston" and developed the concept into his comprehensive chemical theory. Great strength was lent to his ideas as a result of the great variety of inflammable substances from which phlogiston could be produced by the action of one agent, vitriolic acid (H_2SO_4). Indeed, the theory rested on this universal production of phlogiston from all inflammables in this way.

Joseph Black*, writing of Stahl's ideas, says his contribution to chemistry represented the first time that anything like philosophical discussion had been introduced into the subject, and continues:

> But Dr Stahl founded, on the observations which I have now related to you, a body and system of very precise and perspicacious doctrines whose influence connected all the great and important phenomena in chemistry. Observing that the mixture of vitriolic acid with every inflammable substance produces the same sulphur and that the substance was no longer inflammable, he inferred with great propriety that all inflammables imparted one and the same substance to the acid . . . He called it phlogiston . . . The truly essential principle and material of fire I began to call phlogiston [he says], the principle which is ignitable, inflammable and most easily raised to heat. Adding this to any body renders it inflammable and taking it away, renders it non-flammable.[4]

Stahl put forward his theory or rather his development of Becher's ideas in his *Fundamenta Chymiae . . .*[5] in 1723 and soon it became widely accepted in Europe as the chemical explanation of all phenomena involving combustion. However, the exact nature of Stahl's principle posed as perplexing a problem for the chemists as Newton's aether had for the mechanistic philosophers. Just as the latter desired to identify the theoretical aether with a manifest substance having experimentally demonstrable properties so did the chemists for phlogiston. The 'mechanical' philosophers directed their attention to the aethereal particle and came to identify it with electricity: the 'chemical' philosophers directed their attention to the inflammable particle and came to identify it with fire or light or some modification of these. After all, it was obvious that during combustion these substances appeared to be leaving the burning body just as phlogiston was believed to do.

The real crux of the difference of opinion between the mechanical and chemical philosophers stemmed from their different views as to the cause of heat. The former, as has been seen, adopted the Baconian concept of heat as a manifestation of the vibration of parts of a body.[6] They supposed there were two kinds of matter, "gravitational, inert" particles and the subtle, aethereal particles and that the oscillations of the latter (which create heat) brought about the cohesion of the former, which cohesion was exhibited as the elasticity of the body. The chemical philosophers allowed that motion attended the generation of heat but maintained that heat depended on a "simple, primary ingredient present in all natural bodies," the principle of inflammability or phlogiston.[7]

The extremely influential French chemist, Joseph Macquer*, writing in the middle of the century gives the following all-embracing description of this inflammable principle:

> *The Matter of the Sun, or of Light, the Phlogiston, Fire, the Sulphureous Principle, the Inflammable Matter, are all of them names by which the Element of Fire is usually denoted. But it should seem, that an accurate distinction hath not yet been made between the different states in which it exists; that is between the phenomena of Fire actually existing as a principle in the composition of bodies, and those which it exhibits when existing separately in its natural state. In the latter state we may properly give it the names of Fire, Matter of the Sun, of Light and of Heat, and may consider it as a substance composed of infinitely small particles, continually agitated by a most rapid motion, and of consequence, essentially fluid.*[8]

And later Macquer describes this fluid as:

> *. . . so subtile, so active, so difficult to confine, so capable of penetrating into every other substance in nature.*[9]

The exact nature of phlogiston and its relation to light and heat obviously posed a real problem for chemists and this led later to the development of a number of theories,[10] which postulated that phlogiston either was light or a modification of it, within bodies. The details of these need not concern us but the general concept of a subtle, active particle becoming activated in some way so as to allow the emission of heat and light is important because, as Black says of Stahl's theory, its influence ". . . connected all the great and important phenomena in chemistry."[4]

The mechanical philosophers had found in aether a universal agent capable of bringing about motion, but it had the drawback of being theoretical – hence the efforts to identify it with electricity. The chemists, by mid-century, had a universal agent, phlogiston, which although equally theoretical had the advantage of manifesting itself by the production or release of light from bodies in which it was supposedly activated. The fact that it was believed to be light itself or a 'compound of light' made chemists feel that it had a much more valid claim to a real existence than the aethereal fluid of Newton's imagination. Light was a sensible phenomenon while nobody had ever experienced the aether. As a result of this the rôle of the aether began to be questioned and after mid-century we find writers such as Bryan Higgins* denying its responsibility for the effects of attraction and repulsion. In his *Philosophical Essay Concerning Light*,[11] one of the sections is headed as follows: "The Effects called Attraction and Repulsion are not to be ascribed to the Agency of any imagined Ethereal Fluid: Neither is an Ethereal Fluid to be assumed in optical reasoning."[12] Developing his argument, Higgins is led to say that, "as Ether is not the cause of the relations of gross bodies towards each other."[13] he will, "Proceed to show that light itself is a kind *[of phlogiston]* diffused through all known spaces, like the imagined Ether; . . ."[13] In other words, Higgins is suggesting that light fulfils the rôle Newton ascribes to the aether. Macquer referred to phlogiston as a rapidly vibrating small particle.[8] while Higgins considers phlogiston as a "compound of light", the particles of which are mutually repulsive, subtle and rapidly vibrating:

> . . . it moreover appears consistent with the tenour of nature that the parts of Light should repel each other and attract some different kind of matter; and that Light should be condensed and saturated by other matter; and that these should nevertheless form a compound, subtle, elastic, invisible fluid and a tertium quid acting on bodies and acted on by them, in a manner different from that of the actions and passions of Light.[14]

Higgins considered phlogiston as a cause of cohesion in bodies, attracted to other matter and as a result of the mutual repulsion of its own particles, causing the particles of other matter to be brought closer together – exactly as Newton had envisaged aether behaving. Furthermore, he saw the degree of cohesion resulting from this activity as dependent on the quantity of phlogiston present in any body. As an example he refers to the difference between iron and steel magnets. The former he says are made of ". . . martial earth and phlogiston . . ." and differ from steel magnets by containing more phlogiston and have a greater magnetic effect, that is, greater cohesive power, an argument precisely analogous to that used by Browne Langrish on behalf of the aether.[15]

Higgins' ideas have been discussed since they are representative of the general pattern of thought about the nature of phlogiston during the early and middle decades of the century, a pattern which was used to explain a diversity of phenomena viewed as manifestations of the combustion process. Time and time again chemists refer to the various types of combustion resulting from the activation of phlogiston within inflammable bodies. The literature of the time is filled with references to the phenomena enumerated by Newton in his famous 'Query 8', but these are all explained in terms of a phlogiston particle rather than an aethereal one. Thus, the production of calx from a metal was explained in terms of the activation of the phlogiston contained in the metal with the subsequent emission of light particles; putrefaction was similarly explained, as was fermentation, but these two processes were considered as representing a slower and gentler type of inflammation with a consequential smaller emission of light. The production of 'fire-damp' in mines, the light known as Will-o'-the-wisp or ignis fatui and the bubbling, 'vitalizing' properties of spring waters, were all attributed to the activation of phlogiston. Furthermore, this model was used to explain phenomena occurring in living animals for the 'glow' of the glow-worm was also attributed to the activity of phlogiston.

Here was another concept then, waiting to be used by anybody searching for a model of muscular motion based on existing physico-chemical theory. It was accepted that phlogiston was a constituent of living tissues, since they are inflammable and putrefy. Thus if muscles contained phlogiston, its activation could be responsible for the increase in muscular cohesion manifested as muscular contraction, the motion being accompanied by the emission of light and heat. One might then expect a host of theories to have been put forward, analogous to those based on the activity of an aether. But in fact, it is difficult during the first half of the 18th century, to find anything comparable to the detailed theories discussed in the previous chapter. It is true that there is a tacit assumption that muscular motion is due in some way to a process fundamentally the same as that which produces the phenomena listed above but relatively little space is devoted to a specific discussion of it in these terms and there is little, if any, evidence of the phlogiston concept being used as the basis for the experimental investigation of muscular motion.

The reasons for this comparative lack of interest in what was just as valid a model as the aethereal one, are interesting. Although he put forward a chemical theory admirably suited to the explanation of both organic and non-organic phenomena Stahl was a Vitalist[16] and did not consider physiological processes as capable of being reduced to mechanistic events. His followers may therefore have tended to inherit this outlook, whereas the followers of Newton were more than ready to reduce all worldly phenomena to a basic, mechanical pattern of events at the particulate level. At the same time, the general progress in observational biology which was occurring as the 18th century advanced produced a corpus of knowledge which made physicians more cautious in their acceptance of purely theoretical concepts – a caution exemplified by the attitude of the leading physiologist of the time, Albrecht von Haller*.

Haller was not only an immensely learned man, well informed in a wide range of scientific subjects, he was also a careful experimental biologist. His famous treatise 'De partibus corporis humani sensibilibus et irritabilibus'[17] read before the Royal Society of Sciences of Göttingen in 1752, is an expression of his ability not to be carried beyond the legitimate conclusions of his experiments. Glisson had put forward the highly significant concept of 'irritability' in the 17th century – a term he used to describe what he believed was an inherent property of all the elemental parts of living bodies: the ability to move in response to the 'irritation' of a stimulus. This was no more than the biological expression of the philosophical trends of the time and was only partly the result of Glisson's observations.[18] Between the years 1746–1751, Haller and his students made a great number of experiments on various animals using various irritative stimuli. They differentiated between those parts which are truly irritable, for example, muscles and those which are sensible, such as nerves, showing that these two properties of living matter are quite independent of one another. Haller was not prepared to sponsor any mechanical or chemical theory in support of his results. He says:

> But the theory, why some parts of the human body are endowed with these properties, while others are not, I shall not meddle with. For I am persuaded that the source of both lies concealed beyond the reach of the knife and microscope, beyond which I do not choose to hazard many conjectures . . . for I am persuaded that the great source of error in physic has been owing to physicians, at least a great part of them, making few or no experiments, substituting analogy instead of them.[19]

Haller was prepared to go no further than to describe biological phenomena in as far as he could by careful observation. In terms of muscular motion he was prepared to say that muscles were 'irritable', but he was not prepared to attribute this irritability to any specific physical or chemical cause.

Writing more specifically of muscular motion in his *First Lines of Physiology*,[20] Haller again limits himself to a general description of events and dismisses hypotheses as unworthy of discussion. His views are the result of his experimental investigations and he explains the phenomena he has observed in the most cautious and empirical terms. Thus he differentiates most carefully between the 'nervous power' brought to a muscle by the nerve (and responsible for the setting in action of voluntary muscles) and the *vis insita* which is the force inherent in a muscle and brings about motion in the absence of nervous stimulation (involuntary motion).

> *This force* [the nervous force] *is not the same with the* vis insita. *The former comes to the muscle from without; whereas the other resides constantly in the muscle itself. The nervous power ceases when life is destroyed; after which the other, from certain experiments, appears to remain a long time: it is also suppressed by tying a ligature on the nerve, by hurting the brain, and by drinking opium. The* vis insita *suffers nothing from all these: it remains after the nerve is tied; and continues in the intestines though taken out of the body, and cut in pieces: it appears in great strength in such animals as are destitute of brain: that part of the body is moved which has no feeling; and the parts of the body feel which are without motion. The will excites and removes the nervous power but has no power over the* vis insita.[21]

Having described the biological situation, Haller refuses to speculate on the ultimate physical cause:

> *But the direct manner by which the nerves excite motion in the muscles, is so obscure, that we may almost for ever despair of its discovery. At first, concerning the* vis insita, *we do not indeed enquire; as this seems to be a more brisk attraction of the elementary parts of the fibre by which they mutually approach each other, and produce, as it were, little knots in the middle of the fibre. A stimulus excites and augments this attractive force, which is placed in the very nature of the moving fibre. The other explanations are hypotheses.*[22]

Haller then proceeds to mention some of these hypotheses which he finds wanting, and even goes so far as to deny the possibility of an 'elastic air' or electricity as the cause. The blood does not contain "spherules full of air" and the 'animal spirits' are not of the "nature of an electric torrent."[23]

This tendency to caution is reflected in the works of Haller's disciple, William Cullen*. In his own textbook he does little more than reissue Haller's ideas, giving reference to the above quotations. While he admits that muscular contraction is probably brought about by a process similar to that underlying the elasticity of non-organic bodies, he does not enlarge upon this:

> *As the force of cohesion in the muscular fibres of living animals is much greater than in those of dead ones, it is probable from this and other considerations, that the cause of muscular contraction is an increase only of that same power which gives the contractility of the simple solids and of other inanimate elastics.*[24]

Again, in his manuscript note book entitled *Some Lectures on Fire*,[25] we find Cullen, who did not believe in the existence of an elemental inflammable principle, putting forward the view that combustion with its production of heat and light is the result of the collision of two elastic vapours, one arising from the burning body, the other existing in the air – a sort of *ab externo* modification of the aether theory:

> *Thus heating any oil or sulphur to a certain degree, and they will inflame, provided the air has free access to it and generate light and every such generation of light gives a new birth to fire and it is not propagated from other Bodies but is produced by the Collision of the two elastic vapours arising from the oil, the other the air.*[26]

Cullen attributes the production of light by phosphorous, the Bologna Stone,[27] and various precious gems to the same process. When however he comes to the organic situation he is more cautious:

> *. . . another generation of light is that of several animals, in particular the glow-worm in consequence of Animal life and a peculiar modification of it.*[28]

Reference to the European journals published during these years confirms the opinion that theories of muscular motion involving the phlogistic fluid are singularly absent.[29]

The phlogiston particle did however eventually gain recognition as a likely agent in muscular motion but paradoxically not simply in its historical logical role as the receptor particle, ". . . placed in the very nature of the moving fibre"[7] as Haller describes his *vis insita*, but when there was a strong suspicion that it was identical with the electrical particle! The chemical philosophers would have none of the aether: they postulated only one active particle and it fulfilled the dual role as agent in the nerves responsible for the nervous power and as agent in the muscle, responsible for the *vis insita* – just as the mechanical philosophers allocated both rôles to the aether. But whereas the latter came to identify the aether with the electrical fluid, as discussed in the previous chapter, the chemical philosophers were so convinced of the reality of their concept of phlogiston as a true element that they were led to the belief that phlogiston must be converted into electrical fluid by the animal body, if as indeed seemed likely, the nervous forces were electrical – and the fact that the discharge from an electric machine or Leyden Jar produced convulsive muscular contraction left little doubt that this was so. The real problem seemed to be to decide whether the *vis insita* existed as phlogiston or electrical fluid. By the 1770's however it was becoming increasingly apparent that phlogiston and electricity were one and the same principle – or at least the same matter in different states. This equation was logical both in theory and as a result of experimental evidence. Theoretically they both were considered to be subtle, elastic fluids, endowed with the property of self motion and capable thereby of increasing the cohesion or elasticity of inert matter. And experimentally, the evidence seemed overwhelmingly in favour of this supposition as is admirably shown by Dugud Leslie* in his interesting book dealing with the cause of animal heat.[7] He prefaces his evidence with the following words, which sum up his thesis that the chemical and mechanical philosophers were merely using a different name to describe the same mechanical concept:

> *But to evince what I formerly alleged, that the dispute between the mechanical and chymical philosophers, is in fact, rather about words than things, I shall now endeavour*

to shew that the dense, subtle and highly elastic fluid which the great Newton and all who have contemplated Nature with the utmost attention, have denominated ether, and considered as the one omnipotent animating principle of all natural things upon which every property and phenomenon of material being depends, is one and the same with the phlogistic fluid. A full demonstration of this proposition would, unquestionably, be of very material advantage to the prosecution of natural knowledge; that however we do not absolutely promise, but apprehend that a due attention to facts will prove it to a high degree of probability.[30]

Leslie considers the aether, electricity, light and phlogiston as identical and he marshals his evidence as follows:

1°. It is universally taught by metallurgists that the calcination of metals depends on no other circumstance than the separation of their phlogiston, and their revivification can only be effected by a restitution of that principle; but it appears from the experiments of Padre Beccaria (a) and Dr Priestley (b) that the calcies of metals are returned to their metalline estate by the electric spark. Have we not then every reason to believe that the electric matter is really the phlogistic fluid. (a) Beccaria Misc. Taur. (b): Priestley, Expmts. On Air, Vol I

2°. It was formerly observed that air is diminished in proportion to the quantity of phlogiston with which it is fraught, and it appears from Dr Priestley's experiments that common air loses a fifth part of its bulk by having the electric spark taken in it . . .

3°. In the general account which was given of phlogiston it was alleged that it is not only exempt from the common law of gravity but is even possessed of a power . . . of diminishing the specific weight of the compound into which it enters as a constituent. That the electric fluid is possessed of a similar power appears from all those experiments, in which the reduction of metallic calces is effected by it . . . Besides an ingenious electrician, Abbé Nollet, found that a pigeon lost a fortieth part of its weight, and one sort of a bird, a fiftieth, by being for some time electrified. He even found that several young persons lost several ounces more of their weight than they were wont to lose in the same space of time when not electrified; (c) and with respect to air it is not only contracted in its dimensions, but diminished in its weight by the electric spark . . . (c) Leçons de physique expérimentale

4°. It appears from a number of curious experiments instituted by La Fontana . . . that the electric shock and phlogisticated air, destroy animal life in the very same manner (d). In both instances, animals if not instantaneously killed die universally convulsed. (d) Recherche Fisiche.

5°. The phlogistic fluid and electric fluid coincide in many other particulars besides those already mentioned. Both are attended with light, both produce flame, promote the growth of vegetables, expand fluids, precipitate lime from lime-water and change the blue colour of liquors tinged with vegetable juices to red.[31]

Lastly he says:

6°. The electricity and non-electricity of bodies depend upon the quantity and particular modification of their phlogiston. Various attempts have been made to explain . . . the specific differences between the conductors and non-conductors of electricity; but after reviewing all and collating the facts recited by those truly ingenious philosophers Franklin, Nollet, Beccaria and Priestley, I am induced to ascribe the conducting power of bodies to their being so fully saturated . . . with phlogiston and not to be capable of attracting and retaining any more of it. This opinion is more the plausible, that numberless experiments show, that bodies transmit the electrical matter more or less perfectly in proportion to the proportion of phlogiston which they at that time possess.[32]

After putting forward some examples to substantiate his argument, Leslie continues:

. . . for if the electric and phlogistic matter be what we have reason to believe them, one and the same principle, it by consequence follows that since the Newtonian system accounts the aethereal medium the efficient cause of all the phenomena of electricity; whatever have been ascribed to it are with equal justice and propriety to be attributed to phlogiston . . . It is further to be observed that as the electric aura produces flame, expands fluid, and augments their natural evaporation, and in many other particulars resembles the action of fire, whatever has been advanced in favour of it or the aethereal fluid, in this respect, operates equally in favour of the principle of inflammability.[32]

Leslie's book is concerned primarily with the cause of animal heat. Briefly his theory is that phlogiston is imbibed from the air by plants[33] and therefore comes to form "a great part of their substance". When plants are eaten by animals and digested the phlogiston "recovers its fluid active state" and is diffused through the animal body in the vascular system, by which it reaches all bodily organs and imparts motion to them. Leslie quotes Dr Cromwell Mortimer* as having put forward a similar opinion.

What is interesting is that he specifically uses his theory to explain muscular motion, referring to the production of light from animals during a time of activity. One of the major problems arising from this view of muscular motion was the apparent lack of heat and light produced but Leslie refers to a number of instances in which he believes this is demonstrable *viz* the spark associated with the shock of electrical fish – he quotes the torpedo and *anguille tremblante* of Surinam; the light "known to proceed from some animals, as from cats and other beasts, when they are in pursuit of their prey at night"; the various instances furnished by Thomas Bartholin* in his book *De Causis Lucis Animantium*;[34] the occurrence of sparks when certain ladies comb their hair;[35] and the emission of light during putrefactive processes. Most of these are, of course, discharge phenomena but Leslie's reference to the light of putrefaction shows how a completely different phenomenon could be interpreted logically within the framework of his concept. Having given these examples he feels able to say that:

It may therefore be reasonably concluded that phlogiston is the nutritious matter to which the animal machine owes its accretion, vigour, and constant support; and as the material cause of all muscular motion can only be derived from the aliment it is highly probable that the principle of inflammability after being transmuted by the animal processes into that state, in which it is called the electric fluid, is by means of the nervous system directed to the muscles, and forces them to act, in the same manner as they are forced into action, when the electric fluid is thrown into them ab extra.[36]

Dugud Leslie's book has been discussed for two main reasons; firstly, it gathers together so clearly the sort of arguments that could be used to justify the identity of phlogiston with electricity from both a theoretical and experimental point of view; secondly it is a work devoted to a biological theory of animal heat and specifically identifies phlogiston with the process of muscular motion. However, as Leslie himself indicates, the concept of a phlogiston-electrical cycle in nature, was the brain-child of Joseph Priestley*. The English chemist's comprehensive understanding of the state of electrical knowledge together with his fervent espousal of the phlogiston theory had at an early stage in his career led him to suspect a relationship between electrical and chemical phenomena. His first scientific interest was in the field of electricity and resulted in the publication, in 1767 of his famous account of *The History and Present State of Electricity*.[37] Papers concerned with electrical topics appeared in the *Philosophical Transactions* during the next few years, one of which was entitled 'Experiments and Observations on Charcoal.'[38] He concluded that since both metals (which are conductive *par excellence*) and charcoal were compounds of an earthy base and phlogiston, it was to the latter inflammable principle that both types of compound owed their ability to conduct the electrical fluid. There is thus, at this early stage, the suggestion of a fundamental relationship between the two fluids, a relationship which he could apparently demonstrate in these situations.[31]

Priestley in common with other adherents to the phlogiston theory believed that the phenomena discussed above as manifestations of Newton's Combustion Model (see this book, Chap. 9, Note 11) were associated with the release of phlogiston into the air. Thus the burning of a candle, the breathing of animals, the putrefaction of organic matter, all produced phlogiston which destroyed the 'vital' properties of the air – in as much as these processes ceased after a certain time if carried out in an enclosed space, with no possibility of the accumulating phlogiston escaping. By 1772 he discovered that such a vitiation of the air could be restored by growing green plants in it. In 1772 he wrote a letter to his friend Benjamin Franklin, in which he says:

> *You want to know what I am doing about AIR. I have lately resumed my experiments on that subject with considerable success. I have perfectly ascertained the restoration of air induced by respiration, putrefaction or by the burning of candles, spirits of wine or brimstone matches by the growing of plants. In this purpose I have made use of mint balm, groundsel, and spinach and have found that this effect depends upon the vegetating state of the plants. I have also discovered that air receives, in a great measure, the very same kind of injury from flame, as from respiration etc., but only about one-third in degree.*[39]

Priestley thought the restoration of the air might be due to, ". . . the plants imbibing the phlogistic matter as part of their nourishment." Or because ". . . the phlogiston unites with the vapour that is continually exhaled from them . . ." and ". . . of the two opinions I should incline to the former"[40]

Priestley read a number of papers at the Royal Society during the 1770's on the subject of his experiments on the composition of air and these formed the substance of his book *Experiments and Observations on Different Kinds of Air* which appeared in three volumes during the years 1774–1777.[41] The various individual papers soon appeared in French and Italian translations (both of which would have been available to Galvani) and the *History of Electricity* had been published in French in 1771. It is significant perhaps that between 1775 and 1776 six of Priestley's papers appeared in Italian translation in the *Scelta d'Opuscoli Interessanti*, a journal devoted to the works of European and American scientists, which merited special notice.[42]

Of particular interest is one which appeared in 1775, entitled 'Congetture Intorno all' identità della Materia elettrica e del Flogisto'.[43] This is a translation of Priestley's 'Speculations arising from the consideration of the similarity of the electric matter and phlogiston' which were included in the second edition of his *Experiments and Observations on Different Kinds of Air*.[44] In this, Priestley presents his biological theory of a phlogiston cycle in nature. Referring to the growing significance of electricity in the operations of nature, he says:

> . . . *we were astonished to the highest degree by the discovery of the similarity of electricity and* lightning, *and the* aurora borealis, *with the connection it seems to have with* waterspouts, hurricanes, *and* earthquakes, *and also with the part that is probably assigned to it in the system of* vegetation, *and other the most important processes in nature.*[44]

Priestley continues by referring to the demonstration by John Walsh* of the electrical properties of the torpedo and *anguille tremblante* of Surinam:

> . . . *the most curious discovery of Mr Walsh's that the former of these wonderful fishes has the power of giving a proper electric shock; the electrical matter which proceeds from it performing a real circuit from one part of the animal to the other; while both the fish which performs this experiment and all its apparatus are plunged in water, which is known to be a conducting substance.*[44]

This evidence of an internal circulation of electricity within the torpedo, together with Priestley's strong suspicion that phlogiston and electricity if not identical are but different modifications of the same matter, leads him to his idea of a phlogiston-electricity cycle in nature. He considers certain other facts as further evidence, the most important of which can be summarised thus:

1. "Electrical matter directed through the body of any muscle forces it to contract";

2. phlogiston, or some modification of it, forms the essential element of an animal's nourishment, "from which the source and materials of all muscular motion must be derived";

3. the well-known effect of "vinous and spirituous liquors which consist very much of phlogiston" and which, "instantly brace and strengthen the whole nervous and muscular system; the phlogiston in this case being, perhaps, more easily extricated, and by a less tedious process, than in the usual method of extracting it from mild aliments" and

4. "respiration and putrefaction affect common air in the same manner, and in the same manner in which all other processes diminish air and make it noxious, and which agree in nothing but the emission of phlogiston. If this be the case, it should seem that the phlogiston which we take in with our aliment, after having discharged its proper function in the

animal system . . . is discharged as *effete* by the lungs into the great common *menstruum*, the atmosphere".[45]

Hence, says Priestley:

> My conjecture . . . is that animals have a power of converting phlogiston from the state in which they receive it in their nutriment, into the state in which it is called the electrical fluid; that the brain . . . is the great laboratory and repository for this purpose; that by means of the nerves this great principle, thus exalted, is directed into the muscles, and forces them to act, in the same manner as they are forced into action when the electric fluid is thrown into them ab extra.[46]

Priestley supposes that "the generality of animals" have not the ability to throw this "generated electricity" beyond their own bodies while the torpedo by means of its special apparatus can do so. He is thus led to this interesting conjecture:

> In this case it should seem that the electric matter discharged from the animal system . . . would never return to it, at least so as to be made use of a second time, and yet if the structure of these animals be such as that the electric matter shall dart from one part of them only, while another part is left suddenly deprived of it, it may make a circuit, as in the Leyden phial.[47]

The ideas discussed in the last two chapters reflect the way in which by the mid 1770's the two schools of philosophy had come to consider muscular motion in terms of a physico-chemical model. As we have seen, both were using, basically, the same mechanical model founded on the belief that the degree to which any muscle is 'active' or 'contracted' is a measure of the cohesion or elasticity of its parts. Both believed in the existence in muscle of a vibrating particle, the activity of which produced the degree of cohesion responsible for the muscle's elasticity, in both the flaccid and non-contracted state; both believed in the existence of a vibrating particle in the nerve, capable of augmenting the action of its muscular counterpart, to produce voluntary motion. Both believed that the nervous agent was identical with the electrical fluid, their theoretical surmise having strong backing from the effects of an electric spark passed directly through muscle, but there was no direct experimental evidence for the existence of manifest electrical fluid in the nerves of living (or dead) animals. It was merely known that electricity could pass through animal tissues. Whether it actually did so as a natural occurrence, was another matter.

As to the nature of the particle resident in muscle, there was some difference of opinion. The mechanical philosophers postulated that it was electrified – that the agent responsible for the *vis insita* was in fact a pool of electrical fluid in the muscle, but the chemical philosophers believed this was phlogiston, intimately compounded in the structure of the 'fibres' and perhaps transmuted into an active state identical with electricity as a result of the nervous force. Or perhaps electrical particles had the power to act directly on phlogiston particles without their transformation into the electrical state.[47] After all, muscles were combustible and did ferment and putrefy – they obviously did contain phlogiston, but there was no evidence that they contained electrical fluid.

These ideas reflect the problems facing anyone who wanted to demonstrate the reality of such a physico-chemical model at this time and this was just when Galvani was beginning his investigations. This was what the mechanical and chemical 'philosophers' had to offer him.

Notes

1   See Chap. 6 of this book
2   Becher J. (1667) *Actorum laboratorii chymici monacensis, seu physicae subterraneae*, Frankfurt, John David Zumner
3   Partington J.R. (1961) *A History of Chemistry*, Vol. II, London, Macmillan, p. 644
4   Black J. (1803) *Lectures on the Elements of Chemistry*, Vol. 1, London, Mundell and Sons (eds) for Longman and Rees, p. 391
5   Stahl E. (1723) *Fundamente Chymiae Dogmatico-Rationalis et Experimentalis . . .* Nuremberg, Wolfgang Mauritius
6   Bacon*, Francis (1878) *Novum Organum*, with introduction, notes, etc., by T. Fowler (ed.), Oxford, Clarendon Press, Aphorism XX
7   Leslie, P. Dugud (1778) *A Philosophical Enquiry into the Cause of Animal Heat, with Incidental Observations on several Phisiological and Chymical Questions, connected with the Subject*, London, S. Crowder and J. Robson, pp 175 *et seq.*
8   Macquer P.J. (1758) *Elements of the Theory and Practice of Chymistry*, Andrew Reid (transl.), Vol. 1, London, A. Millar and J. Nourse, p. 7
9   Ibid., p. 9. See also P.J. Macquer, *A Dictionary of Chemistry containing the theory and practice of that Science*, J. Keir (transl.), 2 Vols, London, T. Cadell and P. Elmslie, 1771, for his view of contemporary ideas on phlogiston and its nature
10 For a survey of these theories, see J.R. Partington and Douglas McKie, 'Historical Studies on the Phlogiston Theory – III. Light and heat in combustion.' *Annals of Science*, 1938, Vol. 3, pp 338–371
11 Higgins B. (1776) *A Philosophical Essay Concerning Light*, Vol. 1, London, J. Dodsley
12 Ibid., Section viii, p. 44
13 Ibid., p. 61
14 Ibid., p. 227
15 Ibid., Introduction, p. 181. See also loc. cit., Note 7, p. 179
16 For a brief review of Stahl's views concerning the dependence of living bodies on the presence of a 'sensitive soul', see: Sir M. Foster, *Lectures on the History of Physiology during the 16th, 17th and 18th Centuries*, New York, Dover Publications, 1970, p. 169 *et seq.*
17 (i) von Haller A. (1753) 'De partibus corporis humani sensibilibus et irritabilibus', *Commentarii Societatis Regiae Scientiarium Göttingensis*, Tom. 2, pp 114–158. The contents of the above were read as two dissertations before the Royal Society of Sciences of Göttingen on 22 April and 6 May, 1752
    (ii) For an English translation see: von Haller A. (1755) *A Dissertation on the Sensible and Irritable Parts of Animals*, M. Tissot (transl.), London, J. Nourse
18 Temkin O. (1964) 'The classical roots of Glisson's doctrine of irritation,' *Bulletin of the History of Medicine*, Vol. 38, pp 298–328, where the origin and development of Glisson's ideas are traced
19 Loc. cit., Note 17 (ii), pp 2–3
20 von Haller A. (1779) *First Lines of Physiology*. Translated from the correct Latin edition, printed under the inspection of William Cullen . . ., Edinburgh, C. Elliot
21 Ibid., Chap. XII, p. 196, para. 404
22 Ibid., Chap. XII, p. 197, para. 407
23 Ibid., Chap. XII, p. 198, para. 407
24 Cullen W. (1785) *Institutions of Medicine, Part I, Physiology*, Edinburgh, C. Elliot, London, T. Cadell, pp 70–71
25 Cullen W. 'Some Lectures on Fire, given by Dr Cullen Edinburgh, Anno 1757'. This is a manuscript notebook in the Library of the Royal Society of Medicine, London
26 Ibid., p. 49 *et seq.*

27 See this book Chap. 13
28 Loc. cit., Note 25, p. 52
29 See also *Philosophical transactions of the Royal Society (1750–1780)*, London, *Histoire de l' Académie Royale des Sciences (1750–1780)*, Paris
30 Loc. cit., Note 7, p. 199 *et seq.*
31 Ibid., p. 200 *et seq.* The various references given by Leslie are so sketchy as to be virtually useless. Ample evidence for his suppositions can, however, be found as follows:
(i) Priestley J. (1780) *Experiments and Observations on Different Kinds of Air . . .,* Birmingham, T. Pearson, Vol. I: pp 112–119, 182, 186; Vol. II: pp 219–223, 224, 249, 469–470; Vol. III: pp 277, 409. Ibid., *Experiments and Observations on Different Kinds of Air . . .,* London, J. Johnson, 1775–1779, Vol. I: pp 139, 178; Vol. II: p. 238
(ii) Beccaria G.B. (1777) *A Treatise on Artificial Electricity in which are given solutions of a number of interesting electric phenomena, hitherto unexplained,* London, J. Nourse, p. 304
(iii) Nollet J.A. (1749) *Rechérches sur les Causes particulières des Phenomènes Électrique et sur les effets nuisibles en avantagieux qu'on peut en attendre,* Paris, Frères Guerin, p. 375
(iv) Fontana F. (1775) *Richerche filosofiche sopra la Fisica Animale,* Florence per Galtano Cambiagi Stampatore Granducale, Chap. VIII, para. lxxiii and lxiv, pp 181–183. Presumably Leslie's references are in general as follows: 'Beccaria Msc. Taur.' *Miscellanea philosophica – mathematica dell'Accademia delle Scienze,* Tom. 1, Turin, 1759. 'Priestley, *Experiments on Air* Vol. I' – J. Priestley, *Experiments and Observations on Air . . .,* London, J. Johnson, 1775–1779. J.A. Nollet, *Leçons de physique expérimentale,* Amsterdam, aux Depens de la Compagni, Arkstee and Merkus 1745–1756 – F. Fontana, *Richerche physiche sopra il veleno della vipera . . .,* Lucca, J. Giusti, 1767
32 Ibid., p. 203
33 Ibid., p. 93
34 See: T. Bartholin, *De luce animalium, libri iii, admirandis historiis rationibusque novis referti,* Leyden, F. Hack, 1647. This contains the three books, *De luce hominum; De luce brutorum* and *De Causis Lucis Animantium.* Leslie's reference is merely to "De luce animantium" without any page number. For a good historical account of the phenomenon see J. Priestley, *The History and Present State of discoveries relating to Vision, Light and Colours,* London, J. Johnson, 1772, Vol. II, Section IX, pp 562–587. Priestley refers to "De luce Animalium" pp 183, 184 and 206, all of which occur in the second book, *De luce brutorum*
35 Loc. cit., Note 7, pp 172–173
36 Ibid., pp 173–174
37 Priestley J. (1767) *The History and Present State of Electricity With Original Experiments,* The sources of Science No. 18, Vol. I, New York, Johnson Reprint Corporation, 1966
38 Priestley J. (1770) 'Experiments and Observations on Charcoal', *Philosophical Transactions,* No. 60, pp 211–227
39 See *A Scientific Autobiography of Joseph Priestley,* R.E. Schofield (ed.), Cambridge, Mass., MIT Press, 1966, p. 106, for the letter from Joseph Priestley to Benjamin Franklin dated 1 July 1772
40 Partington J.R. (1962) *A History of Chemistry,* Vol. III, London, Macmillan, p. 277
41 Priestley J. (1774–1777) *Experiments and Observations on Different Kinds of Air,* 3 Vols, London, J. Johnson
42 *Scelta di Opuscoli Interessanti tradotti di varie lingue,* Milan, Guiseppe Marelli, 36 Vols, 1775–1777
43 Ibid., 1775, Vol. XI, p. 48
44 Loc. cit., Note 41, Vol. I, p. 274–275
45 Ibid., pp 276–279
46 Ibid., pp 277–278
47 Priestley tried the effect of the electric spark on Phlogiston. See: J. Priestley, *Experiments and Observations on Different kinds of Air.* See Note 41

* See Biographical Index

12

Hallerian irritability:
a new force in nature?

The application of all physical and chemical theories to the problem of muscular motion were based on analogy. All were conceived in the belief that there is a material agent in the muscle 'fibre' which, by its mere presence, gives muscle its ability to retract and, roused to greater activity by the nervous agent, brings about contraction – and all were dedicated to the view that this material agent can be identified with one or other of the great forces recognised in nature. This reductionism however, of necessity, remained at a purely theoretical level as there was very little in the way of experimental evidence from the practical investigation of animals or man to support this view. The gradual growth, however, of experimental biology during the 17th and 18th centuries and in particular the coincident realisation of the enormous difficulties attached to the devising of suitable experiments – to say nothing of the even greater ones associated with the correct interpretation of their results – led to the cautious outlook referred to previously.[1] There was an increasing number of experimental biologists such as Haller who were prepared to go only as far as ". . . the knife and microscope" would lead them.

The growing confidence of such men allowed them to stand firm against theories based on analogies which might well not be applicable to any particular biological situation. They were prepared to say that they did not know the cause of muscular motion and they were unwilling to admit that the force existing in muscles must necessarily be identified with such fundamental forces as the electrical and phlogistic fluids. Even Newton's universal force of attraction was suspect. It was one thing to assign all the movements of the non-organic universe to such an agent, but why should not a different, equally fundamental, force be responsible for animal movements? Who had shown that the inverse square law was applicable to the intramuscular environment? And whether it was or not, what rôle should be assigned to that prerogative of organic beings, the soul? All these agents were up for consideration as actual active forces in the bringing about of muscular motion; the problem was to identify and relate them in a system within the animal body. The mechanical and chemical philosophers had suggested possible identities for the above agent in muscle: the biologists had the problem of assessing these suggestions in the light of their experimental results.

The most significant contribution to the experimental investigation of muscular motion during the mid 18th century was the publication of Haller's *De partibus corporis humani sensibilibus et irritabilibus*, in 1753.[2]

In this short monograph the author describes, systematically, the results of his experiments, carried out during the decade preceding publication. The purpose of his investigations was to establish which parts of the animal body are 'sensible', which parts are 'irritable' and, most important, whether irritability and sensibility are in any way mutually dependent. He defines his terms thus:

> I call that part of the human body irritable, which becomes shorter on being touched; very irritable if it contracts upon a slight touch, and the contrary if by a violent touch it contracts but little. I call that a sensible part of the human body, which upon being touched transmits the impression of it to the soul; and in brutes, in whom the exist- ence of a soul is not so clear, I call those parts sensible, the irritation of which oc- casions evident signs of pain and disquiet in the animal. On the contrary, I call that insensible, which being burnt, tore, pricked, or cut till it is quite destroyed occasions no sign of pain or convulsion nor any sort of change in the situation of the body.[3]

Haller's experiments were carried out on a great number of animals of different species and he repeated his experiments in order to be as sure as possible of the accuracy of his results. His systematic investigation of sensi- bility and irritability involved the following procedure:

> I took living animals of different kinds, and different ages and after laying bare that part which I wanted to examine, I waited till the animal ceased to struggle or com- plain; after which I irritated the part, by blowing, heat, spirit of wine, the scalpel, lapis infinalis, oil of vitriol, and butter of antimony. I examined attentively whether upon touching, cutting, burning, or lacerating the part, the animal seemed disquieted, made a noise, struggled, or pulled back the wounded limb, if the part was convulsed, or if nothing of all this happened.[4]

Haller's experiments were not carried out merely as a topographical exer- cise, recording the positive or negative results of these assaults on various animal parts. They were intended to demonstrate beyond doubt, that irrita- bility does not depend on sensibility. Now this was contrary to accepted opinion and because of this Haller felt it necessary to repeat his experiments many times so that there could be no question of the validity of his results and the conclusions to be drawn from them. He quotes the origin of the then accepted opinion, *viz* that irritability depends on the presence of nerves in any part of an animal displaying this property. He wrote:

> When Dr Boerhaave [*] had established the doctrine of the nerves being the basis of all our solids, he presently after proceeds to affirm that there was no part of the human body which was not sensible, or capable of some sort of motion and this system which I have elsewhere refuted, was received almost universally all over Europe.[5]

Francis Glisson's original view of irritability was also that it depended on the irritable part having a nerve supply, although later his concept changed and he considered irritability as the inborn property of all living 'fibres'. This idea of an inherent 'life force' in the elemental units of organic bodies was, perhaps, more the result of the philosophical mood of the 17th century than of Glisson's anatomical investigations.[6]

This essentially philosophical concept had been seized upon by various authors who used it as the basis for a medical system which explained all functions and malfunctions of the human body in terms of irritability of the fibres and Haller did not approve of this type of speculative thinking. His aim was to establish, precisely, what fibres or other elements are irritable and whether this property is dependent on the intervention of a nervous pathway the two main sources of what he considered to be, the false ideas of many of his colleagues:

> *A second motive which encouraged me in this work was the readiness with which some celebrated authors have laid hold of the first notions of irritability, so as to make use of this property of our fibres, as a basis of almost an universal system of motion in the human body, and then deduce the functions of the fibres, vessels, nerves, muscles and in short of all our organs. This appears very plain in reading Dr Winter's oration delivered at Franeker in 1746, that of Dr Lup's* De Irritabilitate, *and the thesis of De Magni and La Motte upon the following subject,* Ergo a Vasorum aucta aut diminuta irritabilitate omnis morbus. *For they all agree pretty much in the same opinion, viz.: in deriving all motion from sensation. In which they are joined by Drs Kruger, Nicolai, Whytt, Delius, and some other great physiologists.*[7]

The deductions to be made from Haller's experiments and those of his many students[8] were abundantly clear. 'Irritability' is not the inborn property of all fibres; it is the prerogative of the muscular fibre. 'Sensibility' is similarly the prerogative of the nerve. In other words, the irritability of a muscle fibre is the result of a force existing in the muscle fibre itself, since any muscle fibre can be stimulated to display irritability in the complete absence of any nervous connection with the animal body:

> *. . . And, at the same time, I shall demonstrate that irritability does not depend on the nerves, but on the original fabric of the parts which are susceptible to it.*[9]

This demonstration that the source of irritability lies in "the original fabric" of the muscle fibre was in fact the biological confirmation of the theoretical surmise of the various mechanical theories we have considered. Any notion of the muscle fibre as a perceptive or sensible element was disproved and furthermore, any notion of another perceptive element, that is, in the parts of the brain and nervous system, as being essential to the exhibition of irritability was proved false. The nervous system was to be considered in terms of an auxiliary mechanism by which agent(s) capable of arousing or dispelling irritability could be brought to the muscle. The life-force was in the muscle itself.

Haller's demonstration was enormously important because inevitably the whole problem of why a muscle is capable of moving *per se* seemed to be involved with the problem of life itself – self-movement being one of the distinguishing properties of animal life. The fundamental difference of opinion which developed in the 17th century was between those who believed that the essential attribute of life is the ability to perceive and Glisson, who believed that the ability to move lay at the root of the different views developed during the 18th century, as referred to by Haller above.[10]

His great controversy with Robert Whytt* was concerned with the location of the agent responsible for irritability. The Edinburgh anatomist, in company with others believed this lay within the nervous system:

> Upon the whole there seems to be in a man one sentient and intelligent PRINCIPLE, which is equally the source of life, sense and motion, as of reason; and which from the law of its union with the body, exerts more or less of its power and influence as the different circumstances of the several organs actuated by it may require. That this principle operates upon the body by the intervention of something in the brain or nerves, is, I think likewise probable: though as to its particular nature, I presume not to allow myself in any uncertain conjectures; but, perhaps, by means of this connecting medium the various impressions, made on the several parts of the body either by external or internal forces, are transmitted to, and perceived by the mind: in consequence of which may determine the nervous influence variously into different organs, and so become the cause of all the vital and involuntary motions as well as of the animal and voluntary.[11]

Whytt's insistence that all muscular motion depends upon the activity of an agent capable of perception – "a sentient principle" puts the seat of irritability in the nervous system. Since he also associated intelligence and reason with this principle it had all the requisites of the human rational soul. Haller can therefore say that:

> . . . the celebrated Dr Whytt has attributed all the motions of the human body to the force of a stimulus; but with this difference between him and the others, that he imputes irritability to the soul, which feeling the impression of the irritation, occasions the contraction of the fibre.[12]

The fact that excised portions of muscles are capable of exhibiting irritability forced Whytt to the view that the soul is divisible and separable into as many parts as the body, a view which Haller could not accept. Haller believed the seat of the soul was in the brain since he recognised it as the force responsible for the initiation of rational, intelligent acts. Since abscission of any part of the body from the brain separates it from any control by rational thought, Haller could not identify the force he had demonstrated in excised muscle fibres with the soul as he had defined it. Because of this fundamental difference between the outlook of Whytt and Haller, stress tends to be put on the vitalist outlook of the former. Because he associated the qualities of irritability and soul, Whytt's essential identification of 'irritability' with sensibility of perception tends to be obscured.

The enormously important fact which Haller established was that it was to the nature of the muscle fibre that investigators must turn their attention.[13] The theories of Whytt and others, identifying irritability with an agent in the nervous system, were apparently wrong. However the soul or nervous forces might exert their effect, there was a force to be identified within muscle itself. But what was the nature of this force? Or had they revealed a unique and as yet unrecognised force, perhaps existing only in the muscle fibres of man and animals? This was the burning issue between philosophers all over Europe in the mid-18th century. Had Haller merely located the site of action of an already recognised universal force or had he revealed the existence of a new organic motive agent, obeying as yet unknown laws of motion?

Haller's own views regarding the nature of irritability are cautiously summed up as follows:

> What therefore should hinder us from granting irritability to be a property of the animal gluten the same as we acknowledge attraction and gravity to be properties of matter in general, without being able to determine the cause of them. Experiments have taught us the existence of this property, and doubtless it is owing to a physical cause which depends upon the arrangement of the ultimate particles, though the experiments we can make are too gross to investigate them.[14]

This statement really leaves the matter open although Haller's suggestion would seem to be that irritability is due to a (known) physical cause manifested only in the particular structure of the muscle fibre. However he also said that: ". . . this power of producing motion is different from all the other properties of bodies."[15] and proceeded to distinguish it from elasticity, citing as evidence the fact that irritability is decreased on drying a body while elasticity is increased. Irritability is the property of moist (and young) bodies, elasticity is the property of hard bodies. Whatever Haller really envisaged as the true nature of his force, many of his disciples interpreted his statements as meaning that irritability is quite different from "attraction and gravity" which are the properties of "matter in general". This was not just an example of a general physical force manifesting its activity in a rather special way in animals, but a newly discovered primordial agent acting according to its own special laws. A new 'vitalist' versus 'non-vitalist' division of thought arose between those who adopted this view and those who believed that further experimental investigation would certainly identify it with one of the great forces recognised as responsible for the motion of elemental particles, in general.

The belief that Haller had revealed the existence of this vital force was in large measure responsible for the impact which his treatise made. It was as though a physiologist had, at last, produced irrefutable evidence of an organic agent able to hold its own with those demonstrated by physicists and chemists. Haller's experiments were repeated all over Europe and countless animals suffered countless tortures at the hands of those wishing to verify or dispute the accuracy of his results.

In no country was the problem of the nature of irritability more avidly studied than in Italy. Italian physicists, chemists, anatomists and physicians in all the northern universities were busy repeating Haller's experiments. The anatomists were anxious to verify or confound this astounding reversal of their previous views as to the sensitivity of such structures as ligaments, tendons, the pleura and meninges.[16] Boerhaave's authority had been absolute and his concepts deeply entrenched, and now his pupil, Haller, had proved that such concepts did not stand the test of the experiment. The physicists and chemists were anxious to reveal the nature of irritability and identify this agent in muscle with one of their own law-abiding forces.

The intense interest in these problems shown by Italian scientists is reflected in the publication in Bologna in 1757 of a two-part volume devoted to the collected works of various European authors. The title, *Sulla Insensitivita ed Irritabilita Halleriana*,[17] emphasises the novelty of the fact that Haller's experiments had shown the insensibility of parts of the body previously assumed to be sensible. The first part contains the works of authors favouring Haller's theories; the second, those of authors not in accord with them. In his preface to the Rome edition, Giorgio Vincenzo Petrini* says he was induced to undertake the publication of these various dissertations for the benefit of the public since copies were too rare in Italy and the material too good and useful, "a great number of people being interested in the matter, including philosophers, physicians, surgeons and the curious."[18] Petrini translated most of the articles into Italian so as not to present to the public a book composed of many languages.

Petrini's preface is a good example of the kind of way in which many Italians considered irritability: he is representative of what I have called the new vitalist point of view. Having dealt with Haller's experimental results *vis-a-vis* the insensibility of structures previously believed to be sensible he turns to irritability, coming straight to the fundamental issue of its nature.

Referring to the significance and portent of Haller's discovery, he says that it alone, without any of the author's other great contributions to science, would assure the glory and immortality of his name. Petrini sees it as a discovery which:

> . . . *illuminates the machine of the animal body in as great measure as Sir Isaac Newton's Attraction illuminates that of the great world. The one is created by Nature for the macrocosm, the other the microcosm.*[19]

He elaborates his reasons for this view, thus:

> *Before these forces were discovered, only hypothesis had been offered in explanation of so many marvellous phenomena; but not even these were successful in rationalising confused concepts. Attraction finally brought the great planetary system into broad daylight, and gave us the analysis of light and colours: and now, today, Irritability comes along to do the same for the regulation, mechanism and movement of animals, returning the human spirit to its rightful place and revealing to us the mood of its actions. All the efforts made by the philosophers and physicians up to this point led only to false conclusions. I will content myself with noting as evidence, the useless endeavours of the followers of Stahl, as well as of those who opposed him – those who wished to explain animal motion as a result of a purely mechanical force rather than by considering the actions of the animal as a whole. It is true that some more judicious men trod the middle path, making the soul master and arbiter of spontaneous animal movements only and ascribing necessary movements such as the rhythmical beating of the heart, the peristalsis of the stomach and intestines, etc., to a mechanical arrangement, but this mechanical disposition, without a force to set the organs in motion, was like a sumptuous set of tools which pretended to work themselves but lacked the force that would set them in motion. The insight and expertise of a mind such as Haller's was needed to expose this force . . .*[20]

Petrini is quite sure that irritability is a force unlike any other so far recognised despite Haller's cautious remarks as to its probable nature. He illustrates his view that "Irritability is a natural property of the animal fibre, and independent of any recognised principle, whatsoever,"[21] by reference to such forces as attraction and elasticity. Towards the end of his paper he says that it remains for him to prove that "Irritability does not depend on any force known up until this time. There are only two which can have any similarity with it; these are attraction and elasticity."[22]

He dismisses any similarity between irritability and attraction since the latter force serves only to bind together the elemental particles of matter and there is no rationale for attraction being responsible for rhythmical movements such as are seen in the heart. As for elasticity this property is most obvious in those parts of the animal which are devoid of irritability, *viz* the skin, tendons, arteries, etc. Furthermore, heat decreases elasticity but increases irritability. The heart becomes more elastic on desiccation, but, at the same time, loses all irritability. He therefore concludes that:

> *Irritability is not therefore an effect of elasticity and must not be confused with it; it is a virtue, different from all others known before now, a property of the animal fibre in every sense necessary to the life, function and entire economy of the animal and given to him for that reason by the provident hand of the architect, in Nature.*[23]

A somewhat similar point of view is put forward by Haller's pupil Johann Georg Zimmerman*, at the very beginning of his article. In his opening paragraph, he defines irritability in a way similar to his teacher and then goes on to say:

> *There are two sorts of elasticity. The first I call* simple, *the second,* animal *or* innate. *The simple must not be confused with the animal, which in my particular view, is properly called irritability. Simple elasticity is rendered intelligible by Mechanics; but what we have called animal, belongs to the particular Physics of the human body, and that of animals . . .*[24]

And towards the end of his article, Zimmerman refers to Hartley's ideas *apropos* attraction and the part this plays in muscular motion. In his view, they fail to explain anything:

> *Neither does Hartley (with all respect to so great a man) explain anything with his force of attraction. Attraction and the celebrated pre-arranged harmony are voices, which but echo a theory based on ignorance.*[25]

Zimmerman, like Petrini, insists that irritability is a force distinct from Newton's attraction or the elasticity of non-organic bodies.

One of the most striking phenomena to be taken into consideration in any theory as to the nature of irritability is the fact that some parts of the animal body appear more irritable than others, for example, the heart which beats rhythmically without any apparent stimulus brought about by the intervention of the will and which will even continue to beat rhythmically for some considerable time after separation from the body. This organ appears to be the most irritable of all, the intestines, bladder and other 'involuntary' organs somewhat less so, while the muscles which seem to act only at the command of the will, appear to be much less irritable. This was explained, by those accepting the Hallerian view, as being due to the uneven distribution of a specific motive agent, throughout the animal body musculature. Zimmerman adopts this view and questions what the nature of such an agent may be:

> *How then can Irritability be explained by the composition of the fibres? How is the fibre of the heart different from that of another muscle . . . ? What is this material that is distributed with such inequality, causing one part to be more irritable than another.*[26]

Zimmerman, however, will not be drawn on the ultimate nature of this agent, he simply describes it as being responsible for animal movement by depriving animal parts of their inertia:

> *It seems to me that one can only say, in general, that irritability is a property of such (animal) bodies, that it contains within itself the cause of its motion, and that in consequence of this, it renders these bodies quite devoid of inertia. In a similar way, I have said above, that irritability is concerned with life. In this sense, irritability deserves to be numbered among the primary properties of bodies, being that which belongs to animals and which perhaps is the only one by which we live.*[26]

It is not for him to postulate causes, only to describe phenomena. Consciously or subconsciously he echoes Benjamin Franklin's words: "We can content ourselves with ignoring the causes since we know the phenomena."[27]

The animal body "contains within itself the cause of its own motion" but Zimmerman does not believe that this self-moving matter operates in the non-organic situation.

These references to the views of two of the contributors to the Italian book devoted to the subject of irritability indicate a reluctance to identify the force 'irritability' with any known agent – and this view was held by many others. It was accepted that there was a specific, self-moving agent in the animal muscle fibre, and that the mechanical activation of this agent was responsible for muscular motion. What was not acceptable to them was the view that this agent could necessarily be identified with any agent thought to be responsible for non-organic phenomena, a 'vitalist' view.

On the other hand there existed at this time a group of men who, accepting the same basic model as their 'vitalist' colleagues, were convinced that the force of irritability is indeed a material, self-moving agent but not an agent restricted solely to the animal muscle fibre. Their self-moving agent had a general activity in the universe and was responsible for events inside and outside the animal body.

Some of the theories based on this concept were discussed in previous chapters. As an example of the championship of this outlook is the letter written by Padre Lettore "N.N."* in reply to Giacinto Fabri*, Professor of Medicine and Surgery in Bologna. This letter appeared in the Italian volume of collected works referred to above[17] under the title *Saggio fisico Intorno alla Irritabilita Halleriana del Padre Lettore N.N. in reposta al chiarissimo Signor Dottore Giacinto Fabri.*

Fabri had asked N.N. to give him his views on the fundamental nature of irritability, based only on "reference to physics". Having accepted Haller's experimental results without reservation, N.N. says:

> Since I must be involved with thinking, as much as with the anatomists knife in rec-
> ognising the features of this new irritability, I will seek out, not only its existence but
> also its nature, because that series of experiments which seems ordained to persuade
> us to accept it [that is, as a new force] will not be able to convince us so easily if by
> intellectual rationalisation, we cannot recognise it to be of such a character that its
> operations must be ascribed to laws already recognised.[28]

N.N. then proceeds to define the term "primordial quality", showing that such a term can only be referred to a quality existing in the ultimate element of bodies – that is, not as a result of the arrangement of such elements. Thus "the extension of bodies, gravity, attraction, solidity and other such princi-ples" are defined by him as primordial, since:

> . . . they are in the elements, taken by themselves and their conjunction only means
> that they combine together to exaggerate and bring into greater view the same quality
> which is found in them individually.[29]

He says he cannot accept irritability as a primordial quality which operates by itself, independently of other known forces if it cannot be demonstrated as a universal force distributed throughout nature, its action proportional to its mass and obeying constant laws. Within these terms of reference he can-not accept irritability as a new force. He asks:

> Is this irritability we find in the muscle, a result of the union of the fibres which com-
> pose it or are even the fibres, themselves, irritable? And do these fibres have their irri-
> tability solely as a result of the union of the little filaments of which they are composed
> or are the little filaments themselves irritable? And do the filaments become irritable
> when they develop into filaments or are they irritable as a result of the parts from
> which they are formed? And, since these parts circulate in the blood before being in the
> filaments were they irritable when they were in the blood or as soon as they are sepa-
> rated and variously joined do they become irritable finally, in becoming filaments? And
> since the blood was first of all chyle, the chyle was food and food can be said to be any-
> thing; and since we can extract at least spirits capable of refreshing man from almost
> anything, I ask, are these very delicate filaments, which filaments are irritable; are
> they so in being blood, chyle, food, or in being something from which food is formed?[30]

He then answers his own question "Since the elements of animals are the same as those of any other body whatever, nothing can be found in animals which cannot be found in other bodies".[31] How can irritability be considered as a quality specifically animal? N.N. continues by saying that if irritability is a force specific to animals other bodies must have their specific forces:

> Since therefore the animal species are distinguished by this life force which moves
> them and causes them to act in this way, there is no body in nature which may not
> similarly have its own prerogative from which it gets its name and its effects are
> recognised. In like manner if we admit a force of irritability in animals because life is
> found in them of which other bodies are deprived, stones would want another force,
> metal another or fluids and solids would want a force of their own . . .[32]

To postulate so many forces is no more irrational than to propose a specific force in animals. N.N. suggests that this cannot be and that irritability depends on the particular arrangements of the animal parts, not on the presence of a new or specific agent:

> It seems to me that the life of an animal is not derived from some particular force existing in it, but rather from the marvellous conjunction of so many diverse forces which, while they exist in other bodies acting partly, unite in the animal body and particularly in man who may be called a compendium of nature.[32]

which was what Haller had suggested!

N.N. considers the fundamental force in nature is Newton's attraction and the motion of parts of a body must be recognised as the manifestation of varying degrees of this force. The parts of some bodies cohere rigidly; others to a much lesser degree (c.f. solids and liquids). The irritable parts of the animal body are related to the non-irritable as liquids are related to solids, that is, their elemental parts are disposed to be set in motion more easily – but N.N. does not invoke Newton's aether as the agent responsible for coherence.

He refers to the great advances made as a result of Newton's fundamental discovery of the way in which particles interact in various circumstances and is sure that the great interest shown in irritability by scientists from widely different branches of philosophy will uncover the special conditions underlying its action. All natural forces are a manifestation of the activity of Newton's 'attractive force' – irritability no less than those forces studied by botanists, chemists, physicists, astronomers and even those who study the nature of ideas and theology.

Elasticity and irritability are simply effects and the use of such terms depends on the circumstances in which attraction is seen to work on the motion of elemental parts. Why should not the disintegration of any body by fire be referred to as 'irritability of its parts'? To deny that 'irritability' is no more than the manifestation of the motion of elemental parts, obeying general physical laws is to deny that:

> ... irritability reigns in all those bodies which are disintegrated by fire, although the breaking up of bodies in this way is nothing else but the irritation of their parts, which are obliged to vibrate and oscillate – that is to say manifest their irritability – as a result of its action.[33]

Newton's fundamental model for motion is the fundamental model of N.N. for irritability, a model which he hopes to see investigated so as to "render this new force universal".[34] He believed Bologna had men with the ability to do this and refers to various eminent scientists of the time – men of the generation who, if not actually teaching the young Galvani, were there to influence him. He refers to "the immortal Beccaria" whose work on phosphorus and light should lead him to greater discoveries *apropos* the physical nature of irritability. As to the mathematical analysis of its laws, who better than: "the most profound Balbi [*] . . ." Perhaps Galeazzi* and Laghi*, ". . . so cautious and shrewd in their observations and deductions . . ." will solve the problem. Perhaps Eraclito Manfredi*, Menghini*, Molinelli* or Monti* will find the answer. What might the celebrated physicist Laura Bassi or her equally noted husband Guiseppe Veratti do to identify the physical nature of irritability? The latter had frequently demonstrated the activity of the electrical fluid in the human body, might one not hope to see him demonstrate irritability in non-organic bodies!

And finally N.N. suggests the "elegant" Zanotti*, President of the Bologna Institute, as another scientist with the ability to unravel this mystery.

The message from N.N. to Fabri is clear. Irritability is a universal physical force at work in the animal body. It obeys laws which must be discovered and in Bologna there were men tackling this problem with the ability to solve it.

Notes

1 See Chap. 11 of this book
2 von Haller A. (1753) 'De Partibus corporis humani sensibilibus et irritabilibus', *Commentarii Societatis Regiae Scientarium Göttingensis*, Tom. 2, pp 114–158. The contents of the above were read as two dissertations before the Royal Society of Sciences of Göttingen on 22 April and 6 May, 1752
   (ii) For an English translation see A. von Haller, *A Dissertation on the Sensibility and Irritable Parts of Animals*, M. Tissot (transl.), London, J. Nourse, 1755
3 Ibid., (ii), p. 4
4 Ibid., (ii), p. 6
5 Ibid., (ii), p. 5
6 See (i) O. Temkin, 'The classical roots of Glisson's doctrine of irritation' *Bulletin of the History of Medicine*, 1964, Vol. 38, pp 298–328, where the origin and development of Glisson's ideas are traced
   (ii) Legée G. (1974) 'Un concept né en Angleterre et son évolution aux xviiie et xixe Siècles: Le concept d'irritabilité', *Proceedings of the 23rd International Congress of the History of Medicine, London, 1972*, Vol. I, pp 615–623
7 Loc. cit., Note 2, (ii) p. 3 Haller's references are to; F. Winter, *Oratio inauguralis de certitudine in medicina practica . . .*, Franeker, G. Coulon, 1746. J. Lups, *De irritabilitate*, Leyden, E. Luzac, jnr, 1748. The thesis by De Magni and La Motte entitled *Ergo a vasorum aucta aut diminuta irritabilitate omnis morbus* (not identified)
8 It seems surprising that Haller found the cornea of the eye insensitive. Not having demonstrated the fine corneal nerves he must have deduced its insensitivity on the basis of his theory rather than an experimental fact. He says, "But I do not find that the cornea has any nerves and it may be pierced with a needle without occasioning any pain" (Loc. cit., Note 2, (ii) p. 24). Similarly it is interesting that he found no evidence of the irritability of the arteries despite the fact that they have a muscular coat (Ibid., p. 30). And again he finds the ureters devoid of a muscular force "as indeed there has never been any muscular fibres plainly shown in those canals". (Ibid., p. 32).
9 Ibid., (ii), p. 25
10 Loc. cit., Note 6 (i)
11 Whytt, Robert (1751) *An Essay on the Vital and other involuntary and other Motions of Animals*, Edinburgh, Hamilton, Balfour and Neill, p. 291
12 Loc. cit., Note 2, (ii), p. 45
13 Ibid., (ii), p. 40. Haller suggests that the force resides in the glutinous, mucous fraction of the muscle fibre, "because this when it is pulled, endeavours to shorten itself.
14 Ibid., (ii), p. 42
15 Ibid., (ii), p. 43
16 Innumerable workers repeated the experiments relating to the sensibility of various parts – particularly the tendo achilles and the meninges of the brain. The collected works referred to below (see Note 17) are taken up with the recital of a vast number of these.

17 (i) *Sulla Insensitivita ed Irritabilita Halleriana*, Opuscoli di vari autori raccolti da Giacinto Bartolomeo Fabri, 2 Vols, Bologna per Giriolamo Corciolani, ed Eredi Colli a S. Tommaso d' Aquino, 1757. A similar publication appeared in Switzerland
(ii) *Mémoires sur la nature sensibles et irritable des parties du corps animal*, 4 Vols, Tissot (transl.), Lausanne, M.M. Bosquet, 1756–1760
18 Ibid., (i) p. 13
19 Ibid., (i), p. 6
20 Ibid., (i), pp 6 and 7
21 Ibid., (i), p. 8
22 Ibid., (i), p. 9
23 Ibid., (i), pp 9–10, c.f. Haller's remarks, which his pupil reiterated
24 Ibid., (i), p. 74
25 Ibid., (i), p. 118
26 Ibid., (i), p. 120
27 See: *Benjamin Franklin's Experiments: A new edition of Experiments and Observations on Electricity* with a critical and historical introduction by I. Bernard Cohen (ed.), Cambridge, Mass., Harvard University Press, 1941, p. 219, para. 19
28 Loc. cit., Note 17 (i), p. 211
29 Ibid., (i), p. 212
30 Ibid., (i), p. 213
31 Ibid., (i), p. 215
32 Ibid., (i), p. 216
33 Ibid., (i), p. 226
34 Ibid., (i), p. 227

* See Biographical Index

13

The scientific background to the study of irritability in Bologna

It is significant that N.N. could cite so many Bolognese scientists who were involved with the problem of the nature of irritability and whom he felt could demonstrate its universality as a force in nature. All these men, whatever their particular scientific interest, had in common a reductionist outlook and a dedication to the experimental method, for in Bologna there was a deeply held view that in order to find the answer to any particular problem one must be prepared to turn to any or all of the various branches of scientific knowledge. This attitude was expressed by Jacopo Sandri,[1] the foremost contemporary medical teacher, with reference to the problems of medical science and is reflected in the comprehensive scientific outlook of the medical teachers of the time.[1]

The new mechanistic philosophy had been introduced into Bologna University by Francesco Maria Zanotti who was appointed to the Chair of Philosophy in 1718. He resigned from this in order to succeed Matteo Bazzani* as Secretary of the Institute in 1723 and as its President in 1766. His influence during his long term of office as Secretary was enormous.

Zanotti's early education was in a Jesuit school and then at the university in his native Bologna. He became accomplished in Greek and Latin as well as Mathematics and his facility with the classical languages enabled him to read the ancient philosophers comprehensively. He made a detailed study of these in order to understand the roots of scholastic philosophy and then turned his mind to 17th century authors, particularly Descartes* and Malebranche* whose ideas he favoured. According to his biographer, Giovanni Fantuzzi, writing in 1778,[2] he did much to introduce these ideas into the school of philosophy, which ". . . still had a taste for the scholastics . . ."[3] despite the contemporary success of the experimental study of anatomy by the Faculty of Medicine and that of hydrostatics by the mathematicians. His enthusiasm for the new experimental philosophy was, however, much more theoretical than practical. He was a philosopher of science rather than an experimenter.

Fantuzzi considered that Zanotti's most important contribution to the scientific milieu of Bologna was the introduction of these new mechanistic ideas. He says he was the first to explain the Cartesian theory of vortices, light, colours and motion, which were ". . . completely new in Bologna at that time . . ."[4] However the ideas of Descartes were soon to be replaced for when, a few years later, the Newtonian system reached Bologna, Zanotti turned his mind to it, expounding Newton's ideas in his lectures, explaining the attraction of the heavenly bodies, the refrangibility of light, the consistency of colours, etc, in terms of the Newtonian theory. He exhorted his students to apply themselves to the study of Newton since by this time, he considered it the true explanation of natural phenomena since it was derived ". . . from reason and not from custom or caprice."[5]

As a result of his interest in Aristotelian philosophy, Zanotti attempted a reconciliation between the surviving elements of this and the new theories of Newton and Descartes. In the early 18th century the Newtonian theory of attraction became applied not only to physical and biological phenomena but also to moral and philosophical issues and Zanotti was one of the first to try to apply Newtonianism to ideas, presenting his theories in the form of an argument in his book, *Della Forza Attrativa delle Idee*, in 1747.[6]

He took part in the Leibnizian-Cartesian[7] controversy and was involved with the moral doctrines of Maupertuis*, publishing his ideas in volumes which appeared in the 1750's.[8] Throughout his long academic career, Zanotti preached Newtonianism to Bologna and in 1762 published his definitive exposition of Newton's Theory in a work entitled *De Viribus Centralibus*.[9]

This was the man who set the scene for the development of experimental science in Bologna, who in his rôle as Professor of Philosophy introduced Newtonian theory to the University and in his rôles as Secretary and President of the Institute was the father figure in the scientific society of Bologna, guiding, criticising, editing and evaluating the scientific work of his time – a reductionist who believed that even ideas obeyed Newton's laws.

When Zanotti relinquished the Chair of Philosophy in 1723, it passed to Gaetano Tacconi*, who taught Galvani pathology. Tacconi himself was a pupil of Lelio Trionfetti* and Matteo Bazzani, the first and second Presidents of the Institute. Having completed three years of his medical course, Tacconi delivered a public oration entitled 'Dissertatio pro instauratione studiorum medicam artem respicientium',[10] which brought him great acclaim. His theme dealt with the best ways of teaching, learning and practising medicine or in other words, the scientific and moral education of the physician. The general and important nature of this theme indicates the breadth of approach of this young man to his subject and his appointment to the Chair of Philosophy at the age of 34 is evidence of his inclination and ability as a general scientific thinker. Laura Bassi was his pupil and protegée and it was as a result of his teaching that the celebrated Bolognese physicist developed into one of the leading Newtonian scientists in Italy.

But Tacconi's talents were not of course restricted to general philosophy. When Valsalva* the first anatomical dissector in the University, died in 1723, Tacconi was suggested as his successor, a post in which he was highly successful. Four years later he was lecturing from the Chair of Anatomy and after eight years he was promoted to the post of Senior Physician in the Santa Maria della Mortes hospital where he was able to devote himself to the study of surgical pathology. Tacconi is known to have taught Galvani pathology but there can be little doubt that he also taught his pupil the Newtonian approach to medical science.

Galeazzi, Galvani's father-in-law, is referred to by N.N. as a cautious and astute philosopher whose mind might be expected to reveal the secrets of irritability.[11] It is certain that experiments with this in mind were carried out by 'Gli Inesperti' in that little laboratory in Galeazzi's house and there is little doubt that Galeazzi's approach to the nature of irritability was that of a reductionist. Like Tacconi he was a product of Trionfetti's philosophic teaching and like Tacconi his range of scientific interest and ability was very wide. At the age of 25 (in 1711) he was elected deputy Professor of Experimental Physics in the Bologna Institute (Jacopo Beccari* occupying the Chair at this time), succeeding to the Chair in 1734, when Beccari took over the Chair of Chemistry.

As a young man Galeazzi travelled to Paris where, at the time, Italians were very welcome. He met Malebranche, Réaumur*, Fontenelle*, Homberg*, the younger de Lahire*, Varignon* and Louis Lemery* among others and wrote home long scientific letters to Beccari giving descriptions of instruments and ideas currently in vogue in Paris. When he returned home two years later, he was promoted to the university Chair of Philosophy, which he held for 40 years.

Galeazzi, who tends to be remembered as an anatomist, wrote on chemistry, physics and medical practice as well as anatomy and like many 18th century scientists had the naturalist's interest in geographical, geological and biological phenomena.

As a chemist he was interested in the argument current in the Paris Academy as to whether iron which is so widely encountered in nature is a composite or simple body, in the language of the Paris Academy at that time a 'product' or an 'educt'. Étienne François Geoffroy* was the leading champion of the former and Louis Lemery of the latter view. On his return to Italy Galeazzi undertook numerous experiments with the naturalist Guiseppe Monti, and as a result of these he was led to support Lemery's view. During the course of these experiments he examined the varying quantities of iron found in plants, animals and various parts of different species of living things. This investigation was extended to include the human body and studies were made of the inhabitants of different localities, that is, areas rich or poor in iron. The results of his analysis appear in the *Bologna Commentaries* under the title, 'De Ferreis particulis quae in corporibus reperiuntur'.[12]

As a physicist Galeazzi turned his mind to the variation of readings obtained from different instruments being used for any particular measurement. The French scientist Guillaume Amontons* had bequeathed a great number of barometers, thermometers and hygrometers etc, to the Paris Academy and Galeazzi had become interested in them during his visit. On his return he carried out a number of experiments aimed at studying the cause of the variation in the expansion of certain fluids used in the thermometers and concluded that this was due to the variations in the quality of the air introduced into them.[13] He also studied the variability of barometers and studied the nature of temperature changes *in vacuo*.[14]

His anatomical studies covered a wide field and included the investigation and description of the disposition of the muscular wall of the stomach, the disposition and connections of the lacteals, the formation of renal and biliary stones.[15]

As a naturalist he set off, in 1719, on a journey to the hills of San Pellegrino, in company with Luigi Ferdinando Marsigli*. The latter was interested in the geological formation of the terrain while Galeazzi was concerned with meteorological and biological phenomena. He climbed Pradalbino and Monte Maggiore where he encountered fossil scallops, oysters and other marine animals and some pieces of the famous phosphoric stone of Bologna (see later in this chapter). He found sea urchins in such numbers that it seemed as if the whole hill was composed of them. Galeazzi studied these fossil creatures and carried out various barometric determinations. He collected various materials from an erupting volcano and when he returned to Bologna subjected them to various chemical analyses.

Galeazzi taught Galvani anatomy but it is obvious that he must have passed on to his son-in-law much of his general knowledge and interest in experimental chemistry, physics and the study of nature.

Tacconi and Galeazzi both show a comprehensive approach to scientific problems – an approach which we have noted was typical of the Bologna attitude at this time. Hard and fast lines between different areas of study were not drawn and a wide understanding of all branches of scientific knowledge were believed to be necessary for the solution of any particular problem.

Other teachers such as Monti, Caldani*, and Manfredi, all shared this attitude which Jacopo Sandri had urged on those who would solve the problems of medicine. Its general influence on Galvani must have been very strong and particularly through Galeazzi who was so close to him. However the teacher who seems to have had the most specific influence on the development of Galvani's concept of the nature of irritability was Jacopo Beccari, who held the Chair of Chemistry.

Jacopo Beccari, like Galeazzi and Tacconi, was taught philosophy by Lelio Trionfetti then Bologna's most eminent teacher. As has been noted, philosophy was to a great extent still dominated by scholasticism but Trionfetti was both a botanist and naturalist and these interests doubtless influenced his young student.[16] After a period of studying chemistry, physics and botany, Beccari entered the school of Jacopo Sandri. Sandri was one of the most illustrious students of Marcello Malpighi*, who ran a private medical school under the aegis of the University. He was impressed by the enthusiasm and ability of his young student and made him a member of the newly formed society 'Gli Inquieti'[17] which met regularly at his house. A year before Beccari received his Laureates in philosophy and medicine in 1704, he read two papers to this group which was to develop into the Academy of Science of Bologna. The manuscripts merely described as *Dissertationes duae* are in the Academy of Science of Bologna.[18] One was concerned with the electrical properties of amber and various other bodies, the other with the basic nature of the combustion of bodies. In this he attacked the new ideas of the English chemist John Mayow developing his arguments in a masterful style.[18]

His view was that such bodies must contain sulphureous and saline particles which by their interaction cause the production of sufficient heat to transform them into flame. Thus we see that right at the beginning of his career, Beccari was interested in the nature of Newton's combustion model, an interest which underlined much of his later work.

In 1705 he was appointed lecturer in philosophy and a year later of medicine in the University. By 1711, he had so impressed his colleagues and teachers that he was appointed to the Chair of Experimental Physics in the Institute, his friend Galeazzi acting as deputy.

Zannoti said of Beccari's qualifications for the Chair of Physics:

He had been taught extensively in geometry and in all the philosophical sciences, being as experienced and as learned as the greatest savant. He knew so thoroughly the matters of metaphysics, especially those which the princes of the new philosophy like Descartes, Malebranche, Leibniz and others brought forth, that he was able to explain them in a scholarly way and readily to demonstrate them. But he excelled as well in the knowledge of physics being ever faultless in his ingenuity of experiment and in his theoretic discourses.[19]

Two botanical papers were read in 1705[20] and then in 1706 Beccari wrote an essay on the inflammable, sulphureous emanations from fissures and cracks in rocks.[21] Another paper, undated, deals with the same topic. Beccari describes a journey he made to Pietramala on the Tuscan slopes of the Apennines – a location well known for the production of inflammable gases.[21]

Much later in 1728, we find Beccari writing to the English Newtonian, William Derham*, on the nature of the *ignis fatui* of the marshy areas near Bologna. (Derham had recently proposed Beccari as a FRS). The Italian scientist did not believe the phenomena was due to the light emitted by glow-worms or fireflies but rather to the combustion of vapours emitted from fissured ground. However, as to their exact nature he would not say since these evanescent lights were most easily and constantly seen in bitterly cold weather and when it was raining and he could not feel these conditions could possibly favour combustion. Furthermore, he had never found evidence of a conflagration at the site of the phenomenon.[22]

In 1711 he accompanied Count Marsigli, his friend and colleague, on an expedition to Monte Peterno, primarily at the instigation of Marsigli who wished to collect further evidence concerning the famous Bologna Stone which abounded in this locality (see earlier in this chapter).

An excellent account of the history of this mineral is given by Priestley in the first volume of *The History and Present State of Discoveries relating to Vision, Light and Colours*.[23] It was first discovered according to Priestley by a Bolognese shoemaker named Vincenzo Cascariolo, some time around 1630. Cascariolo had been searching in the neighbourhood of Monte Peterno for what Priestley calls "... some chemical secret ..."[24] He made the astonishing discovery that this rock, when placed in a dark place after previous exposure to light, was plainly visible as a result of light issuing from it. As Priestley says, such a remarkable fact could not fail to engage the attentions of philosophers and soon all over Europe they were examining specimens and writing about it. Marsigli was one of these. He published his treatise in 1698.[25]

The significance of the property of Bologna Stone lay in its apparent ability to store light and re-emit it from its body. The fact that this emission could be stimulated by heat added further interest – and seemed to substantiate a corpuscular view of light as postulated by Newton. Newton includes these phenomena in his 8th Query as a manifestation of his model for the motion of parts of the body.[26] Heat representing the external force could be presumed to set in motion aethereal and sulphureous particles within this stone, forcing the emission of super-abundant light particles which had previously been absorbed by the stone during its exposure to light. In fact this could be explained as one of the gentler, slower types of combustion, analogous to the organic processes supposedly involved in putrefaction, the glow of the glow-worm, the light produced by *ignis fatui* etc – and the light resulting from muscular motion. This, however, was not the only view adopted. Granted that a material view of light was accepted, there was the problem of whether the light imbibed was the same as that emitted. Was the Bologna Stone acting merely as a temporary store or did the exposure to light kindle into activity other light particles, dormant in the pores of the stone. Zanotti and later, Padre Giambattista Beccaria* conducted experiments aimed at elucidating this, the former coming to the conclusion that the afferent and efferent lights were different, the latter concluding they were the same.

From one point of view it is interesting that Beccari along with his companions collected numerous specimens of this stone and according to Priestley:

> These gentlemen took a great deal of pains with the chemical analysis of this fossil, by which they thought they had discovered in it some sulphur and also an alkaline salt.[27]

Beccari continued his study of the Bologna Stone by building a special dark room in his house where he was able to observe its behaviour. During the same visit to the Bolognese hills he also discovered that the earth there contained the mineral remains of myriads of minute animalculae which came to be known as 'Rotaria Beccari'.[28]

In 1724 he once again returned to his interest in fossilised testaceans. Marsigli had donated a wonderful collection of these to the academy and Beccari shared the general interest in them. Apparently, scientists in Bologna were "completely absorbed in dactyls" (the name given to these creatures by Beccari).[29] Monti, Galeazzi, Eraclito Manfredi and many others were busy studying them.

Beccari took his studies a step further forward by visiting Ancona where he obtained living examples of these tiny creatures, presenting a paper describing the results of his studies under the title 'De Luce Dactylorum'.[30] According to Pini his biographer:

> He [Beccari] asserted that these animals while still enclosed in stone emit a tenuous light similar to that of some worms. In the living state, but removed from their shell, they shine vividly because their investing pellicle is translucent, and they shine even

more if they are rubbed. The juice expressed from their body, has no less splendour. The light which shines from them is white, tending towards blue, and seems more concentrated in those appendices of muscular semblance, which the animal extrudes and retracts and which Réaumur considers as organs for absorbing and expelling sea water.[31]

Here is the overt suggestion that the moving parts of an animal contain a specially great quantity of light, or of a matter which releases light either *per se*, or when activated by rubbing. The analogy with the Newtonian model is obvious.

Beccari continued his study of the phosphorescence of substances other than the Bologna Stone and found that nearly all natural bodies could be seen to emit light although their ability to do so varies enormously and depended, in some cases, on activation by rubbing or heat.[32]

Both Dufay* working in Paris and Beccari had recognised the luminous properties of diamonds at about the same time and both continued to extend their investigations to other bodies. Despite Beccari's demonstration that an enormous number of bodies both organic and non-organic possessed this phosphorescent property he was never able to communicate it to water or metals "Almost all vegetable and animal substances, when thoroughly dry had this property".[32] But, says Priestley, "To metals and water he could never communicate the least degree of light, which is something remarkable, and deserving particular notice, as these substances agree in the property of being conductors of electricity."[33] Priestley's remark is evidence of the way in which he (and Beccari no doubt) were equating the behaviour of phosphorescent bodies with activation of 'phlogiston' within metals or the conducting tissues of an animal, as a result of the 'external agent' electricity.

Beccari continued his experiments on the phenomenon of phosphorescence which led to an interest in the ability of light to change the intimate structure of bodies[34] *viz* the purple colouration induced in a quantity of *luna cornea* exposed to the sunlight – although it was Schulze* who made the discovery that the effect depended on the presence of silver.

Perhaps Beccari's best known claim to fame is one that had nothing to do with light or combustion. He was the first to separate the gluten fraction of flour – a task of analysis which he himself describes as ". . . a thing of little labour . . ."[35]

If one tries to recognise a significant bias in the type of investigation undertaken by Beccari it seems fair to say that he was fundamentally concerned with the intimate structure of bodies and their ability to emit light.

He maintained a correspondence with the famous Italian electrician, Father Beccaria, and one of his letters to his friend touches on his view of the importance of electricity as an agent in bringing about chemical changes within the human body:

I cannot deny that I am a little flattered by the honour you deigned to pay to my prediction that the electric vapour could one day become an agent capable of bringing about new events in chemistry. But only your perspicacity and dexterity could do what my presage forecast. If the electrical vapour has been able to accelerate vegetation in plants, why could it not promote or otherwise modify the solution, fermentation and other such things untried by chemists.[36]

In another letter to Galeazzi, discussing the action of electricity on the human body he says that it:

. . . does not only act by introducing very smooth, active particles into the electrified body particles capable of setting in motion, sharpening and altering the configuration of the smallest particles of fluids, but acts also by shaking, irritating, or invigorating the solids; those moving little elastic machines . . .[37]

Beccari is merely referring to electricity the rôle of which, as we have seen, was generally ascribed to it as the agent which provokes irritability. While Haller himself made no use of electricity as a stimulating agent producing irritability, after the introduction of Leyden Jars and electrical machines in the mid-century countless experiments were made in which it was directed through the various parts of animals and its ability to convulse muscles was common knowledge as Priestley has shown.

Two examples of the use of electricity in this way are interesting as an illustration of the sort of experiments that were being carried out at this time – the results of which were obviously widely known among Bolognese scientists.

Father Beccaria, the foremost Italian electrician at this time, was a devoted admirer of Franklin's views and was responsible for the dissemination of the latter's theory throughout Italy. In 1753 he produced a two volume work on the nature of artificial and natural electricity which appeared in English translation in 1776.[38] Here he describes an experiment on a cock as follows:

We fastened the cock to a chair, its wings were tied to the highest cross-stick of the back of the chair; a man held its head and its left leg was left at liberty, for the surgeon to operate on it. The thigh being stripped of all its common ligaments, without lacerating its fleshy fibres, I began to send sparks through the several muscles which remain united and in their natural position successfully. I used my usual jars [Leyden Jars], which contain at most half a pint; with one hand I held the belly of it, to which was fastened a brass chain; with my other hand and a stick of sealing wax I managed the other end of the brass chain; I presented this end of the brass chain to the extremity of the muscle, and the hook of the bottle to the other extremity; and the passage of the spark being thus evidently determined, I constantly made the following observations

I. Any of the muscles when traversed by the spark was vehemently contracted so that it always compelled the hand of the surgeon to give way.

II. The contraction of the muscle always was attended with a sudden and proportionally violent swelling of it; meanwhile, the places where the membrane which parts one muscle from another, was inserted between them, remained depressed.

III. In the place through which the spark ran, the membrane which vested the muscle, from moist and smooth became in an instant dry and wrinkled the direction of the wrinkles being transversal to the length of the muscle, and a very conspicuous vapour or smoke arose over that place.

IV. The dryness the wrinkles and the smoke continued after the spark had passed; but these different accidents afterwards gradually vanished so that the membrane partly recovered that kind of gloss, which is the result of moisture; another spark being sent afresh the same appearances again took place.

V. While one muscle was thus contracted, a kind of general contraction was observable in all the muscles contiguous to it; and there was hardly a muscle in the thigh that remained in a quiet state, which I have considered as a visible proof of the expansion of the shock into lateral parts.

VI. For several seconds after the passage of the spark, small convulsions took place in the muscle, and it was during that time that the above-mentioned wrinkles began to lessen and a new moisture gradually appeared on the muscle.[39]

The production of these very violent contractions associated with injury of the animal tissues was seen by Beccaria as likely to shed light on the normal, physiological act:

From these violent contractions of muscle, a vast field is now opened for conjectures about the cause of the voluntary contractions of muscles.[40]

He proceeds to equate such violent contractions with those produced when an animal is killed by an electric shock or lightning and makes the point that, in these cases, the quantity of electrical fluid passing is so great that it "... injures the whole system itself and renders it unfit for performing again its vital functions".[40] The greater the quantity of electrical fluid, the larger the animal that can be killed, the more violent its contractions, the greater the attendant damage by burning. The suggestion that a sufficiently small quantity of electricity may be able to produce physiological contraction in the absence of side effects is implicit, but Beccaria does not indulge in this speculation since "... Such inquiries are too foreign to our subject to engage in them at present ..."[40]

Even more interesting is the description of a series of experiments carried out by Marc Antonio Caldani, who was Professor of Anatomy in Bologna University from 1755–1761 and almost certainly a teacher of Galvani.[41] In his letter to Haller (read in the Academy of the Institute of Sciences of Bologna on 25 November 1756)[42] he describes a vast number of experiments on the sensitivity of various parts and then turns to the question of irritability. He examines the response of tissue to such stimuli as needle pricks and the application of burning metal rods and then deals with the results of electrical stimulation:

All the parts of a frog, whether living or dead are set in motion by the electrical spark. This is specially seen in their intestines, which when electrified, contract vigorously; and one can by this means awaken movement in them and make it last a good time even although it had previously ceased. Likewise we also extracted electric sparks from the intestines of some cats and I observed that these produced movements of a magnitude that I could not have brought about by another external stimulus. We laid bare the crural nerves of a frog, and dividing them close to the vertebral column at their point of issue, we arranged them so that they lay over a little wooden spoon, each one forming four little bends, I held an electrified iron rod near them, at a distance of two, three and even more inches, but the muscles of the inferior limb always contracted violently. All this happened with the mere thrust of the electrical material without extracting any electric spark. After the space of fifty minutes we found these nerves to be desiccated and inflexible. We pricked them with needles, we pinched them with our fingers, without any contraction of the lower limbs. On bringing the electrified point near to them however, the usual movements were observed, although they were weaker. The same thing was done to the crural nerves of two other frogs and the result was in no way different. The chest of a cat was then opened and we pinched the diaphragmatic nerve with our fingers, as a result of which the diaphragm at once contracted. We then brought an electrified iron window-catch near the same nerve and the diaphragm was always convulsed even when all other stimuli failed. It was beautiful to see that when we withdrew a spark from any part of a frog, whatever, even some other frogs which were lying together on the same table, were set in motion.[43]

Electricity as Caldani demonstrated, was obviously the external biological stimulus *par excellence* and it could act at a distance. Was it the normally occurring one and if so what process did it set in motion in muscle?

Notes

1   Sandri was recognised as the most esteemed pupil of the famous Marcello Malpighi (1628–1694). The latter had been in Florence when the famous Accademia del Cimento was formed in 1657 at the instigation of Ferdinand II, the Grand Duke of Tuscany. In this atmosphere, among colleagues devoted to the new scientific learning, he had collaborated with his friend Giovanni Borelli and on his return to Bologna in 1660 was one of the founder members of the Accademi della Traccia which was based on the same ideals and constitution as the older and more renowned Florentine Societies (other Bolognese academies founded during this period were: Accademia della Rosa, della Spada, della Mano, della Croce e della Ede). As with the Royal Society in London these formed a meeting place for scientists of widely differing disciplines but with a common belief in the value of the experimental method. There was a common medium for the exchange of ideas out of which grew the realisation that scientific problems might derive their solution from the concept and methods of more than one branch of science. Sandri was brought up in this intellectual atmosphere and interpreted the problems of medical science in this way. His "Saggi Medici" read before the Accademia degl' Inquieti in 1694 (four years after its foundation) were concerned with a purely physiological topic, the nature of the blood, yet Sandri, ". . . at every step, confirmed his theories by reference to the authority of Galileo, Bacon, Toricelli, Borelli, Malpighi, Redi, Harvey, Willis, Mayow, Graaf, Boyle, Leeuwenhoek and others who expanded the frontiers of science through experiment . . ." In the opening pages of his "Saggio Primo", Sandri refers to the scientific principles on which the study of medicine should be based, stating that a knowledge of chemistry, mechanics, anatomy and other subjects is necessary. See: Medici, 'Cenno Storico Intorno le Accademie Scientifiche di Bologna . . .', *Memorie della Società Medico-Chirurgica di Bologna, Sequito agli opuscoli da essai pubblicati,* Bologna, Tipografia governativa-alla Volpe, 1847, Vol. 4, pp iii–xxiii. See page xv

2   (i) Fantuzzi G.F. (1778) *Notizie della vita e degli scritti di Francisco Maria Zanotti,* Bologna nella Stemperia di S. Tommaso d'Aquino
    (ii) See also *Enciclopedia Italiana di Scienze, Lettere ed Arti, Instituto della Enciclopedia, Italiana,* Fondata di Giovanni Treccani a Roma, Milan, Rizzoli and Co., 1937, Vol. 35, p. 886

3   Ibid., (i), p. 15

4   Ibid., (i), p. 19

5   Ibid., (i), p. 20

6   Zanotti F. (1747) *Della Forza Attrativa delle Idee,* Naples. The publishers of this work (and Note 9) cannot be traced. Fantuzzi who includes a chapter on Zanotti's publications in the work referred to above (Note 2 (i), pp 25–46) is careful to give full references to other works, for example Note 8, but fails to give details of the publisher of these two. Other sources consulted, have also failed to supply the information

7   At this time there was a division of opinion between philosophers as to whether the force by which a body is self-moved (and is called Life), is measured by its velocity (the Cartesian view), or by the square of its velocity (Leibniz's view)

8 Zanotti F. (1752) *Della Forza de' Corpi, che chiamano viva*, Bologna per gli Eredi Constantino Pisarri e Giacomo Filippo Primodi, Impressori del S. Officio con lic. Di sup.

9 Zanotti F. (1762) *De Viribus Centralibus*, Bologna (see Note 6)

10 Tacconi G. (1853) 'Dissertatio pro instauratione studiorum medicam artem respicientium' was an oration which was not published. See: M. Medici, *Della Vita e degli Scritti degli Anatomici e Medici fioriti in Bologna*, Bologna, Tipografia a S. Tommaso, d'Aquino, p. 4

11 See Chap. 12 of this book

12 (i) Galeazzi D.M.G. (1746) 'De Ferreis particulis quae in corporibus reperiuntur', *De Bononiensi Scientiarum et Artium Instituto atque Accademia Commentarii*, Bologna, Tipis Laelii a Vulpe Instituti Scientiarum Tipographi, Tom. 2, Pt II, pp 20–38
   (ii) See also, M. Medici, 'Elogio di Domenico Maria Gusmano Galeazzi', p. 8, contained in loc. cit., Note 10

13 Galeazzi D.M.G. (1746) 'De Thermometris Amontoniasnasis conficiedis', *De Bononiensi Scientiarum et Artium Instituto atque Accademia Commentarii*, Bologna, Tipis Laelii a Vulpe Instituti Scientiarum Tipographi, Tom. 2, Pt II, pp 20–38

14 See 'De Calore et Figore in vacuo', *De Bononiensi Scientiarum et Artium Instituto atque Accademia Commentarii*, Bologna, Tipis Laelii a Vulpe Instituti Scientiarum Tipographi, 1745, Tom. 2, Pt I, pp 312–315

15 Loc. cit., Note 12 (ii), p. 10 *et seq.*

16 See Eliot F. Beach, 'Beccari of Bologna, the discoverer of Vegetable Protein', *Journal of the History of Medicine*, 1961, Vol. 16, pp 354–373

17 Ibid., p. 356

18 See Giovanni Pini, *Jacopo Bartolomeo Beccari*, Bologna, Licinio Cappelli, 1940, Chap. II, p. 25. The dissertation on the combustion of bodies does not appear to have a title; the other was entitled 'Phylosophicae meditationes de succino et de rei ipsius aliorumque similium corporum attractione'

19 Loc. cit., Note 16, p. 358

20 'Observatio et cogitata circa odoriferarum plantarium Folia' read on 26 November 1705. 'Semi delle piante' was read in the same year, and two other essays concerned with botanical subjects appeared during the next two years. 'De Plantarum Vegitione' and 'Della Diligenza della natura nel formare e conservare tutte le cose e in particolare le piante'

21 Loc. cit., Note 18, p. 26

22 Derham W. (1729–1730) 'Of the meteor called the Ignis Fatuus, from observations made in England, by the Reverend Mr W. Derham, F.R.S. and others in Italy, communicated by Dr Thomas Derham . . .' *Philosophical Transactions*, Vol. 36, No. 411, pp 204–214, especially pp 206–215

23 Priestley, Joseph (1772) *The History and Present State of Discoveries relating to Vision, Light and Colours*, London, J. Johnson, Vol. I, p. 361 *et seq.*

24 Ibid., Vol. I, p. 361

25 Marsigli L.F. (1698) *Dissertatione Epistolare da fosforo minerale o sua della pietra illuminabile Bolognese*, Leipzig, s.n.

26 See Chap. 9 of this book, Note 11

27 Loc. cit., Note 23, Vol. I, p. 362

28 Beccari was the first to describe this species of foraminifera found in the sandy areas of Bologna and the Adriatic. It was given the name Rotaria Beccari as a gesture to Beccari whose priority in its discovery was not originally recognised. See: loc. cit., Note 18, p. 29

29 Loc. cit., Note 18, pp 30–31

30 Beccari J.B. (1745) 'De Luce Dactylorum' *De Bononiensi Scientiarum . . .*, Bologna, Tipis Laelii a Vulpe Instituti Scientiarum Tipographi, Tom. 2, Pt I, pp 248–273

31 Loc. cit., Note 18, p. 31

32 Loc. cit., Note 23, p. 368

33 Ibid., p. 369

34 Ibid., p. 379

35 Loc. cit., Note 16, p. 362

36 Loc. cit., Note 18, p. 34

37 Ibid., p. 54

38 Beccaria, Giambattista (1776) *A Treatise upon Artificial Electricity* . . . Translated from the original Italian of Father Giambatista Beccaria, Professor of Natural Philosophy in the University of Turin, London, J. Nourse

39 Ibid., p. 270

40 Ibid., p. 272

41 Galvani graduated in 1759 so it seems likely that he was a pupil of Caldani. Tommaso Laghi, another Bolognese anatomist had tried the effect of stimulating muscles electrically. See: T. Laghi, 'De insensibilitate, atque irritabilitate Halleriana' *De Bononiensi* . . ., Bologna, Tipis Laelii a Vulpe Instituti Scientiarum Tipographi, 1757, Tom. 4, pp 208–217. See also: Hebbel E. Hoff, 'Galvani and the Pre-Galvani Electrophysiologists', *Annals of Science*, 1936, Vol. I, pp 157–172

42 *Sulla Insensitivita ed Irritabilita Halleriana*, Opuscoli di vari Autori raccolti da Giacinto Bartolomeo Fabri, Bologna, Girolamo Corciolani (ed.), Eredi Colli a S. Tommaso d'Aquino, 1757, Vol. I, pp 269–336

43 Ibid., p. 331

* See Biographical Index

14

Early life and initial research
of Luigi Galvani

Luigi Galvani was born on 9 September 1737 in the family home in Bologna. His father's house is still standing although the old Via delle Case has been renamed the Via Marconi and a busy bank now occupies the attractive terracotta building despite attempts to retain it as a memorial to the famous scientist.

Luigi's father, Domenico Galvani, following in the family tradition was a goldsmith and jeweller, an occupation which seems to have been followed by the Galvani family from the time of its move from Argenta to Bologna in about 1650. His mother, Barbara Foschi, came from a well-to-do background. She was his father's fourth wife and brought him as part of her dowry this house in the Via delle Case, where her own family had lived in considerable comfort and affluence. Luigi's step-brother, Francesco, was an advocate and taught Canon Law in the Bologna Studio. Tenure of this appointment brought certain privileges and status to the family, so that Luigi's home life was in every sense comfortable and secure and presumably conducive to his intellectual development.[1]

Virtually nothing is known about Galvani's childhood and early schooling. It was the common practice for boys of his class to receive their earliest lessons at home from their parents, progressing later to the care of such Jesuit tutors as the renowned Lelio Trionfetti and presumably Galvani's earliest education followed this pattern.

At the age of 15 he was enrolled at the Oratorio of the Filippine Fathers which had been attended by the sons of the best families in Bologna since the time of its foundation in 1612.[1] Galvani was a devoutly religious man all his life and while he was attending the Oratorio decided on a theological course of study with a view to taking Holy Orders. This may well have been the result of his period of work with a charitable Order whose concern was with looking after the dying. Pupils at the Oratorio had to undertake some form of social work during their school career and Galvani spent some time with this Order and this may have influenced him. Fortunately for posterity, his obvious ability in his general school studies did not pass unnoticed and one of the priests dissuaded him from his proposed course, suggesting that it would be unwise to commit himself to a religious life at such an early age, particularly as his aptitude for natural philosophy was so marked.[2] The young Galvani therefore turned to medicine, a career in which he no doubt felt he could combine his scientific bent with the practical care of the sick he had already experienced during his hours in the Convent. He was enrolled in the Faculty of

Medicine of the University of Bologna[3] at a relatively early age at a time when Francesco Maria Zanotti was President of the Bologna Institute and he had as his teachers such men as Jacopo Bartolomeo Beccari, Gaetano Tacconi, Domenica Maria Gusmano Galeazzi and Giovanni Antonio Galli*.

The young student continued to show his aptitude for natural philosophy and was soon recognised by these men as being of more than usual ability and integrity. This latter quality, together with a gentleness of manner and modesty was characteristic of Galvani throughout life and led to his being held not only in respect but in sincere affection by his teachers and colleagues.[4]

In one particular instance this bond of affection developed into a family relationship for Galvani married Lucia, the daughter of Galeazzi his anatomy professor, and their life-long devotion to one another is one of the most charming episodes in the history of science. Lucia was apparently well educated as were many women in 18th century Italy and may well have been destined for a university career had she not married and devoted herself to helping her husband with his work.[5] The education of women in scientific subjects was not at all uncommon in Bologna in the early 18th century and the highest university appointments were open to them. In Galvani's lifetime the aunt and teacher of Lazaro Spallanzani*, the famous Laura Maria Caterina Bassi-Verati* opened a school of experimental physics having been granted a Chair in the University in 1732. A protegée of Tacconi who also taught Galvani she became renowned throughout Europe for her learning and had considerable influence on the development of the experimental study of physics in Italy at this time. Yet another contemporary of Galvani, Anna Morandi-Manzolini*, held the Chair of Anatomy and was famed as a teacher. She was extremely skilful in making wax models of anatomical parts for demonstration purposes and three years after she died when the Anatomy Theatre was dedicated, Galvani delivered an oration entitled *De Manzoliniana Supellectili*,[6] referring to the wonderful collection of models she had left and paying tribute to her skill as an anatomist and teacher.

Galvani almost certainly met his future wife in her father's house where the latter held private classes in anatomy to which Galvani was invited. They were married in 1760, a year after he received his Laureate, and he and his bride set up house in the Galeazzi home. Soon after this his father-in-law, together with various colleagues formed a small scientific society disarmingly called 'Gli Inesperti', to which of course Galvani belonged. One of the rooms in the house was equipped as a laboratory and regular meetings and scientific discussions were conducted there by the group up until the death of Galeazzi in 1775.

In 1762, three years after receiving his Laureate in philosophy, Galvani publicly defended his thesis 'De Ossibus'[7] in which he included what he considered the most important facts relevant to the chemical composition, structure, formation, nutrition and diseases of bone. A year previously he had been appointed alumno (student) at the Academy of Sciences and during the period prior to the defence of his thesis his time was divided between clinical work in the Bologna Hospitals and anatomical research. Two university dissertations resulted from the work done during this period, both of them reflecting the interests and research work of his Professor of Pathology, Tacconi, during the previous two decades. The first of these was the thesis to which we have just referred and the second dealt with the effects of the ingestion of Rubbia or Robbia by chickens.[8] Both Tacconi* and Duhamel* separately in Paris had been experimenting with the red die extracted from the plant madder and had noted its ability to stain animal tissues. The famous French naturalist had been carrying out some experiments on the growth of wood with Buffon* in 1737 when Hans Sloane* told him of the ability of madder to colour the bones of animals which ate it. Duhamel then carried out a long series of experiments confirming the English results, publishing his own in the Memoirs of the French Academy (1739–1741). He became interested in the formation and growth of bone and came to believe that new bone was formed by the addition of layers of osseous tissue originating in the periosteum – analogous to the growth of ligneous tissues in the outer part of the stem of plants. His ideas dispelled the belief that fractures were healed by the exudation of an 'osseous juice' and it came to be realised that it was the periosteum which supplied the tissue which eventually became new bone. The whole problem of the new bone formation interested Galvani's teacher, Tacconi, and this must have contributed to Galvani's choice of topic for his thesis.

Early the following year he delivered a public dissertation which dealt with the anatomy of the renal tract of birds.[9] According to the 19th century historian, Michele Medici, both his thesis and this dissertation met with acclaim in university circles[10] and doubtless combined soon afterwards to secure for Galvani the appointment of Honorary Lecturer. He appears to have been a lucid and interesting teacher whose lectures were crowded not only with young medical students for whom they were compulsory, but by many older practitioners who were anxious to keep up-to-date and extend their knowledge.

In his dissertation on the urinary tract in birds[9] he made use of a novel means of displaying the anatomical configuration of the renal system. Finding maceration an inadequate technique, he devised an original procedure which he termed "a new method of injection". Knowing that birds' urine coagulates smoothly into a sort of white mud if its flow is halted, he ligated together the ureters of a bird allowing the urine retained in the renal system to distend it and harden into a white cast which was the replica of the parts containing it. In this way he was able to demonstrate the intricacy of the renal architecture. He saw a multitude of uriniferous tubules appearing as white threads and was able to follow the many convolutions of these. He followed this up by injecting the arteries and veins, tracing their course into the renal lobules and thus indicating the differences in their disposition in birds as compared with quadrupeds.[10]

He traced the origin of the ureter and displayed its entrance into the bladder, showing that the valve-like mechanism, responsible for preventing urinary reflux, resulted from its oblique transit through the vesical wall and was exactly similar to that found in quadrupeds (c.f. Galen's description of the analogous structure in apes which he likened to the lid of a dovecote).[11]

Galvani then turned his attention to the intimate structure of the ureter. He describes three coats, but these were not analogous to the coats described today *viz* an outer fibrous, middle muscular and inner mucous. His 'outer coat' is the peritoneum; his middle coat is denser and thicker and contains an abundance of blood vessels and irregularly arranged 'fibres' – identified nowadays as the outer fibrous coat. He described his 'inner' coat as thicker than the others and presenting the colour of the muscular coat of the intestine (he is referring here to what we would now call the 'middle or muscular coat', since the internal coat is for us the mucous lining).

In his 'inner coat' with its irregularly disposed fibres, Galvani recognised some running parallel to the length of the ureter. These he guessed were of a muscular nature and responsible for ureteric movements. With his colleague, Francesco Bibiena* he went on to give proof of this conjecture by applying a stimulus to them and obtaining a contractile response. According to Medici, no one before Galvani had recognised three coats in the ureter and while it had been assumed that muscular fibres were present, they had never been demonstrated. Galvani's work was well contrived and carried out, and added to the available knowledge of the comparative anatomy of the renal system in birds.

The anatomical tables which Galvani produced as illustrations for this work received praise from the famous Johannes Müller in his publication *De Glandularum Secernentium Structura Penitiori . . .*[12] The content of Galvani's research as well as the clear exposition of the papers he read at this stage in his career, won him acclaim from the University and in April 1763 he was offered the appointment of Honorary Lecturer in Medicine by unanimous vote. By this time he was 25 and beginning to be embarrassed by his financial dependence on his father-in-law. The following year, therefore, he requested that his honorary appointment be translated to a paid one.[13] He had to wait until 1768 however, before he was given the post of paid lecturer, although he gained an income of 100 Lire per annum by his appointment as Curator and Demonstrator of Anatomy at the Museum of the Institute of Science in 1766. He succeeded Erco Lelli* who, like Anna Morandi, was famous for his ability to make superb anatomical models. These, carved from wood or fashioned from wax, were inherited by Galvani whose appointment required him to lecture to medical students, painters and sculptors. He was eventually granted the post of paid lecturer in consideration of his research contributions to the University and for the anatomical dissections he had performed at Galeazzi's house as well as in the Saint Orsola Hospital (under Professor Galli) and in the Hospital for the Dying.

In the intervening years Galvani had given several more Latin dissertations to the University, two[14,15] on the effects of the ingestion of Robbia by animals and another on the excretion of urine in birds.[16]

In 1767 he read a dissertation entitled 'Desquistiones anatomica circa membranam pituitariam'. The manuscript of this was found in the Archives of the Academy some years after his death and published with certain others in the volume of collected works by the Academy of Sciences of Bologna in 1841–1842.[17] In this dissertation Galvani described certain corpuscles of varying sizes situated in the "pituitary membrane", that is, the mucosal lining of the nose (pituitary here referring to its phlegm producing properties). Galvani prepared his material for examination by maceration with a solution of black ink and examined it with a lens. He described these corpuscles in the anterior part of the nasal septum and inferior turbinate and says some are visible, even to the naked eye. Pressure on them resulted in the expression of a watery fluid, the tubercles becoming depressed after this manoeuvre. Galvani concluded that the larger of these tubercles was responsible for the production of a fluid which humidified the anterior nares. The Secretary of the Academy, Canterzani, added a note to the manuscript to the effect that Tacconi (whose opinion had obviously been sought) had given him back the dissertation saying that the material required better proof.[18]

In the following two years Galvani became interested in the anatomy of the ear and read four dissertations on the structure and function of this organ in birds and various species of animals, including man. By 1772, he was apparently ready to gather these separate treatises into a single volume and have it published in the Commentaries, but in the same year, Antonio Scarpa* published his book *De Structura fenestrae rotundae auris et de tympano secundario anatomicae observationes*[19] a work containing much of the research and observations of Galvani. Through this publication, Galvani lost much of the honour due to him but it was in part his own fault. Many of the academics at Bologna were slow to publish their results and Galvani was no exception as we see here and later in the case of his famous Commentary on muscular motion in animals. As Medici points out, the publication of Commentaries was a slow procedure, the sixth volume in which he intended publishing his collected works not coming out until 1783![20] Whether the two anatomists worked entirely independently is difficult to say. Scarpa certainly spent some time in Bologna when he was a student and when he might well have heard of Galvani's ideas. However this may be, Galvani contented himself with publishing a paper dealing only with those things not noted by Scarpa or in which he differed from Scarpa in his interpretation. This paper entitled 'De Volatilium Aurae'[21] dealt systematically with the external, middle and internal ear of birds and made original observations on the presence of structures homologous with those in man. He discussed the function of the ossicles and inner ear and postulated theories of sound perception.

Apart from the two dissertations in 1775 and 1776 on the same topic, which he incorporated in 'De Volatilium Aurae' and two further on cataract, read in 1779[22] and 1781[23] his other dissertations may be said to relate essentially to the problem of animal movement. It is interesting that the point at which Galvani really became involved in experimental work on the problem of animal motion, more or less coincided with the death of his father-in-law in 1775. Perhaps while Galeazzi was alive he felt constrained to restrict himself to such work as he felt Galeazzi wished him to do or again, with the latter's increasing age, his teaching burdens on his behalf may have occupied too much of his time. (In 1769 Galeazzi, owing to failing health, had given Galvani the task of continuing the teaching of practical anatomy in their house.)

He was certainly busy as a teacher of anatomy at this time. In 1772 he held the famous 'Carnival' course of public lectures in anatomy with great success.[24] This course was so named for two reasons. The need for avoiding very hot weather which would have resulted in the rapid disintegration of the cadavers meant that the most favourable time for holding the course coincided with the Carnival season. Furthermore, it was common for revellers, complete with costume and mask, to stroll into the audience of the anatomical lectures as part of the evening's diversion. There were 16 lectures in the course. In the first and last, the meeting finished at the end of the lecture, but in the others the audience was free to participate in the proceedings and ask questions. Artists, students and philosophers all took part in the lively disputes which arose and no doubt a good time was had by all. After the lecture, the lecturer came down from his chair, and proceeded to demonstrate his teaching on a prepared cadaver, in the centre of the theatre. Apparently, during Galvani's course of lectures, there was nobody able to dispute with him – so masterful was his presentation – and his lectures ended in tumultuous applause. When he was asked to give the course again in 1779 however he declined, giving poor health as his reason. This was certainly true but by 1779 he was also deeply involved with his experiments on muscular movement and doubtless did not wish to break off to give the course of lectures.

This brings us to the stage at which Galvani's work on muscular movement was beginning to engage his attention more or less exclusively as a research topic. Of course he was still actively engaged in the practice of clinical medicine and with university teaching, and continued to be so throughout his life.

The early stage in Galvani's professional life shows us that he was first and foremost an anatomist in the widest and best sense of the term. The nature of his thesis, which dealt not only with the structure of bones but also with their chemical composition, formation, nutrition and disease, is an early indication of his ability to consider both structure and function. The logical development of anatomy as a tool of scientific investigation, is mirrored in the development of Galvani's work. From basic descriptive work he progressed to the study of comparative anatomy as a means of reaching his ultimate goal. Thus we see him investigating and comparing homologous structures in the ears of birds and various species of animals, including man, and as a result of this, attempting a theory of sound perception.

In the investigation of muscular function, he felt the 'structure' of muscle needed to be known at a much more intimate level than that offered by the dissection technique of gross anatomy, but we have no records of any such investigations of the architecture of muscle in the *Commentary* of 1791. As Galvani quite rightly thought the secret of a muscle's ability to contract in response to a nervous stimulus lay hidden in its most intimate structure, far beyond the reach of the scalpel or microscope. Nothing short of chemical investigation would reveal this secret and it was with the technique of chemistry that Galvani made his first attack on the nature of muscle. The reasons that led him to this view are the substance of the next two chapters.

Notes

1 Tabarroni G. (1970) 'Luigi Galvani', extract from Grand Antologia Filosfica Milan, ed. Mazorati. Vol. XXI, p. 3 (By kind permission of the author from galley proofs)

2 See Candido Mesini, 'L' Uomo Galvani', Galvaniana, Bologna, The Committee for the bicentenary of the birth of Luigi Galvani 1937. This is a digest from an article which was published in the newspaper *Avvenire d'Italia*, Milan, 16 October 1937. According to *Nouvelle Biographie Generale*, Paris, 1858, Vol. 19, p. 353, it was Galvani's parents who dissuaded him from a theological career

3 In Bologna, at the time of Galvani, the University and the Institute of Science were two distinct entities: the University had its seat in the Archiginnasio, situated in the square then called Piazza della Pace and now named after Galvani. The Institute had its seat in the Piazza Poggi, the present seat of the University. The Institute, which had been created in 1714 by Count Luigi Ferdinando Marsigli, could be regarded as a superior Faculty of Science and was the active nucleus of scientific life in Bologna recognised and appreciated abroad (Simeoni, L. *Storia dell' Universita di Bologna*, Vol. II, Bologna, Zanichelli, 1947, p. 125). The Academy of the Inquieti which came into being around 1690 at the instigation of those wishing to give special emphasis to the experimental aspect of scientific research, met in the Institute and took its name. The Academy which was then heavily endowed by the Bolognese Pope, Benedetto XIV was also named Benedettina. See G.C. Pupilli, *Luigi Galvani, Bologna, Universita degli Studi*, 1956, p. 455, Note (1) (this is an extract from *Studi e memorie la storia dell' Universita di Bologna*, Nuova Serie, Vol. I)

4 Medici M. (1857) *Compendio Storico della Scuola Anatomica di Bologna . . .*, Tipi., Governativi della Volpe e del Sassi, p. 362

5 Fulton J.F. and Cushing H. (1936) 'A Bibliographical study of the Galvani and Aldini writings on Animal Electricity', *Annals of Science*, Vol. 1, pp 239–268. See p. 240

6 Galvani L. (1777) *De Manzoliniana Supellectili Oratio Habita . . .*, Bologna, per Lelio Dalla Volpe

7 Galvani L. (1762) 'De Ossibus', Thesis Physico-Medico-Chirurgicae, Bologna, per la Stamperia a S. Tommaso d' Aquino

8 See *Notizie relative a Luigi Galvani*, Memorie dell' Accademia delle Scienze dell' Instituto di Bologna, Tipi Gamberini e Parmeggiani 1853, Tom. 3, p. 172, where Galvani's dissertations are listed (their titles in Italian.) This 'Dissertation in Latin on the effects of Rubbia ingested by chickens', was read on 28 January 1762. The reference given is to Thesis XIII in the Archives of the Bologna Institute[†]

9 Galvani L. (1767) 'De renibus atque ureteribus volatilium', *De Bononiensi Scientiarum et Artium Instituto atque Accademia Commentarii*, Bologna, Tom. 5, Part II, p. 500. The dissertation referred to in the text and read on 25 February 1763 is printed here together with a similar dissertation read on 20 March 1766

10 Loc. cit., Note 4, p. 363

11 Singer C. (1956) *Galen on Anatomical Procedures*, London, Oxford University Press, p. xiii

12 Muller, Johannes (1830) *De Glandularum Secernentium Structura Penitiori . . .*, Leipzig, L. Vossius, pp 12, 23

13 Loc. cit., Note 2, p. 8

14 See loc. cit., Note 8. The dissertation is listed as 'Dissertation in Latin on the effect of Rubbia taken in the food on the bones of animals'. It is referred to as thesis XIII in the archives of the Bologna Institute. It was read on 21 February 1765[†]

15 Ibid., Dissertation in Latin on the Rubbia stain contained in the bones and other parts of the bodies of animals taking it in their food. This accompanied by a note which says that as the session of 14 July was open to the public, Galvani would be re-reading his dissertation on 21 February[†]

16 See Note 9. This is the dissertation read on 20 March 1766

17 See L. Galvani, *Opere Editie ed inedite del Professor Luigi Galvani* . . ., Bologna, Tipografica di Emidio dall' Olmo, 1841, p. 45 (various paginations)

18 Loc. cit., Note 8, p. 172

19 Scarpa A. (1772) *De Structura fenestrae rotundae auris et de tympano secundario anatomicae observationes*, Modena, Apud Societatem Tipographicam

20 Loc. cit., Note 4, p. 365

21 Galvani L. (1783) 'De Volatilium Aurae' (comprising the dissertations read at the Institute in the years 1768, 1769 and 1770 together with those read on 6 April 1775 and 25 April 1776, *De Bononiensi Scientiarum* . . ., Bologna, Ex. Tipographia Instituti Scientiarum, Tom. 1, p. 58. See also loc. cit., Note 8

22 Loc. cit, Note 8, p. 173. This dissertation is listed as 'Dissertation on an artificial cataract and on the morbid condition [of cataract]'. The reference given is to Collected Reports 3, 5 and 5. It was read on 24 March 1779[†]

23 Ibid., 'Dissertation in Latin on cataract'. The reference given is to Collected Reports 3, 4 and 5. It was read on 8 March 1781

24 Loc. cit., Note 2, p. 9

* See Biographical Index
[†] Efforts to obtain the latin titles to these dissertations have been unsuccessful.

15

Galvani's introduction to the study of animal electricity: the physical basis of irritability (Phase I: 1770–1780)

From what has already been discussed, it is not difficult to understand why Galvani should have become interested in the problem of what makes a muscle irritable. The experimental demonstration of a physical basis for this physiological function must have offered one of the most exciting of challenges and at the same time one of the most difficult of investigations, to a man whose first interest was in functional anatomy – and who found himself working in the scientific atmosphere of mid-18th century Bologna.

The first evidence that we have of Galvani's active concern with this topic of popular scientific interest, is contained in a list of dissertations read before the Academy of Science of the Institute. This list, written in the hand of Sebastiano Canterzani (then Secretary of the Bologna Academy) is among the manuscript documents bequeathed to the Bologna Academy by Galvani's nephew, Giovanni Aldini*. It refers to the following papers read by Galvani during the years 1772–1774,[1] 'Su l'irritabilita Halleriana' (9 Aprile 1772), 'Sul moto musculare nelle rane' (22 Aprile 1773) and 'Azione dell'oppio ne' nervi delle rane' (20 Gennaro 1774).

Unfortunately the manuscripts of these dissertations are lost and so while we know that Galvani had begun to think about the nature of Hallerian irritability some time before 1772 and that he had presumably carried out some experiments on frogs before 1773, we have no access to his ideas from his own words. There is a note written on the front of Canterzani's list stating that all these dissertations were to be returned to the author as he was collecting them with a view to their publication in the *Acts of the Academy*, so Galvani presumably thought that they were the considered expression of his views at that time.

The third dissertation, the last of this trio concerned with muscular motion, dealt with the action of opium on frogs' nerves and deserves consideration. This was a topic in which Galvani seems to have been interested over many years for we have evidence that he read a dissertation before the Academy some time during the last year of his life (1798) and that it was based on the results of his work on this subject.[2]

In the Archives of Bologna University are certain papers belonging to the Accounts Department. These contain lists of expenses incurred by various members of the Academy in the preparation of their dissertation material and among these is a reference to Galvani's purchase of various items including opium.[3] That Galvani was still, in the last year of his life, interested in the effect of opium on frog muscle irritability is also evidenced by the words of his niece, Camilla dal Pane who describes how she helped him with certain of his experiments. She told Sylvestro Gherardi*, the Italian physiologist who wrote the report on Galvani's unpublished papers (which were collected and published from 1841–1842), that she was employed for a number of weeks ". . . to make the frogs Galvani was experimenting on, swallow opium and mercury every morning, by means of a little funnel inserted in their mouth's . . ."[4]

The significance of Galvani's interest in opium resulted from the drug's ability to destroy irritability. The nature of the action of ingested opium on the animal body was a subject of great interest during the second half of the 18th century because of this property. It seems to share this proclivity with other substances such as viper venom, the poisonous substances used by South American Indians to arm their arrows, the poisonous juice exuded by certain polyps, and certain other juices obtained from various vegetables and other plants.[5] The way in which such varied organic substances brought about their effects was widely studied since it was believed that an understanding of the way in which irritability could be destroyed might give a clue to the mechanism by which it was normally manifested, and this was doubtless the rationale of Galvani's experiments. Both Robert Whytt and Felice Fontana*, among others carried out a number of experiments aimed at understanding the action of opium and the way in which they interpreted their results reflect their different views of irritability. Whytt, whose ideas appeared in *An Account of some experiments made with opium on Living and Dying animals*,[6] was convinced that opium acted primarily on the nervous system – the brain, spinal cord or nerves supplying the muscle exposed to its action. Any other action on the muscle fibre destroyed its irritability only as a result of rendering it unfit to respond to the nervous force brought to it:

> Opium does not only destroy the moving power of the muscles of animals by intercepting the influence of the brain and spinal marrow, but also by unfitting the muscular fibres themselves or the nervous power lodged in them, for performing its office . . .[7]

Referring to Haller's view that irritability is independent of nerves, Whytt argues against Haller's experiments questioning:

> . . . is it not reasonable to conclude, that the tremulous motions of irritated muscles, after their nerves are tied, proceed from the integrity of the nervous filaments below the ligature and the nervous power still remaining in them or in the muscular fibres themselves?[8]

Galvani's dissertation title refers to the action of opium on the nerves of frogs which tends to suggest that he adopted a view similar to Whytt's. That this was so, or at least that he was undecided at this stage and later as to the true seat of irritability, is further borne out by his quoting a view similar to Whytt's in an essay written ten years later in 1782.[9]

Fontana's view of irritability was Hallerian and he therefore sought the answer to the action of opium in its ability to destroy the intimate structure of the muscle fibre. In his book, *Ricerche Fisica sopra il veleno della vipera* . . ., published in 1767,[10] he considered the action of opium along with that of viper venom and certain other organic poisons which appeared to him to destroy irritability in a similar manner. He was also convinced that 'mephitic vapours' similarly killed animals by destroying irritability and during a stay in Bologna artificially produced "vapours of sulphur", "vapour of a solution of iron filings in nitrous acid" and demonstrated that they brought about the death of frogs by reducing the animals muscles to a flaccid, non-irritable state.[11]

One of the great paradoxes of the action of opium and these other toxins seems to be their ability to cause convulsions in small doses, while in greater doses, or acting over a longer period, they lead to total muscular inactivity. Fontana reflects on the similar property displayed by electricity, "Electricity occasions death by depriving the heart and fleshy fibres of their irritability . . ."[12] but paradoxically:

> . . . this same electricity is notwithstanding one of the strongest stimulants to the muscular fibres that are known. It restores life by exciting irritability, in the very animals in which it had an instant before destroyed it.[12]

The physical process which Fontana believed the various agents produce is putrefaction of the muscle fibre, which was envisaged as a forcible separation of the particles accompanied by the expulsion of inflammable airs – a succession of events that he must therefore have supposed to occur during muscle stimulation by any or all of these agents including electricity and the as yet unidentified physiological nervous agent. The only stipulation required would be the activity of a small enough quantity of the activating agent – a conclusion similar to that reached by Beccaria.[13]

Whatever views Galvani may have put forward in these early dissertations, we do know that as late as 1778 he was carrying out the investigation of irritability in much the same way as other European workers, for Gherardi refers to a manuscript dated "a di 4.1778" which describes the stimulation of frogs by the usual array of irritants such as:

> . . . needle punctures, longitudinal cuts in the spinal medulla, incision of the ventricle, intestines, crural nerves and vessels of the lower abdomen, opening of the auricle of the heart, the pericardium . . . as well as irritation of the crural nerves and ventricle with oil of tartar.[14]

There are manuscript notes of various experiments carried out at this time, experiments which were concerned essentially with the variation in pulse-rate associated with such procedures as have been noted above, but no reference to electrical stimulation occurs. Gherardi was apparently surprised by this omission,[14] but the significance for his studies of the effects of electricity would seem to be that it gives a *terminus ad quem*.

In the same year however, Galvani was also involved with a series of chemical analyses on the various parts of frogs and vipers. These would seem to have started as a repetition of the type of experiment Priestley was carrying out during the 1770's. The English chemist's analysis of the content of various 'airs' evolved in different situations, including the parts of plants and animals, was one of the topics of current scientific interest and as has been noted, his papers were available in Italian translation.

Reference to these experiments occurs in a series of manuscript sheets which Gherardi collected together as Plico I (Fascii A-H) and which he believed represented the earliest of Galvani's unpublished writings.[15] They contain material of the outline sketch for a dissertation which it would appear Galvani intended to read before the Academy under the title 'Sul l'aria contenuta nelle diverse parti degli animali'. Although Gherardi stresses that Galvani's dissertation was mainly concerned with the quantities of 'inflammable air'[16] which various parts of his animal bodies were found to yield, it would seem that this stress becomes significant only as the dissertation progresses and that initially Galvani wished to carry out a completely comprehensive chemical analysis of all the parts of the animal body, liquid and solid, and to estimate all the various gases such as 'fixed air' and 'inflammable air' yielded by them. This is certainly what he himself says he was doing and what the title of his dissertation suggests ". . . nobody before myself has been dedicated to examining, with all diligence the principles of the various parts of animals their nature and quantity . . ."[17]

It is not possible to know the details of these experiments without direct reference to the manuscripts. Gherardi however says that:

> In these chemical experiments the author [Galvani] employed combustion, boiling and putrefaction as methods [of analysis]. He also appears to have used freezing; but in the case of the chapter devoted to freezing, as in that devoted to boiling, the actual pages cannot be found. For this reason we have only notes on experiments involving combustion and putrefaction.[18]

It seems however from Galvani's reference to Priestley (see below) that his own methods were similar to those carried out by the English chemist.

The first experiments were apparently carried out on liquids. Galvani says that he always analysed the same weight of an animal part, that is, 3 drachms, and that the troughs in which he exposed these parts to combustion, "were not made of iron or any other metals, like those employed by Priestley in the similar researches but were made of terracotta, vitreous both inside and out."[19]

Gherardi makes reference to an interesting note by Galvani on his analysis of the residues from blood and milk left after combustion:

> We did not omit to examine the caput mortuum both of milk and blood, which we were able to collect accurately, and discovered that it contained not a little iron, because without any other preparation, save stirring the caput mortuum with a finger, it was liberally and copiously attracted by the magnet. This occurred with a smaller quantity of milk than blood: the caput mortuum of milk was two grains less than that of blood.[20]

The presence of iron in blood had already been demonstrated by Vincenzo Menghini, but Galvani's was the first demonstration of its presence in milk – an interesting by-product of his general analysis of the parts of the animal body and in the tradition of the type of chemical analysis carried out by his teachers, Beccari and Galeazzi, the latter being especially concerned with the distribution of iron in nature.

When Galvani had finished the various fluid parts he turned his attention to the solid parts. Gherardi quotes from pp 14–15 of the dissertations' notes:

> When the solid parts were also examined by the same method, the quantity of inflammable air recovered varied according to the part thus treated and it was not without amazement that I discovered the most in nerves, an intermediate quantity in muscles, minimal amounts in bone and virtually none in tendons.[21]

Suddenly, for some reason, Galvani's attention is riveted by this discovery that muscles and nerves yield a higher quantity of 'inflammable air' than other solid parts. Up until this point, 'inflammable air' does not seem to have had any particular significance compared with other airs in his systematic analysis.

The clue to the explanation of Galvani's surprise can be found in a note on page 35:

> Nowadays the action of electricity on inflammable air is [well] recognised; [we know] what a small amount of the former is required to set in motion and increase the elasticity of the latter.[18]

Galvani is referring to the recent discovery by his fellow-countryman Alessandro Volta*, that various 'inflammable airs' could be made to explode by allowing the electric spark drawn from an electric machine to pass through them in the presence of 'dephlogisticated air'. This reaction between electricity and 'inflammable air' was to provide Galvani with his first ideas for a biophysical model of muscular motion and hence his excitement at his experimental demonstration that muscles and nerves contain predominately high quantities of 'inflammable air'. Volta's experiments are remembered today as the first demonstration of the synthesis of hydrogen (inflammable air) and oxygen (dephlogisticated air) to form water and are contained in a series of letters he wrote to his friend Carlo Guiseppe Campi*, during the years 1776–1777. Volta however, was little concerned with the production of water from his 'inflammable air' His letters to Campi unfold the development of a chemical concept based on his belief in the phlogiston theory of combustion and it is this concept that influenced Galvani's thinking at this stage in his investigations. Volta's ideas are so relevant to Galvani's that a consideration of the Volta-Campi correspondence seems justified.[22]

Carlo Campi had discovered a natural source of 'inflammable air' in San Colombet and had written to his friend to tell him about it. In his first letter to Campi written on 14 November 1767 Volta tells his friend that he has also discovered the existence of a naturally occurring 'inflammable air' on the shores of lakes Como and Verbano (Maggiore). Volta had been walking round these lakes poking his walking cane into the stagnant putrid marshy ground in these situations and had seen the evolution of bubbles of an air which burned spontaneously. Volta collected specimens and examined them, coming to the conclusion that this type of 'inflammable air' was identical to that discovered by Campi:

This air burns very slowly with a blue flame the same as that which you have discovered. In order to ignite it and see its flame in all its beauty, it is necessary that the mouth of the jar (in which it is contained) should be a little wide; if it is too narrow when you present a lighted taper there will truly occur a great number of successive little explosions.[23]

In his second letter, Volta goes on to suggest that this naturally occurring type of 'inflammable air' is quite distinct from that which is produced by the action of acids on metals and that it is responsible for the phenomenon known as *ignis fatui* (will-o'-the-wisp):

I would also like to be sure of its identity with regard to ignis fatui. *Several circumstances indeed lead me to believe that they are nothing else than an inflammable air which is released from swampy ground since they seem common in marshy areas.*[24]

Volta calls his newly discovered 'inflammable air', 'native marsh air' (methane). Two characteristics of this air particularly interested the Italian physicist: its explosive nature and the fact that it was produced naturally as the result of purely organic processes. His long third letter to Campi is devoted to speculations as to why this (and to an even greater degree, the inflammable air produced from metals) should be explosive. One of the problems posed by the phlogiston theory was the nature of the difference between the noxious, suffocating, phlogisticated air, resulting from combustion or the respiration of animals and 'inflammable air', the inflammability of which was seen as depending on its phlogiston content. Both airs apparently contained phlogiston but were obviously of different compositions.

Volta seeks to explain this difference by postulating that whereas the phlogiston particles in 'phlogisticated air' are only loosely bound to the host particles of atmospheric air, into which they have passed as a result of combustion or respiration, the particles of phlogiston in 'inflammable air' are rigidly bound and form an integral part of it: each particle of 'inflammable air' being joined to a particle of phlogiston in such a manner that only the force of a flame can separate them – with a resulting explosion:

I think, on the contrary, that the integral parts of inflammable air never lose their phlogiston, that they swim among the particles of common air, by which they are surrounded, without changing their nature, that it is only they that are truly inflammable, and that the others [common air particles] *contribute nothing to this save their aptitude to receive their discharge . . . The phlogiston of inflammable air does not therefore separate from its base spontaneously and by the sole contact of common air, as is the case with air which is merely phlogisticated. The latter, has only need to be shaken in water for a fairly brief time in order to be deprived of its phlogiston. In order to dephlogisticate the former it is, similarly, sufficient to agitate it in water, but this needs to be much more vigorous and for a much longer time and plants which restore phlogisticated air so well and so readily, rendering it once more salubrious, have never deprived inflammable air of the inflammability of which it appears to be singularly tenacious. The action of a living flame is the only situation which produces this effect, that is to say, the only force bringing about a true decomposition – and this violent decomposition, where this separation of phlogiston from its base, as well as its passage through common air, seems to be necessary, are perhaps the only thing necessary for producing any and every sort of inflammation.*[25]

Having developed his theory as to why 'inflammable airs' are explosive, in his long third letter, Volta opens his fourth letter by apologising to his friend for all the conjecture he has presented to him without any experimental evidence to verify them. In order to repair this he says:

> . . . here I am, a flask of inflammable air in one hand, the other ready to set in motion the electric machine. Prepare yourself for facts – absolutely new facts, much better than conjectures.[26]

Not unnaturally, it occurred to Volta to try to explode his 'inflammable air' by means of the electric spark. The 'firing' of vinous spirits by this means was a well known phenomenon and it was therefore logical to expect the 'electric fire' to act on the phlogiston of 'inflammable air' in an analogous way. Volta suggests that Campi would expect that a considerable electrical force would be required to bring this about, but tells his friend that this is not so. All it requires is a little skill, particularly in the case of marsh air:

> Doubtless you imagine that this requires a very strong electricity, such as that which is commonly necessary for igniting the spirit of wine and essential oils: you are greatly mistaken. All it requires is a little skill above all for igniting the air of marshes on which the experiment only succeeds under certain conditions; it occurs with the air extracted from metallic substances as a result of their solution in acids, with much greater facility than you can imagine. I need only present the mouth of a jar full of this air to the plate of my big electrophorus at the moment I lift it off the base. The spark and sometimes only the brush which arises from the edges of the jar . . . are sufficient to ignite the air.[26]

Volta describes an even more striking experiment where he brings an electrified conductor close to the mouth of a siphon stuck down over the opening of a flask in which iron is dissolving briskly in sulphuric acid:

> The sparks which left from the conductor and often the brush or star alone, ignited the air which was given off and the flame, once excited, continued to burn and to consume the new aliment which was continually supplied to it.[27]

So much for the ignition of the 'inflammable air' produced from metals. In the case of his 'marsh air', Volta had to resort to the device of a spark-gap which he insinuated into the mouth of the jar containing the gas, when he was again just as successful in causing its ignition.[28]

Having demonstrated that a small quantity of electric fluid can bring about the ignition and explosion of the two types of 'inflammable air' he recognised, Volta returned to his original idea that the *ignis fatui* of the marshes is in fact nothing more than the ignition and explosion of his naturally occurring 'native marsh air'. All he needed to justify his theory was a suitable source of naturally occurring electricity to act as the provocative agent. He did not need to look far for the extensive observations of his fellow-countryman, Padre Beccaria, on the variations in the electricity in the atmosphere, supplied the answer. Volta suggests:

> Cannot atmospheric electricity come more specifically to our help? Not only that which is manifested in stormy weather when the sky is full of clouds and vapours, but even that which is there during serene weather and shows a diurnal variation as the celebrated

*Padre Beccaria has discovered after long and exact determinations and has described in
a short work entitled,* dell' Elettricita terrestere atmosferica a cielo sereno, 1775.[29]

This theory of a naturally occurring spontaneous ignition of the 'inflammable air', of putrefying marshes by electricity present in the atmosphere served Volta as the model for a much wider concept of the interaction between electricity and naturally occurring 'inflammable air'. He sets forth his fully developed thesis in his fifth letter to Campi. He attacks those who, like slaves, consider electricity as the all important natural force in nature suggesting that ". . . every spark, every ignited vapour, every fire, every flame, every conflagration is nothing else but a simple electric fire".[30]

Volta sees many of the grand events of nature as due to the interaction of electricity with naturally occurring 'mephitic or inflammable airs', similar to his 'native marsh air'. He realises that this is against commonly held views and says to Campi:

> *I leave you to guess what the outcry would be if we dared to usurp some new portion
> of the territory of electricity. If we dared to say, for example, that volcanoes and earth-
> quakes are simply the effects of inflammable air enclosed in subterranean caves and
> mixed with common air in suitable proportions so that once ignited it is able to explode
> suddenly throughout a very long stretch of ground; that the* aurora borealis *is likewise
> engendered by the inflammable air gathered in the upper reaches of the atmosphere . . .
> If we admit that only lightning is truly electrical in nature and donate these other
> functions to inflammable air, restricting the role of electricity to that of igniting these
> others by means of the thundering spark between clouds . . . What a vast field of ideas
> and conjectures are opened up to the man who would rebel against electricity.*[31]

Volta's concept is concerned entirely with the physico-chemical explanation of naturally occurring events in terms of the activation of 'inflammable airs' by relatively small quantities of electrical fluid. He is concerned to make it clear that he was the first to discover this naturally occurring type of 'inflammable air' and points out in a foot-note that Priestley:

> *. . . has never spoken of the inflammable air which is engendered by plants and
> animals disintegrating under water and which can be easily produced from the depths
> of every type of ditch and lake.*[32]

This concept of atmospheric electricity reacting with naturally occurring 'inflammable air' is undoubtedly the model Galvani was to adopt. There is no doubt that he was aware of Volta's ideas since the latter used the explosive properties of suitable mixtures of 'inflammable' and 'dephlogisticated airs' to produce a "pistol" which he describes for Campi in this same fifth letter.[33] Furthermore, a model of this pistol was presented to the Bologna Academy in 1770 and Galvani refers to this in his dissertation notes.[34] It would seem likely that Galvani began his investigation of the various airs yielded by animal parts some time during 1777 and became aware of Volta's ideas at some stage after he had begun his experiments. At this point his own results suggested the possible significance of the action of atmospheric electricity on the naturally occurring 'inflammable air' in the muscles and nerves of his experimental animals. His appreciation of the possible application of Volta's general thesis to his specific problem is evident from a second note which occurs on page 35 of his dissertation.[18] Here he talks of the importance of electricity in the, ". . . great mutations and variations which occur in the atmosphere. . ."[34] and wishes to deduce similar changes in the animal economy. He suggests that ". . . the correspondence between this and the other group of changes is brought about or depends on the influx of electricity on the inflammable air in the parts of animals."[35]

At this time (1778) there can be little doubt that Galvani believed that the mechanism underlying the excitation and contraction of a muscle was dependent on the same chemico-physical changes postulated by Volta as responsible for certain other naturally occurring phenomena. The hypothesis was entirely logical within the framework of contemporary thinking and must have seemed to be substantiated by his obtaining such a high yield of 'inflammable air' from the parts of the animal concerned with the function of muscular motion

During the next two years, Galvani was evidently busy carrying out experiments on frogs (and other cold blooded animals) with a view to understanding and demonstrating the intimate mechanism underlying the response to, electrical stimulation and thus eventually explaining the naturally occurring physiological mechanism.

We have no manuscript records from this period but fortunately we do have a considerable number of manuscript notes dating from December 1780 onwards. The earliest of these, dated "delle 6 Novembre 1780" contains details of electrical experiments and refers to the use of frogs, ". . . prepared in the usual manner . . ."[36] so that it can be assumed that similar frog experiments had been performed at some time earlier than this – during the period 1778 – November 1780.

The year 1780 seems to mark the stage at which Galvani began his systematic investigation of the action of electricity on frog muscles and nerves. Although there are records of these various experiments which he carried out during the 1780's, none of these were published during his lifetime and it was not until the publication of the famous *De viribus electricitatis in motu musculari Commentarius*[37] of 1791 that the world was given access to the results of his work and his interpretation of the significance of his results.

Our next chapters will deal with these investigations.

Notes

1 Gheradi S. (1841–1842) *Opere edite ed inedite, del Professore Luigi Galvani raccolte e publicate per cura dell Accademia delle Scienze dell' Instituto di Bologna*, Bologna, E. Dall' Olmo, p. 16
2 Ibid., p. 67
3 Ibid., pp 67–68
4 Ibid., p. 68. Camilla dal Pane was the daughter of Galvani's brother Giacomo, with whom he spent the last years of his life in the family house in the Via delle Case
5 These various toxic agents, believed to operate in a similar manner are now known to exert their action at different sites in the nervous system, for example, the poison used by American Indians, curare, acts at the neuro-muscular junction, preventing

the normal action of acetylcholine released by the nerve supplying a muscle; opium
has a selective depressive and stimulatory action on the Central Nervous System
(CNS) as well as a tonic action on muscle fibre; most snake venoms contain neuro-
toxins which depress the CNS

6 Whytt R. (1768) *The works of Robert Whytt M.D. . . .*, published by his son. Printed for
    J. Balfour, Edinburgh, by Balfour, Auld and Smellie, p. 309

7 Ibid., p. 324

8 Ibid., p. 325

9 *Memorie ed Esperimenti di Luigi Galvani con la iconografia di lui e un saggio di bibliografia
    degli scritti*, Bologna, Licinio Cappelli Editore 1937, pp 3–31, which contains the
    'Saggio della forza nervea a sua realazione coll' elettricità', dated 25 Novembris 1782,
    pp 7–8

10 Fontana F. (1767) *Ricerche Fisica sopra il veleno della vipera . . .*, Lucca, Jacopo Guisti

11 Fontana F. (1795) *Treatise on the venom of the viper . . .*, Translated from original French
    by Joseph Skinner, 2 Vols, 2nd edn, London, John Cuthill, Vol. 1, p. 92

12 Loc. cit., Note 11, p. 96

13 See Chap. 13 of this book

14 Loc. cit., Note 1, p. 12

15 Ibid., p. 5

16 'Inflammable air' was the name given to any gas produced during combustion;
    Priestley made no distinction between such gases as hydrogen, carbon monoxide and
    methane

17 Ibid., p. 8

18 Ibid., p. 7

19 Ibid., p. 9

20 Ibid., pp 8–9

21 Ibid., p. 11

22 See (i) 'Lettra del Sig. D. Alessandro Volta sull'aria inflammabile native delle palido,
    Milano 1777', *Scelta di Opuscoli Interressanti . . .*, 1777, Vol. 28, pp 43–78
    (ii) *Lettres de M. Alexandre Volta sur l'air inflammable des marais, auxquelles on a ajouté
    trois Lettres du même auteur tirées du Journal de Milan*, Strasbourg, J.H. Heitz, 1778

23 Ibid., (ii),'Prèmiere lettre', p. 9

24 Ibid., (ii) 'Deuxième lettre', p. 21

25 Ibid., (ii) 'Troisième lettre', pp 31–32

26 Ibid., (ii) 'Quatrième lettre', p. 49

27 Ibid., (ii) 'Quatrième lettre', p. 51

28 Ibid., p. 52

29 Ibid., p. 53

30 Ibid., (ii) 'Cinquième lettre', p. 58

31 Ibid., p. 59

32 Ibid., footnote p. 61

33 Ibid., p. 68 *et seq.* Volta also discusses his "pistol" in three letters written to Sig. Marchese
    Francesco Castelli.
    See: Lettra I, 'alla Construzione di un Moschetto e d'una Pistola ad Aria inflamma-
    bile', *Scelta di Opuscoli Interessanti . . .*, 1777, Vol. 30, pp 86–96
    Lettra II, 'Sul medisimo soggetto' Ibid., Vol. 30, pp 97–109
    Lettra III 'Sul medisimo soggetto', Ibid., Vol. 31, pp 3–24

34 Loc. cit. Note 1, p. 7

35 Ibid., p. 8.

36 Loc. cit., Note 1, p. 233

37 Galvani, Luigi (1791) 'De viribus electricitatis in motu musculari, Commentarius,'
    De Bononiensi Scientiarum et Artium Instituto atque Accademia Commentarii, Bologna,
    Ex Tipographia Instituti Scientiarum, L. della Volpe, Vol. 7, pp 363–418

* See Biographical Index

16

The effects of artificial electricity on nerves
(Phase II: 1780–1783)

When Galvani eventually published the results of his investigations into the basis of muscular motion, in 1791, his readers were presented with a well organised monograph purporting to describe the course of his work over an unspecified length of time:

> . . . a brief and accurate account of the discoveries in the same order of circumstance that chance and fortune in part brought to me, and diligence and attentiveness in part revealed.[1]

Thus *De viribus electricitatis in motu musculari, Commentarius*, appeared as a commentary divided into four parts, each of which was devoted to a particular aspect of Galvani's story, the four parts being arranged so as to present the supposedly logical development of his work and ideas; *viz*:

Part I   *The Effects of Artificial electricity on Muscular Motion*
Part II   *The Effects of Atmospheric electricity on Muscular Motion*
Part III *The Effects of Animal electricity on Muscular Motion*
Part IV *The Effects of Animal electricity on Muscular Motion: Conjectures and some Conclusions*

In effect, Parts I and II examine the results of the experimental or artificial stimulation of the nerves (and muscles) of certain animals by electricity coming from a source outside the animal body while Parts III and IV deal with the mechanism by which Galvani believed muscular excitation and contraction are brought about *in vivo* that is, the physical changes underlying the activation of muscles by nerves. The four parts of his commentary fall naturally, therefore, in two sections, Parts I and II concerned with the investigation of the purely mechanical – and in no way necessarily normally occurring – action of electricity on nerves and muscles, and Parts III and IV which are concerned essentially with a physiological process. As will be shown by reference to his experimental notes and essays published a number of years later, Galvani did not pursue his investigation of these two topics in precisely the chronological order suggested by the *Commentary* but since the sub-division is convenient, it seems reasonable to analyse his work under these two headings. This chapter will therefore deal with his examination of the effects of applying an external source of electricity to the nerves and muscles of various experimental animals.

As has been noted already, Galvani probably began his series of electrical researches at the end of 1780, his first recorded experiment being dated

6 November of that year. Almost exactly two years later, he wrote a little essay in which he put forward the rationale for the work he had been carrying out during this period and summed up the state of his ideas at this time. This paper, unpublished until 1937, was entitled 'Saggio della forza nervea a sua realazione coll' elettricita' and dated 25 November 1782 (the *1782 Essay*).[2]

Galvani's opening paragraph makes it quite clear that the problem he was trying to solve was the identity of the 'nervous force' or 'animal spirits'. Was the subtle fluid which he believed ran through nerves, and acted upon muscles, identical with or related to ordinary electrical fluid as produced *ex vivo*; that is, in the atmosphere or by electric devices?

> *Although not a few anatomists have believed that electrical fluid is either a component of that most subtle fluid which they, with reason, consider runs through the nerves or indeed is, the very nerve fluid itself, I thought it not unuseful to make various experiments on these same nerves in the hope that the truth might be discovered or that at least, some light might be shed on the obscurity in which these nervous phenomena lie.[3]*

He continues by explaining what he means by 'nervous action' and how he intends to examine it. He considers that electrical fluid 'acts on nerves' when by its application he can produce in these nerves "some perceptible action appropriate to them" *viz* sensation or muscular motion – the only two possible effects.[4] Since, however, sensation is a subjective phenomenon he does not consider it so amenable to experimental analysis as muscular motion which can be seen by the eyes of the observer and provoked by various, purely mechanical agents acting on the nerves. He refers to the two types of muscular motion he recognises and which we now term 'voluntary' and 'involuntary,' designating the former type of motion "primary" and the latter "secondary".[5] In this paper he says he is going to confine his attention to 'primary' movements for although the mind or will is involved in such movements, this does not mean that, ". . . a mechanical agent, applied to their nerves, does not excite them *[the muscles involved]* equally as well *[as the will]*".[6] He dismissed the investigation of "secondary" movements to a later treatise.

So what Galvani set out to investigate was the purely mechanical effect of electrical fluid on nerves supplying what we term voluntary muscles and in order to do this, he says he must exclude any other agents capable of producing a similar result, that is, the mind, the brain, or any other extraneous animal parts. He therefore chooses as his experimental subjects non-living (and in the first place cold-blooded) animals prepared as follows:

> *Frogs, which on account of their number and ease of access in all seasons, have been used for our experiment, were cut transversely below their anterior limbs, then skinned and eviscerated, leaving only their posterior limbs joined together through the insertion of the long crural nerves, these latter being either loose and free or suspended from the spinal cord which again was either left intact in the vertebral column or taken out and separated in part or whole from the latter as will be shown later.[7]*

The vast majority of Galvani's investigations were carried out on frogs and other cold-blooded animals such as salamanders and vipers since these responded readily and vigorously to electrical stimulation but he also adapted his techniques to the examination of warm-blooded animals, carrying out *in vivo* as well as *in vitro* experiments in a number of different species.

In the previous chapter it was suggested that Galvani derived his original ideas as to the physical basis of muscular excitation and contraction from his fellow-countryman, Volta: that he postulated that in some way, small quantities of electrical fluid, present in the atmosphere, enter the animal body, reach the brain and thence pass along the nerves to reach the muscle fibres where they react explosively with phlogiston[8] – a variant of Priestley's theory.[9] Hence the need to see if the experimental application of a known, extraneous supply of electrical fluid either from the atmosphere or produced artificially in the laboratory, would mimic exactly, the physiological situation. But the problem was not so simple as this, as Galvani was well aware. Assuming as he did, that nerves contain an intrinsic fluid, which he refers to as 'the nervous force' or 'animal spirits', which might or might not be identical with artificially produced electrical fluid, the "application" of electrical fluid to such nerves could theoretically produce muscular contraction for a number of different reasons. Firstly, if the 'electrical fluid' were identical with the fluid in the nerves, all he might be doing was to increase the quantity of the normally occurring physiological agent and in fact reproducing at will the normal situation. But if the two were not identical, electrical fluid had to be considered as a non-physiological excitant and the mode of its action on the nerve fluid analysed in terms of the action of a primary on a secondary or intermediate agent – particularly as it was reasonable to expect his prepared nerves to contain a certain residual quantity of intrinsic fluid. That Galvani was open minded as to whether his electrical source was merely a mechanical agent taking the place of the will, or whether it was to be regarded as a substitute for the nervous agent, or indeed to be regarded as representing the will plus nervous agent becomes apparent from his experimental notes during the period under consideration. The point has been stressed not only in order to make the analysis and understanding of his ideas clearer but in order to do justice to Galvani's ability to assess the complexity of his problem. Galvani had a habit of tidying up his ideas and presenting his current views without reference to their development, no less in the case of the *1782 Essay*,[2] than that of the *Commentary* so our first clues as to how his ideas progressed are to be found in his notes of experiments carried out during the months of November and December, 1780.[10]

In a later chapter,[11] an analysis will be made of the theoretical basis of Galvani's procedures with reference to the state of electrical theory at the time he was working, but for the moment it seems more logical historically to examine the progress of his ideas and deduce from his own words how he envisaged that the various electrical phenomena were produced. In the first place then, we need not assume more than that Galvani considered the electrical fluid as being composed of subtle, mutually repulsive particles and that he could produce a supply of it by means of various electrical, devices which had come into use during the mid-century, *viz* the electrical machine, the Franklinian Square, the Leyden Jar and the electrophorus.[12]

Now the essential feature of the earlier experiments of 1780, as far as Galvani was concerned, was that in all cases he was apparently applying electrical fluid directly to the nerves of his animal preparation. Most of the manoeuvres involved the use of the Franklinian Square (charged by an electrical machine) although there is reference to the use of a Leyden Jar on one occasion.[13]

In the first recorded experiment, dated 6 November, he says:

> In a frog, prepared in the usual manner, a large discharge from the Franklinian Square having been made to pass through the spinal cord, . . . the dependent muscles contracted.[14]

This experiment was the first of a series in which he examined the effect of such a discharge applied respectively to the spinal cord, crural nerves and thigh muscles themselves. Since in the case of the direct application of electricity to muscle he obtained no contractions (or very feeble ones) although previous stimulation of the appropriate nerve had given positive results, he comes to believe that "the nervous force" is greater than "the muscular force" and proceeds to carry out further experiments which convince him that in fact, a muscle can only be made to contract as the result of the previous stimulation of its nerve supply. This view, that the irritability of voluntary muscles is absolutely dependant on the presence of nerves may be said to be the first deduction made from this series of experiments. Any feeble contractions obtained as a result of the direct stimulation of muscle were explained by Galvani as resulting from the prior stimulation of very small, invisible portions of nerves hidden within the muscle body – a view which we have seen already was held by many contemporary anatomists.

The second deduction Galvani draws from experiments carried out at this time concerns the possible influence of the direction taken by the electric fluid applied to a nerve. In experiment 5, carried out on 2 December, he demonstrates that the direction has no influence on the production of contractions:

> Exp. 5 In other frogs, prepared as in expmt. 1 one crural nerve was isolated and divided; then the discharge of the bottle (Leyden Jar) was directed in such a way that first it passed from the feet to the spinal cord, then from the spinal cord to the feet. In the first case, movements took place as a result of the passage (of electricity) almost equally in both limbs, in the second, movement was always greater in that with an intact nerve.[15]

Galvani turned his attention to the quantity of electrical fluid required to act upon a nerve in order to produce muscular contractions. Experiments carried out in November had suggested to him that it was difficult to force electrical fluid through nerves and on 29 December he carried out further experiments which seemed to him to prove this. He placed his frog-preparation on a large plate of glass to which he applied the conductor of his electrical machine, and found that:

> . . . with the first and every turn of the machine there was a corresponding contraction of all the muscles of the limbs, and this was so, for a various number of revolutions of the handle.[16]

Further turning of the handle failed to produce contractions as did touching or even striking the glass plate with a conducting rod, but similarly touching or, stroking the animals limbs led to further activity. He found that with up to 15 "touchings" he could produce 15 corresponding contractions, but after this the limbs remained motionless. After allowing the animal to rest for a short time, once more turning the machine handle produced one or two contractions.

Galvani interpreted these results as a demonstration that the conductor does not easily discharge its electrical fluid into the nerves:

> Corollary 1° – The conductor is not discharged freely through the nerves, there always remains a little quantity of it [electrical fluid] which is drawn through the nerves to the muscles by touching. This shows how difficult is the passage through nerves.[17]

Galvani then went on to repeat this type of experiment, bringing very light bodies up close to the conductor of his machine:

> While the animal was being touched and gave contractions and retouched without giving contractions, very light bodies were brought near to the conductor. These were attracted upwards, a manifest sign of that very small quantity of electrical fluid which remained in the conductor and in consequence of which the latter was not totally discharged . . .[18]

He then repeated a similar type of experiment using a frog-preparation lying on a discharged insulated Franklinian Square. He turned the machine 15 times, obtaining contractions, continued to turn the handle (with no resulting contractions) and then touched the conductor, "close to the machine and in consequence far from the animal", producing contractions at each touch. On touching the inferior surface of the Square, he produced a last few, weak contractions before the limbs became inactive. During these last "touchings" light bodies brought up to the conductor showed no movements, even though after a period of rest, further turning of the handle, followed by touching of either surface of the Square, produced contractions. He had only to turn the handle of the machine a few times and then touch the surface of the Square in order to produce contractions.[19]

We have seen how Galvani interpreted his touching of the frog limbs as a means of drawing electrical fluid through the nerves. In these last experiments he believed that the ultimate contractions produced by touching the surfaces of the Square resulted from a pulling of tiny quantities of electrical fluid from its surfaces – fluid which had passed from the prime-conductor as a result of only one or two turns of the handle. No signs of this fluid's presence were apparent in that there was no spark, no smell nor any signs of movement in the light bodies near the conductor – the ultimate source of any fluid going to the Square.

In his corollary he reiterates this:

> In order to have muscular contractions it is therefore sufficient to have a quantity of electrical fluid so small that it does not manifest itself by any of the usual signs of electricity, not even by the attraction of light bodies.[20]

Bearing in mind that Galvani's object was to demonstrate experimentally that the intrinsic nervous fluid is identical with or contains particles identical with those of artificially produced electricity, his achievement by the end of 1780 can be summarised thus: very small quantities of known, artificially produced electrical fluid, passing along a nerve in either direction with respect to its dependent muscle can mimic the physiological stimulus for muscular contraction. He had no real evidence that any electrical fluid other than that which his electric machine supplied, was involved in the physiological process he had set in motion. His "nervous fluid" was still a completely unidentified substance. Galvani was aware of this and early in 1781 he has a note at the end of a series of experiments which reflects his striving after evidence not so much for the possibly artificial effects of artificial electricity, but for some hint that the nervous fluid is electrical. He reflects:

> In all the experiments carried out this year, as well as in many others, a certain irregularity and anomaly has been observed, not only associated with the use of different frogs, but even when the same have been used; this shows to what degree the nervous force is variable, inconstant and changeable, as is the electrical fluid: this could be an argument in favour of believing that this force is the same as electricity.[21]

But this is only circumstantial evidence as Galvani knew. All the experiments he had carried out to date involving the direct application of electricity to nerve, had been done before and he was no nearer his goal of identifying the nature of the 'animal spirits' – a fact he admits in the *1782 Essay*:

> All these methods of exciting muscular contractions by means of the artificial application of electric fluid are already known to some and I have not set them forward in order to propose new facts but solely in order to proceed with a logical synthesis . . .[22]

However, on 26 January 1781, a chance observation is recorded as follows:

> *Exp. 6°. A frog prepared as expmt. 1°, day 17, was placed on an unarmed glass plate which in turn was resting by means of its four feet on the same varnished table as the machine; when my wife or somebody else brought a finger up to the conductor, and extracted sparks and at the same time, I rubbed the crural nerves or spinal cord with a bone-handled scalpel or only touched the spinal cord and nerves, contractions occurred, although there was no conductor on the glass plate supporting the frog. They occurred in the same way whether or not the person who discharged the conductor touched the table, and irrespective of the distance away of the little apparatus supporting the frog provided that it was on the same table as the machine.*
>
> *Removing it to another table which was either in contact with or separated from the one supporting the machine, in the presence or absence of a conductor between the tables, no movements occurred. The phenomenon was constant and indeed astonishing. It occurred whether I was touching the table or not, whether my wife was touching it or not.*
>
> *Warning. Those movements therefore which have sometimes occurred in the frog when it was lying on an unarmed glass plate and its nerves touched with some conductor or other, there being no possible communication by means of the conductor between the machine and glass plate, must have arisen as a result of that certain unknown cause which brought them about in this experiment, although one must take heed that they sometimes occurred when the machine was quiet while those occurring in this experiment never appeared if the machine [handle] was not turned and the conductor actually discharged.*[23]

This apparently chance observation caused Galvani great surprise and seemed to be of such significance to him that when his *Commentary* appeared, 10 years later, it was "the novelty of the phenomenon" which was given pride of place as the event which set in motion the series of experiments on which his theory of muscular motion was based.[24]

The features of the experiment which seem to have astonished Galvani are the necessity for the production of a spark and the lack of communication between the electric machine and the glass plate. The reason for his astonishment becomes apparent as his investigations proceed.

His next move was to cover the spinal cord with an insulating paste composed of oil and sulphur. With the paste applied, however, touching the crural nerves resulted in precisely the same brisk contractions. Even covering the nerves and nearly all the frog, leaving only a tiny portion of either the spinal cord or nerve exposed, resulted in the same contractions when the nerves were touched. Galvani interprets these results thus:

> *And yet in all these cases the electric fluid of the electric atmosphere of the conductor* [prime-conductor] *or the disc was not able to enter or accumulate in either the muscles or nerves and even when it could have,* via *that small uncovered portion of nerve, the effects ought to have been scarcely less, yet the effects were the same, the contractions almost equally strong and so the electric fluid of the electrical atmosphere of the conductor or the disc, does not appear to be the author of the phenomenon.*[25]

Galvani is now convinced that the electric fluid (electricity) produced by the machine is not responsible for the contractions produced in these experiments. He can bring about contractions whenever a spark is produced and those occurring with the first spark are identical with those produced as a result of many sparks. One would have expected (he reasons) that the contractions would grow in strength with an increase in the size of the electric atmosphere[26] of the conductor, that is, with an increasing number of turns of the handle but, he says, the contractions are as strong at the appearance of the first spark as with the hundredth. The essential factor seems to be the production of a spark. The phenomenon takes place when the distance between the prime-conductor and his preparation is as much as six feet, but, he reasons this distance is beyond that to which one can believe the atmosphere of a spark is dispersed. If the electric atmosphere is responsible, the contractions should take place as a result of turning the handle of his machine without the extraction of a spark, and might indeed be expected to be greater in these circumstances. Again, if he places his frog close up under the prime-conductor, contractions should result, but in fact he finds that leaving his frog under the prime-conductor for a long time still produces no contractions. Finally, when he places a conductor on the glass plate, anterior and close to the spinal cord and touching the ground, no electrical vapour, or at least very little, ought to be able to accumulate, but the contractions are still the same, so they cannot be due to the electric atmosphere, produced by the electric machine![25] In this last experiment Galvani obviously sees the conductor as a depôt capable of mopping up the electric fluid before it can reach his frog preparation.

So these contractions of 26 January 1781 are produced in rather a different manner from those occurring as a result of the 1780 experiments and hence Galvani's astonishment. The earlier series, as he admitted, dealt with the effects of forcing electricity into his nerves, but now he has evidence of contractions when it seems certain that no electric fluid can be entering the nerves and none of its expected effects can be demonstrated. Since, however, the contractions in both cases seem to be identically produced, surely there must be a source of electrical fluid within the nerves themselves? In other words he has at least strongly suggestive evidence that the intrinsic nervous fluid acts like or is in fact like ordinary artificially produced electricity. No wonder Galvani saw this experiment as a crucial one.

Having decided that the electricity from his machine does not enter the frog nerves he puts forward the following model as a hypothesis explaining his results:

> There is therefore, existing in the nerves, a most subtle fluid which is excited to motion by the blow, by the vibration, by the impulse of the spark, communicated to the air and to a most subtle fluid which is in the air and to the smallest parts of the glass or of other bodies which the glass supports, and this is the author of this phenomenon. These vibrations are not extinguished by touching the glass with a light body, even in many places, and are at a maximum if this body is elastic; they are extinguished or at least weakened if brought about by the use of a poorly elastic body. When the glass plate is touched by a conductor lying on it, the effects are undiminished, but if the glass plate is held in the palm of ones hand or by the fingers, the effects diminish or fail; hence when the glass plate supporting the frog is placed on the same table (as the electric machine) the movements are always greater, because these impulses are more easily and certainly communicated. When the glass supporting the frog is held in the air or placed on a separate table, the tremors are difficult to obtain and more languid, and contractions are less.[27]

This note "Corollary 1°" to the previous experiments shows quite clearly how Galvani was interpreting his results. He makes no analogy between this series of experiments and those carried out with the Franklinian Square and Leyden Jar during 1780. Having established to his own satisfaction that electrical fluid, in the form of the electrical atmosphere, produced around the prime-conductor of his machine can play no part in the production of his contractions, he is able to adopt a purely mechanical theory which interprets the action of the spark as an impulse or force which is transmitted *via* subtle particles in the air and other bodies touching his frog, eventually setting in motion or increasing the vibration of subtle particles in the nerve fluid. But these subtle particles in the nerve have to be electric; because touching the frog's nerves with non-conductors does not produce contractions, while touching them with a conductor does.

> Corollary 2° This fluid set in motion and vibrated by the impulse and vibration of the spark is the electric fluid, for if you apply a cylinder of glass or old (dry) bone to the nerves or spinal cord no movement is produced but if you touch these with any different body, metal, a finger or something else the phenomenon is produced and there are contractions.[28]

Galvani's hypothetical model is almost pure Newtonianism – the only difference between the two models resulting from Galvani's espousal of a hollow nerve theory. Newton envisaged his aethereal vibrations as being transmitted to solid nerves while Galvani believes he has evidence that the vibrations of subtle particles in the electric atmosphere are transmitted *via* other subtle particles in the air and contiguous bodies to the subtle fluid particles within the nerve. He must have felt he had indeed begun to demonstrate experimentally that the Newtonian theory espoused so readily by 18th century philosophers had a reality as the physical basis of nervous action.

In the *1782 Essay*, in which this mechanical view of the role of the electric machine is put forward, Galvani explains his interpretation of the 1780 experiments using the Franklinian Square, when contractions were produced without the production of a spark, that is, at the mere turning of the machine handle.

He quotes an experiment involving a prepared frog placed inside a bottle. The spinal cord was transfixed by a small metal hook to which was attached a suitable hooked iron wire. This wire passed upwards through the neck of the bottle sealed completely by a waxed cork. In this way the bottle could be suspended from the prime-conductor of the machine, allowing the frog to hang vertically, limbs downward, inside it.

In the first place Galvani hung the bottle on the prime-conductor and began to turn the handle of his machine. No muscular contractions were produced. When however, he removed the wire a very little way from the conductor, sparks occurred at the gap produced and so did contractions of the muscles. He explains the difference between the two situations as depending on the fact that:

> . . . *in the first case, the torrent of electric fluid goes placidly, without meeting any resistance from any conductor or other while in the second case, it meets with a resistance in the little stratum of air placed between one conductor and another, and in consequence the electric fluid is constrained to exert some impulse, some greater effect in order to overcome the said resistance. Therefore an impulse of electric fluid equal to that which is adequate to forcing its way across a little stratum of air is sufficient, when applied to nerves to excite the contraction of their corresponding muscles.*[29]

Applying this idea to previous experimental results when contractions were produced in the absence of a spark, he says:

> *But not only the force, or the impulse exerted by the electrical fluid in overcoming a little of the stratum of air, in order to enter, run along and issue from the nerves or their contiguous bodies, is sufficient to act on these in the aforesaid manner, but also that which it adopts in passing through and running over bodies which are not perfect conductors, as over armed Franklinian Squares, and going to the above-mentioned nerves and their contiguous bodies or conductors.*[30]

So put into more general terms, Galvani is saying that it is not a spark *per se* which is necessary: nerves can be stimulated by an extremely small quantity of electrical fluid, provided it can be made to exert an 'impulse' such as is necessary to overcome any resistance, whatever this resistance may be. It is the motive force of the artificially produced electric fluid and not any other intrinsic quality which is acting on the fluid in the nerves and in turn stimulating the appropriate muscles to contract.

Thus by the first month of 1781, Galvani seems to have been convinced of the electrical nature of the nervous juice: thus he believed he had strong evidence that he had demonstrated what had for a long time been a conjecture.

Now considering the overriding importance of this evidence in the analysis of the physical basis of irritability – it was the key fact upon which Galvani was to build his whole theory of muscular motion – his evidence is worth further examination. His theory depends on his interpretation of the physical events taking place when muscle contractions were produced in the experiment of 26 January 1781. From his reasoning it is quite clear that he considers the situation different from that normally occurring when electrical changes are brought about in a body as a result of its being brought near a source of electrical fluid. The experiments just described make it obvious that, in general, Galvani regarded electrical phenomena as due to the movement of a quantity of electrical fluid from one situation to another along a pressure gradient from regions of higher to lower density through bodies which offered varying degrees of resistance to its passage. Thus he reasoned that if the muscular contractions are due (as he apparently would have expected) quite simply to the accumulation of electrical fluid in the nerves of his frog preparation, to their being 'charged' with electrical fluid, he would have expected these contractions:

1. To occur without the necessary accompaniment of a spark;

2. To be proportionately more vigorous as the charge or accumulation of electricity in the neighbourhood of the prime-conductor increased (that is, to increase with the number of times the handle was turned);

3. To be more readily produced the nearer his preparation was to the prime-conductor (the density of the atmosphere surrounding the prime-conductor decreasing with distance).

This reasoning gives us a fairly clear picture of Galvani's interpretation of the electrical events occurring in the neighbourhood of a charged conductor and since his frog's contractions did not seem to occur in a manner consistent with this, explains why he adopted a different and special explanation for their occurrence. He believed that an infinitesimally small quantity of electrical fluid directed at a point in the frog's nerve would cause contractions provided its particles had sufficient vibratory motion to activate the particles of the intrinsic nervous juice. In terms of a physical model the frog-preparation could not, apparently, be considered as behaving like a mere conducting body, capable of imbibing electrical fluid throughout its entire mass: the agency of the extrinsic fluid from the applied electrical atmosphere ceased at or before its contact with the nerve. All that was apparently required was that a sufficient (although small) quantity was able to activate intermediary particles to a state of vibratory motion adequate to activate the nervous juice.

If Galvani had believed that his preparation was behaving like a mere conductor in the vicinity of a charged body, his whole case for the nervous fluid's identity with electricity would have been invalidated and so he was at pains to accumulate evidence which would corroborate the validity of this crucial distinction. From the time of the discovery of 26 January 1781 until February 1783 (the months during which he continued to be concerned with the action of artificial electricity) he had this problem in the forefront of his mind; time and time again there are references to experiments which seem to prove that the accumulation of electrical fluid from the atmosphere of his machine's conductor cannot be the cause of his frog's contractions. To quote just a few examples:

On 3 February 1781 he described an experiment (See Fig. 1 on p. 161 of this book) with the usual frog preparation. A long iron wire was attached to the spinal cord of the preparation which was lying on a table near the electric machine in one room, the wire being led through the doorway into a second room, where it was held by an assistant. On closing the communicating door, and extracting a spark from the machine, the usual vigorous contractions occurred. Galvani says this is:

> A manifest indication that the contractions do not arise from the electrical fluid communicated by the electrical atmosphere to the nerve or to the person touching the wire.[31]

The electrical atmosphere does not pass through closed doors!

On the same day, he covered the whole of his frog-preparation with a wet cloth, extracted a spark and noted the usual contractions.[32] When he then took a larger wet cloth and arranged it so that one end was wrapped around the spinal cord (the proximal end of his preparation with respect to the machine) and the other free end draped under a long conducting wire which reached the ground, he found the same, undiminished contractions when a spark was extracted. He interprets this as further proof that the electrical fluid from the prime-conductor's atmosphere is not the agent responsible for the contractions since, if it were, the contractions should be diminished in this second experiment as a result of the soaking up of a part of that atmosphere by the conductile, wet cloth, before it can reach the frog's nerves.[33]

And again on 8 February 1781, he produced contractions in one and the same frog using first the discharge of a Leyden Jar, then that of a Franklinian Square. Since he considered that the quantity of fluid produced (on discharge) by the Jar was much greater than that of the Square, the fact that contractions were equally strong in both cases seemed to him to offer further proof that it is the vibration rather than the amount of fluid that is significant.[34] Similarly he noted that contractions produced by extracting a spark from his electric machine were always of greater magnitude than those obtained following discharge of the Leyden Jar, although he was certain that the quantity of fluid "extracted" from the latter was very much greater. Other references to this point of distinction occur throughout his notes: it is as though he must constantly reassure himself that his frog-preparation is not in fact acting as a mere conductor, producing contractions in proportion to the quantity of electrical fluid it can soak up.

However a quantitative consideration did influence his investigations and he was aware of this, for within the context of his thinking it was obvious that the force necessary to produce contractions must exceed a critical level of potency which could be expected to depend on such factors as quantity of electric fluid vibrating, its degree of vibration, the distance from its source to point of application on the nerve, the ease with which it could reach this point, etc. And furthermore and most strikingly, he was aware of the way in which individual experimental animals varied in their response to such a stimulus – a result of the "varying strength of the nervous force" possessed by them. These relationships were put forward by Galvani in Part I of his *Commentary on Muscular Motion* as a series of laws governing the production of muscle contractions in response to the application of artificial electricity.

Our next chapter will deal with this section of the *Commentary*, its content, its interpretation by Galvani's contemporaries, and its analysis within the framework of present day concepts.

Notes

1 Galvani, Luigi (1953) *Commentary on the effects of Electricity on Muscular Motion*, M. Foley (transl.), I. Bernard Cohen (ed.), Norwalk Conn. Burndy Library, p. 45
2 *Memorie ed Esperimenti di Luigi Galvani con la iconografia di lui e un saggio di bibliografia degli scritti*, Bologna, Licinio Cappelli Editore 1937, pp 3–31, which contains the 'Saggio della forza nervea a sua realazione coll' elettricità', dated 25 Novembris 1782, pp 3–31
3 Ibid., p. 3
4 This is a direct reference to Haller's work. See Chap. 12 of this book, Note 2
5 Muscular movements are today classified as 'voluntary' when they are performed in response to the will, 'involuntary' when they occur without this intervention. Galvani has merely elected to choose a different terminology. It is apparent from the way that he sets out his essay that he had every intention of dealing with 'secondary' or 'involuntary' movements at some later date
6 Loc cit., Note 2, p. 4
7 Ibid., p. 5
8 See Chap. 15 of this book
9 See Chap. 11 of this book
10 Loc cit., Note 2, See 'Esperimenti del Mese di Novembre 1780', pp 233–237 and 'Esperimenti del Mese di Decembre 1780', pp 238–244
11 See Chap. 17 of this book
12 See Appendix II of this book, where an account of these devices is given
13 Loc cit., Note 2, 'Esperimenti del Mese di Decembre 1780, Die 2° Decembre, Esp. 5°', p. 238
14 Ibid., 'Esperimenti del Mese di Novembre 1780, Giorno 6 Novembre, Esp 1°', p. 233
15 Ibid., 'Esperimenti del Mese di Decembre 1780, Die 2ª Decembre, Esp. 5°', p. 238
16 Ibid., 'Esperimenti del Mese di Decembre 1780, A di 29 Decembre, Esp 1°', p. 242
17 Ibid., 'Esperimenti del Mese di Decembre 1780, A di 29 Decembre, Corollario 1°', p. 242
18 Ibid., 'Esperimenti del Mese di Decembre 1780, A di 29 Decembre, Corollario 2°', p. 243
19 Ibid., 'Esperimenti del Mese di Decembre 1780, A di 29 Decembre, Esp 2°', p. 243
20 Ibid., 'Esperimenti del Mese di Decembre 1780, A di 29 Decembre, Corollario, p. 244
21 Ibid., 'Anno 1781 – Gennaro, Esperimenti, Giorno 24 Gennaro 1781, Riflessione', p. 252

22 Ibid., 'Saggio della Forza nervea . . ., ', p. 9. Galvani's reference would of course apply
   to the experiments carried out by Caldani and Beccaria quoted in Chap. 13 of this book
23 Ibid., 'Anno 1781, Gennaro, Die 26 Gennaro, Esp. 6°', p. 254
24 Loc cit., Note 1, p. 47
25 Loc cit., Note 2, 'Anno 1781, Giorno 31 Gennaro, Esp. 2°' p. 256
26 Galvani is using the term in use at that time to describe the area immediately surrounding a positively charged conductor. This was envisaged as being loaded with
   the surplus electrical fluid given off by the conductor. For details of this concept and
   its development, see Chap. 17 of this book
27 Loc cit., Note 2, 'Anno 1781, Giorno 31 Gennaro, Corollario 1°', p. 257
28 Ibid., 'Anno 1781, Giorno 31 Gennaro, Corollario 2°', p. 257
29 Ibid., 'Esp. 9°', p. 10
30 Ibid., 'Esp. 10°', p. 11
31 Ibid., 'Esperimenti del Mese di Febbraro 1781, Die 3ª Febbraro 1781 Esp. 2°', p. 260
32 Ibid., 'Esp. 3°', p. 261
33 Ibid., 'Esp. 4°', p. 261
34 Ibid., 'Giorno 8 Febbraro 1781', p. 267

17

The effects of artificial electricity on muscular motion: 1791

From as early as the beginning of 1781, Galvani had convinced himself that his frog-preparation was not behaving as a mere passive conductor of electrical fluid accumulating in it as a result of its proximity to a charged source. Between 1781 and 1783 when he was particularly concerned with experiments involving the stimulation of muscular contractions under just these circumstances, he believed the physical stimulus was a vibration. When he came to write Part I of his *Commentary*, in which he eventually presented the public with the results of the work undertaken during this period, he was still wedded to the same concept. Unfortunately, Galvani limited his published account to a description of certain experiments from which he had deduced a series of laws concerning the relationship between the 'strength' of his stimulus and the production and 'strength' of the contractile response obtained. The reader is given no parallel account of the conceptual background to these experiments, no hint that Galvani considered the electric fluid supplied by his machine as a purely mechanical extrinsic force rousing a naturally-occurring intrinsic electrical agent which, in turn, acted upon the frog's muscles. Galvani considered the rôle of the electrical machine as analogous to that of the brain in relation to the nerves and not as a replacement for the nervous force itself. All the laws he derived were interpreted by him as reflecting the ease with which the force of any given, vibrating quantity of artificial electricity could reach his frog's nerve and increase the vibration of a nervous fluid contained in its central canal. At the stage when this occurred, he considered that a purely physiological process took over, although the frog-preparation would at the same time, coincidentally, act as a mere passive conductor. Galvani's use of such expressions as "electricity flowing into nerves" etc, is unfortunate as this phrasing fails to convey the true nature of his model.

He opens his account with a description of the discovery made on 26 January 1781. This is substantially the same as the one occurring in his experimental notes although his wife is described merely as 'an assistant':

Having in mind other things I placed the frog on the same table as an electrical machine . . ., so that the animal was completely separated from and removed at a considerable distance from the machine's conductor. When one of my assistants by chance lightly applied the point of a scalpel to the inner crural nerves . . . of the frog, suddenly all the muscles of the limbs were seen so to contract that they appeared to have fallen into violent tonic convulsions. Another assistant who was present when we were performing electrical experiments thought that he observed that the phenomenon occurred when a spark was discharged from the conductor of the electrical machine . . .[1]

The assistant directed Galvani's attention to this "unusual phenomenon" and from this, we are told, arose the series of investigations aimed at elucidating its cause. Now, instead of proceeding to describe the experiments of 31 January which had led Galvani to formulate his hypothesis, the *Commentary* goes on to analyse the route by which the electrical fluid supposedly reached the frog's nerve. Thus Galvani demonstrates that the phenomenon only occurred if the conductible part of his scalpel (that is, the metal blade or nails in the handle and not the bone handle itself) touched the nerve at the time a spark was withdrawn from the electric machine. As a result of this he says:

> . . . *we began to suspect that perhaps when we held the bone handle in our fingers there was no way for the electric fluid to flow (by whatever means) into the frog but when we took hold of the blade or nails and brought them in contact with the frog, a path was opened.*[2]

He would have conveyed his idea more accurately, perhaps, if he had said there was no medium along which the vibrations of the electric fluid could be conveyed to the nerves unless a conducting body was in contact with them. This he confirms by showing that if he touched or even rubbed the nerves with a clean dry glass rod, no contractions ensued at the discharge of a spark, but on replacing the glass rod with an iron one, they occurred once more.

Galvani's next problem was to determine whether he himself was an essential part of the conductile pathway and so he repeated the experiment, applying the iron rod to the nerves but this time without holding it in his fingers. The result being negative he replaced the original iron rod with a much longer iron wire to see if this extra quantity of conducting material would compensate for the absence of his own body – with positive results. He makes no reference to the fact that his body was in contact with the earth nor does he tell us whether his long iron wire was grounded although in his illustration (Fig. 1) it is shown as dangling over the edge of the table to reach the floor (KK, Fig. 1).[3] All Galvani is concerned with is the need for a conducting pathway of such dimensions that the vibrations of the electrical fluid can be conveyed to the nerves and stimulate them:

> *From these observations it became clear to us that not only was a conducting substance that touched the nerves required to produce the phenomenon, but also one of determined size and length. Hereafter for the sake of clearness rather than brevity, allow us to call a conducting substance of this sort a nerve-conductor.*[2]

His analysis of the conducting pathway continues with an examination of the significance of the lie of his frog-preparation in relation to the electric machine. He fixed a small metal hook through the spinal cord of the frog and attached to it a nerve-conductor found to be of adequate dimensions. Varying the position of his preparation so that first the nerve-conductor and then the frog was directed towards the prime-conductor was found to make no difference to his result – brisk contractions ensuing in both cases.

Separating the frog's nerves from the electric machine by a relatively great distance, that is, well beyond the atmosphere surrounding the prime-conductor, did not prevent the production of contractions, provided a long

Fig.1. Diagram of apparatus and layout of Galvani's experiments. Copied from Luigi Galvani (1791) *Commentary . . ., 3 Disegni Inediti delle Esperienze di Galvani* edition. Courtesy of Guido Tabarroni.

enough conducting medium was used. Galvani demonstrates this in the
following way:

> *We suspended a long iron wire, . . . FF* [See Fig. 1, FF should be EE – it is incorrect
> in the original Latin text of the *Commentary* and the translation], *by silk threads
> and thereby insulated it as the natural philosophers say. Then we fastened one end by
> a silk thread to a nail, F, driven into the wall; the other end we carried away from the
> electrical machine through various rooms as far as the wire reached. To the latter at
> point C, we joined another iron wire, B, from whose end a frog was suspended. For the
> sake of convenience we enclosed the frog in a glass jar, A, whose bottom was covered
> with some conducting material, e.g., water or very small lead shot of the kind used by
> hunters (the latter brought about the best experimental results). When a spark was
> discharged from the conductor of the electrical machine, the limbs of the prepared frog
> moved, even at so great a distance – which was truly extraordinary – and almost
> jumped. The same phenomenon occurred when the frog was removed from the glass
> jar and was hung in a similar manner from the conductor, EE. This happened much
> more quickly if some conducting body, which was in contact with the earth, were
> fastened to the feet of the animal.[4]*

Galvani tells us that the iron wire EE (I have used the correct letters EE as
shown in the figures published with the *Commentary*), was of "one hundred or
more ells in length".[5] His next move was to see if he could "milk off" some
of the electrical fluid passing along the nerve-conductor before it could reach
the frog's nerves. He did this by removing the silk threads and attaching the
long wire directly to the metal hinges of the various doors in his house. The
rationale appears to be similar to that which he applies on many occasions
and the diminished contractions he achieved as a result of this manoeuvre
seemed to confirm his view that the stimulus was passing from the machine
towards the frog and that there was a quantitative relationship of some kind
between the size of the contractions and the quantity of electrical fluid
thrown into the nerve-conductor by the vibration of the spark. It is interesting that when he was carrying out these experiments on 4 January 1782, he
made a note to the effect that they demonstrated what an exceedingly small
quantity of electricity is required as a stimulus:

> *Having calculated how much electrical fluid must be dispersed in its passage through
> the various rooms and in contact with various conducting bodies, the amount re-
> quired to excite the contractions is very much smaller than one would believe.[6]*

In this last series of experiments, it will be noted that he refers to the significance of conducting bodies attached to the feet or muscles of the preparation,
particularly if they are grounded. He also became aware of this as a result of
an experiment he performed in order to see if the electrical fluid is equally
distributed in all directions by the prime-conductor of his machine. He describes the arranging of a number of frog-preparations in a circle around the
latter, the nerve-conductors being set radially and lying proximally with respect to the frogs. At the discharge of the spark all the frog limbs contracted
in unison "particularly" when a conducting body was attached to their feet,
the reaction being even stronger if this were grounded. Galvani remarks:

*Consequently when we became aware of the usefulness or even the necessity of fasten-
ing conducting bodies to the feet of the animals, we were eager to attempt new experiments embracing the problem. Once these were performed, it became clear that the
conducting bodies which we attached to the muscles to bring about contractions either
were at times sufficient by themselves to produce this effect without a nerve-conductor,
or at any rate, made no small contribution to the effect. Moreover the larger the conducting bodies were and the more they were possessed of a strong conducting power
the greater were the contractions, particularly if the conductors were in contact with the
earth. They were at least as effective as those conductors which we were accustomed to
attach to the nerves. Hereafter we shall call these conducting bodies muscle-conductors
to distinguish them conveniently from the so-called nerve-conductors.*[4]

Galvani does not give any reasons for the efficacy of the muscle-conductor
per se or, when in contact with the ground, and in particular he does not
specify in which direction he considers the electrical fluid is flowing when this
conductor is in use. Now, logically, if he was concerned solely with the ease
with which the vibrations of artificial electricity could reach his frog's nerve,
the muscle-conductor should be considered merely as another afferent pathway, the only difference being that in this case, the artificial electricity would
have to pass in a centripetal direction through the muscle before reaching the
nerve which it stimulated. From this point of view, the efficiency of a muscle-
conductor would depend on factors identical with those operating in the case
of a nerve-conductor *viz* its dimensions and intrinsic nature (good or bad conducting material) – which is what Galvani found to be true. On the other hand,
in various experimental notes, for example, those dated 29 December 1780 he
talks of touching the animals' legs and "inviting" the electrical fluid to flow
through the nerves to the muscles. There is no doubt that Galvani considered
the earth as a conducting body of insatiable capacity and that putting the earth
in contact with electrical fluid resulted in a discharge of that fluid into it. In
fact, Galvani considered a muscle-conductor as an afferent pathway in some
situations and an efferent in others but he does not make this clear to the
reader. Perhaps this is a suitable occasion for discussing the problem in general.

Briefly, Galvani considered the role of the muscle-conductor in three situations with regard to its distal end:

Case 1. The distal end was in contact with the earth.

Case 2. The distal end was in contact with an electric or insulating body.

Case 3. The distal end was free in the air.

In case 1, Galvani seems to have seen earthing as a means of attracting
electric fluid towards and through the frog-preparation and hence *via* the
muscle-conductor to earth. He does not say whether he considered this contributed to the production or magnitude of muscle contractions as a result of
an increased vibration of particles of extrinsic electric fluid reaching the
nerve, or as an increased vibration of the particles of intrinsic nervous electricity acting on the muscle, or by some other mechanism. There seems little
doubt however, that in this situation he considered that the muscle-conductor
was acting as an efferent pathway.

In case 2, the muscle-conductor was regarded as an afferent pathway, acting as a means of directing artificial electricity towards his frog's nerve. That
this was Galvani's view is quite apparent from his interpretation of the results
of numerous experiments carried out in the early 1780's, some of which we
will be discussing later in the chapter. Bear in mind that Galvani appreciated
that the direction of flow of electricity in his frog-preparation was of no significance provided its vibrations could reach a point on the nerve and stimulate it. Also, with his purely mechanistic view of electrical fluid as composed
of vibrating particles, it is easy to see how he would envisage the action of an
insulating body placed at the point where the stimulating artificial electricity
was entering the distal end of the muscle-conductor from the air: it acted
rather like the walls of a squash court, propelling the particles into the muscle-
conductor with increased force towards the muscle and hence to the nerve.

In case 3, it is difficult to be sure how he considered its action although
most probably as an afferent pathway, less useful than in case 2, because the
electrical fluid was not forcibly directed towards it.

Various ambiguities are apparent in Galvani's reasoning. It is, for example.
surprising that he did not see an analogy between the situation of an earthed
man touching his frog's nerve with a conducting body (the crucial experiment
of 26 January 1781) and the numerous experiments in which he considered
an earthed or non-insulated conductor as a pathway draining off electrical
fluid before it could reach his frog's nerve. He never appears to have shown
much interest in the earthing or non-earthing of a nerve-conductor.

Having established the efficacy of nerve and muscle-conductors, Galvani's
next aim was to try to prevent the flow of electrical fluid along these conductors towards his frog-preparation and thus show that it is indeed the
necessary stimulus. He used the basic apparatus referred to above,[3] consisting of a very long wire attached to a short conductor transfixing the frog's
spinal cord, the frog being suspended in a glass bottle. In the first case he attempted to obstruct the flow by joining the long and short conductors by
means of a silk thread and in the second case by separating the opposing
ends of these conductors although leaving them as close together as possible
without their actually touching. In both these cases he failed to obtain contractions. On the other hand. When he laid his frog-preparation on a non-
conducting slab with its nerve-conductor separated from the spinal cord or
nerves by "several lines" or even "a thumb's width", contractions were brisk
at the extraction of a spark.[7] Even placing the muscles on a conducting slab
(while leaving the spinal cord and nerves on a non-conducting surface) did
not prevent contractions occurring, although if the nerves were placed on a
conducting surface, no contractions appeared. Galvani does not suggest any
reason for the different results obtained. In the first experiment he doubtless
assumed the vibrating particles of electric fluid were unable to enter the
short wire transfixing the spinal cord, as a result of the obstruction provided
by the insulating silk thread. Similar reasoning could be applied in the case
of the air gap between the two wires, the vibrations travelling along the long
wire being dissipated into the air at this point and not gathered into the

second wire. In the experiment with a shorter conductor as opposed to the 100 ell wire[5] (that is, nearer the machine) Galvani almost certainly envisaged the vibrations as being more vigorous and the electrical fluid arriving at the gap as rebounding from the insulating slab to enter the spinal cord or nerves more easily than in the situation of the previous experiments. In the case of their being supported on a conducting slab, he would assume the vibrating fluid was running away through this and therefore not entering the nerve.

At this stage he makes the following statement:

> Consequently, when these different problems were investigated and their results confirmed in a long series of experiments, we felt permitted not only to attribute the phenomenon of muscular contractions to electricity, but even to consider the conditions of the experiment and certain laws by which it was bound.[8]

He feels "... permitted ... to attribute the phenomenon of muscular contractions to electricity ..." but what electricity? The natural assumption of anybody reading the description of experiments as set out in the *Commentary* would be that the artificial electricity produced by Galvani's machine was charging his frog-preparation and bringing about contractions in a probably quite unnatural way. At no point does Galvani mention the critical reasoning behind his belief that the nervous fluid is electrical and acting as the physiological intermediary – set in motion, albeit unnaturally by the vibration of the electric fluid thrust out by the machine.

Galvani's 'laws' confirm what he might well have anticipated on the basis of his hypothesis; they are altogether in keeping with his idea of the stimulus depending on the ease with which an adequate supply of vibrating electricity could influence his frog's nerve:

> Muscular contraction of this sort, then, seemed to us within certain limits to stand in a direct proportion to the strength of the spark and of the animal as well as to the length of the conductors, particularly the nerve-conductor. They seemed to stand in an inverse proportion, however, to the distances from the conductor of the electrical machine. These contractions, moreover, appeared generally stronger to us when the animal was set on the same table with the electric machine and the table was covered with an oily coating, or when the animal was removed from the table and laid on a non-conducting, rather than a conducting substance.[9]

He notes however, that the relationship between these quantities is proportional only within certain limits:

> I have said, to be sure, that a direct proportion seemed to me to be maintained in the contractions, but only within certain limits. It has been found, for example, that if you shorten a nerve-conductor of a length which is sufficient to bring about contractions, the contractions do not diminish but disappear. If, however, you lengthen it, the contractions in fact grow stronger but only up to a certain point, beyond which – however far you extend the nerve-conductor – the contractions are augmented imperceptibly, if at all. The same can be said about the other elements of proportion I have set forth.[9]

In other words, there is both a minimal level of stimulus for the production of contractions and a maximal level of response on the part of the muscle, a physiological relationship which Galvani almost certainly attributed to the ability of the nervous fluid to respond to the electrical vibrations and in turn, that of muscle to respond to the stimulus of the nervous fluid. He does not specify what he means by "strength of contraction" but in fact this could only be a measure of the number of muscle elements roused to activity, since, as we now know, any muscle fibre is capable of responding in only one way to an adequate stimulus, that is, by maximal contractions. Galvani of course was unaware of this, but his observation of the response of muscle to varying strengths of stimulus is accurate as regards the existence of a threshold value and ceiling of response.

Galvani's laws of proportion for the behaviour of frogs' muscle in response to the stimulus of his electrical machine's spark sum up the essential results of his experiments and appear to the reader of the *Commentary* to contain the most important facts that he wishes to transmit. Other experiments referred to later in Part I serve merely as an attempt to confirm what has already been demonstrated with the electric machine. They consist of (a) experiments involving the use of other devices for the production of artificial electricity and (b) experiments designed to prevent this electricity from reaching the frog.

The first variant involved the use of the Franklinian Square. Galvani says that he expected the discharge from one of these to bring about even greater contractions but to his astonishment no contractions occurred when the Square was made to produce a flash (he does not give any reason for this failure but it must be assumed that his Square was of too low a capacitance).

His next series of experiments involved the use of 'negative electricity'. He describes the insulation of his electrical machine and the man who turned it. The frogs were set on a glass plate and the machine operator held an iron rod in his free hand which was close to the usual frog-nerve-conductor. The operator extracted sparks from neighbouring objects, the frog responding with muscle contractions on each occasion. 'Negative electricity' was also involved in experiments using the Leyden Jar:

> We set a nerve-conductor . . . at a certain distance from the negative surface of a Leyden Jar. We then produced sparks . . . from the positive surface, as the natural philosophers say, or that surface to which electricity had been given. The frogs reacted in the same way as with positive electricity. It is notable that this even occurred when the iron wire which served as a nerve-conductor was at some distance from the external surface of the Jar and when it was completely enclosed by a long glass tube and the frog itself was confined in a glass receptacle. The only requirement was that the open end of the tube touched the outer surface of the aforementioned Jar. These same contractions were obtained, moreover, if a spark were produced from the hook of a Leyden Jar at the same time as it was being charged with electricity, as they say, or a little later. They also occurred if a spark were emitted either in the same place in which the Jar was being charged, or else after it had been removed at a distance from the electrical machine.[10]

Now while Galvani talks of 'positive' and 'negative' electrical fluids, it is quite obvious from his description of the Leyden Jar that he recognised only one electrical fluid which he considered to be in excess in a body which is 'positively' charged, and in deficit in a body 'negatively' charged, *viz* the hook and outside of a Leyden Jar are considered as respectively positively and negatively charged. At no point in his experimental notes does he refer to two different fluids but always theorises in terms of the movement of one, that is, he adopts the Franklinian view (See Chapter 10 and Chapter 18 of this book).

As a final source of 'negative electricity' he extracted sparks from the under surface of a Franklinian Square, on the upper surface of which he had placed his prepared frog and which was being charged from his electrical machine. This time he obtained contractions but only while the electrical machine was being turned, or on rare occasions, immediately after it had stopped. All that these experiments with 'negative electricity' were apparently demonstrating is that the direction of flow of the fluid within the frog parts is immaterial provided it hits the nerve with sufficient vibratory force at some point – a fact that Galvani believed he had established in 1780.

For the sake of completeness he used the electrophorus as a last source of electricity. Extracting a spark from the plate, he obtained his usual contractions but only at short range and even then the contractions were weak: presumably the electrophorus was a poor supplier of electrical fluid!

The second group of experiments, comprised further and more rigid attempts to exclude artificial electricity from his frog-preparation:

> Now then to place the results of the experiment beyond all doubt, we sought in various ways to prevent the electric fluid from the electrical machine from passing (in whatever way this might be done) into the animal and its conductors.[11]

He says that he set about this by placing his frog inside a glass jar, the mouth of which was glued to an opening in the party-wall between the room housing his electrical machine and that adjoining it, in such a way that the jar was in the same room as his machine but the nerve-conductor hung down in the second room. When a spark was extracted from the machine, the usual contractions resulted. When this procedure was reversed, so that the conductor was placed in the jar and the frog hung where the conductor had previously been, the usual contractions resulted on the extraction of a spark. These experiments were first carried out in February 1781 and in his notes Galvani gives more details of his procedure, laying stress on the fact that the mouth of the jar was sealed with wax.[12] A glass cylinder was passed through this wax and extended through the hole in the wall so that the frog's nerve-conductor which was made to pass through its lumen and thus into the other room was completely insulated. Galvani would certainly have expected that his glass jar would prevent the entry of electrical fluid into the frog's nerve-conductor, just as his other insulating procedures did, and yet he was able to produce contractions that were as vigorous as ever.

Without hinting in any way at the significance that this observation held for him, he proceeds in the *Commentary* to describe experiments in which the exclusion of the electrical fluid was apparently even more rigid.

In order to do this he designed a little device consisting of two bottles one inverted on the other, the two joined by a cork stopper, which was firmly and copiously waxed into position. The frog hung by its hook, suspended in the lower jar by an iron wire which descended from the upper jar through the cork to transfix the hook. The iron wire in the upper jar, the nerve-conductor, was in contact with lead shot, as were the feet of the animal, in the lower jar.[3] Galvani placed this device on an insulated table near his machine (See Fig. 1 (Fig. 6) on p. 161 of this book) extracted sparks and observed the usual contractions, contemporaneous with each discharge. Here was yet another example of the power of the machine to act as a stimulus in a situation where there seemed no possibility that electrical fluid could be conveyed from the prime-conductor to the nerve-conductor and where the other striking feature was the synchronous relationship between the discharge of a spark and the contraction of the frog's muscles.

It seems surprising that at this stage in the *Commentary* Galvani does not elaborate on the real significance these observations held for him. In fact all he does is to make an extremely oblique and difficult statement concerning the cause of the contractions:

> *. . . After these results had been seen, I would easily have given up my original postulation that the electricity, excited in the conductor of the electrical machine, in some manner or other motivated these muscular movements through the discharge of a spark, had not the experiments which were carried out above – and the growth of a certain strong suspicion that the phenomenon certainly ought not to be ascribed to the electricity on the inner surface of the jar working on the animal and its conductors at the time a spark was discharged – recalled me to my first opinion.*[13]

This paragraph is all that Galvani offers the reader of Part I of the *Commentary* by way of a clue as to how he is interpreting his results. He suggests that his original, and still held view, is that the movements are: ". . . motivated in some manner or other through the discharge of a spark . . ." but he does not tell his reader anything of the theory he believes underlies this phenomenon.

His experiments with the double bottle device, as described in the *Commentary* and in much greater detail in his notes, are the key to an understanding of the theoretical basis of his ideas. We know from his own words that he viewed the electrical fluid produced by his machine as being composed of actively vibrating particles which were launched into the air in little packets or little atmospheres around each spark.[14] Furthermore, we know that he believed that the production of these sparks was almost always the necessary accompaniment of contractions, the synchronous nature of the extraction of a spark and muscle contraction being one of the features of his experiments which impressed him most. We also know that he viewed electrics or insulators as bodies which obstructed the passage of vibrating electrical particles, causing them to be reflected or rebound from their surface, while conductors allowed them to pass along a gradient from an area of relative excess to one of relative deficiency. So how was he to explain the fact that, when his frog-preparation together with its conductors was completely enclosed inside the double-bottle, not only did he produce contractions, synchronous with the extraction of a spark, but these were even more vigorous than when the frog was not so insulated? How did he envisage that the vibrating force of the particles of electric fluid reached the frog's nerve?

The very first insulating experiments carried out in January 1781 had convinced him that the electrical atmosphere from his machine flowing smoothly into his frog's nerve was not the stimulus for muscle contraction and at this early stage he was impressed with the significance of the electric machine spark as a means of producing a mechanical impulse – an impulse which happened to use electrical fluid as its medium, for artificial electricity seemed to be an agent capable of exerting great vibratory force when present in extremely small quantities.

In March 1781, he performed experiments which demonstrated that if he separated the upper and lower bottles of his apparatus, allowing the long nerve-conductor to stretch between them, the contractions produced at the extraction of a spark were less vigorous than those obtained when the two bottles were joined together as already described.[15] This difference was also present when the experiments were performed with the bottles under the dome of an air-pump. Reducing the pressure resulted in an absence of contractions if the two bottles were separated, while if they were joined, contractions were as vigorous as ever, even with very low pressures. Galvani offers the following as possible explanations:

> It is always observed, outside the machine as well [that is, outside the dome of the air-pump] that when the bottles are separated – A – the contractions diminished in force relative to the contractions which we had when the bottles were united, one over the other – B – This seemed to arise either from the tremors which were more easily communicated and were more united and intense in the little machine B than in A, since in this latter case, they could be dispersed by the air, or again by the electrical fluid developed in the glass by the tremors. These tremors could not be dispersed from the little machine B, since being made of glass, this was perfectly insulated and they were therefore constrained to go to the frog's conductor. In the little machine A, they were able to disperse through the air, since this is not as perfect an insulator as glass. All this occurred more easily and in greater strength under the pneumatic machine, since a vacuum is a better metallic conductor and in consequence a better disperser of electric fluid.[16]

This explanation suggests that Galvani is undecided as to whether the electrical fluid impelled against the little machine B (joined bottles) actually passes through its walls to reach the frog-conductor or whether its arrival at the external surface of the bottle causes an equal amount of electrical fluid to be discharged from the internal surface and that this latter is the vibratory stimulant for the frog's nerve. This in fact is what he is saying in the *Commentary* but he never brings the matter to a head by saying that his originally and still held view involves the belief that electrical fluid can pass through glass.

At the end of 1781 he performed experiments in which he brought about contractions in his frog-preparation when he placed it in the little machine B, under the dome of an air-pump. He had brought the little ring, attached to the end of the chain leading to the prime-conductor of his machine in contact with various parts of the external surface of the receiver and on extracting a spark, obtained vigorous contractions. In this case each bottle composing B had a little hole bored in it to allow the free passage of air. Galvani reflects thus:

It seems then that the upper surface of the receiver must have been discharged; how therefore, when this was discharged was the phenomenon produced if the electric fluid, existing naturally in the frog's bottle, was not set in motion, and being directed toward the glass of the bottle passed through it, to reach the internal surface of the receiver ? To say this, truly seems difficult; and equally difficult that at the discharge of a spark, the most subtle part of the electrical or other fluid which I will call animal electricity, was not able to pass through glass and be carried to the frog.[17]

This question of whether electrical fluid can pass through glass was still worrying Galvani the following year. We find him carrying out experiments with different thicknesses of glass for example flower vases and wine bottles, trying to see if their thickness has an effect on the ability of electrical fluid to pass through them and concluding that perhaps it does pass more readily through thin glass although on the other hand, it could be that thin glass discharges electricity more readily.[18]

At the beginning of 1783 he was still open minded about the problem. He describes experiments with the frog in the usual single jar – A. This was placed on a table near his electrical machine with the conducting wire at a certain distance from it. When he then touched the outer surface of the bottle, there were no contractions at the extraction of a spark.[19]

In a second experiment he placed a long iron wire under the base of the bottle A in such a way that a portion of it touched the table before passing downwards to reach and touch the ground. He found that when he pressed the wire hard against the table with the flat of his hand, the contractions previously obtained at the extraction of a spark ceased. If then instead, he touched the iron wire beyond the table, and held it between his fingers contractions reappeared. He gives two explanations for these results which are interesting as an illustration of his concept of electrical phenomena:

The phenomenon seems to depend on the differing charge of the superficial surface of the bottle by the electric atmosphere and on the differing degrees of immersion of the conductors in the atmosphere, for when I touch the bottle with my hand and I am immersed in the atmosphere, being a bigger conductor and having a greater surface area, I led off more [electrical fluid] than the internal iron wire, I led off more I say, to the superficial surface of the bottle, than the frog-conductor and as a consequence the outside [of the bottle] cannot be freely discharged and the inside cannot be adequately charged for the excitation of contractions.

The same holds true when I squeeze the iron wire against the table. Whereas, when I touch the iron wire beyond the table, since I am not immersed in the atmosphere of the conductor [prime-conductor] therefore I discharge the external surface more, that is a greater quantity of electric fluid is carried to the frog. Another explanation, perhaps more probable – When I touch the bottle with my hand on the iron wire on the table, I appropriate for myself a part of the atmosphere which ought to go to the external surface and in consequence impede the adequate discharging of the internal surface, and hence the development of a sufficient quantity of electrical fluid, by the glass, and its subsequent passage via *the spinal cord to the conductors.*[20]

Two points seem worthy of note here. Firstly that Galvani is well aware of the Franklinan concept of the reciprocal balance of charge on opposite sides of an electric *per se* (this is a substance in which an electric force can be excited and accumulated by friction) – a point which he refers to elsewhere[21] and secondly that he considers the electricity "developed by the glass" or repelled from the inner surface as a result of a cumulation of electricity on the outer surface, passes in a centripetal direction from the frog's feet to its muscle and spinal cord and hence toward the conductor. This seems logical when there is only one bottle and the frog-conductor is exposed outside it, but strangely enough, when on other occasions he refers to experiments with the two bottles he always assumes that if contractions are due to this electricity from the inner surface, it must pass in a centripetal direction from muscles to nerves. This seems illogical as in theory it could just as easily pass in the opposite direction. However Galvani never seems to have considered it this way. As he saw it, the stimulus was provided either by fluid from his machine passing through glass and then in a centrifugal direction in the frog or by the electrical fluid normally existing on the inside of the bottle and dislodged by the impact of this fluid (from the machine) on its outer surface. In the latter case he considered this fluid passed centripetally in the frog.

This discussion has taken us some way from the *Commentary* but has, I hope, served to explain Galvani's rather difficult paragraph. He continues his discussion in the *Commentary* by referring to the movements of an electrometer placed inside the little instrument (elsewhere this is called machine B). He says that these helped to persuade him that it was not the electricity on the inside of the jar that was acting as an excitant:

> Not only did subsequent experiments that were undertaken, but more particularly the motions of an electrometer placed inside of the little instrument, completely confirm my suspicion. For the very light shot [balls] and wires [straw leaves] within the electrometer immediately changed position and were separated from one another when the electrical machine was turned. When the sparks were discharged however, they were restored to their former position and resumed contact.[13]

Galvani's explanation is very similar to the one he offered for the behaviour of an electrometer attached to his frog-conductors, in an attempt to relate the flow of electricity in them with the production of contractions:

> Thus we attached a small electrometer, fashioned after the design of the renowned Volta, to the conductors. We covered one side of the straw leaves of the electrometer with very thin tin foil, that they might be more suitable for the experiment. At first, when the conductors were insulated, the leaves were frequently drawn apart from one another at the turning of the electrical machine, but at the production of a spark, they often fell together. When the wires were freely conducting, then however, the leaves did not withdraw from each other at all at the turning of the electrical machine. It was only at the discharge of a spark that they gave little jumps and vibrations which clearly seemed to indicate some passage of electricity – through the conductors of the animal when contractions were produced.[11]

These quotations merely reflect Galvani's view of the stimulus as a vibratory force passing in a forward direction towards his frog's nerve. Separation of the electroscope leaves, an indication of the accumulation of electrical fluid in the conductors, accompanied the phase of turning the machine, but was absent at the moment when a spark was extracted and the vibratory force came into being.

Obviously in the case of the non-insulated conductors Galvani envisaged extremely small quantities of vibratory fluid being projected into them at the extraction of a spark – a little fluid under great pressure causing a momentary charge and therefore momentarily separating the electroscope leaves – as compared with a lot of fluid at low pressure which would produce a sustained charge and sustained separation of the leaves.

What does appear certain from these remarks, is that Galvani does not believe that a sudden loss of electric fluid is indicated by his electrometer and that this could be the stimulatory factor. However, he did consider the possibility but by the time he came to write the *Commentary* had decided against it.

In December 1781 he performed experiments involving the stimulation of his frog in the single bottle – A. On this occasion he found he could sometimes produce contractions without the extraction of a spark when he touched the outside of the bottle and he adds this significant remark at the end of his notes:

> *Another reflection. – Since however contractions occur without the extraction of a spark, merely by touching the bottle, then when the [electrical] machine was turned, so it can be said that even the mere motion of force and impulse acquired by the electric atmosphere as a result of turning the disc, sets in action the electrical fluid of the glass, the internal surface is discharged and the electrical fluid goes through the conductor of the frog to the frog placidly and accumulates at the bottom of the bottle without exciting contractions. So that, when I touch the bottle at the spot where there is lead shot, discharging the external surface, then that [electrical fluid] which is at the bottom of the bottle leaps upwards through the frog and through the spinal cord to the conductor of the spinal cord, to be deposited on the internal surface, if we suppose the whole of the outer surface, to be discharged, and it leaps there, invited by this disequilibrium, with a force and blow which is greater than its natural and placid diffusive force, and in consequence, excites contractions.[22]*

A year later however Galvani carried out further experiments which seemed to prove to him that this restitutive flow of electricity was not in fact the stimulus to contraction:

> *Esp. 1°. A bottle containing a frog-preparation with a little conductor – but one that sufficed to produce contractions at the extraction of a spark – was brought up to the fire which was issuing from the conductor of the machine in such a way that the frog-conductor did not disturb or sensibly alter this fire . . . After very many turns of the machine, the spark was extracted but no contractions resulted.*
>
> *Esp 2° The bottle was then brought up [to the conductor of the machine] in such a way that the frog-conductor sensibly changed the fire and altered it, that is so that the said conductor [frog-conductor] received the electrical fluid which previously issued from the conductor of the machine in the form of fire but now was seen no longer as fire but only as a luminous point at the extremity of the conductor: the spark was extracted from various parts of the conductor, but there were no contractions.*
>
> *Corollary:- The contractions of the frog do not therefore depend on electrical fluid collected in the bottle which is restored to the [prime] conductor of the machine at the time the extraction of a spark dissipates either the greater part or all of the electric*

fluid contained in the conductor, particularly as there are no contractions even in the act of extracting the spark and after turning the machine, and in consequence in restituting to it a part of the electric fluid removed from the conductor at the extraction of a spark.[23]

These experiments are some of those which Galvani refers to in the *Commentary* as having helped to persuade him that his contractions resulted from a forward and not a reverse flow of electricity in his frog. As a result of these he was increasingly led to the view that electrical fluid from his machine could pass through glass, although he does not give the reader of Part I of the *Commentary* an adequate description of his ideas. The *Commentary* describes his experiments with the pneumatic machine as a means of assessing whether he could produce contractions in the presence of a vacuum and he finds that he can. (as we have already seen from his notes).

The crucial fact that Galvani faced and on which he based his whole concept was the dependence of contractions on the presence of a spark but as we have seen he found that on certain occasions, contractions occurred in the absence of the discharge of his machine and we have discussed how he rationalised this in his notes. In the *Commentary* he refers to this point in a paragraph in which he describes the production of contractions when the nerve-conductor is set:

> *. . . as close to the conductor of the electrical machine . . . as possible and then if the plate of an electrophorus were lifted from the resin disc, or if (when the electrophorus had been set at a considerable distance from the aforementioned conductor) the same plate were brought very near to it, in both cases without a spark discharge.*[24]

This result would seem to contradict Galvani's early findings as a result of which he had conceived his entire theory, yet he makes no comment on its significance. In his notes referring to the crucial experiment of 26 January 1781, he defends his view by suggesting, among other things, that if he placed his frog very close to the conductor of the machine, he should obtain contractions without the discharge of a spark, were such contractions due to the accumulation of fluid in the frog preparation, but by 1791, he chooses to ignore this crucial piece of evidence.

The rest of the *Commentary* refers to experiments carried out in warm-blooded animals. The only point of interest they raise is Galvani's remark that ". . . the prepared animals which were subjected to the electrical experiments became putrefied and rotten long before those that had not been exposed to electricity"[25] a suggestion perhaps that the process of muscular contraction resembles that of putrefaction?

Notes

1 Galvani L. (1953) *Commentary on the effects of electricity on muscular motion*, M.G. Foley (transl.), I. Bernard Cohen (ed.), Norwalk, Conn. Burndy Library, p. 45
2 Ibid., p. 48
3 Ibid., p. 93
4 Ibid., p. 49

5   An ell varies in different countries from 45 inches (English) to 27 inches (Flemish). It
    seems unlikely that the wire was 375 feet long!
6   See *Memorie ed Esperimenti Inediti di Luigi Galvani* . . ., Bologna, Licinio Cappelli
    Editore, 1937, 'Esperimenti del Mese di Gennaro 1782, Die 4a', p. 340
7   Loc. cit., Note 1, p. 50. A line = ½th of an inch
8   Ibid., p. 50
9   Ibid., p. 51
10 Ibid., p. 52
11 Ibid., p. 53
12 See loc. cit., Note 6, 'Esperimenti del Mese di Febbaro 1781, Giorno 4 Febbaro 1781',
    p. 262
13 Loc. cit., Note 1, p. 54
14 Loc. cit., Note 6, 'Esperimenti del Mese di Gennaro 1783, Die 21a– Januarij', p. 375
15 Ibid., 'Esperimenti del Mese di Marzo 1781, Marzo Giorno 1°', p. 279
16 Ibid., p. 281
17 Ibid., 'Esperimenti del Mese di Decembre 1781, Die 28a Ejusdem,' p. 331
18 Ibid., 'Esperimenti del Mese di Gennaro 1782, Die 2a Januarij', p. 338. Also,
    'Esperimenti del Mese di Gennaro 1783, Die 14a Januarij, Collario', p. 369
19 Ibid., 'Esperimenti del Mese di Gennaro 1783, Die 2a Januarij', p. 357
20 Ibid., p. 358
21 Ibid., 'Anno 1781 – Gennaro Die 17a Januarij', p. 250
22 Loc. cit., Note 6, 'Esperimenti del Mese di Decembre 1781, Die 14a Decembre', p. 321
23 Ibid., 'Esperimenti del Mese di Gennaro 1783, Die 17a Januarij', p. 369
24 Loc. cit., Note, 1, p. 55
25 Ibid., p. 56

18

A critical examination of Galvani's experiments and conclusions

In order to understand the way in which Galvani's ideas were received by contemporary philosophers we must take into consideration the way in which such electrical phenomena were being interpreted at that time. Electricians of the second half of the 18th century were almost unanimously indebted to Benjamin Franklin for the basis of their concepts and knowledge. I. Bernard Cohen has pointed out the extent of the influence that the American philosopher had both at home and in Europe. His concepts, terminology and experimental techniques brought order to what had been previously an area characterised by bizarre and apparently contradictory phenomena. Cohen says:

> No one who makes even a superficial examination of the literature of electricity during the 18th century can escape the recognition of the commanding role of Franklin after the mid-century and the eventual universal adoption of the concepts and even the language he introduced into electricity for the first time.[1]

Franklin's ideas, based on the results of his experimental work, were conveyed to England in the letters he wrote to his friend, Peter Collinson, FRS* and as a result of this appeared in the *Philosophical Transactions* between the years 1747 and 1750. His papers were published in book-form by Edward Cave[2] in 1751 and when this work was brought to the attention of Georges-Louis Buffon*, the latter arranged for a translation into French to be made by François Dalibard*, which appeared in 1752.[3] Franklin's Philadelphia experiments were performed before Louis XV by his master of Experimental Philosophy, Monsieur De Lor, and these were received with such applause and enthusiasm that the latter went on to perform the famous Sentry-box experiment.[1] All over Europe these experiments were repeated before fashionable audiences and editions of Franklin's work appeared in other European languages, an Italian version coming out in 1774.[4] The practical application of Franklin's ideas in the use of lightning rods became known to the masses throughout Europe, but to the philosophers his achievement was the introduction of a concept which explained successfully most of the phenomena they recognised and served as a fruitful model for the further development of electrical science.

We have already touched on Franklin's ideas and seen how they were the logical development of the Newtonian theory of an aether. We have noted how anybody considering a model for muscular motion, in the mid-18th century, would be led to view electricity as an active agent in terms of its capacity to act as a fluid composed of subtle mutually repulsive particles. Particles which on being brought into contact with the particles of other matter, have the power to set them in motion. From what we have already learnt of Galvani's ideas, it is apparent that he adopted just this view: his theory is Franklin's with particular emphasis on the Newtonian roots from which it was derived.

Any theory however, may be viewed as the statement of a transition view in the development of our knowledge of a subject and Franklin's is no exception, containing as it does, elements which owe their origin to pre-Franklinian concepts as well as others upon which the future development of the subject was to depend. Franklin's theory represented the *avant-garde* position in the mid-century, but by the time Galvani was carrying out his experiments and indeed long before the publication of the *Commentary*, new concepts had taken its place.

Three major developments in thought occurred during the 18th century, with respect to the explanation of electrical phenomena:

1. The evolution and sophistication of the concept of an 'effluvium' as being responsible for electrical charge. Franklin's designation, the 'electrical atmosphere', applied to the excess of electrical fluid situated around a 'positively' charged body is a natural development of the idea of an effluvium.[5]

2. The differentiation between 'electrics *per se*' and 'non-electrics' or, as we would say, between dielectrics and conductors.

3. The appreciation of the polarisation of charge induced in any insulated conductor, placed in proximity to a charged source.

Now from Galvani's own words, it is apparent that he was quite *au fait* with the concept of an 'electrical atmosphere,' that he was not altogether happy about the position of glass and the ability of electrical fluid to pass through it, and most important that he had no real understanding of the concept of the polarisation induced in an insulated conductor.

His devotion to Franklin's ideas is apparent when he reflects on the results of his experiment with the pneumatic machine. He feels that electricity must pass through glass yet, he reflects, "To say this, truly seems difficult . . ."[6] One of the cornerstones of Franklin's theory was the fact that the electricity cannot pass through glass – time and time again the American philosopher expounded this view as a basis for his explanation of the working of the Leyden Jar. In a letter to Collinson, dated 29 July 1750, he puts forward the tenets of his theory. In paragraphs 27 and 28 he remarks as follows:

> 27. *It is said in Section 8, of this paper, that all kinds of common matter are supposed not to attract the electrical fluid with equal strength; and that those called electrics* per se, *as glass, etc., attract and retain it strongest, and contain the greatest quantity. The latter may seem a paradox to some, being contrary to the hitherto received opinion; and therefore I shall now endeavour to explain it.*

> 28. *In order to do this, let it first be considered,* that we cannot by any means we are yet acquainted with, force the electrical fluid through glass. *I know it is commonly*

thought that it easily pervades glass; and the experiment of a feather suspended by a thread, in a bottle hermetically sealed, yet moved by bringing a rubber tube near the outside of the bottle, is alleged to prove it. But, if the electrical fluid so easily pervades glass, how does the vial [Leyden Jar] *become* charged *(as we term it) when we hold it in our hands? Would not the fire thrown in by the wire, pass through to our hands, and so escape into the floor? Would not the bottle in that case be left just as we found it, uncharged, as we know a metal bottle so attempted to be charged would be? Indeed, if there be the least crack, the minutest solution of continuity in the glass, though it remains so tight that nothing else we know of will pass, yet the extremely subtle electric fluid flies through such a crack with the greatest freedom, and such a bottle we know can never be charged. What then makes the difference between such a bottle and one that is sound, but this that the fluid can pass through the one, and not through the other.*[7]

Galvani who was obviously acquainted with Franklin's views, must have indeed found it hard to admit that he could not reconcile his theory with this view.

The question of the passage of electricity through glass was considered by Galvani over a long period of time and for various reasons he chose to believe that in fact glass does transmit its subtle particles: he seems to have been fully conversant with Franklinian theory although he chose to reject one of its fundamental principles.

Franklin's idea of an electrical atmosphere was a straightforward development of the earlier concept of an effluvium.[5] The atmosphere was seen as being composed of particles of electrical fluid lying in a zone round any conductor so 'charged' or loaded that there was no room to accommodate such a quantity of fluid within the structure of its own material:

But in common matter there is (generally) as much of the electrical as it will contain within its substance. If more is added it lies without upon the surface, and forms what we call an electrical atmosphere: and then the body is said to be electrified.[8]

Now the result of placing an uncharged, insulated conductor in this Franklinian atmosphere would be simply to produce an atmosphere of similar nature around it, that is, the whole body would become 'charged' in a like manner. There is no reason why any part of the body should be considered as having a greater acquisition of electric fluid than any other. Bringing up such a body to the positively charged prime-conductor would simply be seen as immersing the body in the excess electrical fluid extruded around the latter and all parts would be considered as developing a positive charge. But as Priestley pointed out, this inevitable deduction from Franklin's theory was not what in fact happens if the experiment is carried out. All parts of the insulated conductor do not acquire a positive charge similar to that of the prime-conductor: the part of any such body nearest to the prime-conductor becomes negatively charged while the opposite end, that furthest from the prime-conductor, acquires an equal and opposite positive charge.

The demonstration of a negative or opposite charge in the proximal end of an insulated conductor had been first made in the previous century by Otto von Guericke* although there does not seem to have been any reference to its significance until the middle of the 18th century. Speaking of von Guericke, Priestley says:

> But the most remarkable experiments of this philosopher were two which depend upon a property of the electric fluid that has not been illustrated till within these late years: viz that bodies immerged in electric atmospheres are themselves electrified, and with an electricity opposite to that of the atmosphere. Threads suspended within a small distance of his excited globe, he observed to be often repelled by his finger brought near them, and that a feather repelled by the globe always turned the same face towards it like the moon with respect to the earth. This last experiment seems to have been wholly overlooked by later electricians, though it is a very curious one and may be made with such ease.[9]

Later in Period IX, Section V, of his book where he goes on to consider "Electric Atmospheres", Priestley again refers to the lack of reference to this interesting and fundamental discovery. Speaking of the experiments carried out by the 18th century electrician John Canton*, relating to this he remarks that they:

> . . . demonstrate a remarkable property of all electrified bodies which has often been referred to in the course of this history, but which had not been attended to before. . . It is, that the electric fluid, when there is a redundancy of it in any body, repels the electric fluid in any other body, when they are brought within the sphere of each others influence, and drives it into the remote parts of the body; or quite out of it, if there be any outlet for that purpose. In other words, bodies immerged in electric atmospheres always become possessed of the electricity contrary to that of the body in whose atmosphere they are immerged . . .[10]

Now this appreciation of an opposite charge in the proximal end of the body is only half way to appreciating the polarisation which occurs but what is interesting is that there is a reference to the adjustment or re-organisation of electrical fluid within a body, brought about by an adjacent charged source. This would appear to have been a new concept which later, in the hands of Johann Karl Wilcke* and Ulrich Theodor Aepinus* (the latter particularly), was developed into an appreciation of the polarisation of conductors in regions of electrical influence. This marks the point at which the electrical atmosphere which had developed from the concept of an effluvium became converted into a 'sphere' of influence. While earlier workers, including Franklin, when he became aware of this polarising effect, still clung to the mechanical notion of an exodus of fluid from the charging source, Aepinus denied this and considered the atmosphere merely as the region through which the force of this source acted: that is, force acting at a distance on the basis of attraction and repulsion. There was no question of electrical matter passing from the charged source to the conductor it was affecting. The experimental demonstration by Aepinus showing this polarity in conductors was extended to include electrics and led to his conclusion that conductors and electrics differed as regards their electric properties in degree only and not kind; that is, any difference in behaviour depended on the ease or difficulty with which electrical fluid could move within them, from one part to another.

With the publication of *Tentamen Theoriae* . . . by Aepinus in 1758,[11] these ideas became available to informed electricians and by the 1770's they were well established. It was therefore against this theoretical background that Galvani's investigation of the effects of artificial electricity on his frog-preparation would be examined by 'the philosophers' to whom he so often refers. As an example of an informed up-to-date view of the time, the description given by Tiberius Cavallo*, FRS, and friend of Volta, serves very well. In his book, *A Complete Treatise of Electricity* . . . (1777),[12] dedicated to the famous British electrician William Watson*, Cavallo set out to describe the contemporary state of electrical knowledge, adding descriptions of certain of his own experiments where he felt these were of value. The book was meant to serve as a comprehensive textbook and as such is useful for our purpose. In Part I, Chapter V, Cavallo deals with the problem of "Communicated Electricity", arranging his remarks so as to deal with the effects of super-inducing electricity on an electric, an earthed conductor and an insulated conductor, respectively.

In the case of an electric, for example, a glass tube, he considers that electrical fluid is:

> *confined . . . and remains and is perceivable upon the glass in as much as it is surrounded by air, which is an Electric; and as the air is in a more or less perfect electric state, so that virtue is retained upon the glass longer or shorter; and because the air is never the perfect Electric, therefore the excited tube can never preserve the required electricity perpetually, but is continually imparting some of it to the contiguous air or the conducting particles that float in that element, till at last it quite loses its powers. If a finger, or any other conductor be presented towards an excited Electric, it will receive a spark, and in that spark part only of the Electricity of the Electric; but why not all? Because the excited Electric being a non-Conductor, cannot convey Electricity of all its surface to that side to which the Conductor has been presented . . .[13]*

Cavallo now continues by considering the effect of placing an earthed conductor close to an excited electric:

> *Whenever a Conductor communicating with the earth is exhibited at a convenient distance to an excited Electric, it acquires on that exhibited side an Electricity contrary to that possessed by the Electric: this Electricity increases the nearer it is approached, and at last as there is an eager attraction between Positive and Negative Electricity, the Conductor receives a spark from the Electric and so the balance is restored. If this Conductor does not communicate with the earth, but is insulated and approached to the excited Electric as before, then not only that side of it which is towards the Electric but the opposite also, will appear electrified, with this difference, however, that the side, which is exposed to the influence of the Electric, has acquired an Electricity contrary to that of the excited Electric, and the opposite side an Electricity of the same kind with that of the Electric. These two different Electricities of the Conductor increase as it comes nearer to the Electric, and at last, the former receiving a spark from the latter, becomes throughout possessed of the same Electricity with the Electric, from which it has received the spark. All these effects will happen in the same manner if between the excited Electric and the approaching Conductor there is interposed some other Electric substance besides air; as for instance, a thin plate of glass, rosin, sealing wax etc., but then a spark can never come from the excited Electric to the Conductor,*

except it forces or bursts its way through the interposed electric as it always does through air. This displacing of the air is what causes the noise that attends a spark, and that noise is more or less loud in proportion to the quantity of Electricity, and to the resistance it meets with in its passage.[14]

Cavallo proceeds in logical fashion to discuss what happens when an insulated conductor, having been electrified by an excited electric, is "approached by another Conductor communicating with the earth":

An insulated Conductor having received the Electricity from an excited Electric (in which state it is said to be electrified by communication) will act in every respect like the excited Electric itself except, that when it is approached by another conductor communicating with the Earth, the former gives one spark to the latter, and by that discharges all its Electricity. The reason why an electrified conductor loses its Electricity all at once, when touched with another Conductor communicating with the earth and not part of it only like the excited Electric, is because the Electricity belonging to the whole of the Conductor is easily conducted through its own substance, to that side, to which the other Conductor is presented. Hence it appears that in general, the Electricity discharged from an electrified Conductor is much more powerful, than when discharged from an Electric; for the Conductor may acquire a great quantity of Electricity from an Electric by receiving spark after spark, and afterwards if touched, discharge it all at once and not by little and little as it was received.[15]

A little further on in his chapter, Cavallo makes this brief reference to the effect of electricity on insulated animal bodies, similarly situated "Electricity, strongly communicated to insulated animal bodies, quickens their pulse, and promotes their respiration . . ."[16]

Cavallo's description of the events associated with the situation of an insulated conductor in the vicinity of a charged electric demonstrate his familiarity with the concept of movement of charge within such a body, with its resulting polarisation. Galvani's frog-preparation was just such an insulated conductor and logically could be supposed to exhibit this same internal redistribution of charge when placed within range of the electrical machine, the handle of which was being turned. However, in the typical situation of Galvani's experiments, this polarising force was suddenly removed by his presenting a finger to the prime-conductor and withdrawing a spark. For the first full contemporary explanation of this precise situation we have to turn to a work published in 1780 by Viscount Mahon, FRS, third Earl of Stanhope*. His book which was given a comprehensive review in *Medical Commentaries* in the year 1780 included a new term, "the returning stroke".[17] Lord Mahon describes experiments which:

. . . will shew, in what manner, remarkable Effects may be produced by conducting Bodies under certain circumstances being placed in an insulated situation within an electrical atmosphere, at small distances from each other.[18]

These experiments were carried out with a prime-conductor, PC, and two brass cylinders with three-quarter balls at either end, the first of these, AB, being 18 inches long and having a diameter of 2 inches and the second, EF, 40 inches long and having a diameter of 3¾ inches. A was placed 20 inches

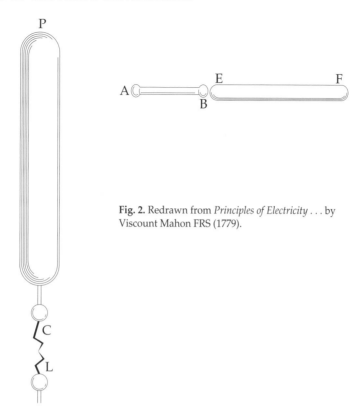

Fig. 2. Redrawn from *Principles of Electricity . . .* by Viscount Mahon FRS (1779).

from PC and E was placed ¹⁄₁₀th inch from B. A large brass ball, L, was so placed as to form a place of discharge for PC. Lord Mahon continues:

> *The three Bodies PC, AB and EF being placed with respect to each other, . . .* [See Fig. 2, above] *I electrified the prime conductor PC.*
>
> *All the time, that the Prime-Conductor was receiving its plus Charge of Electricity: there passed a great number of weak (red or purple) Sparks from the end B of the near Body AB, into the End E of the remote Body, EF. Sometimes the Electricity passed, from B to E, in a white stream. When the Prime-Conductor PC, having received its full charge, came suddenly to discharge, with an Explosion, its superabundant Electricity upon the large brass Ball L, which was made to communicate with the Earth: which having been gradually expelled, from the body AB, and driven into the Body EF (by the superinduced elastic electrical Pressure, of the electrical Atmosphere, of the Prime-Conductor PC (whilst it was charging) did suddenly return, from the body EF, into the Body AB, in a strong bright Spark; at the very instant, that the Explosion took place upon the ball L. This I call the electrical returning Stroke.*[19]

This sudden readjustment of electrical fluid with an insulated charged conductor was to become recognised among late 18th century electricians by Mahon's term the 'returning stroke' a term which describes very vividly the idea of a sudden reverse flow of charge. Mahon extended his experiments to show that human beings behave in a manner precisely similar to the metal

conductors and used the returning stroke as an explanation for the death of
persons, insulated or not, standing beneath charged thunder clouds and
near but not in contact with each other or some conducting body, provided
these conductors were not well connected with the earth. He postulated that
if such persons were "strongly superinduced by the electrical atmosphere of
the cloud" they could be injured or even killed as a result of the 'returning
stroke' of electricity flowing through their bodies at the moment the cloud
discharged to earth.

Here then was the contemporary model for the explanation of the electrical events taking place in Galvani's frog-preparation. The contraction of
his frog-preparation would be seen as resulting from the stimulating effect
of a sudden readjustment of electrical fluid brought about by the discharge
of the prime-conductor. However, in Part I of the *Commentary*, Galvani gives
no hint that he thinks this is the mechanism by which his frog-preparation
was being stimulated. In fact we know, from his notes that he was well
aware of this theory since he used it as a possible explanation for the results
of his experiment of December 1781 and similarly, experiments carried out
in January 1782 were obviously based on the recognition of this electrical
situation, although his results led him to reject it as the true explanation of
events.[20] By the time he wrote Parts III and IV of the *Commentary* however,
Galvani had quite definitely adopted a 'returning stroke' mechanism to explain the result of his electrical machine experiment, an interesting change of
heart which will be explained later (See Chapter 20 of this book).

It is now known that the spark discharge is associated with the production of both an alternating and direct current in conducting bodies placed
within its sphere of activity. The former, which consists of high frequency
oscillations of the order 10 to 3×10^7 kilocycles per second, need not concern
us here since such a range is well above that capable of acting as an excitant
of nervous tissue.[21]

The production of a direct current is described by S.G. Starling and
A.J. Woodall, as follows:

(Redrawn
from Ref. 22.)

*That a charge produces a potential gradient in its neighbourhood may be shown by em-
ploying an insulated conductor AB which is divided into two parts, the parts being in
contact. On bringing a positively charged body C, near to B a potential gradient exists,
B being at a higher potential than A. Hence a current takes place in the conductor and
will flow from B to A until the accumulation of positive charge at A and the accumulation of the negative charge on B restore the whole of the conductor to uniform potential
when the current ceases. If the two insulated parts are separated while C is still present, the charges on A and B may be found by testing with a charged electroscope to be
respectively positive and negative. If instead of separating A and B, we at the same
time remove C, we at the same time remove the potential gradient due to it, and the
reverse potential gradient due to the accumulated charges will cause a current from A*

to B until the potential of the conductor is again uniform. We may note here, that when there is no current in a conductor, there must be a uniformity of potential throughout it; in fact the distinction between a conductor and an insulator is that a potential gradient cannot exist in a conductor without producing a current while in an insulator a potential gradient can exist even when there is no current.[22]

If we consider the charge developed across any capacitance exposed to a potential gradient, where:

q = charge (coulombs)

v = potential difference across ends of the capacitance (volts)

c = capacitance (farads)

$q = cv$

then any increase in potential or capacitance will tend to increase the quantity of charge developed.

Now, Galvani's insulated frog-preparation can be considered as a capacitance exposed to the potential gradient developed across it as a result of its proximity to the charged prime-conductor of the electrical machine. Its behaviour can be explained in terms of the relationship above ($q = cv$), in as much as the effectiveness of any electrical stimulus for nervous tissue depends, among other things, on the development of a certain quantity of charge across it, within a certain time. If this critical level of charge is developed rapidly enough (and acts for a sufficient period) excitation of the nerve occurs. Hence we can predict the various results obtained by Galvani on this basis, variation in these results depending on whether the prevailing relative values for capacitance and potential difference across the preparation, resulted in the development of a critical level of charge in a critical time.

Variations in conditions affecting this may be considered thus:

1. Factors tending to increase potential across frog-preparation
    a) Earthing of the preparation (which brings it into contact with zero potential)
    b) Decrease in the distance between the charged prime-conductor and the frog-preparation
2. Factors tending to increase the capacitance of the frog-preparation
    a) Increasing the effective conductile mass by the attachment of a nerve-conductor
    b) Increasing the effective conductile mass by the attachment of a muscle-conductor
3. Factors tending to vary the time factor
    a) The induction phase which allows a relatively slow charging of the frog-preparation
    b) The discharge phase which takes place very much more rapidly

The muscular response obtained by Galvani was, however, the result of two effects, one physical and the other physiological. It depends on the quantity and rate of supply of charge, factors determined by the relationships:

$$q = cv$$

$$\frac{dq}{dt} = i \text{ (where } i = \text{ current flowing in amperes)}$$

and, the limits of the physiological response imposed by 'all-or-none' be-haviour of individual nerves and muscles. (Muscle and nerve cells can only respond or not respond – they cannot partially respond.)[23]

Considered then, in terms of present day concepts, the various results he obtained with artificial electricity can be explained as follows:

1. **Lack of a physiological response during the induction or charging phase**
   This would result from the relatively long time required to develop the critical quantity of charge, that is, dt is relatively large:

$$\frac{dt}{dq} < \text{ critical level (t = time during which q acts)}$$

2. **Lack of a physiological response during redistribution or discharge phase, when the preparation is not earthed**
   This would result from an inadequate value for q. Earthing the preparation increases both the potential difference across it (v), and the capacitance (c) thus increasing the charge (q):

$$\frac{dq}{dt} \text{ is increased and becomes adequate as a stimulus}$$

3. **Lack of physiological response in the absence of a muscle or nerve-conductor (of adequate mass)**
   This would result from too low a value for a capacitance (c), resulting again in a low value for charge (q). Increasing the capacitance (without increasing the value of the potential difference (v) through earthing the preparation or bringing it nearer to the charged prime-conductor) could be sufficient to increase the charge so that dq/dt is adequate during the discharge phase.

   N.B. Galvani's observation of the effectiveness of unearthed conduc-tors and the even greater effectiveness of the earthed ones.

4. **Increase in the physiological response resulting from a decrease in the distance between the charged prime-conductor and the frog-preparation**
   Here the resulting increase in potential difference (v) across the prep-aration, increases the charge (q) and therefore the contractile response (within the physiological limits).

These few examples show how some of the results obtained by Galvani can be explained in terms of the quantity of charge developed in his frog-preparation as a result of its situation in a collapsing electric field and the development of a direct current of sufficient strength (and at a rapid enough rate) to stimulate the frog's nerve.

Laboratory study of Galvani's experiments

Certain of Galvani's experiments were repeated by the author of this book and the results, in general confirmed. It was not felt necessary to imitate his experimental procedure in detail. A spark was produced in the laboratory by means of a high voltage direct current generator of the type generally used in the teaching departments of colleges, etc. The generator was set up at one end of the bench with its spark balls (diameter 9 cm) separated by a gap of 4 mm and at a height of 15 mm above the bench. The apparatus was modified to produce a single spark at 15 kv. The experimental frog was stunned, decapitated and dissected as rapidly as possible to produce a preparation similar to that used by Galvani. It was placed on a clean dry porcelain dish, supported on a non-conducting stand so as to be opposite the spark gap at a height of 15 cm above the bench, and so orientated that its spinal cord and nerves lay towards the spark gap and its legs and feet away from it. A metre rule was fixed to the front of the bench so that its zero marking was opposite the spark gap and its length was parallel to the length of the frog preparation. Various lengths of iron wire (diameter 0.048 cm) between 5 cm and 100 cm long were cut and labelled and used as 'nerve-conductors.'

The first experiment attempted was a demonstration of Galvani's original discovery. The frog-preparation was set up at an arbitrary distance of 35 cm from the spark and a screwdriver with an insulated handle was applied to the right nerve, the author holding the screwdriver by the handle and the metal part touching the nerve. At the emission of a spark no twitch occurred but on holding the metal blade itself, the whole right frog leg was seen to contract. This was repeated many times, with the same result.

Further experiments were then carried out in an attempt to verify the relationships between the various components of the experiment described by Galvani and which he expressed as laws governing the magnitude of the frog's contraction. It was found in the first place that increasing the length of the nerve-conductor allowed its proximal end to be situated at increasing distances from the spark, in order for a twitch to be just visible – that is, in order to produce a minimal adequate stimulus. No twitch resulted with a 5 cm wire, irrespective of its situation, but the use of 10 cm, 20 cm and 40 cm wires resulted in a twitch at 5.5 cm, 10 cm and 29 cm, respectively in the distance between its proximal end and the spark. Doubling the length of the nerve-conductor from 40 cm to 80 cm only allowed an increase of 1 cm (29–30 cm) in this distance.

These experiments were carried out without the frog-preparation being earthed. Earthing allowed the distances at which various conductors were effective, to be increased, but the overall pattern was the same. Doubling the voltage at which the machine discharged, doubled the distance at which any nerve-conductor was effective again within limits, and there was the same potentiation by earthing. Maintaining various lengths of nerve-conductor at a fixed distance (34 cm) from the spark resulted in differences in muscular response. As longer and longer conductors were used, more and more muscles became involved. With a 20 cm conductor, the toe was seen to twitch, with 30 cm, the foot and calf was affected and with 40 cm, the whole leg was involved. Increasing the wire to 50 cm and 60 cm did not alter the response significantly. Again, earthing potentiated the results obtained, within limits. From these results, it was felt that the description given by Galvani was accurate.

The next stage in the investigations was an attempt to associate the frog's response with a definite physical event. The spark generator was arranged next to the frog-preparation which had a 10 cm nerve-conductor attached to it and a train of sparks produced. The oscillatory field was detected and displayed on an oscilloscope. In this way it was seen that the high frequency field from each individual spark (strongly at 100 KHz) was being modulated at the very much lower frequency of the spark train rate (the frog twitched synchronously with the slower modulation of the spark train – that is, at the major collapse of the static field). Exposing it to the higher frequency oscillatory current had no exciting effect on muscle contraction, as was anticipated. This demonstrated quite clearly that the stimulus to Galvani's frog was a direct current resulting from the collapse of the static electric field induced by the prime-conductor of his machine and that any high frequency alternating current produced as a result of the electromagnetic radiation emitted by a spark discharge either had not sufficient energy to effect it or was of an unsuitable frequency – a result already indicated by the linear as opposed to inverse square relationship obtained above.

As regards the laws drawn up by Galvani for his frog's behaviour, we must consider them therefore in terms of the static field induced by the prime-conductor. On this basis they describe the behaviour of an insulated conductor exposed to such a force. Galvani does not suggest that his frog's contractions might be limited by the physiological nature of its response, except in general terms, that is, "lively" recently killed frogs produced better contractions than "less lively" ones. Repetition of his experiments made it clear that an increase in magnitude of the contraction described by him depended on the involvement of an increasing number of muscles. In fact two effects, one physical and the other physiological, were involved. His demonstration that a requisite quantity of electricity was necessary to bring about contraction at all, showed that any current of less than that value had no observable effect on the nerve and muscle. Increasing this current, increased the contraction of individual muscles and increased the number of muscles involved. That no further increase in contraction resulted beyond certain limits was a manifestation of the limits imposed on the quantity of charge available to the preparation owing to its situation in the potential gradient of the field and its capacitance, but also of the limit imposed on the response of a muscle by the nature of its functioning. For any one muscle, which is composed of a number of fibres, any increase in contraction can only be the result of the stimulation of an increased number of fibres since any single fibre contracts to its maximal extent if it contracts at all. Since any one group of fibres is supplied by a nerve fibre which also responds to a stimulus in this 'all or none' fashion, once all the fibres in a muscle contract, the muscle has contracted maximally and no available increases in charge supplied to it, will increase the magnitude of its contraction.

To sum up, the muscular response obtained by Galvani was the result of two effects, one physical, the other physiological. It depended on the quantity and rate of supply of charge, factors determined by the relationships:

$$q = cv$$

$$\text{and} \quad \frac{dq}{dt} = i \; (i = \text{current flowing})$$

and the limits of the physiological response inspired by the 'all or none' behaviour of individual muscles.[23] The precise rôles played by these factors in Galvani's actual experiment is impossible to say since we have no quantitative values for his experiments any more than we have access to the individual frogs he was using.

Notes

1 Cohen, I. Bernard (1966) *Franklin and Newton: An Inquiry into Speculative Newtonian Experimental Science and Franklin's work in Electricity as an Example thereof.* Now published for The American Philosophical Society by Harvard University Press, Cambridge, Mass., p. 17

2 Franklin, Benjamin (1751) *Experiments and Observations on electricity made at Philadelphia, in America, and communicated in several letters to Mr P. Collinson of London,* London, E. Cave

3 Dalibard, Jean François (1752) *Experiénces et observations sur l'Electricité. par Franklin.* Paris

4 *Scelta di Lettre e di Opuscoli del Signor Beniamino Franklin,* transl. from English, Milan, 1774

5 The use of the term "effluvium" in this context would appear to date from the writings of William Gilbert (1540–1603) whose experiments on magnetism and electricity led him to consider the cause of the movement of a body towards any electrified body, such as rubbed amber. Referring to the ancient view of Plutarch who believed that amber contains a flame-like substance which is emitted and attracts bodies when its path is cleared, as it were, as a result of friction, Gilbert postulated rather the emission of "exceedingly attenuated humours" which passing from the amber to the attracted body mechanically transport it towards the latter (See William Gilbert, *De Magnete,* P. Fleury Mottelay (transl.), Dover Publications, New York, 1958, *et seq.*). In the 17th century, the effluvium developed a much sturdier nature. In the mind of Robert Boyle the "attenuated humours" became transformed into "viscous strings" which leaving the attracting body, stretched out and fixed on the attracted body. He postulated that the elasticity or retracting power inherent in the strings was then responsible for the movement of the attracted body back to the attracting one. (See Marie Boas Hall, *Robert Boyle on Natural Philosophy An Essay with selections from his writings,* Indiana University Press, Bloomington, 1965, p. 251 and J. Hartman, 'Succinta Succini Prussici Historia et demonstratio,' *Philosophical Transactions,* 1699, Vol. 21, No. 248, pp 5–40.

The electricians of the first half of the 18th century maintained the concept of an effluvium and developed it into the 'electrical atmosphere'. The ability of any electric to act as a source of electrification was seen as a result of the ease or difficulty with which its electrical effluvium could reach other bodies and influence them. One constantly meets the concept of impedance to the movement of the effluvium as an explanation of various experimentally observed phenomena. Thus we find such early workers as Francis Hauksbee (d. 1713) referring to the failure of electrical attraction to the resistance that moisture gives to the movement of the effluvium. (See Chap. 10, Note 63 of this book and J. Priestley *History and Present State of Electricity*, pp 21 and 29).

John Theophilus Desaguliers (1683–1744) worked within the same concept, referring failure of electrification to the presence of moisture which "intercepted the electrical effluvia" (See *Philosophical Transactions*, 1732–1734 pp 418–439). He did not however always use the same term, effluvium referring variously to "the electrical stream or virtue" and "electrical emanations" in order to describe the concept of a material emanation. Charles Dufay (1698–1739) similarly used a variety of expressions to describe the material responsible for electrical attraction *viz* "la vertu électrique", "la matière électrique", "l'électricité", "les écoutements électrique", etc. But he also introduced a new term, "le turbillon électrique" in order to explain repulsion between two similarly charged bodies. The latter term described an atmosphere or envelope of electrical fluid surrounding charged bodies although Dufay did not give a detailed description of his ideas. However, from the tourbillon it was but a short step to the 'electrical atmosphere' conceived of by Franklin and described by I. Bernard Cohen in his book on Franklin and Newton. The concept of a material emission from a charged body remained throughout all these theories and was not abandoned until the second half of the 18th century

6 *Memorie ed Esperimenti Inediti di Luigi Galvani . . .*, Bologna, Licinio Cappelli Editore, 1937
7 *Benjamin Franklin's Experiments, A new edition of Franklin's Experiments and Observations on Electricity.* With a critical and historical introduction, by I. Bernard Cohen (ed.), Harvard University Press, Cambridge Mass., 1941, p. 227
8 Ibid., p. 214
9 Priestley, Joseph (1966) *The History and Present State of Electricity . . .*, The Sources of Science, No. 18, New York and London, Johnson Reprint Corporation, Vol. I, p. 11
10 Ibid., p. 287
11 Aepinus, Ulrich Theodor (1758) *Tentamen Theoriae Electricitatis et Magnetismi*, St Petersburg. Acad. Sci.
12 Cavallo, Tiberius (1777) *A Complete Treatise of Electricity in Theory and Practice, with original experiments*, London, E. and C. Dilly
13 Ibid., p. 30
14 Ibid., p. 31
15 Ibid., p. 33
16 Ibid., p. 37
17 Viscount Mahon, Charles, FRS (1779) *Principles of Electricity; containing diverse new Theorems and Experiments, together with an Analysis of the superior advantages of high and pointed Conductors and an Explanation of an electrical returning Stroke, by which fatal effects may be produced even at a vast distance from the place where the Lightning falls*, London, printed for P. Elmsly in the Strand
18 Ibid., p. 75
19 Ibid., p. 77
20 See Chap. 17 of this book
21 See Bernard Katz, *Nerve Muscle and Synapse*, McGraw Hill, New York, 1966, p. 21
22 Starling S.G. and Woodall A.J. (1953) *Electricity and Magnetism for Degree Students*, London, Longmans Green and Co., 8th edn, p. 108
23 Adrian E.D. (1913–1914) The all or none principle in nerves *Journal of Physiology* 47: 460–474 – Muscle and nerve cells can only respond or not respond – they cannot partially repond.

* See Biographical Index

19

Galvani's investigations: the nature of the irritable particle in muscle (Phase III: 1782–1783)

In the previous two chapters we have analysed the way in which Galvani developed his idea that the process of exciting muscular contraction depends on the mechanical agitation of electrical particles composing or contained in a naturally occurring nerve-juice ('animal spirits'). He believed that the vibratory impulse produced by his electrical machine at the moment of discharge was analogous to the action of the brain, exerted as the will, and mechanically passing on its activity to the nerve fluid. His experimental findings considered together with the theories of Priestley and Volta might well have suggested that the nature of the impulse exerted by the brain was itself electrical but he does not examine this part of his model – nor indeed was he in a position to do so. All he was at pains to point out was that the action of the electrical machine was a particularly efficient form of stimulus to nerve fluid but a stimulus acting as mechanically as any other *viz* cutting, pricking, burning, etc.

By 1781 then, Galvani almost certainly believed that he knew the nature of the essential material components of his model: the intermediate particle in the nerve juice was electrical, the receptor particle in muscle was phlogiston or some manifestation of this, and the primary particle in the brain was quite possibly electrical. But the following year he was led to the view that the active particle in muscle was also electrical in nature, thus unifying his concept into one which depended entirely on the interaction of electrical forces within the animal body.

Gherardi refers to a manuscript in which Galvani puts forward the idea that electrical fluid is the element material responsible for a number of phenomena which he saw as analogous. He says:

> This fasiculus is a dissertation in Latin on a rather curious subject. By comparing the changes which these three phenomena manifest, i.e., the electric fire, resplendent at the extremity of the conductor of a charged Leyden Jar, the ordinary flame, and the respiration of Animals, where they are subjected to certain common conditions in the atmosphere, it was conjectured that the phenomena themselves had a common principle in the electric fluid; that this existed in a very pure and simple form in the aforementioned electric fire, and was variously joined with diverse material principles in flame and in respiration [that is, exhaled gases].[1]

What Galvani is suggesting is that electrical fluid is the essential element of inflammability and motion; he is restating 'the phlogiston theory' as the 'electrical fluid theory.' The possibility that phlogiston and electricity might be identical or closely related materials had, of course, been considered (see Chapter 11 of this book) but the key to his ideas is to be found once more in the writings of his fellow-countryman, Volta. Galvani's statement would appear to have been based specifically on the results of a series of experiments carried out by Volta in the Spring of 1782, a description of which can be found in his collected works.[2]

Volta refers to the fact that he had:

> . . . *finally succeeded in obtaining distinct signs of electricity both by the simple evaporation of water and by various chemical effervescences.*[3]

The initial experiments were carried out in the company of Antoine Laurent Lavoisier* and Pierre Simon de Laplace* while Volta was staying in Paris the two Frenchmen being in fact the first to carry out a successful demonstration of the phenomenon. Volta describes the experiment in some detail as follows:

> *This happened* [that is, a successful outcome] *on April 13th and the manner of carrying out the experiment was this. A large metal plate was insulated in an open garden. Attached to this plate was a long iron wire which terminated in contact with the disc or shield which rested on the marble slab, the latter being continually kept dry and warm by means of some coals. Having arranged this, we passed some warming pans containing smouldering coals on the aforementioned plate and allowed the combustion to flare up for a few minutes as a result of a gentle breeze which was blowing: then, on removing the shield from its contact with the metal wire and thence from the marble, and on lifting it in the usual way, the expected signs of electricity appeared when Signor Cavallo's new electrometer was brought up to it, the two straws separating: on examination this electricity proved to be* negative.[3]

The experiment was repeated, this time placing four jars containing iron filings and water on the metal plate instead of the warming pans. Oil of vitriol was poured into the jars with the production of a brisk effervescence and when this began to subside the disc was once more removed and tested for signs of electricity and once more was found to be charged negatively.

Further experiments of this nature, involving various reactions which produced fixed air and nitrous air succeeded equally well in producing a negatively charged disc.

Experiments carried out in Paris however, involving the simple evaporation of water, seemed to indicate a positive charge on the disc but when further experiments were repeated in London the following month, once again a negative charge was demonstrated.[4] This time Volta described throwing water on to burning coals contained in warming pans which were found to be negatively charged following the evolution of steam.

As a result of these various experiments, Volta reflected that:

> *If bodies which resolve into vapours or an elastic fluid are charged with electric fire at the expense of other bodies, and consequently cause them to be charged negatively; when once more the same vapours become condensed, would they not seek to deposit this charge and as a result produce signs of positive electricity?*[5]

Volta said that he had many ideas as to how he could put this to the test of experiment but preferred to discuss the way in which he considered this phenomenon is related to the electricity in the atmosphere. Once again Volta is at pains to put forward a general theory to explain what he considers to be analogous events in nature:

The experiments carried out to date, to which we have referred, although few, all concur to show us that the vapours of water and in general the parts of every body, which is being volatized, carry away with them a quantity of electric fluid at the expense of the fixed bodies which remain, leaving them therefore, negatively charged, in no way different from the manner in which they carry away a quantity of elementary fire leaving them cooled. Hence it can be inferred that bodies resolving into vapours or becoming aeriform acquire a greater capacity with respect to electric fluid, just as they acquire a greater capacity with respect to common fire or calorific fluid. Who would not be struck by such a pretty analogy, in which electricity brings light to the new doctrine of heat and in exchange receives from it? I am speaking of the doctrine of latent or specific heat, as it is called, the seeds of which Black[*] and Wilke[*] have shewn with their stupendous discovery and which has been so promoted by D. Crawford[*] following the experiments of D. Irvine.[*][6]

Volta's application of this idea to the electrical content of the atmosphere need not concern us here: what is interesting with reference to Galvani's thinking is the experimental evidence Volta puts forward to suggest that there is not only a loss of heat to the atmosphere when combustion – of any type – takes place but also a loss of electrical fluid. In other words, if the model for muscular motion was to be considered as a manifestation of the combustion model, the process taking place in muscle could be interpreted as the interaction between an intrinsic electric fluid brought by the nerve interacting with an intrinsic electrical fluid resident in muscle – the reaction resulting in a loss of positive electricity rather than phlogiston. That Galvani had Volta's experiments in mind when he wrote his dissertation is certain from the fact that he refers to "the recent discovery" that the vapours of volatile bodies carry away with them electrical fluid, and that "without doubt" the remaining parts "carry negative signs". These remarks occur on the penultimate page among the conjectures referred to above and echo Volta's phrases extremely closely, so that it must be assumed that the dissertation was written some short time after the publication of Volta's work in 1782.[7]

The concept of phlogiston as the active particle in muscle was, of course, to suffer an even more radical blow as a result of the revolutionary ideas of Volta's erstwhile colleague, Lavoisier. During the 1770's the French chemist had been carrying out quantitative experiments which led him eventually to attack the concept of phlogiston as the basis of combustion. By 1783 he was in a position to say that phlogiston was an imaginary material and that the combustion of substances resulted in the acquisition of part of the atmospheric air rather than the loss of phlogiston.[8]

In a memoir entitled 'Reflections on Phlogiston' he put before the Académie Royale des Sciences his definite theory of combustion, showing how all the changes which had previously been attributed to the loss of Stahl's phlogiston could equally well be explained in terms of the acquisition of a simple principle, 'pure air' or 'vital air' (today named oxygen). Criticising the protean nature attributed to phlogiston by chemists in the past he continued:

> All these reflections confirm what I have advanced, what I set out to prove, and what I am going to repeat again. Chemists have made phlogiston a vague principle, which is not strictly defined and which consequently fits all the explanations demanded of it. Sometimes it has weight, sometimes it has not; sometimes it is free fire, sometimes it is fire combined with earth; sometimes it passes through the pores of vessels, sometimes these are impenetrable to it. It explains at once causticity and non-causticity, transparency and opacity, colour and the absence of colour. It is a veritable Proteus that changes its form every instant![9]

A summary of the general facts of combustion follows and then the French chemist concluded his memoir with the following words:

> My only objective in this memoir is to extend the theory of combustion I announced in 1777 to show that Stahl's phlogiston is imaginary and its existence in the metals, sulphur, phosphorous and all combustible bodies a baseless supposition and that all the facts of combustion and calcination are explained in a much simpler and much easier way without phlogiston than with it. I do not expect that my ideas will be adopted at once; the human mind inclines to one way of thinking and those who have looked at nature from a certain point of view during a part of their lives adopt new ideas only with difficulty; it is for time therefore, to confirm or reject the opinions that I have advanced. Meanwhile I see with much satisfaction that young men, who are beginning to study the science without prejudice, and geometers and physicists, who bring fresh minds to bear on chemical facts, no longer believe in phlogiston in the sense that Stahl gave to it and consider the whole of this doctrine as a scaffolding that is more of a hindrance than a help for extending the fabric of chemical science.[10]

Towards the end of 1782, only a few months after Volta had been collaborating with Lavoisier and Laplace, the two Frenchmen began their famous series of experiments based on what the Italian physicist had deemed ". . . the stupendous discovery of Black and Wilcke . . ."[7] Black's crucial experiments had shown that both ice in melting, and boiling water during its conversion to steam, absorb large quantities of heat and at the same time revealed an excellent means of estimating any quantity of heat in terms of the amount of ice it can melt. Lavoisier and Laplace applied this principle to the construction of the first ice calorimeter with which they estimated the heat produced by various chemical reactions.

The extension of their work to the measurement of the heat produced by various living animals during fixed periods led to their demonstration that respiration is a slow combustion process during which oxygen from the air is transformed into carbon dioxide, accompanied by the evolution of a quantity of heat which maintains the animal temperature at a constant normal value. Lavoisier and Laplace however considered that this process took place only in the lungs:

Respiration is therefore a combustion, admittedly very slow, but otherwise exactly similar to that of charcoal; it takes place in the interior of the lungs, without the evolution of light, since the matter of fire set free is immediately absorbed by the moisture of those organs: the heat developed in this combustion is communicated to the blood which passes through the lungs and thence diffuses through the whole animal system.[11]

Lavoisier had destroyed the concept of phlogiston as the material lost during combustion but the concept of the loss of "matter of fire" which equals "heat substance" was retained and in the hands of Volta was equated with loss of electrical fluid. How natural for Galvani to adopt this aspect of the combustion model and use it as the basis for his model of muscular motion, analogous to respiration.

By 1783 then, ideas were abroad which would inevitably lead Galvani to the conjecture that the most likely model for muscular motion was one involving electrical changes in the muscle which resulted in its loss of electrical fluid. In Part III of the *Commentary* he describes the experiments which led to his choice of model and we shall consider these in the next chapter.

Part II of the *Commentary* deals with the effects of atmospheric electricity on muscular motion and contains a description of experiments carried out between April and October, 1786, some with the help of his nephew, Camillo Galvani*. It is not proposed to deal in any detail with these experiments since their results add little to our analysis of Galvani's ideas. They demonstrated what he had anticipated, namely, that the lightning flash could be substituted for the spark of his electric machine, as the prime stimulus to muscular contraction. Franklin's demonstration that the lightning flash is in fact an electrical discharge phenomenon[12] was ample reason for Galvani to test its efficacy on his frog preparation. It is interesting to see how Galvani used the knowledge he had gained with his electrical machine experiments in order to gain maximum effect from atmospheric change:

Therefore in the open air, we set up and insulated a long conductor, appropriately made of iron, . . . and fastened one end of it to a high part of the house. When a thunderstorm arose, we fastened the nerves of prepared frogs or the prepared limbs of warm blooded animals to the other end . . . Then we attached to their feet another similar conductor of the greatest possible length so that it might reach down to the water of the well, . . . As we hoped the result completely paralleled that in the experiment with artificial electricity.[13]

In the last paragraph of Part II, Galvani refers to the fact that no contractions were produced when his animal preparations were exposed to "heat flashes" or "summer evening heat lightning". He adds that:

No contractions took place at all, perhaps because heat flashes of this kind either do not have their source in electricity or if they do, they occur a great distance away and operate in a completely different manner from lightning. This is a question however that would be of particular interest to the natural philosophers.[14]

Doubtless he had Volta's theories in mind.

Notes

1   Galvani L. (1841 and 1842) *Opere edite ed inedite del Professore Luigi Galvani raccolte e pubblicate per cura dell' Accademia delle Scienze dell' Istituto di Bologna*, Bologna, Tipografia di Emidio dall'Olmo. See 'Rapporto', p. 23

2   Volta A. (1816) *Collezione dell' Opere del Cavaliere Conte Alessandro Volta . . .*, Firenze, Nella Stamperia di Guglielmo Piatti

3   Ibid., Tom. 1, Parte II, p. 271

4   Ibid., p. 273

5   Ibid., pp 274–275

6   Ibid., p. 275

7   See loc. cit. Note 1, 'Rapporto', pp 23–24

8   Lavoisier A. (1783) 'Réflexions sur le Phlogistique, pour servir de developpment à la theorie de la Combustion et de la Calcination, publiée en 1777,' *Mémoires de l'Académie Royale des Sciences*, pp 505–538

9   See: McKie D. (1952) *Antoine Lavoisier, Scientist, Economist, Social Reformer*, London, Constable, p. 116

10 Ibid., p. 117

11 Ibid., p. 107

12 Cohen, I. Bernard (ed.) (1941) *Benjamin Franklin's Experiments: A new edition of Franklin's Experiments and Observations on Electricity*, Harvard University Press, Cambridge, Mass. See 'Letter V', p. 201 *et seq.*

13 Galvani, Luigi (1953) *Commentary on the effects of electricity on muscular motion*, M.G. Foley (transl.), I. Bernard Cohen (ed.), Norwalk, Conn., Burndy Library, p. 57

14 Ibid., p. 58

* See Biographical Index

20

The effects of animal electricity on muscular motion: Galvani's definitive model in 1791

We have seen how the events of 1782–1783 would have tended to lead Galvani to the view that the physical changes responsible for muscular movement were entirely electrical in nature. His problem was then that of explaining the observed facts of neuro-muscular activity in terms of contemporary electrical knowledge. His attempt to do this was first put before the public in Parts III and IV of the *Commentary*, although two Latin dissertations written in 1786 and 1787 and a third read at the Institute in 1789 (but unpublished during his lifetime), have substantially the same content.[1] The earlier one, dated 30 October 1786 was written at the end of a series of experiments carried out during the previous two months and entitled 'Experiments with metals making various contacts with muscles and nerves' (September 1786), 'Experiments on the electricity of metals in cold blooded animals' (13 October 1786), 'Experiments using a conducting arc, with a hook in the spinal cord and a metal wire in one leg, the frog being placed on a glass slab' (20 October 1786). There is no question that Galvani was developing his theories as to an all electrical model for muscular motion long before 1786 – certainly by 1782 when he first became impressed by the apparent similarities between the properties of the Leyden Jar and that of his neuro-muscular preparation. Apart from the experimental notes referred to above however we have no details of the precise way in which his ideas developed and these notes in fact add little to what he has to say in the *Commentary* itself and in which he purports to explain the experimental basis for his theory.

Part III opens with the now famous description of how Galvani says he set about investigating the effect of the "ordinary quiescent electricity" of the atmosphere on prepared frogs. He tells us that he chose to do this as a result of observing the behaviour of certain prepared specimens which were hanging up on the iron railings of his balcony by means of brass hooks which transfixed their spinal cords – a purely fortuitous arrangement. He had noted odd, apparently random activity among the specimens at times when there was no lightning and the weather was in no way stormy. This, he says had led him to the view that the small quantities of electrical fluid in the atmosphere might be responsible for the contractions. However, long periods of observation failed to confirm this view and somewhat in exasperation he tells us, he began pressing the brass hooks against the railings in an attempt to see whether this manoeuvre would bring about contractions at different times related to possible variations in atmospheric electricity. In fact he did manage to set the frogs' muscles in action in this way but it became evident that this activity was simply the result of pressing the hooks against the railings and that possible variations in the content of atmospheric electricity were of no causal significance:

> *Since I had upon occasion remarked that prepared frogs, which were fastened by brass hooks in their spinal cord to an iron railing which surrounded a certain hanging garden of my home, fell into the usual contractions not only when lightning flashed but even at times when the sky was quiet and serene, I surmised that these contractions had their origin in changes which occur during the day in the electricity of the atmosphere. Hence with confidence I began diligently to investigate the effects of these atmospheric changes on the muscular movements I witnessed and I repeated the experiment in various different ways. Therefore at different hours and for a span of many days I observed the animals which were appropriately arranged for this purpose, but scarcely a motion was evident in their muscles. I finally became tired of waiting in vain and began to press and squeeze the brass hooks which penetrated the spinal cord against the iron railing. I hoped to see whether muscular contractions were excited by this technique and whether they revealed any change or alteration related to the electrical state of the atmosphere. As a matter of fact, I did observe frequent contractions but they had no relation to the changes in the electrical state of the atmosphere.[2]*

Galvani goes on to give his initial explanation for the apparently unexpected results he obtained:

> *Now since I had observed these contractions only in the open air and had not yet carried out the experiment elsewhere, I was on the point of postulating that such contractions result from atmospheric electricity slowly insinuating itself in the animal, accumulating there and then being rapidly discharged when the hook comes in contact with the iron railing.[2]*

The belief that contractions could result from the gentle passage of small quantities of atmospheric electricity in his frog-preparation is interesting. It will be remembered that these frog-preparations consisted essentially of spinal cord, crural nerves and leg muscles, that is, there was no brain present and therefore the prime-mover in the physiological situation was absent. Furthermore, any *ex-vivo* analogue of the brain such as the electrical machine or lightning, was also absent in this particular case. The concept of atmospheric electricity passing into the living animal and reaching the brain whence it was in some way elaborated and passed out in the motor nerves as the nerveo-electrical fluid has been referred to already. However one must remember that such a concept necessarily involved two functions for the brain, that of elaborating the nerve fluid and also that of acting in some unknown way, as the mechanical stimulus necessary to arouse it to the degree of vibration required for it to act as a muscle stimulus. In order to explain the action of atmospheric electricity, in this case, Galvani, logically, had to explain how it was sufficiently aroused to act as the prime stimulus to his nerveo-electrical fluid. To be clear as to the way he was thinking it must be remembered that the single stimulus of the brain was equated in his mind with a compound *ex vivo* stimulus, that is, small quantities of artificial electricity set in motion by such a force as the spark of the electrical machine. This is a complicated concept when other physiological components such as the 'nerve juice' and presumably the 'muscle juice' are considered as having electrical properties similar to that of artificial electricity and the whole picture is further complicated by the fact that Galvani still does not at this stage mention that he believes in the existence of an intrinsic electrical component.

Galvani's reason for pressing and squeezing the hooks against the railings may well have been a mere act of desperation with no rationale behind it but it could be considered as a clumsy attempt to supply the atmospheric electricity with the mechanical stimulus it lacked. When Galvani found that bringing the two metals together was the significant manoeuvre for bringing about contractions, the uppermost thought in his mind was obviously that he had suddenly, at the moment of contact, opened up a capacious conducting pathway and in order to explain it, he turned to the theory he had, on the whole decided against, when he was carrying out his earlier experiments with the electric machine and the double-bottle arrangement. For the first time in the *Commentary* he quite definitely postulates that the mechanical stimulus can be supplied by a sudden loss of electrical fluid from his frog-preparation. We know that he had considered this explanation from his discussion of the December 1781 experiment (see Chapter 17 of this book) but that he had seemed to favour an 'overcharging' rather than a 'discharging' theory at this stage. Now, however, he postulates what, in fact, is a 'returning-stroke' mechanism and as we shall see he continues to adopt this model from this point onward in the *Commentary*.[3] Although this is the first time in the *Commentary* that he states explicitly that the stimulus can arise from a sudden loss of electrical fluid, he may well have been tending towards this explanation as early as 1782 when he became aware of Volta's experiments showing the loss of electrical fluid during the combustion process. In theory, his frog-preparation had to lose electrical fluid during its active phase, if he were to equate the two processes; and if he were to make the other equation with the activity of a discharging Leyden Jar it seemed equally necessary, so there was good reason for him to adopt this view.

However, Galvani soon had to abandon this early idea that atmospheric electricity played any part in the production of contractions, not only as a result of the garden fence observations but also because when he brought a frog-preparation indoors and placed it on an iron plate, pressing the brass hook down on to the latter, caused brisk contractions each time the hook and plate made contact. Repetition of this experiment moreover, in different places and at different times and with different metals, still produced similar results, although he did find that such contractions varied according to the metals used. Furthermore, when the metals were replaced by non-conductors or poor conductors such as: "glass, gum, resin, stones and dry wood"[2] no contraction took place.

As a result of these events, Galvani goes on to make the quite logical deduction that whatever is causing these contractions does not apparently come from the atmosphere and must therefore reside in the metals or in the frog-preparation. Furthermore, since it passes through the conductors but not through non-conductors, either the metals or the frog-preparation contain a store of electrical fluid which is capable of being set in motion and as a result of this, cause muscular motion. He then remarks "These results surprised us greatly and led us to suspect that the electricity was inherent in the animal itself".[4]

Galvani can hardly be telling the whole truth since we know that he not only suspected but was convinced that the nerves contained an intrinsic nerveo-electric fluid as a result of completely different experiments performed at an earlier date. Doubtless this previous conviction was mainly responsible for his deciding in favour of the animal and not the metals as the site on this occasion.

Now if we consider that Galvani was almost certainly looking for a model based on the concept of a loss of electrical fluid from the muscle at the time of stimulation, his obvious need would be to demonstrate some sort of circuit between muscle and nerve, and *vice versa* if he were to explain the physiological phenomenon of constantly recurring muscular activity. The electrical situation in the muscle prior to stimulation had presumably to be recoverable before a second stimulation could occur. Evidence for just such a circulation of electrical fluid seemed apparent to Galvani as a result of certain experiments he goes on to describe.

The first of these seemed to demonstrate that animal electricity could flow through Galvani's body and return to the frog to act once more as a stimulus:

> *Furthermore, while I held in one hand a prepared frog with a hook fastened in its spinal cord in such a way that it stood on its feet in a silver box, with the other hand I struck the top of the box on which the frog's feet rested, or its side, using some metallic instrument. Contrary to expectation, I saw the frog react in violent contractions as often as I used this technique.*[4]

Further experiments with his Jesuit friend Rialpus, confirmed this view. When Rialpus held the frog as Galvani had done, but the latter struck the silver box, no contractions occurred, but when Galvani then held the frog in one hand while holding Rialpus' hand in his other and Rialpus then struck the box, contractions occurred each time this was done. Galvani says "To our joy and surprise, contractions immediately took place, only to disappear if we separated our hands."[4] He is convinced that ". . . these results seemed sufficient to indicate an electrical flowing-out, as it were, of nerve fluid through the human chain . . ."[4] and goes on to confirm this view by introducing conductors and non-conductors into the "human chain", and showed that contractions only took place if Rialpus and he joined hands *via* conductors. These results apparently convinced Galvani that:

> *a kind of circuit of delicate nerve fluid is made from the nerves to the muscles when the phenomenon of contractions is produced, similar to the electric circuit which is completed in a Leyden Jar . . .*[4]

Now we know that Galvani had been struck by the resemblance between the properties of the Leyden Jar and his frog-preparation in 1782, around the time he would have been abandoning the concept of phlogiston as the active constituent in muscle. As one continues to read his account of his work in

Part III, it becomes obvious that he is absolutely dedicated to this analogy: the muscle-nerve preparation is a store of electrical fluid which can be considered as manifesting electrical properties similar to its non-organic model. Behind all his experiments and their explanations one can recognise his wish to justify this analogy. As we have seen, he first became convinced that the frog-preparation contained an intrinsic store of electric fluid as a result of the series of experiments following on his discovery of 26 January 1781, but now he seemed to have had this belief confirmed and to have further demonstrated a circulation of this fluid between the essential parts of his preparation. The analogy with a Leyden Jar must have seemed very inviting: Franklin's writings on the physical properties of the Jar had made it very much in the news and it can easily be seen how Galvani would have seen similarities between the behaviour of a Leyden Jar being repeatedly charged and discharged and the activation and recovery phases characteristic of neuro-muscular functioning.

Galvani does not mention his earlier evidence for an intrinsic animal electricity but seems to suggest that this was his first indication of its existence. His evidence for assuming this to be the case results from the contemporary ignorance of the potential existing across the two different metals coupled in his circuit. As he quite naturally and logically assumed, the metals could only be acting as a conducting pathway – on the whole more convincing reasoning than that which originally led him to his view in 1781.

Galvani is so convinced of his interpretation of events that he fails to see the true significance of his own valid observation that if the metals composing the various parts of the conducting arc are similar, the contractions are absent, whereas if they are dissimilar, vigorous contractions result:

> We have frequently observed, moreover, that the following unusual and remarkable technique which stimulates the weakened reactions of prepared animals – namely the use of a diversity and variety of metals for the conductors of the arc or the conducting plate – is extremely effective in contributing to and augmenting muscular contractions, and without doubt is much more satisfactory than the use of one and the same metal.[5]

The true interpretation of Galvani's observations was of course made by Volta and formed the theoretical basis for the construction of the Voltaic battery, which was launched on the scientific world at the end of the century.[6] But Galvani was thinking in a quite different way, convinced that his 'metallic arc', which he saw as a simple conducting pathway between the frog's nerve and muscle, was acting in exactly the same way as any metallic conducting arc joining the conducting rod of a Leyden Jar to the outside of the Jar. The next obvious assumption he had to make was that two different parts of his frog-preparation were acting as the electrical equivalents of the conducting rod and outside of the Jar, that is, carrying an equal and opposite charge:

> From the discovery of a circuit of nerve fluid, (an electric fire, as it were) it naturally seemed to follow that a two-fold and dissimilar, or rather an opposite, electricity produces this phenomenon in the same way that the electricity in the Leyden Jar or the magic square [Franklinian Square] is two-fold whereby it releases in these bodies its electric fluid in a circuit. For, as the natural philosophers have shown, a flow of

electricity in a circuit can take place only in a restoration of equilibrium and occurs chiefly between opposite charges.[7]

The likelihood that the equal and opposite charges occurred in "one and the same metal" seemed remote to him and as he says, "contrary to nature" and so his next task was to try to demonstrate such a situation within the parts of such a preparation. Quite obviously Galvani was envisaging the presence in the frog of some element which had insulating properties similar to that of the glass of the Leyden Jar or the glass plate in the Franklinian Square – a not unreasonable supposition that all the parts of his organic preparation were not equally good conductors of electricity:

> *After these discoveries had been duly noted it seemed quite possible to me that the two-fold and opposite electricity could be found without delay in the prepared animals and that either one component has its seat in the muscle and the other in the nerve or both are present in one or the other as the natural philosophers assert to be the case in the tourmaline stone.[8]*

He had no difficulty in envisaging the possibility that the equal and opposite charges might exist in either the nerve or muscle since he considered both to be composed of heterogeneous elements, but as we shall see from the experiments he performed and more especially from the deductions he drew, he had, at this stage, made up his mind that the insulating barrier lay between the muscle and nerve and not within either of these. Not long after this however, he came to envisage the nerve as a passive conductor and assumed the site of the barrier to be intramuscular – a closer analogy with the Leyden Jar.

The *Commentary* continues with a description of these experiments, the first of which were aiming at demonstrating the nature of the electricity displayed by the nerves. Galvani compares the effect of moving "a glass rod" and "one of *[rubbed]* sealing wax, near the severed spinal cord of frogs which I had freshly killed in preparation for the experiment". In the first case (not unsurprisingly) no contractions occurred, while in the second case (very surprisingly!) they did occur and "even at a distance of four and more lines, provided that the spinal column had been encased in tin-foil as we mention below."[8]

Why Galvani expected this manoeuvre to produce a stimulus to contraction is difficult to understand and why it did, if it did, is even more difficult to explain. Presumably the tin-foil produced a traumatic irritation of the very fresh spinal cord and this was responsible for any odd spasms produced. The third manoeuvre involved the turning of the disc of the electrical machine:

> *. . . in numerous revolutions, in order to learn whether the greater supply of electricity accumulated in the disc excited muscular contractions which the [glass] rod could not do. The result, however, was the same: not the slightest movement occurred in the muscles.[8]*

Again one can only be surprised that Galvani thought such a procedure would be successful. Having performed numerous experiments previously to show that in order to act as a stimulus the electrical fluid must be subjected to a sudden force,[9] such as the rapid movement induced by offering it a discharge pathway, it is strange that he should have abandoned this concept even temporarily. What he in fact says he deduced from these results was that nerves carry a positive charge:

> *Thus we learn from these experiments that nerve electricity is positive, since the natural philosophers demonstrate that only opposite kinds of electricity can bring about the customary effects and movements.*[8]

In other words, the 'positive electricity' or flow of electrical fluid produced by turning the disc of his electric machine had no effect while the 'negative electricity' or relative lack of electrical fluid, was successful, and therefore, the nerves must be 'positively' (oppositely) charged. The experimental results described are of little value and Galvani's reasoning is even less. However, when he came to repeat these procedures on muscles he has to admit that he was unsuccessful:

> *Then we turned to an investigation of muscle electricity. We undertook the same experiments with the muscles as we had done before with the nerves but could observe no movements in the former with either the application of positive or negative electricity.*[8]

Galvani's readiness to accept the evidence for a 'positive charge' in nerves was a result of his desire to show that the nerve in his preparation was positively charged relative to the muscle. Leyden Jars were normally charged by bringing their conducting rod and hook up to the prime-conductor of the electric machine, thus making this positive with respect to the equally negatively charged outer surface of the Jar. One begins to see the way in which Galvani wishes to make the analogy.

However, having failed to find evidence of a negative charge in muscle, Galvani turned once more to the study of nerves since they seemed to "react more favourably to our experiments". He says that he repeated experiments similar to the original ones with the electrical machine (Part I of the *Commentary*), "using the same techniques we had used earlier when we experimented with it through the discharge of a spark." This time, however, the electrical machine was replaced by a rubbed stick of sealing wax and apparently contractions were produced ". . . except that they, that had responded earlier to the force of electricity in the spark, were much less intense with the sealing wax."[8]

How Galvani obtained contractions by the mere holding of a stick of rubbed sealing wax near his frog-preparation is difficult to explain. Perhaps he again became frustrated and started prodding the fresh nerve end with the wax, obtaining contractions as a result of trauma. There certainly seems to have been some wishful thinking on his part!

Galvani was obviously not too happy with his results so far and went on to cover the nerves with metal foil, copying, as he saw it, the technique employed by contemporary electricians who armed the surfaces of their Franklinian Squares and Leyden Jars with metals. His result pleased him:

> *Through this device in a remarkable way such forceful muscular movements developed that even without an arc, contractions were produced through one single contact by a body of either a conducting or non-conducting nature when the nerves were armed, provided that the animals had been recently prepared and were still lively. This device,*

moreover, also greatly increased the efficacy and usefulness of the arc and other instru-
ments, and finally brought about contractions that were extremely violent, of long
duration, and essentially constant in animals (that were vigorous before dissection)
even with the arc or the body removed which touched the armed nerves.[10]

These results could have occurred for a number of reasons. Galvani does
not specify whether his brass hook was present in any of these experiments
and his diagrams do not help to elucidate this point. If in fact a brass hook
was transfixing the spinal cord, pressure by any body conducting or otherwise
would be enough to bring the hook into contact with the tin-foil and create a
little voltaic cell capable of stimulating contractions. If no brass hook was present and contractions occurred in the absence of an arc, presumably the minor
trauma produced by touching the tin-foil with a non-conducting body was
sufficient to bring about contractions in these highly excitable tissues. Galvani
stressed the fact that the specimens were lively and freshly killed and indeed
it is not uncommon for such preparations to go into spontaneous spasmodic
contractions in the absence of any experimental manoeuvres so that this
must be assumed to be the explanation of the contractions produced "... even
with the arc or the body removed which touched the armed nerves."

Galvani, however, was sure that arming his nerves gave rise to bigger and
better contractions as a result of the same principles as underlie the technique of arming Franklinian Squares.[11] He describes further experiments in
which he arms his nerves with various metal amalgam pastes and then applies his arc to the paste and to the muscles – another way of producing a
Voltaic cell in fact, but for him further evidence of the similarity between his
preparation and the Franklinian Square or Leyden Jar.

Galvani, it would seem, was convinced by now that when he placed one
end of his conducting arc against the brass hook and the other against the
muscle, he was seeing the results of the flow of animal electricity (intrinsic
nerveo-electric fluid) from the nerve to the muscle *via* the arc. He still had no
evidence as it were, for the electrical state of the various parts of the muscle,
for example, that the external surface was relatively negative to the inner cut
surface. His attempts to do just this, however met with little success. He performed one curious manoeuvre in which he placed one end of his arc on
bare muscle and the other in contact with the metal foil arming another part
of its surface. Not unsurprisingly, no contractions were regularly produced.
Presumably he might have envisaged the possibility of some inequality in
the electrical charge of different parts of the surface of a muscle – the obvious
rationale to his procedure. Similarly, no contractions resulted when he connected the "internal surface of the muscle" with the outer. This latter result
must have been very disappointing to him, particularly as he so readily produced contractions when he connected the nerve with the muscle, by means
of his arc. Somewhat sadly he reflects:

We carried out these experiments to discover the seat of animal electricity but
it became evident to us that this problem, which could not be sufficiently clarified
by experiment, must be left primarily to conjecture. But of this we shall write later
on.[12]

He was disappointed because if his analogy with a Leyden Jar were to be valid, an inequality of charge somewhere between the parts of the muscle had to be demonstrated. The "seat of animal electricity" had to be in the muscle and the nerve had to be acting as a mere conductor of intrinsic electrical fluid.

This really is about as far as Galvani reached in his pursuit of experimental evidence for his Leyden Jar model. As he himself says, the problem had to be left to conjecture. The remaining pages of Part III of the *Commentary* are devoted to his thoughts on the similarity between artificial and animal electricity and certain experiments which seemed to substantiate his claim for the existence of an intrinsic animal electricity. Thus we find him partially covering the nerves and muscles with a non-conducting substance ("silk cloth completely saturated with oil in which pitch had been dissolved") and finding that contractions were completely absent.

Remarking that animal electricity seemed to pass through conducting bodies more readily than through non-conductors (a point of similarity with ordinary electricity), he was led to compare the various metals as regards their conducting powers for animal electricity and concluded that such metals as silver and gold are superior in this respect to lead and iron. In like manner he also found that aqueous fluids were better conductors than oily fluids.

This in turn led him to investigate the relative conducting powers of the parts of his frog but all he seemed to discover was that all animal tissues seemed to conduct pretty easily, a fact he attributed to their being bathed in natural fluids. Dried parts, however, which had been dissected some time previously, appeared not to conduct animal electricity. His experiments consisted essentially of introducing pieces of such tissue into his circuit with the arc and armed nerves.

The conducting powers of the all pervading 'natural juices' supplied Galvani with a physiological answer to the problem of how his 'neuromuscular Leyden Jar' was discharged in the animal body. Experiments which he performed on the whole animal, wherein one end of his arc was applied as usual to an unarmed nerve while the other was placed on "any part of the body, you wish, lying intact in its natural position, which in some way responds to the muscles associated with these nerves" produced the usual contractions.

This seemed strong evidence that the body fluids took part in the circuit of animal electricity he envisaged as taking place and other experiments he carried out seemed to confirm this opinion. He concludes:

> *Clearly the phenomena of these contractions cannot be sufficiently well explained unless one assumes that the internal moisture present in the bodily parts affords an entrance and passageway to the circulating animal electricity.*[13]

and adds "Now can these phenomena bring any light to bear on the hitherto obscure cause and circumstances of the co-operation of the nerves?"[13]

Galvani was sure he had the answer to this problem, yet with due caution he remarks that his deductions are open to criticism on the grounds that his arc and other experimental apparatus could be said to be acting as a source of irritation and so he wishes to:

> . . . discover the mode and reason whereby these same muscular contractions might be obtained without the nerves or muscles being touched by any body, in any way.[14]

He tried to do this in a number of ways. Firstly, he connected the muscle of his preparation to one side of a Franklinian Square and the nerves to the opposite, and then joined the two surfaces of the Square by a conducting arc at points quite separate from those where the frog parts touched. When contact was made, contractions occurred. Galvani explains his rationale for believing that this result rules out a mechanical stimulus as follows:

> For if the fluid flowing through the nerves were electric and if the contractions were stimulated by its flowing out from the nerves to the muscles, then I could easily perceive from this type of experiment that it was the same as if I brought an arc in contact with the muscles and nerves themselves, without there being any suspicion that a mechanical stimulus had been applied to them.[14]

Again he is unaware of the significance of the contact of the metal arc and the metallic arming of the glass plate of the Square.

His most impressive demonstration of this belief however seemed to result from the following experiment. The spinal cord and nerves of the frog were placed in one beaker of water and the feet in another, the preparation thus forming an arc between the two beakers. On merely connecting the two water surfaces with his metallic arc, contractions occurred – a sure indication for him that no stimulating body was irritating the frog, although the true cause for the contractions was again the formation of a Voltaic cell.

Other apparently corroborative experiments are described, including some of a similar nature on living animals, both cold and warm-blooded, the latter with a view to explaining neuro-muscular function in the normal and abnormal state in man and thus, as we shall see, forming the basis of a theory of neuro-pathology. However, Galvani merely indicates this in Part III: the dénouement of his complete hypothesis is presented in Part IV, which he aptly entitles, *The Effects of Animal Electricity on Muscular Motion, Conjecture and some Conclusions*.

This animal electricity is "seen most clearly" in the muscles and nerves, he goes on:

> Its special characteristic, not recognised before, seems to be that it courses strongly from the muscles to the nerves or rather from the latter to the former and directly enters an arc, a chain of men, or other conducting bodies which lead from the nerves to the muscles by the shortest and most direct course possible, and passes in all haste from one to the other through them.[15]

He might seem to be suggesting that he is unsure whether the animal electricity is going from the muscle to nerve or nerve to muscle, but it is quite apparent really, from what has just been discussed, that he is describing what he considers to be the two parts of his physiological circuit. On stimulation, he believes, the electricity first passes from the depth of the muscle, centripetally in the central canal of the nerve then returns in some way *via* parts outside the nerve and muscle to the external surface of the muscle, thus completing its circuit. This physiological analogy with the Leyden Jar (or any other condenser) depends on the presence of a boundary material separating regions of equal and opposite charge for, as Galvani says:

> From this, two facts are particularly evident, namely that a two-fold electricity is present in these bodily parts, one positive, as one supposes, the other negative, and that each is completely separated from the other by nature: otherwise, if there were a state of equilibrium, no movement, no flow of electricity, and no phenomenon of muscular contraction would take place.[15]

However, the problem of locating this boundary zone was beyond his experimental powers. Having, for various reasons, decided to liken his neuromuscular preparation to a Leyden Jar, he hypothesises that the boundary in fact lies within the muscle itself. He justifies this by suggesting that, although, as he believes, he has demonstrated that the nerves are positively charged, they in fact are mere conductors carrying electric fluid or positive charge, from the inside of the muscle. (c.f. the conducting rod of a Leyden Jar). He suggests that nerve substance is not homogenous and that while the main part of a nerve, visible beyond the muscle is a mere conducting pathway, that part of the nerve hidden within the depths of the muscle and in contact with its internal surface, is in fact positively charged – a store in fact of electrical fluid. Any muscle is a collection of fibres each of which acts like a little Leyden Jar:

> If one admits these conclusions, then perhaps the hypothesis is not absurd and wholly speculative which compares a muscle fibre to something like a small Leyden Jar or to some other similar electrical body charged with a twofold and opposite electricity, and by comparing a nerve in some measure to the conductor of the Jar; in this way one likens the whole muscle, as it were, to a large group of Leyden Jars. Anyone who has supposed that a muscle fibre, although simple at first sight is composed of solid as well as of fluid parts (substances that produce in it no slight diversity), will readily admit that a twofold and contrary electricity having its seat in one and the same muscle is not far from the truth: for sensory perception, which is present throughout the fibre, clearly indicates that the nerve substance found therein is wholly different from muscle. Indeed since this nerve substance, which is present throughout the fibre, neither constitutes a nerve nor is perceptible to the eye but is perceived only by feeling, what hinders our supposing that it is at least partially dissimilar to the substance of the visible nerve, or is arranged in a different way, and for this reason has perhaps an electrical nature, but that it is extended as conducting nerve outside of the muscle fibre? But perhaps this may become clearer from what we will say a little later on about nerves.[16]

The anatomical facts available to Galvani were simply not adequate to his problem, but his guess that a boundary exists separating organic tissues carrying opposing electrical charges has turned out to be a very good one in terms of present day concepts of the electrical changes across the nerve membrane in particular and organic membranes in general.[17] Without the necessary anatomical knowledge, Galvani could do little else to support his inspired guess than to cite analogies between the physiological situation and that seemingly present in the mineral tourmaline and his beloved Leyden Jar. Galvani, as he admits, was so impressed by the latter that he felt bound to accept it as the true model of the events taking place in the animal body:

> But however this may be, we feel sure that the argument of causes and phenomena between the streaming out of electric fluid from a Leyden Jar and our contractions is so noticeable that we have scarcely, and not even scarcely, been able to be diverted from this hypothesis and comparison and to restrain ourselves from ascribing a similar cause to the former and the latter.[18]

He quotes three main instances of what he considers to be analogous behaviour of a Leyden Jar and his frog-preparation. Three techniques bring about the discharge of the former and produce muscular contractions in the latter, *viz*:

1. Connecting the conducting rod of the Jar with another body . . . "especially . . . of a conducting nature . . ."
2. The . . . "application of an arc . . .", that is, a conducting pathway between the conducting rod and the outside of the Jar
3. ". . . through the discharge of a spark from the conductor of an electrical machine . . ."

Similarly muscular contractions can be produced:

1. ". . . through the contact of an armed nerve, which we have made a muscle-conductor . . ."
2. ". . . through the application of the ends of an arc to this nerve, as well as to the muscle . . ."
3. ". . . through the discharge of a spark . . ."[19]

These three techniques appear to Galvani to be working in the same way and further, the efficacious one for bringing about the discharge of the Leyden Jar, that is, the application of an arc, is also the most efficient means of producing muscle contractions. Again, he finds it is difficult to discharge the Jar with the arc if an adequate length of conducting rod does not project beyond its mouth and similarly, it is difficult to produce muscle contractions if the nerve does not project for an adequate length beyond its insertion into the muscle.

The most cogent similarities however, between the working of these two electrical stores, seemed to exist as a result of their behaviour in the presence of the electrical machine spark. Galvani had noted the "brush discharge" glowing from a charged Leyden Jar, standing in the dark and had seen how, gradually, this disappeared after an interval of time. On standing the Jar near the electrical machine and withdrawing a spark, the brush discharge could be made to reappear and this as often as the machine discharged – just as frog contractions could be produced, synchronously with each spark. The brush discharge, glowing at the extremity of the conducting rod, was seen by Galvani as a leak of electrical fluid from the inside of the Jar, up the conducting rod - a leak which apparently appeared spontaneously for some time after charging the Jar but which could also be pulled, as it were, by the discharge of a spark from the machine. Again he makes it quite clear in which direction he now considered the electrical fluid was flowing: the discharge of a spark from the machine depleted the Leyden Jar just as he envisaged it depleting the nerve and muscle (and their conductors).

The analogous behaviour seems further to be exemplified by the efficacy of a grounded conducting rod attached to the outside of the Jar in one case, or to the muscle in the other. In one case, at the discharge of a spark from the adjacent electrical machine, a brush discharge could be revived while in the other muscle contractions could be produced where previously (in the absence of a muscle conductor) they were absent.

Other similarities are quoted by Galvani as confirmatory evidence for his hypothesis, which he eventually described in detail. One problem which he had to explain was related to the electric nature of the nerves. If they are freely conducting, how is electrical fluid retained within their cavity? He suggests that nerves are either truly hollow or composed of a material "adapted to carrying electrical fluid", while externally they are surrounded by an oily coat which acts as an insulator. In this way their properties seem to be satisfactorily explained, provided it is assumed that the oily coat is only insulating to a degree. When the nerve-force reaches a certain amount, it is able to overcome this insulating barrier and pass through the nerve wall to the external parts (an essential feature of his hypothesis).

Referring to properties which animal electricity has in common both with artificial electricity and that of the torpedo fish (an account of which had been communicated to Franklin by John Walsh* in 1772),[20] Galvani stresses the fact that in the activity of the latter, a circuit is involved from one part of the fish to another, *via* the water. This must have seemed a very convincing analogy of behaviour, and all the more important since the electricity of the torpedo was certainly a form of animal electricity even if it were not altogether evident that it was identical with artificial ordinary electricity. Galvani says he is hopeful that his investigations will throw more light on the mechanism of the torpedo and other related species since, he feels, the basic process involved in the torpedo's activity is similar to that producing muscular activity in all animals. On the other hand a careful examination of the organs of the torpedo should be undertaken since this might be expected to further our knowledge of neuro-muscular excitation.

Finally, Galvani unfolds his complete theory. Dealing with the source of this animal electricity, he suggests that this is almost certainly the cerebrum:

> For although we have stated that electricity is inherent in the muscles, we are not of the opinion, however, that it emanates from them as from its proper and natural source.[21]

With a somewhat Aristotelian logic he says that since the electrical fluid is passing along all nerves, and all the nerves are connected with the cerebrum, the latter must act as a "single source":

> *Otherwise there would be as many sources as there are parts wherein the nerves end,*
> *and since these parts are completely different in character and composition, they do*
> *not seem to be adapted to activating and secreting one and the same fluid.*[22]

He suggests that the cerebrum extracts electrical fluid from the circulating blood and distributes it *via* the nerves as the active component of the subtle fluid which the brain secretes. Although he does not say so, one must presume the electrical fluid passing centrifugally in the nerves eventually reaches the inner surface of muscle fibres, where it is stored. Leaving this aside, he passes right away to what he believes are the two essential acts in the process of excitation, that is, the recall of this electric fluid from the muscle fibril in a centripetal direction up the central canal of the nerve supply and its return in a centrifugal direction to the external surface of the muscle fibre, *via* parts outside the nerve and muscle. He suggests that four "incitements" are the possible agents responsible for the initial flow of electricity from muscle to nerve:

1. "... The sudden rupture of a state of equilibrium between the internal electricity of the muscles and nerves and the external electricity of bodies in communication with the nerves ..."

2. "... an irritation of these same nerves ..."

3. "... the contact of some body, especially one of a conducting nature, either with the same nerves, or with conducting bodies communicating with these same nerves ..."

4. "... Some sort of stimulation or gentle irritation of the nerve substance, as when contractions are excited by the simple tapping of a soft surface on which a prepared animal lies."[23]

Thus, he says, two elements seem to contribute to the production of muscular movement: some sort of irritation and some disturbance in the electrical equilibrium of the appropriate parts. As examples of the latter, he again refers to the mechanism by which he believes contractions are produced by discharging the electrical machine. At the emission of a spark, he says, electricity is discharged from the air surrounding the prime-conductor and also from the conductors attached to the preparation, making their resultant electricity negative, and hence:

> *... the inner positive electricity of the muscle flows copiously to the nerves through*
> *its own strength as well as that derived from external electricity, whether artificial or*
> *natural, with the result that having been taken up by the nerve-conductors and having*
> *diffused itself through them, it restores failing electricity in them as well as in the*
> *strata of air mentioned previously, and establishes itself in equilibrium.*[23]

In a similar way, he now interprets the results of experiments with his preparation contained in a double glass jar – the results of which seemed to leave him in such perplexity at the time they were carried out. There is no ambiguity now concerning the direction of flow of the electricity:

> *One can apparently attribute the same course and origin to the muscular contractions*
> *which are produced in an animal enclosed in our little glass instrument when a spark*

is discharged: for the internal electricity of the muscle seems to flow to the internal surface of the glass through the nerves and their conductors by reason of the same law of equilibrium. In consequence so much electricity flows to the internal surface of the glass as was removed from the external surface through the discharge of the spark.[23]

And so on. More experiments with the Leyden Jar, more references to his experiments with the arc, all tending to reiterate the same story. Granted that the body fluids can act as an external arc, Galvani's theory is complete.

According to this theory in the living animal, the mind or brain, by means of its inherent powers, can elect to 'stimulate' any point on a nerve and the result of this stimulus is the flow of animal electricity from the inside of the muscle fibre to the point of the nerve thus stimulated (Galvani does not suggest the physical nature of the brain's action but presumably since he considered it as analogous to that of the discharging electrical machine, this too would involve electrical changes). Having reached this certain point in the nerve, its accumulated strength is great enough to overcome the insulating properties of the nerves oily coating and hence it passes out through the latter to enter the fluids or other parts on its external surface. There is thus a disequilibrium produced between the positive charge outside the nerve and the negative charge on the outside of the muscle fibre, and hence the electrical fluid flows back, through the conducting parts to the outside of the muscle to restore the equilibrium.

Certain interesting points arise in connection with this theory. In the first place, Galvani makes it quite clear that the primary stimulus is supplied by the will, but not unsurprisingly he does not hazard any theory as to how he envisages this is produced. The brain serves the function of extracting and elaborating animal electricity from the circulating blood and we are told that this passes out along the nerves, presumably to reach the inside surface of muscle fibres where a certain amount is stored. One wonders whether this supplying of the muscle fibre is something that is envisaged as occurring once – at some early stage of development – or whether as seems more likely, as a constantly recurring process the result of a constant supply of electricity from the food *via* the blood. In the latter case, Galvani would have to explain the effects of a passage of electrical fluid regularly travelling in the opposite direction to that traversed by the animal electricity at the moment it is stimulated to pass from the muscle up the nerve. One cannot help wondering also, whether Galvani envisaged the primary stimulus, acting upon the depôt of animal electricity in the muscle fibre was analogous to that produced by the mechanical action of the brain on that same species of electricity while it was in the vicinity of the brain.

In order to be consistent with the Leyden Jar analogy, stimulation of contractions had to result, it seems, from a centripetal flow of animal electricity and this obviously forced the dilemma of where the flow should end. In the older and simpler mechanical concept of electricity flowing centrifugally to stimulate a muscle there was no problem for quite obviously it would stop when it reached muscle but Galvani's model demanded that some point on the nerve, proximal to the muscle, should be the point at which the electricity should break through and begin its external passage back to muscle. It would be interesting to know what significance Galvani would have attached to the location of this point. Perhaps he conjectured that the will stimulated different parts in order to produce stronger or weaker contractions?

However we may conjecture regarding this model for muscular motion, it seems that Galvani was quite happy to use it as the basis for explaining various malfunctions of the neuro-muscular system. Indeed, the ease with which the occurrence of violent or spasmodic contractions or, in the opposite case, the absence of contractions at all, could be explained in mechanical terms, must have seemed one of the most cogent forms of evidence for its validity.

It will be remembered how he described two main stimuli as being responsible for recalling the electricity from the muscle: irritation and electrical disequilibrium. He uses the irritation produced by 'penetrating humours' and "acid and corrosive substances" to explain the stimulus to various movements. Thus involuntary movements (where the will is not involved) are attributed to the excitation of the nerve by "penetrating and stimulating elements" which "at the same time summon the nerve fluid". If such irritating influences settle on the surface of a nerve, their presence will give rise to prolonged and abnormal muscular contractions:

> It is not difficult to perceive that once these humours have flowed from the vessels and have settled between the surface of the nerve substance and its covering, then contractions ought to be more violent and of longer duration. This happens to be sure because the stagnant acid humours that flowed out will not only irritate the nerve more forcefully but will also furnish quite a suitable type of covering and arc so to speak, for the nerveo-electric fluid.[24]

And so, he continues, in severe rheumatic affections, particularly sciatica, in which he believes this is the case, violent and persistent contractions occur resulting often in permanent contractures. In like manner he explains tetanic contractions as a result of the stagnation of similar humours between various parts of the *dura* and *pia mater*, the ventricles or the cerebrum itself.

On the other hand, paralysis of movement can be explained readily in terms of a stoppage in the circuit of the nerveo-electric fluid, flowing from muscle to nerve, or nerve to muscle. This could be caused, he suggests, as a result of some non-conducting material occupying the centre of the nerve, or if a similar material permeates the normal moisture covering the nerve, or thirdly if corrosive or acid substances damage the texture of the nerves and cerebrum. Epilepsy and apoplexy however, he attributes to a too forceful impulse of 'contaminated' animal electricity against the brain. This is derived by analogy with the destructive as opposed to stimulating effects of electricity applied in great quantities to organic tissues, for example, burning and death resulting from exposure to the lightning stroke.

Old people, he notes, suffer especially from these diseases as a result of the drying of their bodily parts and some increase in the density of the oily substance surrounding their nerves, which together with a decrease in perspiration (which normally causes a diminished loss of electricity from the body) results in an increase in contaminated animal electricity. For like reasons too, any increase in atmospheric electricity (such as at times of storm) will cause the same effects. In fact any building up beyond its normal amounts particularly if it is 'contaminated' by 'stagnant', 'penetrating' humours, will result in this violent, destructive action on the brain which is manifested as epilepsy or apoplexy. So great is the impact of this contaminated electricity that it damages the internal structure of the brain, bursting blood vessels and producing immediate paralysis. The humours thus released, become stagnant and, Galvani says, can be found in various parts of corpses.[25]

Galvani is aware that his theories are open to criticism because of certain difficulties inherent in them. One of these, he says is the fact that:

> ... they are opposed to the common opinion taught in school that muscular motion is activated by an influence of nerve fluid from the brain to the muscular parts not from the latter to the former.[26]

He suggests that the aura felt by epileptics (which he believes is due to the passage of gases from the lower to the upper part of the body) can be stopped by applying a ligature to the leg and that this, perhaps, is an excuse for his conjecture!

The rest of the *Commentary*, deals with the logical application of electro-therapy on the basis of this explanation of neuro-muscular pathology. Applied electrical remedies must:

> ... exert their force on animal electricity and should either augment, diminish or change it and its circuit in some way. For this reason, a physician must of necessity hold this electricity and its state before his eyes especially, in treatment.[27]

Galvani's reference to the various ways of applying external electricity, whether positive or negative, need hardly concern us here. In terms of his beliefs, they aim at supplying or withdrawing electricity from the body according as he believes the lesion under treatment is the result of a lack, surfeit or sluggishness of animal electricity. They include the rather nice idea of attaching (with caution!) muscle conductors to palsied limbs in order to make use of atmospheric electricity, when thunder and lightning rage.[28]

Galvani's theory was presented to the world in 1791 and in the words of the Swiss electrophysiologist, Emil Du Bois Reymond*, the commotion it caused could be likened to that brought about by the upheavals of the French Revolution. Writing more than half a century later he says:

> The storm which was produced by the above named Commentary among philosophers, physiologists and physicians can only be compared to that which disturbed at that time (1791) the political horizons of Europe. It may be said that for ever wherever frogs were to be found and where two different metals could be procured everybody was anxious to see the mangled limbs of frogs brought to life in this wonderful way. The physiologists believed that at length they should realise their visions of a vital power. The physicians whom Galvani had somewhat thoughtlessly led on with attempts to explain all kinds of nervous diseases as sciatica, tetanus and epilepsy began to believe that no cure was impossible and it was considered certain that no-one in a trance could in future be buried alive provided only that he were Galvanised.[29]

Our next Chapter will deal with the fate of Galvani's theory at the hands of his contemporaries and consider its significance in relation to past and future concepts of the mechanical basis of neuro-muscular excitation.

Notes

1 See: *Memorie ed Esperimenti Inediti di Luigi Galvani con la inconografia di lui e un saggio di bibliografia degli scritti . . .*, Bologna, Licinio Cappelli Editore, 1937 –xv,
'De animale electricitate, Die 30a Octobris 1786' pp 33–55 (From manuscripts of the Academy of Science of the Institute of Bologna, bequeathed by Giovanni Aldini, Cart. II, Plico V, fasc. II)
'Electricitatis naturalis, Die 16a Augusti, 1787 B.M.V. Assumptae', pp 57–75 (From manuscripts, Cart. II, Plico IX, B)
'De Musculorum Motu ab electricitate, J.M.H.R,' pp 77–82 (From manuscripts, cart. II Plico. IX, C.) read at the Institute on 30 April 1789
2 Galvani, Luigi (1953) *Commentary on the effects of electricity on muscular motion*, M.G. Foley (transl.), I. Bernard Cohen (ed.), Norwalk, Conn. Burndy Library, p. 59
3 Nevertheless, Galvani was later to use the 'overcharge' theory as an explanation for certain muscular movements occurring physiologically. See Galvani's letter of 8 May 1792, written to Don Bassano Carminati. This is appended to Robert Montraville Green, a translation of Luigi Galvani's *De Viribus Electricitatis in Motu Musculari, Commentarius . . .*, Cambridge, Mass., Elizabeth Licht, 1953
4 Loc. cit., Note 2, p. 60
5 Ibid., p. 61
6 See *The Philosophical Magazine*, London, Davis, Taylor and Wilks, September 1800, Vol. VII, pp 289–311, for an English translation of the letter sent by Alessandro Volta to Sir Joseph Banks, PRS, and entitled, 'On the Electricity excited by the mere Contact of conducting Substances of different kinds.' The original publication, in French, appeared in *The Philosophical Transactions of the Royal Society for 1800*, Part II, pp 403–431
7 Loc. cit., Note 2, p. 62
8 Ibid., p. 63
9 Galvani had of course, sometimes obtained contractions in the absence of a spark. In theory, if he could have induced a big enough charge, quickly enough, this would have provided a stimulus to his preparation
10 Loc. cit., Note 2, p. 63–64
11 See Appendix II in this book. The Franklinian Square consisted of a plate of glass having a lead sheet on both of its flat surfaces. The lead plates, when connected in circuit, were of course capable of giving a much more powerful shock than was produced by connecting the surfaces of the glass itself and hence such Squares were usually 'armed' by such conducting plates in order to bring this about
12 Loc. cit., Note 2, p. 65
13 Ibid., p. 67
14 Ibid., p. 68
15 Ibid., p. 73, I. Bernard Cohen remarks in a footnote "The stylistic oddity of this phrase is puzzling; why, if the course of an animal electricity is from the nerves to the muscles did not Galvani say so directly?" The answer to Cohen's query is, I hope apparent, and requires no further comment – Author
16 Ibid., p. 74
17 See Chap. 21 of this book
18 Loc. cit., Note 2, p. 74–75
19 Ibid., p. 75
20 Walsh J. (1773–1774) 'Of the electric property of the Torpedo. In a letter from John Walsh Esq., FRS to Benjamin Franklin, Esq. FRS' *Philosophical Transactions*, Part I, pp 461–487. John Walsh tells the Royal Society of his investigations into the electrical nature of the shock produced by the torpedo fish. This paper contains among others, his original letter to Benjamin Franklin, written from La Rochelle on 12 July 1772.

Having discovered that the upper and the lower surfaces of the fish are charged differently, he was able to "direct his shocks" through various chains of human beings and to demonstrate that if the water or conducting circuit were replaced by non-conductors, no shock occurs. The similarity to Galvani's reasoning is apparent. In a second and further letter, written from Paris on 27 August 1772, Walsh develops his theme and compares the torpedo's electric organs to a Leyden Jar. He tells Franklin in his final paragraph: "He who predicted and showed that electricity wrings the formidable bolt of the atmosphere will hear with attention, that in the deep it speeds an humbler bolt, silent and invisible; he, who analysed the electrified Phial will hear with pleasure that its laws prevail in animate Phials; He Who by Reason became an electrician, will hear with reverence of an instinctive electrician, gifted in his birth with a wonderful apparatus, and with the skill to use it". The similarity to Galvani's ideas is obvious

21 Loc. cit., Note 2, p. 78
22 Ibid., pp 78–79
23 Ibid., p. 80
24 Ibid., p. 82
25 Ibid., p. 84. Such "humours" referred to by Galvani are of course, the result of various pathological conditions pertaining at death for example, circulatory failure, exudates and effusions as a result of inflammatory and neoplastic conditions and so on
26 Ibid., p. 84. Galvani here refers to the fact that previously it had been believed that muscular motion resulted simply from a flow of nervous fluid from the brain towards muscle
27 Ibid., p. 85
28 Ibid., p. 87
29 See H. Bence-Jones, *On Animal Electricity, Being an abstract of the discoveries of Emil Du Bois Reymond*, London, Churchill, 1852, pp 7–8

* See Biographical Index

21

The reception of the *Commentary* and its significance for later theories of neuro-muscular excitation

The oft-quoted description by Du Bois Reymond, of the reception accorded Galvani's *Commentary* (transcribed at the end of the previous chapter) leaves no doubt as to the impact the latter made on a large cross-section of the population of Europe at a time when political events might have been expected to dwarf any scientific achievements. The precise reasons for this are interesting. Leaving aside the popular appeal of seeing the "mangled limbs" of frogs forced into bizarre contortions or the practical interest of physicians in a presumably rational form of therapy for certain diseases; why was the scientific community of Europe so impressed by what Galvani had apparently demonstrated?

Loosely speaking, he is usually credited with having shown the existence of an intrinsic animal electricity, a nervous fluid sharing all the properties exhibited by the ordinary, artificial electricity produced by electricians in their laboratories through such manoeuvres as rubbing electrics with fur, or charging electrical machines, Leyden Jars, etc. The implication is that to everybody's surprise Galvani revealed an unsuspected store of electrical fluid lying within the muscles and nerves of frogs and other animals. Thus, for example we find L. Pearce Williams in his excellent account of the life and work of Michael Faraday*, referring to Galvani's discovery in this way:

> *In 1791 a new imponderable made its appearance when Luigi Galvani announced the discovery of animal electricity produced by living tissue. This fluid, secreted by the nerves, was completely analogous to all the other imponderables except for its connection with life.*[1]

Franklin's theory (or modifications of it), which formed the basis of the ideas currently accepted by electricians on both sides of the Atlantic at this time, depended on the assumption that there is a mutual attraction between the particles of electrical fluid and those of all common matter. As we have discussed in an earlier chapter,[2] Franklin's electrical particles were the direct descendants of Newton's subtle mutually repulsive aethereal particles. They were envisaged as being subtle enough to permeate the pores of all other classes of matter, much as water permeates a sponge. The electricians of the 18th century certainly thought of electrical particles as a generally distributed form of matter. The only difference between various forms of common matter was seen to depend on the strength of attraction exhibited between its particles and the electrical ones: the greater this attraction, the greater the electric or insulating properties of the common matter. In general, Franklin assumed there was "... in common matter as much of the electrical as it will contain within its substance."[3]

Now 18th century electricians were all well aware of the ability of electricity to pass through animal and human bodies and chemical analysis had demonstrated the existence of various types of common matter in organic objects. There was no reason why electrical particles should not have been assumed to be lying within the pores separating the common matter of animal bodies. It wasn't their presence that was really doubted to any degree but their role as the immediate agency of neuro-muscular activation.

Volta, who initially shared in the enthusiasm for Galvani's 'stupendous discovery' and referred to the *Commentary* as containing "... one of the most beautiful and surprising of discoveries and the germ of many others ..."[4] was not impressed because he believed Galvani had demonstrated the presence of electrical particles within the animal body; in fact he was surprised that Galvani was so astonished by his results with the electric machine. His remarks to his friend Cavallo, in the first of a series of letters in which he criticises the *Commentary*, show quite clearly that he considered the frog-preparation as a deferent, the intrinsic electrical particles of which were redistributed as a result of its proximity to the charged conductor of the electrical machine. He says:

> This phenomenon astonished Mr Galvani, perhaps more than it ought to have: for the ability, not only of electric sparks striking the muscles and nerves of animals, directly, but of a current of fluid passing through them, in whatever manner this may be, with sufficient speed, this great ability, I say, of exciting movements, was a fairly well known fact ...

Volta then continues:

> ... besides, it was obvious how ... his frog was effectively exposed to being traversed by such a current. One has only to think back to the well-known action of electric atmospheres or what is called electrical pressure; by which the fluid of deferent Bodies, plunged in the sphere of activity of any electrified Body, is driven and displaced as a result of the force and situation of that Body and held in that state of displacement for as long as the electricity in the dominant Body remains, and which, on removing that force returns to its original situation, little by little, if this is gradually dissipated and instantaneously if this is suddenly destroyed by discharging the Body invested with it, all at once. It is therefore this returning current this reflux of electrical fluid in the different bodies in contact with the frog or near it, its brusque passage from muscle-conductor to nerve-conductor, or vice versa across its Body, and above all when such a current is restricted to the unique canal and space of the nerves, which excites the spasms and the movements in the experiments under consideration.

and then:

> Mr Galvani, who does not seem to have given enough consideration of this action of electric atmospheres and who did not also know of the prodigious sensitivity of his frog, especially when prepared in the manner prescribed (I would say here, that I have

found it almost equally in other little animals such as lizards, salamanders and mice)
was extremely struck by such an effect which would not seem so marvellous to other
physicists. This was perhaps the first step which led him to the beautiful and great dis-
covery of animal electricity *properly speaking . . .*[5]

Volta accepted that the stimulus to muscular contraction was a redistribution of electrical fluid within the frog; what excited him was Galvani's apparent demonstration that such a redistribution could be brought about as a
result of the internal organisation of the animal's body. What Galvani believed he had demonstrated was that the animal body is organised in such a
way that the common, electrical fluid is maintained in a constant state of imbalance at some junctional region within the muscle fibre and that the flow
of redistribution of electrical fluid which tends to redress this imbalance is
the excitatory stimulus for muscular contraction. In other words, the animal
body has an in-built mechanism for sustaining equal and opposite charges
across a certain part of a muscle, and being an anatomist, Galvani assumed
that this faculty depended on its anatomical structure, variations in which
might be expected to be associated with variations in conduction. After all
this is just what Franklin had postulated, in general terms.

One of the most difficult problems in discussing the development of
Galvani's ideas is the fact that he was striving to explain a philosophical
concept in a way which was consistent, not only with his own experimental
results but with contemporary theory. When he began to think about the
problem of the activation of muscle fibres his concept was that of the mechanical interaction of vibrating particles and hence the demonstration that
nervous juice "contained electrical fluid" simply involved the idea of electrical particles bombarding other electrical or phlogistic particles in muscles:
by the time he wrote the *Commentary* he had to think in terms of an electrical
model which fulfilled the requirements of contemporary electrical theory. It
was not enough to say that there is electrical fluid in nerves or muscles.
After all, the mechanical philosophers accepted that anyway. What he had to
do was to show how this fluid could be given the potential for flowing in a
circuit and to do this he adopted the analogy of a Leyden Jar, on the assumption that some intramuscular tissue acted as the glass walls of the Jar
did, separating different levels of electrical fluid.

That certain fishes have this ability to store electrical charge had been
established as a result of the work of John Walsh whose researches into the
electrical activities of the torpedo Gymnotus had demonstrated opposing
charges on the upper and under surface of their bodies. And as we have
noted, he compared the torpedo to an 'animate phial', that is, an animate
Leyden Jar 20 years before Galvani's *Commentary* was published.[6]

Volta was one of the first of the many scientists who became interested in
Galvani's theory, writing with great enthusiasm to his colleagues, all over
Europe on the subject of 'animal electricity'. As George Sarton remarked:

Alessandro Volta devoted himself entirely to the study of these fascinating problems.
Between 1792 and 1800 he wrote more than twenty mémoires on the subject, i.e. animal

electricity. Indeed the history of it during the last decade of the 18th century could be almost reconstructed from his writings alone.[7]

The very first of his many letters was written on 3 April 1792 and addressed to a young medical assistant in the Ospedale Maggiore in Milan. Volta describes various experiments which he has carried out on the subject of 'animal electricity' following upon ". . . the stupendous discoveries of Signor Galvani . . ."[8] Exactly one month later however, we have the first evidence that Volta was suspicious of the explanation that Galvani had given for the production of a current of electrical fluid in his frog-preparation. In certain additions to his first *Mémoire on animal electricity*, delivered on 5 May 1792 at the University of Pavia, he refers to the significance of dissimilar metals in the production of contractions, using a Galvani conducting arc:

> *All this is in agreement with the ideas we have about the influence of nerves and is easy to understand. That however, which is not, and for which I have not yet been able to find a reason is the necessity for dissimilar armatures.[9]*

The story of Volta's eventual explanation of the true significance of the importance of dissimilar armatures is well documented in the history books. Over the years between 1792 and 1800 he proceeded to carry out experiments which culminated in his invention of the Voltaic pile or battery, the details of which he communicated to Sir Joseph Banks*, President of the Royal Society, in the famous letter which appeared in *Philosophical Transactions* for 1800.[10] Pursuing his interest in the significance of dissimilar armatures in the Galvani conducting arc, he had discovered the electro-motive action produced by placing three bodies of different conducting ability in juxtaposition. By multiplying the number of these "triple units" he was able to construct his pile which could produce a shock every time a person touched (or stopped touching) the two terminal conductors thus completing or breaking a circuit. The conductors used by Volta in this case were silver and zinc discs arranged in couplets, each couplet being separated by a pasteboard disc soaked in the third conductor, saline. In another variant the "curonne de tasses", he arranged a series of non-conducting vessels each containing water or saline. A series of metallic arcs so constructed that one end was of copper or brass while the other was of tin or zinc, were immersed in the tumblers, the polarity of the arcs, as it were, being uniform in the series. The power of the electro-lytic cell had been discovered.[11]

Volta was impressed with the fact that his electro-motive force was produced without the presence of an electric as in the Leyden Jar and other devices used for producing a shock at that time. And furthermore, his pile seemed to be capable of a sort of perpetual motion; one had only to complete the circuit joining its terminals and a shock was immediately felt. This was quite unlike the other devices in current use and seemed to Volta to be much more likely to represent the mechanism by which the electric fish produced their physiological shock After all, here was a similar situation with an 'organic pile' having two different charges at either end (the surfaces of the electric organ) capable of giving shocks, to order, without the application of any other *ex vivo* agent. Volta felt that the living animal is unlikely to possess parts of an insulating nature comparable to the glass of a Leyden Jar:

> But neither the humours nor grease especially semi-fluid or entirely fluid, as it is found in living animals, can receive an electric charge in the manner of insulating plates, and retain it . . .[11]

The electric organ of the torpedo, could not, he felt, be compared to any condenser such as the Leyden Jar. He continues:

> To what electricity then, or to what instrument ought the organ of the torpedo or electric eel to be compared? To that which I have constructed according to the new principle of electricity . . .[12]

Just how much Volta believed in this analogy as an explanation of the mechanism involved in the naturally occurring production of the neuro-muscular stimulus one does not know, but certainly, by August 1792 he had demonstrated that Galvani's concept of the Leyden Jar model was untenable. In the first of his letters to Martin van Marum*, written on 30 August he recapitulates the results of his experiments to date, material which is contained in the first two of his *Mémoires* and published in Brugnatelli's *Giornale Fisico-Medico* (May, June and July editions). Referring to Galvani's experiments with an arc connecting nerve and muscle, he says:

> But having varied the experiments much more than he [Galvani] and having multiplied the researches, I have found that the above-described conditions [that is, connection between nerve and muscle] are scarcely necessary. When the nerve is exposed and prepared as above, one can limit the eruption or course of electrical fluid to two more or less neighbouring regions by means of two armatures applied to two spots on the nerve. And the dependent muscles fall into contraction equally well, and the limb twitches in the usual manner although it rests with all its muscle outside the circuit traversed by the current of electricity.[13]

Similarly in his first letter to Cavallo written in the following month (13 September 1792), Volta stresses the failure of Galvani's Leyden Jar model as an explanation of his experimental results. He describes, in some detail to his friend, how he has shown that the electrical current set in motion by the application of dissimilar metals need only pass through a small part of a nerve in order to bring about contraction of its dependent muscle. He describes an experiment in which he used the standard Galvani frog-preparation. He pinched the sciatic nerve, with forceps, a little above its insertion into the thigh and then applied a coin a few lines (12 lines = 1 inch) higher up the nerve, which having been carefully dissected, then was suspended by a thread from a plaque of sealing wax. On applying the base of a feebly charged Leyden Jar to the crushing forceps and at the same time bringing its hook into contact with the coin (thus completing a circuit which allowed the Jar to discharge *via* the nerve) he caused the frog's limb to be convulsed, by this feeble current that passed solely ". . . through a little part of the nerve,"[14] Yet another experiment wherein two coins or discs of different metals were placed either in contact or on the nerve a little distance apart and connected by a conducting arc resulted in muscular contractions, showing that the stimulus for muscular contraction requires only a circuit of electricity within a small portion of the appropriate nerve. Volta remarks:

> Now here are the same effects, convulsions and muscular movements of a most active nature, without the discharge of electric fluid between nerves and muscles as Mr Galvani supposed always occurred and without the need of the ends of a conducting arc communicating between one end and the other of them.[15]

In his second letter to Cavallo (25 October 1792), Volta goes on to show that he can produce contractions by means of a circuit of electrical fluid which passes solely through a muscle or even small pieces of excised muscle:

> (28) Experiment E. Sometimes I cut a leg with one thigh, sometimes the leg alone, sometimes a half or a quarter of the leg of a frog; and having applied as usual the tin foil to one part of the cut piece and the silver foil to another, and having brought these armatures into communication, I always obtained convulsions and movements.

From which Volta concludes that ". . . One can make no comparison between muscle and the Leyden Jar and its discharge in terms of the experiments described here."[16]

By the summer of 1792, Volta had annihilated Galvani's Leyden Jar theory. His experiments proved conclusively, that if muscular motion depends on the flow of a current of intrinsic electric fluid the electro-motive force responsible is not developed across the outside of the muscle and the inside of the nerve as his compatriot had postulated – nor indeed across any parts of the muscle and nerve considered as analogues of the various parts of a Leyden Jar. This was not, however, to deny the possibility that such a current could be produced by some other kind of electro-motive source sustained as a result of a different and as yet undiscovered feature of the internal organisation of the animal economy. Volta was convinced that in the experimental situation the electro-motive force produced by dissimilar armatures caused a current of intrinsic electricity to flow within a motor nerve and that this in turn caused the nerve to stimulate its dependent muscle in some completely unknown and probably non-electrical fashion. In the case of naturally occurring neuro-muscular activity, he was unprepared to say how the flow of intrinsic electricity was initiated. He was even convinced that it was only motor nerves supplying voluntary muscles which depend on an electrical excitation since he was unable to bring about contractions in involuntary muscles, such as the heart, by means of his dissimilar armatures. The view that the immediate stimulus to muscle is not electrical seems strange considering the results of his experiments involving their direct stimulation by means of his dissimilar armatures. He was led to this opinion as a result of experiments in which he stimulated the anterior region of the tongue which he considered as muscle devoid of motor nerves. As he produced no motion (but only a gustatory sensation) whereas on stimulating the posterior region he produced considerable motion, he came to the conclusion that a current of electricity can only act as a stimulus to nerves – in the case of the anterior portion of the tongue stimulating sensory nerves and in the case of the posterior part, motor nerves. He relied on the ancient custom of referring any motion in apparently denervated muscle to those hidden ramifications of nerves so beloved of physiologists.

Volta's experimental findings seemed to leave little if any doubt as to the origin of Galvani's frog contractions and if the concept of an organically produced electro-motive force were to survive, there was a desperate need for fresh experimental evidence to justify it, let alone a new hypothesis to explain the origin and workings of such a force in the environment of the animal body. Galvani and his followers, however, were dedicated to such a concept and so took the obvious course of trying to prove that the action of dissimilar armatures is not essential to the production of muscular contractions in a frog preparation. Furthermore, their various experimental manoeuvres were so successful that by the middle of the last decade of the 18th century, Volta was forced to modify his own concepts in order to explain their results.

The experiments carried out in defence of the concept of an intrinsic organic electro-motive force were of two types: those which showed that contractions could be produced when only one metal was put into a circuit between various parts of the nerve-muscle preparation and those which showed that this result could be achieved even without the presence of any metal at all. Galvani himself had obtained contractions when the ". . . arc, the hook, and the conducting plate are all of iron . . ."[17] But he had also added that these contractions were more often than not "insignificant" and were sometimes "completely absent". Volta's experiments had tended to push the significance of these results into the background but Galvani's protagonists took up this possibly fruitful avenue of attack on Volta as a means of disproving the necessity of dissimilar armatures in the production of contractions. By the end of 1792, this line of attack was well under way. The then current volume of Gren's *Journal der Physik* has a considerable amount of space devoted to the subject of animal electricity and refers to Galvani's experiment employing purely iron armatures and conductors. Gren remarks that following the publication of Galvani's *Commentary*, numerous experiments were carried out by Eusebio Valli* working in Paris in collaboration with Jean Claude Delamétherie* and that these experiments (demonstrated before a Committee of the Académie Royale des Sciences, especially appointed to consider the matter of Galvanism) showed conclusively that if the armatures and the conducting arc were all of the same metal, no muscular contractions could be produced.[18] Valli writing in Rozier's *Journal de Physique* (9 September 1792) describes the results of experiments in which the nerve and muscle armatures were of one and the same metal while the conducting arc was of a different metal. In this event he obtained "some sign of electricity" but had to use different armatures to get really vigorous contractions.[19] As late as September therefore, Valli was still unable to prove that Volta's contention was false.

The following month however a letter from Leopoldo Vacca Berlinghieri* to Delamétherie appeared in the *Journal de Physique*. Describing the results of certain experiments he slips in the following remark without drawing any attention to its significance:

It even suffices to bind one of the front feet of a frog with iron wire and make a communication between this wire and the crural nerves on the thighs [that is, to produce contractions].[20]

The following year however, evidence for the truth of Galvani's original belief began to pour in: 1793 may be called the year of homogeneous metals for it saw the establishment of the truth that dissimilar or heterogeneous metals are not essential in the circuit to produce contractions. In April, Berlinghieri, again writing in the *Journal de Physique*, stated quite categorically that the circuit can be completed by iron alone or ice.[21] In the same year, Valli also published his collected experimental results in book form under the title of *Experiments on Animal Electricity, with their application to Physiology and some Pathological and Medical Observations*,[22] citing crucial experiments which again seemed to show quite conclusively that heterogeneous metals are not essential to the production of contractions in a frog preparation. He was thus able to abandon the opinion he had been forced to accept only one year earlier.

That Valli was delighted to abandon this view need hardly be stressed. He was a devout protagonist of Galvani's theory, convinced that the electromotive force, responsible for producing a flow of intrinsic electricity in the frog, depends on a purely internal, organic agency. Apart from the other aspects of his book there is the interesting description of the way in which he was able to produce contractions without the intervention of dissimilar metals.

Referring to his recently abandoned view he says that since contractions are produced so readily when two metals are introduced into the circuit, one is tempted to believe that the contractions are indeed due to the agency of the metals *per se*. However, he says, when he held a prepared frog up by one foot and merely touched the spinal cord with the blade of his scissors, vigorous contractions took place, provided the frog was a lively one. If, however, the frog's foot was suspended by an insulated, silk thread, or the scissors were insulated, no contractions occurred. And furthermore, the negative results thus obtained could be reversed as soon as the insulation was removed. His prettiest experiment however consisted in hanging the frog's feet through the finger holes of his scissors and then letting the spinal cord gently come in contact with various parts of the blade. This manoeuvre readily produced contractions, although he admits they soon ceased and could be instantly revived and strengthened by the introduction of another metal in the circuit.[23]

During the period between the publication of Galvani's *Commentary* and the emergence of these experimental findings in 1793, Volta had continued his scientific correspondence, writing to various colleagues on the subject of animal electricity and always at pains to point out that the source of the electro-motive force responsible was extrinsic and due to the presence of dissimilar armatures. The publication of results which seemed to disprove his theory however, led him to modify this somewhat and in his first letter to Antonio Maria Vassali-Eandi*, written at the end of 1793 he discusses the problem. Certainly he agrees that contractions can be obtained "In the first moments (though not always)" when similar armatures are used in circuit with a well prepared and therefore highly excitable frog, "But," he goes on:

how can one be assured that the metals used are equal in all respects? They are this merely in name and substance: but the accidental qualities of hardness, temperature, smoothness and cleanness of the surface, of heat, etc., can make them considerably different with respect to the action of electricity, to the ability that is of thrusting the electric fluid in the humid body in contact with them, or attracting it, in the same way as similar differences and other circumstances do . . .[24]

Not content with this conjecture, Volta goes on to describe experiments which show that differences in temperature, lustre etc, between the two ends of a conducting arc made of one metal, will dispose the arc to act as an electro-motive force. He then adds that if Galvani is to maintain his theory of an intrinsic electro-motive force, he must prove that his metal arcs are truly homogenous – a task which he admits is very difficult if not impossible!

The question of the 'purity' or homogeneity of the metal involved was tackled by Galvani's nephew Giovanni Aldini, who carried out a number of well contrived experiments in order to combat Volta's explanation of the positive results obtained in the absence of two dissimilar metals. In 1794 he published a Latin tract entitled *Dissertationes duae*, the substance of two dissertations, the first of which was read in Bologna in 1793 and the second in 1794. Here he describes experiments carried out with carefully purified mercury. In the first of these he used two glass vases, one above the other and joined by a vertical glass tube which acted as a support for the upper one. He placed a prepared frog's crural nerve and its thigh muscle in the lower vase. When the purified mercury was allowed to run down the tube and thus come to be in contact with both the nerve and muscle, contractions occurred. Feeling that these might be due to the mechanical force of the mercury in its descent or due to electricity generated by its rubbing on the glass he designed a second experiment aimed at obviating these criticisms. For this he had made a sort of siphon, one branch of which was many times greater in diameter than the other. He placed the frog muscle in the larger of these and bent the spinal cord over so as to lie in the narrow one. On pouring mercury into the latter, he found that as the mercury rose in the larger branch and eventually reached the muscle, contractions occurred. And finally, Aldini produced contractions by simply suspending the thigh muscle in mercury and gently lowering the spinal cord so that it, too, touched the surface of the mercury.[25]

Volta refers to Aldini's publication in his second letter written to Vassali-Eandi in 1794. Far from being impressed he dismisses Aldini's interpretation of his results, attributing the contractions to the different states of the mercury touching the muscle and nerve. Once purified he says mercury exposed to the air soon loses its lustre and begins to be calcined so that the bright 'living' mercury is covered by a layer of calcined mercury. The contractions produced by Aldini must have depended on the spinal medulla having been immersed in the depth of the mercury and the leg muscle touching only its surface, so that, in fact, the two parts were in contact with mercury existing in two different states.[26]

This discussion of Aldini's work occurs in a lengthy footnote to Volta's main script. At the beginning of this footnote he refers to "another little work"[27] entitled *Dell'uso, e dell'attività dell'arco conduttore nelle contrazioni dei muscoli*. This work, published anonymously in Bologna in 1794, would seem to have been the result of the joint authorship of Galvani and his nephew, Aldini. The precise time of its publication as well as the question of its authorship has given rise to considerable discussion although it appears most probable that it came out in the middle of April. If so, we can date Volta's undated second letter to Vassali-Eandi as later than April.[27]

Volta continues his footnote by saying that the anonymous author has directed all his efforts towards sustaining Galvani's concept of an organically roused animal electricity. The bulk of the footnote is concerned with a discussion of Aldini's *Dissertationes duae* but towards the end, Volta returns to the topic of the "other little work" and its content. He says that the author has put forward some experiments which are in direct opposition to what he (Volta) has maintained, to whit: ". . . that without metals (or carbon) contractions are never produced in the frog – however it may have been prepared." He then goes on to describe the crucial experiment thus:

> The experiments put forward in opposition, to my theory, are as follows: the frog was cut in such a way that the isolated crural nerves together with a small piece of the spinal medulla were hanging freely from the thighs. When, now this half-frog was bent over so that the little portion of the spinal medulla or nerves themselves knocked against the bare thighs, all the muscles were at once convulsed. In this case there was no metal, no other conductor no armature and no arc: that is to say, the arc between nerves and muscles was formed by the nerves and muscles themselves. Therefore the electric charge and discharge exists and takes place entirely within the animal parts; therefore the electricity is inherent and is not adventitous or external.[28]

Volta's description of the experiment states quite clearly the significance of the results obtained by the 'anonymous author'. However, after repeating the experiment a number of times, he found the results so variable that he remained wedded to his conviction that there is no intrinsic electro-motive force. He remarks (as do so many other workers in this field) that the frog must be very young and excitable, that virtually any mechanical stimulus would set off contractions under these conditions and that even those produced are weak, inconstant and of short duration whereas the subsequent application of armatures brings about vigorous movement. In other words, the contractions described by the 'anonymous author' are, he believes, purely the result of mild mechanical stimulation caused by the nerve touching the muscle – a stimulus of greater force than might be assumed he suggests, due to the sudden terminal attraction of the two parts which are bathed in their natural fluids. Volta is still unconvinced and ends his letter to Vassali-Eandi by reaffirming his belief that there is no intrinsic principle which arouses animal electricity and advises his friend to, ". . . abandon these beautiful ideas suggested by the first experiment of Galvani . . ."[29] The nerves and voluntary muscles are simply new types of electrometer of an amazing sensitivity!

If, however, 1793 can be remembered as the year of homogenous metals, 1794 must certainly be remembered as the year which saw the indisputable establishment of the production of contractions without metals, homogeneous or otherwise. This year saw the belief in an organic electro-motive agency proved true. We have noted Volta's reaction to the experiment described in the 'anonymous tract'. Two months later, in June, Aldini published a letter in the *Opuscoli Scelti di Milano*, addressed to the perpetual secretary of the Societa Medisima and editor of the journal, Carlo Amoretti*. Aldini makes it quite clear that the two experiments he describes in this letter are no more than a supplement to those described in the anonymous tract saying that although they demonstrate the insignificant action of metals in the production of contractions:

> . . . *nevertheless, I was not so conceited as not to recognise that they are supplementary to those experiments in a new anonymous tract [Dell'uso, e dell'attività dell'arco conduttore nelle contrazioni dei muscoli] in which the most learned authors develops with singular industry and profound knowledge the most difficult aspects of the theory of animal electricity.*[30]

Aldini continues by saying he is pleased to select two experiments from "that same work" and goes on to describe them as follows:

> *I took a frog which was prepared by immersion in a strong salt solution until vigorous and irregular contractions of the muscles were excited: I then took it out of the water and holding it by one foot, allowed the other to hang free, the trunk with the attached nerves being now upside-down, with a fine glass rod I raised up the spinal cord in such a way that the nerves did not touch the muscle: I took away the glass rod quickly and as soon as the crural nerves and spinal cord fell against the underlying muscle, at that moment, contractions were readily excited. It is easy to remove any suspicion of an [mechanical] excitatory stimulus by applying the described spinal cord to the muscles of another frog; for that same blow, that same impulse, although procured with greater violence does not arouse any muscular motion.*[31]

The second experiment described by Aldini demonstrates the same phenomenon but interestingly Aldini says that, ". . . [it] succeeds without the precaution of any salt solution . . ."[30] Aldini does not make any reference to the significance of soaking the preparation in salt solutions, but it is obvious that he considers it as a necessary precaution in the first experiment; anyway. Volta, as we have noted, does not refer to this in his description of the experiment as it appeared in the original version, that is, in the 'anonymous tract' and as we shall see later, there is no mention of a preparatory soaking in salt solutions in the translation of the original version of this experiment by G.C. Pupilli and E. Fadiga (see following page). The question of the true significance of this point will be dealt with later in this chapter.

Aldini's reference to his experiments as a mere 'supplement' to those set forth in the anonymous tract is particularly interesting as a *Supplemento* to this work did in fact appear in 1794.[32] Again there has been controversy as to the authorship and time of appearance of the latter; most probably it was written by Aldini and Galvani, although much suggests that the experiments described were the brain child of Galvani rather than his nephew. As to the exact date of publication, there is still doubt, although it would seem that this must have been sometime between 12 June and the beginning of November.[33] Both the original tract and its supplement are extremely rare but a translation of the latter appears in *Galvani – Volta*, by Bern Dibner in a publication of the Burndy Library in 1952.[34]

The author of the *Supplemento* opens by referring to the anonymous tract:

> Never having stopped working on animal electricity and since I always tried new experiments after having published the (prior) booklet, I happened to think of trying to learn whether the reactions would be quicker and more vigorous if the animal were left with its natural skin. With this in mind, I made Signor Galvani's usual preparations but I did not peel the skin from the lower members as I had done previously following the steps of the above mentioned author when the experiments proposed in Chapter 9, p 84, was tried, but I left the skin open by a small incision . . .[35]

The original experiment described in Chapter 9, p. 84 is that referred to by Volta above. The anonymous tract, "the (prior) booklet" is, as has been noted, extremely rare (and has not been seen by the author of this book), but G.C. Pupilli and E. Fadiga quote the following description of the experiment from the primary source:

> Let a frog be prepared after the . . . [usual] way; let the crural nerves be severed near their entrance into the vertebral canal, and . . . let them be allowed to hang . . . from the tiny bone thus prepared [that is, each nerve from the bone corresponding to the ileum (sic) arranging the nerve so that it be parallel and external to the thigh]. Then let the natural parts of the thigh be touched [by the same nerves] namely, either by raising the nerves with a non-conducting body and subsequently allowing them to fall freely on the thigh, or by pressing them with the said body into a loose contact, and, if possible, only towards one point of the muscle. When the contact is thus made, contractions on both legs shall be seen to appear . . . It has to be noticed, lastly, that this phenomenon also occurs . . . when only one of the nerves is brought in contact with the corresponding thigh . . . In this case, as is apparent, contractions will be obtained on that side only. This experiment . . . is . . . crucial, in my opinion.[36]

Quite clearly then the original crucial experiment occurred in the anonymous tract itself, although other modifications of it were described in the *Supplemento*. [The author considers John Fulton's and Harvey Cushing's remarks on this point are therefore inaccurate – a fact which emerges from a study of Volta's second letter to Vassali-Eandi as well as from reference to the opening paragraph of the *Supplemento*. Talking of the controversy as to the authorship of the anonymous tract they say:

> The problem is further complicated by the fact that the description of the crucial experiment occurs not in the tract itself but in the Supplemento, on pp 5–7.[32]

And furthermore, if as seems likely, the *Supplemento* was published in the autumn, Volta's second letter to Vassali-Eandi was probably written during the summer of 1794 – between April and November.]

The author of the *Supplemento* goes on to describe experiments similar in all essentials to the one described in the anonymous tract itself, with the exception that the frog retained its skin, contact between the crural nerve and the muscle being made *via* small incisions:

> *The procedure I followed in this experiment was the following. I insulated the nerve located in the hind portion of the thigh from any other adjoining part up to the back of the knee (poplite). I then pulled it out from the thigh and I put a small and very thin glass plate near the popliteal muscle so that it would not come into contact with the muscle in the adjoining parts when I would bend it since otherwise it would disturb the promptness and precision of the experiment. Having done this I took the nerve by means of a very small and very thin glass or rosin cylinder, and I folded it on this cylinder and then I brought it in the direction of the exposed muscle. At this point I suddenly pulled the cylinder away, letting the nerve fall on the muscle. I could also have brought the nerve into contact while still supported on this glass cylinder.[35]*

The contractions are described as "very strong and lasting" whether the muscle was "struck" or "touched lightly". Having performed this experiment the author of the *Supplemento* (apparently quite accidentally) allowed the prepared crural nerve to drop on to a piece of abdominal muscle, severed from the animal, which was lying on an insulating slab. At the moment of contact between the prepared nerve and abdominal muscle contractions occurred – an event which never occurred in the case of skinless frogs. The fact that the abdominal muscle was a separate part of the frog body seems to have impressed the author greatly for in all previous experiments of this nature the circuit was formed by a nerve and its muscle in their physiological relationship, as it were. As a result of further experiments, he tells the reader, he was able to show that contractions were caused by:

> *. . . a hidden arc formed on the nerve by the above-mentioned muscle severed from the animal when the nerve is dropped on the muscle so that it comes into contact with it at various points.[35]*

In order to justify this interpretation of his results he dropped the nerve on hard insulating slabs of glass, sulphur or marble – all of which would apply a greater mechanical stimulus. In no case were contractions seen.

Finally, the *Supplemento* author describes a series of experiments by which he hopes to show conclusively, that the contractions are not the result of the difference in capacity between the nerve and the severed tissues. Briefly, the nerve was wrapped in tin foil and a silver coin laid over the muscle supplied by the nerve in question. On touching the coin with the foil-covered nerve, contractions occurred, whereas if the coin was placed over the other thigh which was completely severed from the animal, a similar procedure gave negative results. The author interprets this thus:

> *Since experience shows the complete opposite it is necessary to conclude that the contractions observed by us recently either do not originate from the difference in capacity between nerve and muscle, or if they do originate from such a difference in capacity, they are not caused by just any odd difference between every muscle and every nerve, but only by the particular and specific difference between a nerve and its*

corresponding muscle. This is impossible, as anybody can see, if there is not a natural pre-existent and pre-determined organisation and connection by which the animal electricity is naturally kept out of balance, and by which this electricity is brought to the muscle either through their mutual contact, through the artificial arc, or by any other change which may occur in the muscle and in the nerve.[37]

When Volta wrote to Vassali-Eandi in the following year, he made no specific reference to the experiments described in the *Supplemento*. His third letter to his colleague, written from Como on 27 October 1795 opens by referring to the way in which most physicists had originally adopted his opinion regarding the origin of the frog contractions, that is, that they were produced by the extrinsic electro-motive agency of dissimilar armatures. He notes however that "a ferment of contrary opinion"[38] had arisen in Italy as a result of the publication of a work by Eusebio Valli, during the previous autumn of 1794. The work referred to is a pamphlet which was published shortly before the *Supplemento*. According to Pupilli and Fadiga, this pamphlet was in fact, Valli's eleventh letter *On Animal Electricity* (the first nine of which appeared in Rozier's *Journal*, the tenth being untraced).[39] It was published in Mantova on 15 October 1794. They describe it as containing 19 original experiments which proved the possibility of exciting contractions without metals and quote from his first, third and fourth experiments:

> *I get hold of an already unsheathed frog, prepared as usual, then I apply my fingers, wetted with blood, to the crural nerves, or rather I touched them with a thigh recently removed from another frog's body. The animal of whose electricity I now become a conductor, jerks slightly and for a short time. If, as often happens, it does not jerk, then I can evoke contractions by applying to the spinal cord or nerves the tip of my tongue or my moistened lips . . .*
>
> *Sometimes the electricity has been lying dormant in the animals organs from the very beginning of the operation. It can be caused to circulate by a second application of the metal stimulator. To this end, a rusted and moistened piece of iron is more active than zinc, gold or silver, taken separately. A slight irritation or simply the gentle heat of my mouth gave me effects perfectly comparable to those of metals . . .*
>
> *After moistening nerves and muscles with saliva I have often noticed that the contractions became stronger if they had been weak, and appeared again when they had been lacking.*
>
> *Mr. Fowler had already noticed, that metals need moisture to exert their power on the nervous fluids, a power which he calls by the new name of* influence. *In my experiments, water could not successfully replace saliva.*[39]

Pupilli and Fadiga chose these particular extracts without doubt to illustrate the stress Valli places on the presence of various saline bodily fluids in the operative circuits, for it is this point which Volta picked up and used to combat Valli's argument for an intrinsic electro-motive force. Perhaps Volta chose to answer the evidence of contractions in the absence of metals by reference, almost exclusively, to Valli's experiments because it was these which allowed him to extend his concept of an external electrical force produced by dissimilar conductors. Referring to the conditions of Valli's experiments Volta says they are:

1° That the body of a frog which has been killed, skinned and completely prepared, is not clean and pure as it would be if washed in water, but on the contrary, dirty, and at least smeared in part with blood or other more or less viscous and tenuous humours: this contaminated condition of the limbs being a circumstance recorded in passing by Valli himself.[40]

If the frog-preparation is thoroughly washed in clean water, Volta continues, no contractions appear when the muscles and nerves are brought into contact. Contraction can only appear when heterogeneous conductors such as two different animal parts, *viz* muscle and nerve, are mutually in contact with a third viscous or saline conductor – such as blood, urine, etc. Such a triad of the heterogeneous conductors will not produce an electromotive force of the magnitude produced by dissimilar metals, but nevertheless is quite capable of providing the stimulus for the weaker contractions recorded in these various experiments. And as further evidence for this view, Volta refers in a footnote to the fact that the author of the 'anonymous tract' used a frog-preparation which had been kept for some time in a bath of saline, prior to experiment.[41]

By the end of 1795, Volta was still convinced that all the contractions produced in frog-preparations were the result of an electrical current produced artificially and externally by some combination of heterogeneous conductors in the presence of a third conductor, but he was having to stretch his argument considerably to draw the line between an artificial extrinsic and a potentially natural and intrinsic force, of perhaps similar origin. A lot had taken place since the original view was put forward – that dissimilar metals were the only element capable of stimulating the electricity in animal nerves. The later experiments of 1794 had forced Volta to a position of considering purely organic elements as acting in a way that was completely analogous with that of non-organic elements acting *ex-vivo*.

The divergence of opinion over the existence or non-existence of an organically aroused electricity in animals continued through the 1790's and when Galvani died in 1798 the question was still disputed. But although the two opposing views seemed so far apart and the problem so far from solution the multitude of experiments performed by so many workers during the years following the publication of the *Commentary* had given those interested in the problem a very great deal of familiarity with the conditions necessary for positive results and it was from this knowledge, acquired slowly and painstakingly that the significant facts emerged.

From what has been discussed so far, it might seem that the only problem facing the inheritors of Galvani's thesis at the end of the 18th century was that of the existence of a physiological mechanism for activating an electrical stimulus to the nerve. But if Galvani and Volta differed on this point, they and their followers did at least agree on the nature of the stimulus. However, many other workers, equally involved in the practical study of nervous action and muscular motion, were far from agreeing that the excitant was in fact electrical. This is not to say that they did not believe that animal bodies have their natural content of electrical fluid but that a flow of such fluid is the physiological antecedent to the activation of nerves supplying voluntary muscles. The basic divergence of opinion was still effectively, that which we have discussed in earlier chapters; the fundamental difference in concept still existed between the "mychanical and chymical philosophers", the former group adopting the view that the stimulus was provided by the activity of electrical particles, the latter were on the whole unconvinced of this and still open-minded as to the exact nature of the 'Galvanic fluid' and how it worked, but instinctively aware that the chemical make-up of the animal parts and the various changes taking place in them, must play a significant role in the processes underlying the normal functioning of the animal body.

It is not surprising therefore to find that many of those who were physiologists, rather than physicists, adopted a sceptical outlook and tended to deny the identity of the Galvanic fluid with electricity. *Medical Commentaries* for the relevant years provide some insight into the different views put forward at this time and indicate how much more fundamental and widespread was interest in the problem of muscular motion than that responsible for the Galvani-Volta controversy. Volume VIII,[42] covering the year 1793 contains reviews of two books dealing with animal electricity: one by Valli, the other by Richard Fowler*. The former, is of course devoted to the belief that the Galvanic fluid is electrical and the editor of the *Commentaries* gives a fair resumé of its contents reviewing the arguments put forward by Valli in defence of this belief.

At the beginning of his book Valli tells his readers that what he is trying to demonstrate is the electrical nature of the nerve-fluid (just as Galvani had done in his essay of 1782). But he points out:

> In order that electricity be in a condition for action, it must exist in two contrary states. This circumstance, presents a strong difficulty viz how is it possible that electricity can be condensed in a body, all the parts of which have the property of conducting this fluid?[43]

However, he concludes, later:

> . . . But our ignorance, with respect to the means which nature employs for the management of the electrical fluid, is not an argument against the existence of animal electricity.[44]

Valli goes on to enumerate his points of evidence, which rest (as did Galvani's) on points of analogy between the behaviour of the nervous and electrical fluids. Thus he says that substances which conduct electricity, likewise conduct the nervous fluid, and *vice-versa*. Furthermore, non-conductors which become conductors of electricity by the acquisition of heat, also become conductors of nervous fluids and cold, which destroys the conducting ability of certain substances with regard to electricity similarly affects their ability to conduct the nervous fluid. He then adds another similarity – quite without evidence – that the velocity of the nervous fluid, "as far as we can calculate"[45] is the same as that of electricity. Other similarities are quoted and Valli goes on to suggest that the muscles are a collection of electric organs or batteries.

Following this not-altogether convincing "demonstration" of the truth of his belief, Valli develops a quite interesting analogy between the way in which an animal maintains its bodily temperature and the way in which it deals with its internal electricity, suggesting that electricity is in some way concerned with the maintenance of a constant body heat. He sees electricity as a fluid universally distributed in the animal body and responsible for the control of all functions:

> *There is then in bodies, which enjoy life, a principle which regulates their temperature according to the necessity of the case. And why should there not be a principle, or force, to accumulate and condense electricity?*[46]

The apparent similarities between the electrical and nervous fluids which convinced Valli, had less success with Richard Fowler whose book, *Experiments and Observations relative to the influence lately discovered by Mr Galvani and commonly called Animal Electricity,*[47] is the second one reviewed by the editor of *Medical Commentaries.* Fowler was not at all convinced that the Galvanic and electrical fluids are identical; he was not even sure that the changes produced in the animal as a result of the application of dissimilar armatures are electrical – a further indication of how complex the whole problem was. He says, "Are the Phenomena exhibited by the application of certain different Metals to Animals referable *[sic]* to Electricity?"[48]

There certainly was no consistent evidence that animal electricity affected the most sensitive electroscopes. He uses the same type of reasoning as Valli in order to examine the question of the identity of the two fluids but comes to a different conclusion since he notes that metallic solutions and animal fluids are better conductors of animal electricity than of ordinary electricity and charcoal, dried wood and ice tend to resist the passage of Galvanic fluid more than that of ordinary electricity. Again he quotes the finding of Walsh as reported by Henry Cavendish* that ". . . the shock of the torpedo would not pass through a small brass chain – but the influence discovered by Galvani passes . . ."[49] Fowler says that he has been unable to detect any signs of electrification of the nerves and ends his argument with what he considers to be the most striking piece of evidence against the identity of the Galvanic and electrical fluids – the fact that the longer the effect of dissimilar metals is in force, the more frequent the contractions produced, whereas the prolonged application of artificial electricity produces putrefaction. He is convinced:

> . . . *that this influence, so far from destroying the contractility of muscles, has a tendency to preserve it. Oxygen is, so far as I know, the only stimulus in nature, whose effects are at all analogous.*[50]

Fowler is quite open-minded and even questions whether magnetism has any concern in the phenomenon discovered by Galvani, although he finds no evidence to support this view.

The following year 1794, *Medical Commentaries* reviewed a work by Alexander Monro* devoted to the same subject.[51] The famous Edinburgh physician and anatomist called his book *Experiments on the Nervous System with Opium and Metalline Substances, made chiefly with the view of determining the Nature and Effects of Animal Electricity.*[52] Like Fowler, Monro was far from convinced that the 'nervous juice' is electrical. The editor refers to Monro's comparison of the various similarities between the two fluids in traditional style and concludes these observations by considering:

> *. . . whether the nervous energy be, or be not, the same with the electric fluid; or with that set in motion by the contact with different metals, which from the singular effect which it shows in animal bodies, has obtained the name of Animal Electricity.*

He continues, "Dr Monro thinks it is clearly proved that the nervous fluid is by no means the same with these."[51] and goes on to give Monro's reason for his opinion.

Monro, apart from noting the difficulties of trying to explain how electricity might be contained within the nerves, refers to the fact that whereas various electrical fish have special organs adapted to its use, other animals have not been so endowed. Again, the nervous power is excited chemically or mechanically and on the other hand destroyed by opium and other poisons, which, he considers, ". . . cannot be imagined to act on the Electrical Fluid."[53] Monro is also troubled by the direction of flow of electricity and 'nerve-juice'. The nervous fluid, he says, prior to stimulation of a muscle, must pass from the main nerve, *via* smaller branches to the muscle (that is, centrifugally) whereas in the experiments quoted (by Galvani and others), the electrical fluid was flowing in the opposite direction. Therefore, he concludes, the two "differ essentially from one another". And finally:

> *5. The Nervous Energy is stopped by a tight ligature or transverse incision of a Nerve, although its divided Parts are thereafterwards placed in contact with each other; whereas the Electrical Fluid, or the Fluid excited by the Metals, passes readily, downwards or upwards, along a Nerve which has been tied or cut.*
>
> *6. After the Limb of a living Animal has been amputated, frequent Convulsions of the same Muscles may be excited by applying Mechanical or Chemical Stimuli to its Nerves, whereas Electrical Matter discharges itself suddenly.*[54]

From all this, Monro concludes that the fluid, which is set in motion by the application of different metals, is electrical or greatly resembles electricity; that this fluid does not act directly on the muscles but through the medium of the nerves, and that "3. That this Fluid and the Nervous Fluid or Energy are not the same, but differ essentially in their Nature."[55] Monro is convinced that the electrical fluid stimulated by metals merely rouses the nervous fluid and that the nature of the latter and its mode of action are quite unknown. He concludes:

> *5. That these Experiments have merely shown a new mode of exciting the Nervous Fluid or Energy without throwing any further or direct Light on the nature of this Fluid or Energy.*[55]

Another voice was that of Erasmus Darwin*, in his book, *Zoonomia or the Laws of Organic Life,*[56] he also refers to the problem of animal electricity. He did not consider that the experiments of Galvani and Volta were conclusive of the identity of electricity and the spirit of animation, and expresses his opinion thus:

> *Nevertheless in muscular contraction . . . there appears no difference in the velocity or pace of it at its commencement or its termination, from whence we must conclude that animal contraction is governed by laws of its own, and not by those of mechanics, chemistry, magnetism or electricity.*[57]

A thoroughly vitalistic outlook, quite unlike those of the various writers we have been considering!

Even Fontana was convinced that the nervous and electrical fluids are different. In a letter to Delamétherie dated November 1792, and quoted in Rozier's *Journal* the following March, the writer, M. Des Genettes, quotes Fontana as follows:

> *In a short time I will publish a work on the new principle of muscular movement, discovered in Bologna by the learned Professor Galvani, and I hope to demonstrate in a rigorous manner, that this principle has nothing in common with electricity and whatever it may be it never brings about contractions and never produces ordinary muscular movements in animals. Thus this obscure principle is reduced to a very pretty phenomenon of which the nature and workings are yet to be determined.*[58]

It would thus seem that the immediate result of Galvani's *Commentary* was to illuminate the size of the problem facing those studying the nature of the neuromuscular stimulus rather than to offer an acceptable answer. While it is probably true to say that the existence of electrical fluid in the animal body was a fairly universally accepted fact, its rôle in the production of normal animal movements was hotly debated. There were those who assumed that its activation, intrinsically (Galvani), was the necessary precursor, those who believed that it could be roused externally and quite artificially (Volta), mimicking and probably, but not necessarily, reproducing the normal process, and those who saw Volta's dissimilar armatures as a stimulus to nerves, not acting *via* intrinsic electrical fluid, but in a completely unknown way.

The man who was responsible for gathering together all these varied opinions, repeating the crucial experiments and producing an analysis of the fundamental findings, was Friedrich Alexander von Humboldt*. A German by nationality who lived for many years in Paris, his two volume work, published in 1797 under the title, *Versuche über die gereizte Muskel und Nervenfaser nebst Vermuthungen über den chemischen Process des Lebens in der Thier und Pflanzenwelt*,[59] set forth his views. The ultimate purpose is to put forward his own theory of irritability, which he is at pains to admit is mere conjecture, but as a background to this and in justification for his opinions, he marshals all the known facts relevant to the excitation of nerves and muscles and analyses their relationship from the standpoint of a physiologist. The theory may have been pure conjecture, but the experimental work, he assures us, has been carried out rigorously and repeatedly so that the evidence gained from his results is undeniable. Humboldt travelled widely in Europe, journeying alone on horseback, armed with the simple pieces of apparatus necessary to carry

out Galvani's experiments and had long hours of solitude in which to pon-
der their results.

In his introduction, he gives his reader a clue as to the direction his ideas
have taken. He says that he has been occupied for several years comparing
many phenomena in living and dead animals and that, ". . . this work has
led to experiments which seem to give a hint as to the nature of the chemical
process of life."[60] This suggestion that he is going to be interested in the
chemical background to irritability is soon elaborated and in the first chapter, where Humboldt is discussing irritability resulting from metallic stimulation, he draws attention to the importance of the state of the animal as well
as the nature of the metallic stimulating agents, in the production of any
physiological response. He says:

> If Galvanism consists of an irritation, it is evident, in the terms of the most basic physi-
> ological notions, that the success of experiments depends as much on the incitability
> and excitability of the organs as on the force of the stimulating cause. It would seem
> that nobody, so far, has paid attention to this factor: one has sought to determine the
> force of different armatures and to distinguish conducting from insulating materials;
> but one has neglected to modify the excitability of the organs employed in exper-
> iments. I have applied myself to the repair of this omission; and in setting myself this
> goal, I have been led to observations which forcefully contradict accepted views on
> metallic irritation.[61]

The variability of the results obtained by different workers carrying out
experiments on neuro-muscular excitation is one of the most striking and
constant features to be noted. Galvani himself remarked on this as did Volta,
Valli and nearly all the others, although generally their observations did not
go further than to note that fresh, young female, frogs during early summer
were most likely to give positive results. As Humboldt quite justifiably remarks, nobody had apparently given thought to the possible reasons for this
or to have devoted any time to a consideration of how this might help in
the understanding of the mechanics underlying the nature of the Galvanic
phenomenon. Humboldt makes the crucial, if obvious, observation that a
mechanical stimulus can take place without any resulting contractions, ". . .
their absence being a result of the inexcitability of the organs."[62] He notes
the fundamental fact that given precisely the same experimental situation as
regards the stimulus (silver and zinc armatures in series with six morsels of
fresh muscle in a conducting arc joining nerve and muscle), contractions fail
to occur in the majority of animals and only after some time in very lively
ones. He therefore goes on to vary the factor "lively" or "not-lively" in various
ways, the exciting stimulus being maintained constant. For instance he discovers that the muscles of frogs which have given up contracting can be
made to contract again by the simple manoeuvre of placing fresh muscle on
the nerve. And again, exhausted fibres regain their sensibility after a period
of rest. Precisely the same sort of thing happens too when the crural nerve of
a mouse, which is no longer capable of responding to a stimulus, is plunged
into an "alkaline solution" or into "oxygenated muriatic acid" and then
chlorine. Humboldt remarks that:

The contraction of the thigh in this case was so strong that the nerve burst asunder from the zinc with which it was armed as soon as the silver forceps supported by an insulator was put in contact with the muscular tissue.[63]

and concludes that:

. . . this makes it evident that the augmentation of incitability can give rise to effects which do not exist at all in circumstances which appear identical.[63]

In fact, Humboldt discovers that he can at will, enhance or diminish the excitability of organs by the direct application of various chemical substances, for example, he can mimic the effect of a very strong stimulus which exhausts a nerve, by plunging the parts in a warm solution of arsenic. Also, ordinary acids painted on nerves diminish their activity and can make an animal tissue pass in seconds from a state of high excitability to the ultimate degree of feebleness. As a result of these findings, he classifies the conditions under which contractions can be produced by Galvanic stimulation into two states: that of excitability which is exalted either naturally or unnaturally and that of diminished excitability – states to which he regrets he cannot assign precise limits, he says for much the same reasons as one cannot always define precisely the temperature at which chemical reactions take place – although it is evident that a rise in temperature makes them possible.

Having established the importance of the chemical state of the reacting organs, Humboldt proceeds to deal with the condition of "exalted excitability" where the conductors are formed solely of animal parts. This discussion which forms the content of his important second chapter deals, as would be expected, with the various experiments without metals described above. He goes on to describe a number of these he himself has carried out and establishes beyond doubt that if a circuit is completed *via* purely animal parts either (a) between a muscle and its nerve or (b) parts of the nerve, contraction can be produced in the muscle involved, provided the excitability of the tissues is adequate. His experiments are briefly as follows:

1. The thigh of a naturally highly excitable frog was separated, its crural nerve quickly dissected and the nerve-muscle preparation laid on a dry glass plate. Humboldt held a sealing wax rod in one hand, the end of which supported a piece of fresh muscle. On touching both the crural nerve and its muscle at the same instant, with the morsel of fresh flesh, strong contractions appeared. In order to overcome Volta's objection that a mechanical effect was involved, the experiment was repeated, substituting dry wood, horn or bone for the morsel of flesh, with negative results.

2. Humboldt then turned to the second thigh which he had put aside for about a quarter of an hour during the previous experiment. Despite the fact that its crural nerve was so insensitive that it had to be strongly pinched with forceps in order to stimulate it, Humboldt found he could repeat the first experiment using the morsel of flesh and produce contractions easily. The experiment was repeated on various other

species and when, as sometimes happened he had a negative result, contractions could be produced by merely plunging the nerves, whose natural degree of excitability was inadequate, into an "alkaline solution", whereupon their excitability was restored.

3. A piece was cut off the terminal end of the crural nerve of several animals and this separated segment laid (by means of a glass rod) so as to touch at the same instant the nerve and muscle. This manoeuvre resulted in strong contractions which, as Humboldt points out, destroyed Volta's supposition that a disturbance of electrical equilibrium can only occur between three substances of a different nature, there being only two (nerve and muscle) present in this case.

4. The crural nerve was held gently in one hand and touched in two places with a morsel of fresh muscle held in the other hand. At once, very brisk contractions occurred, more marked when the nerve was touched near its insertion into the muscle. In order to be assured the result was not due to a mechanical effect, Humboldt again replaced the flesh with dry wood, then horn, etc, obtaining in these cases negative results.

Humboldt's experiments established beyond doubt that Volta's objections to Galvani's thesis were unfounded in the ultimate instance: the extrinsic electro-motive agent of 'dissimilar armatures' had certainly played its part in the production of contractions in certain situations but it was by now obvious that this was not the whole story. We have seen how a number of writers were unconvinced that an intrinsic electro-motive agency producing an internal current is the essential stimulus to motor nerves and Humboldt, as a result of his discovery of the crucial influence of chemicals on the excitability of nerves was quite certain that the stimulus arises as a result of chemical changes within the animal parts. With hindsight we can look back at the strivings of these 18th century reductionists with sympathy. Chemical and electrical phenomena were still considered quite unrelated: the concept of physical chemistry was still in the future and men with the outlook of Volta or Humboldt were tackling a physico-chemical problem from two equally valid viewpoints. The 'chymical' and 'mychanical' philosophers were closer than they could possibly know in their time. Humboldt's ideas seem particularly exciting because he adopted a biochemical philosophy to explain the physical changes underlying the maintenance of excitability in animal nerves, a philosophical concept which was to wait nearly a century for verification at the hands of Walther Nernst*.

In the review of Volume II of Humboldt's book, which appeared in the *Annals of Medicine*,[64] the editors refer to the author's observations on the effects of various chemical substances on the excitability of nerves, particularly to the stimulating effect of alkalis, remarking that if weakly excitable tissues are immersed in such a solution, within four or five minutes:

> . . . *the excitability will be so great, that they will contract on the application of homogenous metals.*[64]

Such an increase in excitability however, can be depressed by opium and restored again by oxide of arsenic, findings which led the author to ask:

> Is it not therefore highly probable that the property of matter to be affected by stimuli depends upon its composition and that everything altering this modifies its excitability.[64]

The editors quote Humboldt's view that ". . . excitability in its most intensive form implies the capability of being changed by external impressions,"[65] and goes on to suggest that inorganic matter undergoing a chemical change may be considered as excitable. However, if a substance such as muriate of tin is changed by the oxygen of the atmosphere:

> . . . it forever afterwards remains insensible to the operation of the same substance while the living animal and vegetable fibre after being excited by any stimulus may be again repeatedly excited by the same stimulus after short intervals. This difference is ascribed by Mr Humboldt to a power in organic matter to retain itself excitable. On this power animal and vegetable life depend; to it we are led by all the vital chemical processes; and it is to be considered as the most important object of physiological enquiry.[65]

Humboldt saw 'excitability' as a state comparable to the vulnerability of matter to the corrosive action of alkaline substances whereas 'excitation' was a state of 'destroyed excitability' or 'exhaustion' and he believed that continuing life implies an ability to counteract the results of excitability. Life depends on a constant interchange of chemicals, reactions in one direction being followed by those in the opposite direction which tend to restore the situation and so forth:

> What is taken in at one moment is given out at the next; and it is solely owing to this opposition that living matter retains its form and mixtures.[66]

In general, Humboldt's insistence that the alternating states of 'excitability' and 'excitation' which characterise animal life are dependent on reciprocally balanced chemical reactions, foreshadowed the way of thinking expressed by Claude Bernard* in his concept of the maintenance of the "milieu intérieur". In more specific terms, his observations on the significance of the chemical state of nerves and muscles in relation to their excitability foreshadowed present day electro-chemical theories of neuro-muscular excitation although the intimate relationship between the chemical and electrical states of tissues in their excitable and excited states was not crystallised until the late 19th century when Nernst enunciated his laws of thermodynamics. Thus the 'chymical philosophers' saw the road ahead earlier than their 'mychanical' colleagues.

After the publication of Humboldt's book there could have been little doubt that if the initiation of neuro-muscular activity is due to electrical changes, the electro-motive agent is intrinsic. The demonstration of electrical currents in nerves, however, had proved extremely difficult for the 18th century experimenters. Many attempts were made, but the results were always suspect, for their recording instruments were simply not accurate enough. Early in the 19th century, a great advance took place when this difficulty was overcome. The discovery in 1820 by Hans Christian Oersted* that a magnetic needle can be deflected by Galvanic currents and the subsequent development of galvanometers proved one of the most important discoveries for electro-physiology. Using an astatic modification of this instrument, the Italian physiologist Leopoldo Nobili* was at first unsuccessful in his attempts to detect electrical currents in nerves but on repeating the old experiment of putting the feet of a frog in one jar of saline and the spinal cord in another and joining the two solutions by means of a conductor such as moist asbestos or cotton, he obtained deflections when his instrument was included in the circuit. He called this current "la corrente propria della rana [the intrinsic frog current]".[67] Nobili's demonstration was of immense significance because it was the starting point for the researches of such workers as Carlo Matteucci* and Emil Du Bois Reymond. The latter, in particular, recognised his debt to the Italian physiologist when developing a theory to account for the existence of such a potential as a constant property of living muscles and nerves during their resting state, and that the electrical changes immediately associated with excitation involve a change in this potential difference. The frog current is the key to the understanding of the results obtained by Galvani and others in the various experiments without metals and for this reason a very brief resumé of the events leading to our present day explanation of these phenomena seems in place.

The most salient feature of this current noted by Nobili is that it is constant. It is manifested as soon as the circuit is completed and the galvanometer shows a deflexion for up to several hours. The frog limbs twitch at the moment of completing or breaking the circuit, but after such muscular contractions are completed, the reading on the galvanometer continues to record a constant deflection. Further analysis of the frog current by Du Bois Reymond during the mid-19th century showed that its origin is in a potential existing between the longitudinal (natural or undissected) surface and the transverse, cut surface of muscles (and nerves).[68] The Swiss physiologist was convinced that this potential exists as a result of a particular internal arrangement of individual units of these tissues which he termed "electromotive molecules", the electrical state of resting muscle or nerve depending, as he postulated, on the fact that the negative poles of these units lie in palisade arrangement along any 'artificial' or cut transverse sections while their positive poles lie along the 'natural' surface.[69]

Du Bois Reymond accumulated a considerable amount of experimental data regarding the electrical behaviour of nerves and muscles, one of his most important discoveries being that if a circuit is completed between the 'natural' and 'artificial' surfaces of nerve or muscle and the intrinsic, constant current noted on a galvanometer, subsequent stimulation of the nerve (or muscle) results in a momentary decrease in the galvanometer reading.

This 'negative variation'[70] as he called it, occurs momentarily at the instant the stimulus is applied and again, momentarily, as it is removed, and in the case of muscle, is accompanied by a contraction of the latter. Du Bois Reymond developed his theory further to account for the electrical changes associated with the negative variation, accounting for the varying electrical states of muscle and nerve during the resting and active phases by suggesting that excitation set in motion electrolytic changes during which the electro-motive molecules swing on their axis, altering their relative positions.[71] He developed his theory quite naturally in the context of contemporary physical models, convinced that some internal arrangement of tissues must exist since he considered it inconceivable that a charged particle or unit could move freely within them. He was a devout admirer of Michael Faraday and modelling his ideas on those of the Englishman, described an "electronic state" of excitable tissues as analogous to the electronic state of metals – giving rise to a term that came into common use among physiologists.[71]

Du Bois Reymond's theories have passed into oblivion, their remaining interest being their indication of the ingenious way in which a physiologist could attempt to explain organic events in terms of the physical models available to him. His recognition of the significance of the difference of potential between the longitudinal and transverse surfaces of muscles and nerves was more correctly the difference between 'natural' and 'artificial' or 'uninjured' and 'injured' regions. Today, as a result of the work of such men as Wilhelm Ostwald* and Walther Nernst, we know that charged particles do move across cells and that electric potential differences occur at boundaries such as the differentially permeable cell membrane which separates electrolyte solutions containing ions of different mobility and concentration.

In 1902, Julius Bernstein* proposed a 'membrane theory' which applied the physico-chemical concepts of Nernst to the problem of neuro-excitation and it is from modifications of this basic model that present day ideas have developed. Many of the advances in this field are relatively recent and due to the study of the giant squid axons which are easier to work with than the smaller nerves of other species: Bernard Katz*, Andrew Huxley* and Alan Hodgkin* having carried out particularly fruitful researches in this field.

Briefly, the nerve cell membrane can be considered as a differentially permeable membrane separating two electrolyte solutions: the external solution (tissue fluid) and the internal, aqueous protein gel of which the cytoplasm consists. In the normal intact state, there is a marked difference in the concentration of the important ions in these two electrolyte solutions, potassium being at a relatively higher concentration within the cell while sodium and chloride ions are relatively in much greater concentration without. In the resting state, the osmotic and electrical forces are such that a potential difference exists across the cell membrane, the inside of the cell being around minus 90 millivolts with respect to the outside. Hence if a circuit is made artificially between the inside and outside of the cell a current will flow. This current can be demonstrated in the laboratory by simply injuring or dividing a nerve at some point (A) and then connecting this point to another undamaged part of the nerve surface (B) *via* a galvanometer, when a constant deflexion will result, indicating a current flowing through the nerve from A to B. This current of injury is in fact, Nobili's intrinsic frog current. If this experiment is carried out on a muscle-nerve preparation, there will be a twitch at the moment of making and breaking the circuit indicating that the current of injury is acting, in this quite artificial situation, as an auto-stimulus to the nerve and thence bringing about contraction of the muscle. The stimulus in this case, is acting at point B, where the current is passing outwards across the membrane. If a direct current (of any external origin) is made to pass in this direction across a nerve membrane, the potential of minus 70 millivolts is reduced and if the stimulus is adequate, the polarity of the membrane becomes temporarily reversed the inside becoming about 40 millivolts positive with respect to the outside. The production of this 'action potential' is the electrical event we identify as excitation of the nerve, the electro-chemical events following upon it, leading to the transfer of the stimulus to the muscle, which in turn responds by contraction. The production of the action potential, which Du Bois Reymond recognised as the "negative variation" can of course be brought about by other external mechanical agents apart from electricity. The common factor would appear to be their ability to depolarise the membrane by means of a transitory injury which momentarily impairs the membrane's permeability properties without inducing the permanent changes responsible for the injury current. In order to maintain the normal internal resting potential of minus 70 millivolts, the cell expends energy pumping sodium ions outwards against their pressure gradient and the electrical potential. The initiation of excitation would appear to be associated with a temporary breakdown in this activity whereby sodium ions enter the nerve cell in increasing numbers, a process which is auto-accelerating as a result of the fact that the conductance of sodium increases as the resting potential is lowered. Once the action potential is reached, the membrane potential is brought to the resting state once more by the influx of potassium ions, the sodium passing outwards to restore the electro-chemical *status quo*.

The source of the electro-motive force responsible for the excitation of contractions in the various 'experiments without metals' was then the artificially circuited 'current of injury', that is, the current produced by the electric potential existing across the nerve-cell membrane. The variability in the results obtained by Galvani and the Galvanists was usually put down to variability in the freshness or excitability of the frogs and it has been noted how often this fact is referred to by workers. This is of considerable importance but even so it would be surprising that positive results were achieved with such apparent ease, in certain experiments anyway, unless one considers the possibility that the excitability of the tissues involved was heightened so as to facilitate the action of the current of injury. Humboldt says he was the first to draw attention to the effect of chemicals on the excitability of animal tissues but it is quite obvious that other workers had become aware of this and that the role of such chemicals must be considered in the explanation of certain of the results obtained.

It will be clear from the electro-chemical considerations described above, that the excitation process is susceptible to modification as a result of an alteration of the concentrations of such important ions as potassium and sodium (among others) in the fluid surrounding the nerve cell. Humboldt discovered this as a result of observation, but it was not until 1908 that the subject was taken up and analysed in any depth. In that year George Mines* wrote a paper which appeared in the *Journal of Physiology* describing the spontaneous movements which occur when amphibian muscles are placed in various solutions.[72] He refers to an experiment described by Ewald Hering* in 1879. The German physiologist had immersed a frog's sartorius muscle in a solution of sodium chloride and noted that it exhibited rhythmic contractions. Hering regarded the saline solution as a liquid conductor which, by closing the circuit, caused stimulation of the muscle by its injury current.[73] Further analysis of the effects of solutions by such workers as Biedermann*,[74] Sydney Ringer*,[75] and Frank Locke*,[76] however, indicated their specific action. Mines makes it clear that, ". . . the muscle in sodium chloride solution is particularly susceptible to the influence of weak constant currents . . ."[77] a fact noted previously by Ringer who had been unable to produce contractions in uninjured muscles (in saline) unless he also stimulated them with a weak current. Similarly, Mines drew attention to the effect of potassium salts which cause an initial increase in excitability followed by a depression.[78]

In a relevant paper by Edgar Douglas Adrian* and S. Gelfan, published in the *Journal of Physiology* in 1933,[79] the authors draw attention to this heightened excitability of nerves and muscles in saline solution and the way in which bathing in this solution makes adequate a weak direct current which would otherwise be an inadequate stimulus. They say:

> *Thus in NaCl there is a much less rapid adaptation to an electric stimulus; as a result a weak constant current might produce a continued excitation and a repeated discharge of impulses. Potential gradients due to inequalities in the surface of the fibre might form a necessary stimulus. But eventually a stimulus of this kind might be unnecessary, for if there is normally an equilibrium between a reaction tending to produce the state of excitation and one tending to counteract it, a failure of the latter would be enough to start a discharge.*[79]

Adrian and Gelfan then turn to the question of stimuli, other than the direct current which will just set off rhythmic contractions in muscles the excitability of which has been heightened by immersion in saline, paying particular attention to stretch, which they consider a minor form of injury. It will be recalled that Aldini's description of an experiment, published in a letter to Amoretti, runs as follows:

> *I take a frog which had been prepared by immersion in a strong solution of salt* until vigorous and irregular contractions of the muscles were excited.[80]

In the English and French editions of Aldini's book *An Account of the late improvements in Galvanism . . .* (1803).[80] The description of this experiment does not refer to the fact that spontaneous contractions were actually produced although the immersion in saline was mentioned: "I immersed a prepared frog in a strong solution of muriate of soda. I then took it from the solution . . ."[81] However in both editions of his book he gives the following description of a variant of this experiment in which he says, "in preparing this experiment in public I obtained several times more than two hundred successive contractions . . ."[82] and elsewhere he describes the contractions as forming "a real electro-animal alarm . . ."[83]

It will be recalled that in this experiment the frog is suspended from his hand by one leg – a situation providing quite enough stretch to trigger off the spontaneous movements occasioned by the treatment with strong salt solution.

One is tempted to the conclusion that, as in these experiments, preparation of the specimen by immersion in strong salt solution was a common occurrence – Aldini certainly seems to have appreciated its value. When one considers the small quantity of injury current necessary for producing positive results in some of these experiments, it is difficult to believe that the muscular contractions which these early Galvanists produced were not due in great part to the ionic content of the strong salt solutions in which they prepared their frog tissues. Indeed, in a highly excitable salt preparation, the merest mechanical pressure of bringing the nerve to the muscle, would result in excitation. Again, in other experiments where two points of the nerve were brought in contact with two separate parts of a muscle – one of which was injured and the other not – the much greater source of potential could more easily and readily result in depolarisation and excitation. If in fact, the specimens used by these various workers were frequently prepared by immersion in saline, it would make the frequent success of their results easier to understand!

Nevertheless, the Galvanists came to the right conclusion. Galvani's concept of an intrinsic electro-motive agency responsible for the excitation of muscular motion has been proved correct. The 'mychanical philosophers' in their way were right as were the 'chymists'. Humboldt's inspired insight into the constantly changing chemical balance which occurs in excitable tissues was certainly very near the truth.

[This book was written to tell the story of man's philosophical and experimental exploration of the matter of motion. It is obvious that while our knowledge of the nature and transmission of the nervous impulse and the way in which muscles contract to produce movement, has advanced greatly even since this book was written, we still have a long way to go to understand the function of the brain as the central focus in the initiation of movement. But that will be for someone else to analyse

As for Galvani himself the *Biographical Dictionary of Scientists*[84] says:

At the setting up of the Trans[Cis]alpine Republic in 1797 Galvani refused to swear an oath of allegiance and was dismissed from his office. He died in the following year, overcome by domestic bereavement aggravated by poverty and criticism of his views.

Volta was also dismissed from his post in 1799 for political reasons, went to Paris, met Napoleon and when the French took over Northern Italy he was reinstated at Pavia as Rector. Ed.]

Notes

1 Williams, L. Pearce (1965) *Michael Faraday*, London, Chapman and Hall, p. 56
2 See Chap. 10 of this book

3 Cohen, I. Bernard (ed.) (1941) *Benjamin Franklin's Experiments, A new edition of Franklin's experiments and Observations on Electricity*, Cambridge, Mass., Harvard University Press, p. 214

4 See *Le Opere di Alessandro Volta*, edizione nationale Milano, Ulrico Hoepli Editore – Librario dell Real Casa, 1918, p. 174. This reference occurs in Volta's first letter to Tiberius Cavallo, written on 13 September 1792, p. 121

5 Ibid., p. 175

6 See Chap. 20, Note 20

7 Sarton, George (1931) 'The Discovery of The Electric Cell', *Isis*, Vol. 15, p. 124

8 Loc. cit., Note 4, p. 3

9 Ibid., p. 39

10 Volta, Alessandro (1800) 'On the electricity excited by the mere Contact of conducting Substances of different kinds.' In a letter from Mr Alexander Volta FRS, Professor of Natural Philosophy in the University of Pavia to the Right Hon. Sir Joseph Banks, Bart., PRS. Read 26 June 1800. *Philosophical Transactions*, Part II, pp 403–431

11 Ibid., p. 430 and *Philosophical Magazine*, Vol. VII, p. 311

12 Ibid., p. 63 and *Philosophical Magazine*, Vol. VII, p. 312

13 Loc. cit., Note 4, p. 122

14 Ibid., p. 181

15 Ibid., p. 182

16 Ibid., p. 188

17 Galvani, Luigi (1953) *Commentary on the effects of electricity on muscular motion*, N.G. Foley (transl.), I. Bernard Cohen (ed.), Norwalk, Conn., Burndy Library, p. 61

18 Gren, Franz Albrecht Carl (ed.) (1792) *Journal der Physik*, Leipzig, J.A. Barth; Sechste Band, p. 378 *et seq.*

19 *Observations et Mémoires sur les arts et métiers, au bureau du Journal de Physique*, Paris, Joseph de Boffe, September 1792, Tom. 41, Part II, p. 185

20 Ibid., October 1792, p. 315

21 Ibid., April 1793, Tom. 42, Part I, p. 289

22 Valli, Eusebio (1793) *Experiments on Animal Electricity, with their application to Physiology and some Pathological and Medical Observations*, London, J. Johnson

23 Ibid., p. 38 *et seq.*

24 Loc. cit., Note 4, p. 264

25 Aldini, Giovanni (1794) *De Animali electricitatis, Dissertationes duae*, Bologna. Ex Tipographia, Instituti Scientiarum. Although English and French editions of this work appeared in 1803 and 1804 respectively, these, like the original Latin version, are extremely rare. However, Aldini's book, *Essai théorique et experimental sur le Galvanisme avec une série d'expériences faites en présence de commissaires de l'Institut Naturel de France, et en divers amphitheatres anatomiques de Londres*, Paris de l'Imprimerie de Fournier Fils, 1804, contains the first and part of the second dissertation. The experiments described appear in *Mémoire VI* (First Dissertation, entitled 'Concernant l'influence des metaux sur l'électricité animale', read at a public meeting of the Academy of the Institute of Science at Bologna. See paras, vi, p. 285; vii, p. 286 and viii, p. 287. For Bibliographical material see John F. Fulton and Harvey Cushing, 'A Bibliographical study of the Galvani and the Aldini writings on animal electricity', *Annals of Science*, 1936, Vol. I, No. 3, pp 259–260

26 Loc. cit. Note 4, p. 276

27 *Dell'uso, e dell'attività dell'arco conduttore nelle contrazioni dei muscoli*, Bologna, A.S. Tommaso d'Aquino 1794. See also *Memorie ed Esperimenti Inediti di Luigi Galvani con la iconografia di lui e un saggio di bibliografia degli scritti . . .*, Bologna, Licinio Cappelli Editore, 1937, xv, pp 473–475

28 Loc. cit., Note 4, p. 280

29 Ibid., p. 281

30 Aldini, Giovanni (1794) 'Memoria inforno al elettricita animale', *Opuscoli Scelti di Milano*, Vol. 17, p. 232

31 Ibid., pp 39 and 232

32 Fulton, John F. and Cushing, Harvey (1936) 'A Bibliographical study of the Galvani and the Aldini writings on animal electricity', *Annals of Science*, Vol. I, pp 239–268. See p. 261

33 See *Memorie ed Esperimenti inediti di Luigi Galvani con la iconografia di lui e un saggio di bibliografia degli scritti* . . . Bologna, Licinio Cappelli Editore, 1937. pp 473–475

34 Dibner, Bern (1952) *Galvani – Volta, A Controversy that led to the Discovery of Useful Electricity*, Norwalk, Conn. Burndy Library, pp 50–51

35 Ibid., p. 50

36 Pupilli G.C. and Fadiga E. (1963) 'The origins of electrophysiology,' *Journal of World History*, VII/2, p. 568

37 Loc. cit., Note 34, p. 51

38 Loc. cit., Note 4, p. 289

39 Loc. cit., Note 36, p. 570

40 Loc. cit., Note 4, p. 294

41 Ibid., p. 295

42 *Medical Commentaries for the year 1793 exhibiting a concise view of the latest and most important discoveries in medicine and medical philosophy*. Collected and published by Andrew Duncan, London, G.G. and J. Robinson, Edinburgh, Peter Hall, 1794, Decade II, Vol. VIII

43 Loc. cit., Note 22, p. ix

44 Ibid., p. xiv

45 Ibid., p. 112

46 Ibid., p. 126. See also p. 147

47 Fowler, Richard (1793) *Experiments and Observations relative to the influence lately discovered by Mr Galvani and commonly called Animal Electricity*, Edinburgh, printed for T. Duncan, P. Hill, Roverston and Berry and G. Mudie, and J. Johnson, London

48 Ibid., p. 1

49 Ibid., p. 46

50 Ibid., p. 53

51 *Medical Commentaries for the year 1794* . . ., Collected and published by Andrew Duncan, London, G.G. and J. Robinson and J. Johnson, G. Mudie, Edinburgh, 1795, Decade II, Vol. IX, p. 47

52 Monro, Alexander (1793) *Experiments on the Nervous System with Opium and Metalline Substances, made chiefly with the view of determining the Nature and Effects of Animal Electricity*, Edinburgh, Printed by Adam Neil and Co., for Bell and Bradfute, and T. Duncan; and J. Johnson, London

53 Ibid., p. 41

54 Ibid., p. 42

55 Ibid., p. 43

56 Darwin, Erasmus (1794) *Zoonomia or the Laws of Organic Life*, London, Printed for J. Johnson

57 Ibid., p. 64

58 Fontana is quoted in a letter entitled 'Sur l'électricité animal' written by M. Des Genettes to Delamétherie which appeared in *Observations et Mémoires sur la physique, sur l'histoire naturelle et sur les arts et métiers, au Bureau du Journal de Physique*, Paris, Joseph de Boffe, March, 1793, Tom. 42, pt I, p. 238. See also Tiberius Cavallo, *A complete Treatise on Electricity in Theory and Practice with original experiments*, Vol. III, London, E. and C. Dilly, 1777, p. 303

59 (i) Humboldt, Friedrich (1797) *Versuche über die gereizte Muskel und Nervenfaser nebst Vermuthungen über den chemischen Process des Lebens in der Thier und Pflanzenwelt*. Posen, Decker und Compagnie
(ii) See also a French edition of Vol. I entitled, *Expériences sur le Galvanisme et en general sur l'excitation des fibres musculaires et nerveuses*, transl. from the German by J. Fr. N. Jadelot, Paris, Didot Jeune, 1799

60 Ibid., (ii), p. I

61 Ibid., p. 19

62 Ibid., p. 20

63 Ibid., p. 21

64 *Annals of Medicine for the year 1799 exhibiting a concise view of the latest and most important discoveries in Medicine and medical philosophy* by Andrew Duncan Senior MD
and Andrew Duncan Jnr, MD, Edinburgh; J. Pillans and Sons, London, W. Mudie,
G.G. and J. Robinson, 1800, Vol. IV, p. 222

65 Ibid., p. 224

66 Ibid., p. 225

67 *Annales de Chimie et de Physique*, July 1822, Tom. 38, p. 225. See also E. Du Bois
Reymond, *Untersuchungen Uber Thierische Electricitat*, Berlin, Reymer, 1848–1884,
2 Vols, Vol. I, p. 103 *et seq.*

68 Bence-Jones H. (1852) *On Animal Electricity being an abstract of the discoveries of Emil Du
Bois Reymond*, London, Churchill, p. 90. This volume is an excellent synopsis, in
English, of the monumental *Untersuchungen . . .*, of the Swiss physiologist

69 Ibid., p. 109

70 Ibid., See p. 130 *et seq.*

71 Ibid., Chap. XXV, pp 174–186

72 Mines G.R. (1908) 'On the spontaneous movements of amphibian skeletal muscle in
saline solutions, with observations on the influence of potassium and calcium chlor-
ides on muscular excitability', *Journal of Physiology*, Vol. 37, pp 408–443

73 Ibid., p. 408. See also, E. Hering 'Beiträge zur allgemeinen Nerven- und Muskel-
physiologie', *Situngsberichte der Mathematisch-naturwissenschaftlichen Classe der Kaiser-
lichen Akademie der Wissenchaften*, Wien, 1879, Vol. 79, Abteilung III, pp 7–32. See 'I,
Zuckung des Muskels in Folge plötzlichen Neben-Schliessung seines Stromes durch
eine leitende Flussigkeit', p. 8

74 Biedermann W. (1880) 'Beiträge zur allgemeinen Nerven- und Muskel-physiologie',
Vol. 81, Abteilung III, pp 74–114. See 'Über die Abhangigkeit des Muskelstromes
von localen chemischen Veränderungen der Muskelsubstanz', pp 74–75 and,
W. Biedermann, *Electrophysiologie*, F.A. Welby (transl.), London, MacMillan, 1896–1898,
Vol. I, p. 221 (A translation of *Electrophysiologie*, Jena, Gustav Fischer, 1895)

75 Ringer S. (1886) 'Further experiments regarding the influence of small quantities
of lime, potassium and other salts on muscular tissue', *Journal of Physiology*, Vol. 7,
pp 2291–2308 and Ringer S. (1887) 'Regarding the action of lime, potassium and
sodium salts on skeletal muscle', *Journal of Physiology*, Vol. 8, pp 20–24

76 Locke F.S. (1893) 'Die Wirkung der physiolischen Kochsalzlosung auf quergestreifte
Musclen', *Pflugers Archives*, Vol. 54, pp 501–524 and, Locke F.S. (1896) 'Of the action of
ether on contracture and of positive Kathodic polarization of vertebrate voluntary
muscle', *Journal of Experimental Medicine*, Vol. I, pp 630–655

77 Loc. cit., Note 72, p. 417

78 Ibid., p. 433 *et seq.*

79 Adrian E.D. and Gelfan S. (1933) 'Rhythmic activity in skeletal muscle fibres', *Journal
of Physiology*, Vol. 78, pp 271–287, See p. 273

80 Aldini, Giovanni (1803) *An Account of the late improvements in Galvanism . . .*, London,
Cuthell, Martin and Murray. See also, Note 25 for details of the French edition

81 Ibid., p. 17

82 Ibid., p. 15

83 Ibid., p. 14

84 Williams, Trevor I. (ed.) (1994) *Biographical Dictionary of Scientists*, Glasgow, Harper
Collins

* See Biographical Index

APPENDICES

BIRTH ORDER OF INDIVIDUALS IN THE TEXT

624BC	Thales	1660	Sloane	1725	Petrini
610BC	Anaximander		Stahl		Walsh
600BC	Xenophanes	1663	Amontons	1728	Black
570BC	Anaximenes	1666	Cowper		Zimmerman
540BC	Heraclitus		Gray	1729	Spallanzani
500BC	Anaxagoras		Valsalva	1730	Fontana
	Parmenides	1667	Bernoulli	1731	Cavendish
493BC	Empedocles	1668	Boerhaave		Darwin E.
470BC	Socrates	1671	Lahire	1732	Berlinghieri
460BC	Democritus	1672	Geoffroy		Wilcke
450BC	Leucippus	1673	Kiell	1733	Monro
428BC	Plato		Stuart		Priestley
384BC	Aristotle	1674	Bazzani	1737	**Galvani L.**
341BC	Epicurus	1677	Lemery		Higgins
304BC	Erasistratus	1680	Robinson	1741	Amoretti
300BC	Euclid	1682	Beccari	1743	Banks
106BC	Cicero		Manfredi		Irvine
99BC	Lucretius	1683	Desaguliers		Lavoisier
46	Plutarch		Réamur	1747	Volta
129	Galen	1686	Galeazzi	1748	Crawford
205	Plotinus	1687	Schultze	1749	Cavallo
1175	Grosseteste	1689	Tacconi		Laplace
1193	Albertus	1690	Mortimer	1750	Marum
1561	Bacon	1692	Zanotti		Scarpa
1568	Harvey	1693	Balbi	1751	Leslie
1579	Van Helmont	1694	Collinson	1753	Galvani C.
1596	Descartes		Pemberton		Mahon
1597	Glisson	1698	Maupertuis	1755	Valli
1602	Guericke	1700	Duhamel	1761	Vassali-Eandi
1608	Borelli		Langrish	1762	Aldini
1616	Bartholin	1702	Lelli	1765	Fowler
1617	Goddard		Molinelli	1769	Humboldt
1621	Willis	1703	Dalibard	1777	Oersted
1627	Boyle	1704	Menghini	1784	Nobili
1628	Malpighi	1705	Hartley	1791	Faraday
1632	Leeuwenhoek	1706	Franklin	1802	Gherardi
1635	Becher	1707	Buffon	1811	Matteuci
	Hooke	1708	Galli	1812	Bernard
1637	Swammerdam		Haller	1818	Du Bois Reymond
1638	Malebranche	1709	Laghi	1834	Hering
	Stensen	1710	Cullen	1835	Ringer
1641	Mayow	1711	Bassi-Verati		Bernstein
1642	Newton	1714	Whytt	1852	Biedermann
1646	Leibniz	1715	Watson	1853	Ostwald
1647	Trionfetti	1716	Beccaria	1864	Nernst
1650	Sandri		Morandi-Manzolini	1871	Locke
1652	Homberg	1718	Canton	1886	Mines
1654	Varignon		Macquer	1889	Adrian
1657	Derham	1720	Bibiena	1911	Katz
	Fontanelle	1724	Aepinus	1914	Hodgkin
1658	Marsigli	1725	Caldani	1917	Huxley

Appendix I

Biographical Index*

ADRIAN Edgar Douglas (London 1889 – Cambridge 1977) studied Natural Sciences at Trinity College, Cambridge. In 1913 he was elected to a Fellowship of Trinity College for his work on the 'all or none' principle of nerves. He broke off his physiological studies at this stage to complete his clinical medical studies at St Bartholomew's Hospital, but returned to Cambridge in 1919 to continue his work and lecture on the nervous system. He was elected FRS in 1923 and two years later began investigating the sense organs, by electrical methods, succeeding Sir Joseph Barcroft as Professor of Physiology in 1937. Adrian produced preparations of a single nerve fibre attached to a single end organ and developed a sophisticated means of increasing his ability to detect the nerve impulses he produced by a constant electrical stimulus. To this end he used the cathode ray tube and capillary electrometer as highly sensitive detectors of small electrical potential and amplified these potentials by using thermionic valves. In this way he showed that when a constant stimulus is applied to an end organ, sensory impulses of a constant intensity pass down the afferent fibre, but that the frequency of these impulses decreases with time and, associated with this decrease in frequency is a decrease of the sensation appreciated in the brain. In other words, stimulation of a nerve can only produce a variable intensity of sensation by variation in the frequency of impulses it produces, each impulse in itself being of a fixed intensity. This work was extended to other nerve fibres. Adrian also studied the sense of smell and electrical activity in the brain. He was awarded the Nobel Prize in 1932 for his work on the behaviour of nerve fibres and among other honours was elected President of the Royal Society for the years 1950–1955. He was made a Baron in 1955.

See: *Nobel Lectures*, Physiology or Medicine, 1922–1941. 1965, p. 301

AEPINUS Franz Ulrich Theodor (Rostock 1724 – Dorpat 1802) studied medicine in Rostock and Jena and was Professor of Astronomy at the Royal Academy of Science in Berlin during the years 1755–1758. His interest in Astronomy was not particularly marked however and he devoted himself to the study of tourmaline, to which he had been introduced by Wilcke who followed him to Berlin. The similarity in properties of tourmaline and magnets together with the magnetic attraction exhibited by the warmed stone, led him to conjecture that electricity and magnetism were basically analogous and this idea is contained in his main work, *Tentamen theoriae electricitatis* . . . (St Petersburg, 1758). As a result of collaboration with Wilcke, Franklin's ideas about the electricity of glass were disproved and the 'air condenser' was shown to behave in a way similar to the Leyden Jar. In 1757 he was elected to the Professorship of Physics at St Petersburg.

See: *Dictionary of Scientific Biography*, 1970, Vol. I, p. 66

ALBERTUS Magnus Saint (Lauingen, Bavaria ?1200 – Cologne 1280) was noted for his wide interest in natural science and for his introduction of Greek and Arabic science to the Medieval world.

See: *Microsoft Encarta 1997 Encyclopedia*

* See List of Abbreviations on p. 288

ALDINI Giovanni (Bologna 1762 – Milan 1834) was the son of Galvani's sister. He was in close contact with his uncle and gave as his oration, on the occasion of his Laureate at Bologna University a eulogy in honour of his uncle. He was made Professor of Physics in the University in 1798, taking over from his teacher Sebastiano Canterzani. He held this chair until 1807 when he was elected to the Council of Milan. Unlike his uncle who was of a modest and retiring nature, Aldini was ready to publicise the discovery of animal electricity at every opportunity. As has been noted, he worked actively in this field, repeating experiments in Italy, France and England and producing the various works noted in the text. Of great importance was his bequest of his uncle's manuscripts to the Academy of the Institute of Science in Bologna. He was interested in the application of electrical therapy in medicine; the construction and improvement of lighthouses; the perfection of Sir Humphrey Davy's safety lamp and he designed a double-layered suit for firemen, the inner layer of asbestos the outer of metal net. This latter project included his ideas for the manufacture and processing of asbestos a material hardly known or used at this time.

    See: (1) *Dizionario Biografico degli Italiani*, 1960, Vol. II, p. 90
        (2) *Dictionary of Scientific Biography*, 1970, Vol. I, p. 107

AMONTONS Guillaume (Paris 1663 – Paris 1705). At an early age he began to suffer from deafness which tended to lead him to a retiring and studious life. His main interests were mathematics and physics and when only 24 years old, he presented a new hygrometer to the Academy of Sciences. He also made barometers although these were not very accurate or consistent in their readings owing to his failure to boil the mercury used in their construction. He wrote a great deal on the subject of such instruments, seeking to find the source of error responsible for such inconsistency and as a result of this work, was elected a member of the Academy. He also wrote on the subject of friction, the use of heat as a means of energy supply for man and he invented an aerial form of telegraph, messages being transmitted along a line of men who simply transferred signals to one another.

    See: (1) *Dictionnaire de Biographie Francaise*, 1936, Tom. Deuxieme, p. 690
        (2) *Dictionary of Scientific Biography*, 1970, Vol. I, p. 138

AMORETTI Carlo (Oneglia 1741 – Milan 1816) studied theology in Pavia and Parma, becoming Professor of Theological Dogma at Pavia University in 1769. In 1772 he went to Milan where he became tutor to the children of the Marchese F. Cusani and at this time turned his mind to more liberal studies including scientific subjects such as chemistry, botany and geology. Between 1775 and 1777 he was a joint publisher of *Una Scelta di opuscoli interessanti sulle Scienze e sulli Arti* and later was solely responsible for this journal. He became increasingly interested in scientific subjects, particularly as related to the cultural and economic development of Italy and wrote various tracts on these subjects. In later life he became active politically and was nominated a member of the National Institute as a result of his work on behalf of Italy.

    See: *Dizionario Biografico degli Italiani*, 1961, Vol. III, p. 9

ANAXIMANDER (Miletus, Asia Minor ?611BC–?547BC) was a Greek philosopher, mathematician and astronomer said to have discovered the obliquity of the ecliptic and credited with introducing the sundial to Greece and inventing cartography. He was a friend and disciple of Thales.

    See: *Microsoft Encarta 1997 Encyclopedia*

ANAXIMENES (Miletus Asia Minor 570BC–500BC) was a Greek philosopher of the School of Thales whose importance lies in his attempt to discover the ultimate nature of reality.
See: *Microsoft Encarta 1997 Encyclopedia*

ANAXAGORAS (Clazomenae nr Izmir ?500BC – Lampsacus, Miletus 428BC) was the Greek philosopher who introduced the notion of 'nous' into the philosophy of origins. His doctrine of atoms prepared the way for the atomic theory of the philosopher Democritus.
See: *Microsoft Encarta 1997 Encyclopedia*

ARISTOTLE (Stagira, Macedonia 384BC – Euboea 322BC) was the Greek philosopher who established the Lyceum in Athens. Numerous texts and treatises on a very wide range of subjects established him together with Plato as one of the most famous of the ancient philosophers
See: *Microsoft Encarta 1997 Encyclopedia*

BACON Francis (London 1561 – London 1626) was educated at Trinity College, Cambridge where he soon became disenchanted with Aristotelian scholasticism. His basic philosophy was that knowledge is the key to controlling man's environment and thus procuring for him a better life in every way. He was dedicated to the experimental study of nature as a means of acquiring this knowledge although his personal talent for experimental science was not outstanding. His importance in the history of science is his recognition of how science could become organised so as to achieve these ends and his influence on the rising generation of philosophers all over Europe was enormous. He published these ideas in *The Advancement of Learning* (London, 1605) and *Novum Organum* (London, 1620). A mechanistic philosopher, he believed that all phenomena could be explained in terms of the shape, size and motion of particles of matter. His conception of heat as simply, the motion of particles, was advanced for his time. Apart from his scientific interests, Bacon was a man of law and letters. He became Lord Chancellor in 1617.
See: (1) Catherine Drinker Bowen, *Francis Bacon,* London, Hamish Hamilton, 1963
      (2) Marie Boas Hall 'In Defense of Bacon's views on the Reform of Science' *The Personalist*, 44, No 4

BALBI Paolo Battista (Bologna 1693 – Bologna 1772) after an early schooling, he studied medicine under Matteo Bazzani and mathematics under the two Manfredi brothers, Eustachio and Eraclito. He obtained his laureate in philosophy and medicine at the age of 25. Four years later he became Lecturer in Logic and commenced public lectures in anatomy and the theory of medicine. In 1734 he became Deputy and assistant to Galeazzi who was Professor of Physics in the Institute an office which he filled with great success until 1770. Apart from his main interest in physics he was a practising physician, anatomist and naturalist and studied the phosphorescent properties of local bi-valves called mitilli or dattili (from their resemblance to dates).
See: M. Medici, (i), 1853, p. 7

BANKS Sir Joseph (London 1743 – Isleworth 1820) is mainly remembered for his Presidency of the Royal Society between the years 1778 and 1820. Soon after leaving Oxford University his talents in the Natural Sciences were recognised by his election as FRS in May 1766. On the death of his father his considerable personal wealth allowed him to join various voyages of exploration, the most notable of which was that made with Captain Cook on board the Endeavour visiting South America, Tahiti, Australia, New Guinea, the East Indies and South Africa. Banks was energetic in collecting specimens of plants and observing animal life, bringing back numerous specimens which formed a priceless collection which is now housed in the Science Museum, London. Not a prolific writer himself, he collected one of the richest scientific libraries of his day, the contents of which are now in the British Museum. In 1778 he succeeded Sir John Pringle as President of the Royal Society. In his early days, his Presidency was unpopular partly because of the nature of his scientific interests which were concerned with natural history rather than mathematics, and partly because of his attempts to reform certain aspects of the way in which the business of the Society was carried out. His great strength of personality, however, and genuine concern for the pursuit of all scientific matters, eventually enabled him to carry out one of the most successful Presidencies of all time.

See: *Dictionary of National Biography*, 1908, Vol. I, p. 1049

BARTHOLIN Thomas (Copenhagen 1616 – Copenhagen 1680) was the second son of Caspar Bartholin, Professor of Anatomy and Religion in the University of Copenhagen. Working in Leyden with Sylvius (Franciscus de le Boe) he produced in 1641 the first of many revised editions of his father's *Institutiones Anatomicae* (1611). After travelling in Europe he returned to Copenhagen to take up the Chair of Anatomy, introducing the new Paduan teaching in his lectures. During these years his most famous pupil and convert, to the new ideas was Nicolaus Stensen. Learning of Pecquet's discovery of the thoracic duct and cysterna chyli in dogs, he dissected the cadavers of two animals and demonstrated the thoracic duct in man (although he overlooked the cysterna chyli). This led him to further researches and the demonstration that the lymphatics form a separate system hitherto unrecognised. His other contribution included the publication of the first Danish Pharmacopoeia *Dispensatorium Hafniense* (Copenhagen, 1658) and he was responsible for the reorganisation of Danish Medicine, ordained by royal decree in 1672.

See: *Dictionary of Scientific Biography*, 1970, Vol. I, p. 482

BASSI-VERATI Laura Maria Caterina (Bologna 1711 – Bologna 1778) was a protégé of Tacconi, who acquired a considerable reputation in Europe as a physicist. Helping Tacconi at her sick mother's bedside, she so impressed him with her ability to understand his teaching, that the Bologna Professor encouraged her to take up the study of natural philosophy and medicine. He instructed her in general philosophy, writing a special tract on logic and metaphysics for her use. In 1732 she was granted a Chair in Bologna University and opened a school of experimental physics. She wrote two treatises; *De Problemata quodam hydrometico* and *De Problemata quodam mechanico*. (See: *Bologna Commentaries*, 1757, Vol. 14, pp 61 and 74). She married the physician Guiseppe Verati and was the aunt of Lazaro Spallanzani, whom she taught.

See: (1) M. Medici, (i), 1853, p. 8
    (2) G. Fantuzzi, (i), 1778

BAZZANI Matteo (Bologna 1674 – Bologna 1749) studied widely in all branches of philosophy, science and the arts. He was appointed first secretary of the Institute by Marsigli and later became President succeeding Trionfetti in 1723. He carried out experiments with Robbia, noting the property of this plant to stain the bones of animals, who took it in their food. (cf. Galvani's early experiments.) His other main interest was in forensic medicine.

See: M. Medici, (i), 1853

BECCARI Jacopo Bartolomeo (Bologna 1682 – 1766).
See: Chapter 13 of this book
See also: (1) Giovanni Pini, *Jacopo Bartolomeo Beccari*, Bologna, Licinio Cappelli, 1940
(2) M. Medici, (i), 1853

BECCARIA Giambatista (Mondovi 1716 – Turin 1781) was a member of the Piarists (Clerks Regular of the Pious Schools), a teaching order. He studied at Rome and Narni and then began his own teaching career, eventually being appointed Professor of Physics at Turin. His interest in electricity began when it was suggested to him that Franklin's ideas, and particularly the demonstration of the lightning experiment would be a useful weapon against the Cartesians who opposed Beccaria's allegiance to the new Newtonian Science. (The Cartesian reduction of electrical phenomena to the vortical motion of a special matter had hardly had success.) Beccaria's first work *Dell' elettricismo artificiale et naturale* . . . (Turin, 1753) was the first exposition of Franklin's view published in Italy and Beccaria became his protagonist for the new theory. He was a highly skilled, ingenious experimenter and other works on electricity followed. He was interested in the electricity of the atmosphere and he was certainly the source of Galvani's ideas on electrical phenomena when he began his researches.

See: *Dictionary of Scientific Biography*, 1970, Vol. I, p. 546

BECHER Johann Joachim (Speyer 1635 – ?London ?1682) was the son of a Protestant pastor. Although self taught he became Professor of Medicine in the University of Mainz (having obtained his MD only two years previously). He left, however, in 1664 to become physician to the Elector at Munich. He travelled widely and was a polymath, writing on such a diversity of subjects as theology, mathematics, philosophy, philology, history and economics and even invented a universal language. His main interest, however, was chemistry. A quarrelsome and vain man he made enemies and was (like Stahl) never elected FRS, the Society not considering him a worthy candidate. Basically his outlook was Neoplatonic and Paracelsian: he believed that minerals as well as plants and animals are endowed with a life-force and grow in the earth from seeds. As a result of his basic philosophy he disapproved of Boyle's mechanical explanations of chemical phenomena and inclined to the views of Sir Kenelm Digby. His virtue as a chemist was his insistence on the importance of analysis as a means of determining the elements.

See: J.R. Partington *A History of Chemistry*, 1962, Vol. II, p. 637 *et seq.*

BERLINGHIERI Leopoldo Vacca (Ponsacca 1732 – Pisa 1812) seems to have been the brother of Francesco, who held the Chair of Medicine in Pisa. Very little is known about him apart from the fact that he lived in Pisa during his early years and then joined the French Army. He wrote papers on various scientific topics such as heat, the nature of phlogiston, electricity and animal electricity.

See: *Poggendorf* (M–Z), 1863, p. 1163

BERNARD Claude (St Julien, nr Villefranche 1813 – Paris 1878). The great physiologist went to Paris in 1832 intent on a career as a playwright but was persuaded to enter the School of Medicine. After qualification he came under the influence of François Majendie in the laboratories of the Collège de France. The adventurous experimentation and critical attitude of the latter, who was determined that the laws of inorganic science are applicable to physiological functions, made a strong impression on his pupil. Bernard adopted the philosophy of his teacher and demonstrated the value of this approach to the science of experimental medicine. His outstanding technical skill in carrying out experiments and his seemingly uncanny powers of observation led to the discovery of numerous physiological facts including the activity of various glands, the experimental production of diabetes, the existence of vaso-motor nerves and animal glycogenesis. His concept of the balanced interaction of physiological functions so as to maintain the "milieu interieur" is one of the greatest biological concepts of all time.

See: Claude Bernard, *An Introduction to the Study of Experimental Medicine*, translated by Henry Copley . . ., New York, Dover Publications, 1957

BERNOULLI Jean (Basel 1667 – Basel 1748) was the brother of Jacob and father of Daniel Bernoulli, two other members of this illustrious scientific family which contributed so much to the development of physical science and mathematics in the 17th and 18th century. With Jacob he was one of the first foreigners to be elected an associate of the Académie des Sciences and of the Berlin Academy. Jean was interested in both chemical and mathematical research. He became MD in 1694 and the following year was elected Professor of Mathematics at Gröningen. Ten years later he moved to Basel where he succeeded his brother as Professor of Mathematics. He was a prolific writer on mathematical subjects, particularly differential equations, the rectification and quadrature of curves, isochronous curves and curves of quickest descent. His *Opera Omnia* were published in Lausanne and Geneva in 1742.

See: *Dictionary of Scientific Biography*, 1970, Vol. II, p. 51

BERNSTEIN Julius (Berlin 1839 – Halle 1917) studied in Berlin and later at Breslau. He became Assistant to Helmholtz in Heidelberg and then was appointed Professor of Physiology at Halle, succeeding F. L. Goltz. While in Berlin he came under the influence of Du Bois Reymond and his main interests came to be in the field of electrophysiology, although he also worked on respiratory and cardiovascular physiology and was interested in the special senses. By means of a ballistic Galvanometer, which he connected to the tissues for brief time intervals, he was able to determine the time course of an action potential in nerve, and thus demonstrate that this electrical change was the true index of the excitatory process passing along it as a result of stimulation. He proposed a 'memory theory' in 1902 to account for this process, basing his ideas on the physico-chemical concepts of Nernst and Ostwald. Through his appreciation that the magnitude and sign of a potential difference existing across a cell membrane depends on its relative permeability to the principal inorganic ions potassium, sodium and chloride, he recognised the fundamental mechanism responsible for the existence and maintenance of the excitatory nature of nerves. Bernstein's theory considered the cell membrane separated a fluid rich in potassium ions internally, from sodium and chloride ions externally and that in the resting state, it was permeable only to potassium ions. Excitation was considered as due to the opening up of pores in the membrane, which allowed the passage inwards of sodium and chloride ions abolishing the resting potential. This concept had to be abolished in 1939 when Hodgkin and Huxley showed that there is a continuous free flux of both sodium and potassium ions across the nerve-cell membrane and further that the excitation process is associated with a temporary reversal and not an abolition of the resting potential.

    See: (1) Edwin Clarke and C.D. O'Malley, *The Human Brain and Spinal Cord,* Berkeley, University of California Press, 1968, p. 213

       (2) Bernard Katz, *Nerve Muscle and Synapse,* New York, McGraw-Hill, 1966

       (3) G. Rudolph, 'Julius Bernstein', in *Founders of Experimental Physiology . . .,* John W. Boylan (ed.), Munich, J.F. Lehmans, 1971, p. 249

BIBIENA Francesco Maria Galli (Bologna 1720 – Bologna 1774) was a pupil of Galeazzi and Beccari, like his contemporary Galvani, with whom he worked on the anatomy of the ureter. He became Professor of Medicine in 1765, a post which he held until his early death at the age of 54. He made a detailed anatomical dissection of the silk-worm in an attempt to find the cause of a fatal disease which caused them to disintegrate into calcareous masses and he investigated the structure of leeches. He became involved, as did other Bolognese anatomists, in the controversy aroused by Haller's doctrine of irritability and read a dissertation on the subject in 1762.

    See: M. Medici, (ii), 1857, p. 324

BIEDERMANN Wilhelm (Bilin 1852 – Jena 1929) studied at Prague University after attending Bruxner Gymnasium. His first interest was in plant physiology but as a result of the influence of Hering (whose assistant he became at Leipzig) he turned to animal and human physiology, carrying out a series of electro-physiological experiments with the latter. He continued this work in Jena where he became head of the Institute of Physiology. He contributed articles to various textbooks of physiology, writing on a wide range of subjects including insects and the nature of irritable substances. Other works were on biochemical subjects including fermentation and the histochemistry of striped muscle. His textbook on electro-physiology is referred to in the text.

    See: Fr N. Schulz, 'Wilhelm Biedermann', *Ergenbisse der Physiologie,* 1930, 30: pp x–xxv

BLACK Joseph (Bordeaux 1728 – Edinburgh 1799) born of Scottish parents he went to school in Belfast and later entered Glasgow University where he studied languages and natural philosophy before turning to anatomy and medicine under Cullen's teaching. He worked for some time in Cullen's laboratory and then moved to Edinburgh where he graduated MD in 1754. He succeeded Cullen as Professor of Anatomy and Lecturer in Chemistry in Glasgow in 1756 but then gave this up to take on the Chair of Medicine, eventually moving to Edinburgh, where, once more, he succeeded his teacher, this time as Professor of Chemistry, a post he held until his death. He had a reputation as a great teacher and his lectures were always well attended. His analyses of various salts were very accurate. In particular he is remembered for his investigation of the composition of magnesia alba (magnesium carbonate). This work which resulted from his search for a harmless solvent for bladder stones, showed that this alkaline salt lost 7/12ths of its weight when heated and that this was due to its content of 'fixed air' (carbon dioxide) and further that limestone (calcium carbonate) reacts with acids giving off fixed air, with a resulting loss of weight.

    See: J.R. Partington, *A History of Chemistry,* 1969, Vol. III, p. 130

BOERHAAVE Hermann (Voorhout, nr Leyden 1668 – Leyden 1738) received his early schooling in Leyden. He graduated at Leyden University in 1690, having distinguished himself by a series of five disputations which earned him a gold medal. His major study had been in theology and philosophy but after graduation, he turned to medicine at Harderwijk University. In 1701 he was appointed Lecturer in Medicine at Leyden and gave private instruction in chemistry, succeeding to the Chair of Botany and Medicine in 1709. He greatly improved the Botanical Garden increasing the content of plants and helping Linnaeus bring about his revolution in the classification of species. His great contribution was due to his ability as a teacher. He brought about a renaissance in Leyden, where medical teaching had fallen into disrepute. He instigated bedside clinical teaching and his methods were so successful that Leyden became the Mecca for medical students from all over Europe. His lectures became the basis for his *Institutiones medicae* ... (Leyden, 1708) and his *Aphorisimi de cognoscendis et curandis morbis* (Leyden, 1709). He was a great synthesiser and organiser of medical theories and his teaching embraced a comprehensive analysis, an eclectic attitude to the older classical theories and the new iatro mechanisms of such men as Willis, Borelli and Bellini. His contributions to chemistry were perhaps greater than those to medicine. He introduced exact quantitative methods and was a skilled experimenter who made biochemical demonstrations for his students. His fame and distinction in Europe was unrivalled.

See: (1) G.A. Lindeboom, *Hermann Boerhaave, the man and his work*, London, Methuen & Co. Ltd, 1968

(2) *Dictionary of Scientific Biography*, 1970, Vol. II, p. 224

BORELLI Giovanni Alphonso (Naples 1608 – Rome 1679) studied mathematics in Rome and was appointed Professor of Mathematics at the University of Messina about 1640. A disciple of Galileo's teaching, he visited Florence in an attempt to learn directly from the great physicist but unfortunately, Galileo died soon after his arrival. In 1650 he accepted the Chair of Mathematics at Pisa and at this time became friendly with Malpighi. While at Pisa, he wrote treatises on mathematics and astronomy as well as his two most important ones, a physical treatise, *De vi percussioni, liber* (Bologna, 1667), and his biological work, *De Motu Animalium* (Rome, 1680–1681). The latter work is an expression of Borelli's iatro-mechanical philosophy, an attempt to explain the physiological basis of animal movement in purely mathematico-physical terms. He dealt with the problems of muscular contraction, the heart beat and circulation, respiration and urine formation as problems of dynamics and while his theories were inevitably inadequate as a result of the lack of facts on which to base them, his concepts were important as they reflected the outlook which was to yield such good results in the field of biology.

See: (1) Sir Michael Foster, *Lectures on the History of Physiology* ..., 1970, p. 62

(2) *Dictionary of Scientific Biography*, 1970, Vol. II, p. 306

BOYLE Robert (Cork 1627 – London 1691). Natural philosopher whose experimental contribution in support of the atomistic hypothesis greatly strengthened the belief in atomism in Europe. He was very influential in encouraging the prosecution of the experimental method in science.

See: *Dictionary of Scientific Biography*, 1970, Vol. II, pp 377–382

BUFFON Georges-Louis Leclerc, Comte de (Montbard 1707 – Paris 1788) received his early schooling at the Collége des Jesuites in Dijon from 1717–1723. He was a student of law in Dijon but gave this up to go to Angers where he is believed to have studied Botany, Medicine and Mathematics. After a visit to Italy he returned to France and began to produce scientific papers. He wrote on the tensile strength of timber and this was followed by a study of probability theory which contributed to his admission to the Académie Royale des Sciences. He then became busy with Botany, translating at this time Stephen Hales's *Vegetable Staticks* (London, 1727). Mathematical interests led to his translation of Newton's *The Method of Fluxions and Infinite Series*, London, 1736) – he is said to have described Newton's binomial theorem independently when only twenty years old – and biological interests led him to microscopical work on animal reproduction. In 1739 he became Intendant of the Jardin du Roi. From then on his fame grew. After fifteen years at the Jardin he had doubled its area and greatly enriched its content of specimens. Buffon's works may be grouped into two categories, the *Mémoires* (Paris, 1737–1752) and *L'Histoire Naturelle* (Paris, 1749). The *Mémoires* deal with mathematics, physics, astronomy, plant physiology and pyrotechnics, while *L'Histoire Naturelle* deals with his view of man as a whole in his environment. Buffon attempted to separate science from metaphysical and religious ideas and rejected idealistic and teleological concepts thus denying Plato, Leibniz and even Newton and basing his theories on the results of sensory impressions. His science was to be derived only from what could be seen, felt or learned from nature itself and this view embraced his explanation of astronomical phenomena just as much as biological events. He was particularly interested in the study of reproduction and favoured epigenesis as the explanation of this. He assumed that nutritive material, having been used to nourish an animal, was then used in the reproduction process, growth having been completed. Such matter received a mould or imprint from the various parts or organs of the animal, these specific imprints determining its role as embryonic material for the next generation. Buffon's work aimed at a comprehensive description of all nature and his eminence as a scientist in Europe reflected his wide knowledge and abilities.

See: *Dictionary of Scientific Biography*, 1970, Vol. I, p. 57

CALDANI Leopoldo Marc-Antonio (Bologna 1725 – Padua 1813) left his native city for Padua when 35 years old. He took over the Chair of Theoretical Medicine and then succeeded Morgagni as Professor of Anatomy. He was taught by Beccari, Manfredi, Tacconi and Molinelli and gained much of his anatomical experience in the Spedale di Santa Maria delle Morte. He became interested in Haller's work on irritability, in company with nearly all the other European anatomists. He became a staunch supporter of Haller's views and defended them in his public lectures, offering his own careful experimental results in support of his words. Unfortunately he was forced to leave Bologna as a result of the professional jealousy of certain colleagues and he made his home in Padua. Haller offered Caldani the Chair of Anatomy at Frankfurt but he declined this, preferring to stay at Padua.

See: (1) M. Medici, (ii), 1857, p. 400
      (2) *Dictionary of Scientific Biography*, 1971, Vol. III, p. 15

CAMPI Carlo Guiseppe. No biographical details were found concerning Volta's friend and correspondent.

CANTON John (Stroud 1718 – London 1772) was sent to London in 1737 to be articled to a schoolmaster with whom he subsequently joined partnership. During this time his interest in electricity led him to perform experiments and he soon acquired a reputation in London as an electrician. He was elected FRS in 1749 and chosen as a member of the Council two years later. He is referred to by Priestley in

his famous *History of Electricity* (London, 1767), as being the first Englishman to repeat Franklin's experiments and verify the identity of lightning and electricity. He
also was the first electrician to demonstrate that air can be electrified by communication. He was also responsible for certain induction experiments which formed the
starting point for the work of Wilcke and Aepinus whereby Franklin's ideas about
the electricity of glass were disproved. Among many discoveries and inventions
were his electroscope and electrometer and his tin/mercury amalgams for increasing the action of the rubber of the electrical machine. He was also interested in the
preparation of artificial magnets and discovered the phosphorescence produced by
mixing calcined oyster shells with sulphur ('Canton's Phosphorus'). He attempted
to popularise science by contributing articles to popular magazine's. He was awarded
the Copley medal of the Royal Society in 1751.
    See: *Dictionary of National Biography*, 1886, Vol. VIII, p. 456

CAVALLO Tiberius (Naples 1749 – London 1809) went to England at an early age
and settled there. When still quite young, in 1775, he published a paper on
Extraordinary Electricity of the Atmosphere observed at Islington and this was reprinted
in Sturgeon's *Annals of Electricity* (London, 1843, p. 158). He was a skilled experimenter and designed a number of electrical instruments, electroscopes and elec-
trometers which were notable for their delicacy and accuracy and were used by
leading electricians including his life-long friend, Alessandro Volta. In 1779 he was
made FRS. Two years later he published *A Treatise on the Nature and Properties of Air
and the permanent Electric Fluids*. He was interested in the composition of air but
while not completely happy with the phlogiston theory, did not advance any new
hypothesis in its place. In 1786 he published his textbook of electricity, *A complete
Treatise on Electricity . . .* (London, 1786) and the following year, *A Treatise on
Magnetism in Theory and Practice* (London, 1787) two works which aimed at a comprehensive account of the current status of these sciences. Towards the end of his
life he became interested in the use of electricity as a form of therapy.
    See: (1) *Dictionary of National Biography*, 1887, Vol. IX, p. 337
         (2) *Dictionary of Scientific Biography*, 1971, Vol. III, p. 154

CAVENDISH Henry (Nice 1731 – London 1810) was the elder son of Lord Charles
Cavendish. After leaving Cambridge University he helped his father with experiments on heat, electricity and magnetism and was elected FRS in 1760. His own
electrical work included many fundamental discoveries. He was the first to determine the electrical conductivity of salt solutions, he differentiated between electrical quantity and intensity and provided experimental proof of the inverse square
law. His chemical work was mainly concerned with the nature and action of the
constituents of air and with the properties of 'inflammable air' (hydrogen). An adherent of the phlogiston theory, he interpreted his experimental results on this basis.
    See: J.R. Partington, *A History of Chemistry*, 1962, Vol. III, p. 302 *et seq.*

CICERO Marcus Tullius (Arpinium, Italy 106BC – executed Rome 43BC) was a Roman
writer, orator and politician. He wrote on many aspects of philosophy in his time.
    See: *Microsoft Encarta 1997 Encyclopedia*

COLLINSON Peter (Windermere 1694 – Essex 1768) was born into a Quaker family
of mercers. Peter joined the family firm and with his brother opened a large business with the American Colonies. A keen naturalist from his youth, he gained the

attention of Sir Hans Sloane and was elected a FRS in 1728. His business interest led him to scientific correspondence with colleagues in America, his most famous correspondent being Benjamin Franklin. In fact, the descriptions of electrical experiments that were carried out in Germany and sent to Franklin by Collinson were the starting point of the American's work in this field. His Botanic Garden at Mill Hill led to many improvements in British horticulture.

See: *Dictionary of National Biography*, 1908, Vol. IV, p. 838

COWPER William (Petersfield 1666 – Petersfield 1709) was apprenticed to a London surgeon in 1682 and began practice in London in 1691. The first edition of *Myotomia Reformata . . .* (London, 1694) was succeeded by a new edition in 1724, which contained various manuscript additions by the author including an historical preface and introduction (See Chapter 10 of this book, Note 15). In 1696 he was made FRS and in 1698 he published *The Anatomy of Humane Bodies* (Oxford), containing superb illustrations. A second edition of this volume, published in Leyden in 1737, gave rise to a controversy over plagiarism of the rights of a Dr Bidlov, a Dutch anatomist some of whose plates Cowper appears to have used.

See: *Dictionary of National Biography*, 1908, Vol. IV, p. 1313

CRAWFORD Adair (?Ireland 1748 or 1749 – Lymington 1795) was a physician at St Thomas's Hospital London and later Professor of Chemistry at Woolwich Arsenal. During a visit to Scotland in 1776 he became aware of Black and Irvine's researches on heat and this led to his own work in this field which he began in Glasgow in 1777. He conceived all bodies as having an 'absolute heat', this latter referring to the quantity of heat they contain, bodies of equal weight and temperature having different quantities of 'absolute heat'. He conceived of a body's ability to receive heat as being proportional to its content of 'absolute heat'. This theory was, of course, based on the current concept of an element of fire or phlogiston which was virtually the same as the 'absolute heat'. He was the first to determine the specific heats of gases (1779) and he went on to make an analysis of the ratio of these qualities of metals and their calces – his interpretation of his results being based on the view that capacity for a body to contain heat is diminished by the addition of phlogiston. He also compared the capacities of the arterial and venous blood, showing that during its passage through the body, the blood gives out the heat which it receives from the air in the lungs. His results were criticised and eventually his theory disproved by the measurements of the specific heats of gases carried out by Delaroche and Bérard who found that the heat of oxygen is lower than that of carbonic acid gas for equal volumes.

See: J.R. Partington, *A History of Chemistry*, 1962, Vol. III, p. 156

CULLEN William (Hamilton 1710 – Edinburgh 1790) attended Glasgow University. In 1729 he went to London and obtained a post as surgeon to a merchant ship in which he went to the West Indies. On returning to London he assisted an apothecary for some months and used this period for intense study. On the death of his father and elder brother in 1731, he had to return to Scotland and set up in practice near Hamilton. From here he attended lectures at Edinburgh University under Monro (Primus), and developed a highly successful surgical practice. He taught William Hunter and later had Joseph Black as his pupil when he was lecturing on Medicine in Glasgow. At this time he was trying to establish a medical school but this venture did not go very well; the school grew slowly. As a result he resigned his post as Professor of Medicine and moved to Edinburgh where he was elected joint professor of chemistry in 1755 and sole professor a few months later. His ability as a teacher, both of chemistry and clinical medicine, soon led to his popularity, and his kindness and interest in the welfare of his students gained him their respect and sincere affection. He eventually succeeded to the Chair of the Practice of Physic and was President of the Edinburgh College of Physicians. Among many publications, his *Synopsis Nosological Methodical* (Edinburgh, 1769) is note-worthy for his exposition of a classification of disease. His *First Lines of the Practice of Physic* (Edinburgh, 1776–1784), was an extremely popular translation of Haller's work. He opposed the eclectic views of Boerhaave, favouring the views of humoral pathologists.

See: *Dictionary of National Biography*, 1908, Vol. V, p. 281

DALIBARD Thomas François (Crannes 1703 – Paris 1779) was a French naturalist, much influenced by Buffon. He was the first to adopt Linnaeus's classification of plants, publishing in 1749 a work entitled *Florae Parisiensis prodomus ou catalogue des plantes qui naissent dans les environs de Paris* (Paris, 1749). At the request of Buffon he translated Franklin's *Experiments and Observations on Electricity*, publishing the French edition in 1752. A second edition in 1756 had a lengthy supplement describing his results when repeating Franklin's experiments.

See: (1) *Dictionary of Scientific Biography*, 1972, Vol. III, p. 535
(2) I. Bernard Cohen, *Franklin and Newton . . .*, p. 488

DARWIN Erasmus (Elston Hall, nr Nottingham 1731 – Breadsall Priory, nr Derby 1802) was educated at Cambridge University. He graduated in Medicine and became a highly successful physician but his scientific and literary interests were far wider than clinical practice. A radical thinker, he had a wide circle of distinguished and influential friends and he was interested and wrote upon such subjects as canals, dispensaries for the poor, sewage, temperance, the application of steam, slavery, flying machines and the care of the insane. *Zoonomia . . .* (London, 1794–1796) contains the germ of the idea of evolution which his famous grandson was to develop into a theory. The basis of this idea was the collection of a great number of accurate observations of animal and plant life.

See: (1) *Dictionary of Scientific Biography*, 1971, Vol. III, p. 577
(2) *Chamber's Encyclopaedia*, 1959, Vol. IV, p. 383

DELAMÉTHERIE Jean-Claude (La Clayette 1745 – Paris 1817) was a journalist and the Editor of *Journal de Physique*. After 1793 he developed the view that Galvanic action was the basis of a vast range of phenomena.

Dictionary of Scientific Biography, 1973, Vol. VII

DEMOCRITUS (Abdera, Thrace ?460BC–?370BC). Greek philosopher who developed the atomic theory of the universe which had been originated by his mentor Leucippus.

See: *Microsoft Encarta 1997 Encyclopedia*

DERHAM William (Stoughton 1657 – Upminster, Essex ?1735) was educated at Trinity College, Oxford where he was admitted in 1675. He graduated BA and became chaplain to Lady Grey of Werke before being ordained Deacon in 1681. He then became vicar of Upminster in Essex and devoted himself to his interests in mechanics and natural history. He became known in scientific circles and was elected FRS in 1702. He contributed a number of papers to the *Philosophical*

Transactions between 1697–1729, these mostly dealing with natural history observations but some later ones reflecting his interest in the mechanism of clocks and watches. He delivered the Boyle lectures in 1711 and 1712. These were published under the title *Physico-Theology or a demonstration of the Being and Attributes of God from his Works of Creation* (London, 1713). One year later his *Astro-Theology . . .* (London, 1714) was published, the latter purporting to demonstrate God's attributes from a survey of the heavens. He became Canon of Windsor and President of St John's College, Oxford.

See: (1) *Dictionary of National Biography*, 1888, Vol. XIV, p. 392
     (2) *Dictionary of Scientific Biography*, 1971, Vol. IV, p. 40

DESAGULIERS John Theophilus (LaRochelle 1683 – London 1744) was the son of a Protestant pastor. In 1685 the revocation of the Edict of Nantes caused his father to flee from France to England bringing his child with him. At Oxford University, John Theophilus succeeded James Keith as lecturer on experimental philosophy, continuing his lectures in London when he left Oxford. In 1714 he was made FRS and became their Demonstrator and Curator, being held in high esteem by Sir Isaac Newton. His writings covered a wide range of subjects within the realm of experimental philosophy and he was responsible for a number of practical inventions such as a ventilator for the House of Commons. He received the Copley Medal of the RS in 1741.

See: *Dictionary of National Biography*, 1908, Vol. V, p. 850

DESCARTES René (LaHaye, Poitiers 1596 – Stockholm 1650) was educated at the Jesuit college of La Flèche in Maine where he soon showed a great talent for mathematics. While at school he became a friend of Mersenne who later, at his convent in Paris introduced Descartes to the leading scientists in Europe. Descartes reaction against the scholastic Aristotelian tradition resulted in his famous *Discourse on Method* (Leyden, 1637) in which he devised rules for the study of the world from first principles. As a practical means of learning about the world at large, he enlisted in a foreign army in the Low Countries and on the Danube. At this time, he formulated his concept of the application of algebra to geometry and from which the branch of mathematics known as co-ordinate geometry has developed. His philosophical speculations embraced all branches of science from astronomy to biology and his theories regarding man as a machine are contained in Part V of *The Method* under the title 'Le Monde'. He was a philosopher and not an experimental scientist and his contribution to science was essentially his ability to see the significance of interpreting all natural phenomena within a rational, mechanistic framework. This outlook has been the basis for the progress of science from the 17th century onwards and Descartes' writings have been in no small way responsible for this. He died in Stockholm where he went at the request of Queen Christine of Sweden.

See : (1) Sir Michael Foster, *Lectures in the History of Physiology . . .*, 1970, p. 57
     et seq.
     (2) *Dictionary of Scientific Biography*, 1971, Vol. IV, p. 51

DU BOIS REYMOND Emil Heinrich (Berlin 1818 – Berlin 1896) although born in Berlin and spending virtually his whole professional life there, Du Bois Reymond was the son of a Swiss father and French Huguenot mother. After studying general scientific and philosophical subjects at Berlin and Bonn Universities he was persuaded to turn to medicine by his friend Eduard Hallman who was assistant to

Johannes Müller. After an initial period of work as anatomist in the University, he began what was to become a life-long study of electrophysiology. In 1840 Müller gave him Matteuci's newly published *Essai sur les phénomènes électrique des animaux* (Paris, 1840) and this seems to have been the starting point for his researches. Essentially a physicist and mathematician he found the phenomena of muscle and nerve excitation a vehicle for his philosophical concepts and experimental dexterity for he had no great love for medicine *per se*. He came to this study steeped in the philosophy of materialism, determined to demonstrate the physical laws applicable to this branch of animal physiology. In January 1843 he published his first paper, 'Abriss einer untersuchung über den sogennanten Frochstrom und über die electrichen Fische' (Poggendorf's *Annalen der Physik und Chemie*) and by this time was well advanced with the first volume of his monumental *Untersuchungen über thierische Elektrizität* (Berlin, 1848–1884). In 1845 he founded the Physikallische Gesellschaft together with Brücke and Helmholtz, these three young biophysicists together with Ludwig forming an association which was to have so much influence on the development of 19th century German physiology. He was elected to the Prussian Academy of Sciences in 1851 (and made its perennial secretary in 1876) and became Professor of Physiology in Berlin University when Müller died in 1858. The latter part of his life was concerned with the establishment of a new Institute of Physiology in Berlin and with his duties as Rector of the University from 1868–1870 and from 1882–1883. His immense intellectual vigour in wide-spread areas apart from experimental science fitted him admirably for this post and during these later years he revealed these talents through the various university orations which he delivered. His contributions to electrophysiology were both practical and theoretical. His ability to design and develop new pieces of electrical apparatus such as highly sensitive galvanometers, non-polarizable electrodes, switches, etc., made the task of detecting small organic electrical currents feasible and his rigorous attention to experimental detail was of great influence on his students. His main contributions were his demonstration that an electrical potential exists between the cut end and surface of a muscle or nerve together with his discovery that at the moment of excitation of these structures, this resting potential is lowered momentarily. His theories as to a model for the events taking place in these structures rested on contemporary electrical work by Faraday and Ampère and were displaced later in the 19th century by theories based on Nernst's thermo-dynamic considerations.

  See: (1) *Dictionary of Scientific Biography*, 1971, Vol. IV, pp 200–205
       (2) Chapter 20 of this book, Note 29
       (3) Emil Du Bois Reymond, *Jugendbriefe von E. Du Bois Reymond an Eduard Hallman*, Berlin, Dietrich Reimer, 1918, p. 120

DUHAMEL Henri Louis du Monceau (Paris 1700 – Paris 1782) first achieved scientific recognition with his explanation of the cause of a blight which attacked the saffron plant, in 1720. This work which showed the effects were due to a parasite, earned him membership of the Académie des Sciences. He was a true polymath with wide interests in scientific subjects, botany and chemistry being his earliest affections. His most important chemical work at this time, "Sur la base du sel marin" was read in 1737. In this paper he argued that soda and potash were the essential fixed alkalis in salt. His interest in plants led to his appointment as Inspector General of the Navy, an appointment which led to his publication of several prints on the properties and management of various woods used for battleships. His main contributions,

however, were in the field of Agriculture. He visited England in 1750 and noted the great advances in English methods of land cultivation, publishing *Traité de la culture des terres . . .* (Paris, 1750–1761) which was an exposition of the book *Horse-Howing Husbandry* (1733), written by the Englishman, Jethro Tull. Unfortunately the French did not adopt these ideas and their agriculture failed to improve as did the British.
  See: *Dictionary of Scientific Biography*, 1971, Vol. IV, p. 223

EMPEDOCLES (Agrigento, Sicily ?499BC–430BC) was a Greek philosopher, statesman and poet. He believed that all things are composed of four primal elements earth, air, fire and water and that these were acted upon by love and strife. He also formulated a theory of evolution.
  See: *Microsoft Encarta 1997 Encyclopedia*

EPICURUS (Samos 341BC–270BC) was a Greek philosopher who taught in Mitilini and Athens and wrote extensively. Epicureanism is the philosophy of his ideas and is described by Lucretius in the poem *De Rerum Natura*.
  See: *Microsoft Encarta 1997 Encyclopedia*

ERASISTRATUS (Iulis now Kea ?304BC–?250BC) was the Greek anatomist who founded a school of anatomy in Alexandria and described the nervous and vascular systems.
  See: *Microsoft Encarta 1997 Encyclopedia*

EUCLID (active around 300 BC) was a Greek mathematician, whose chief work, *Elements,* is a comprehensive treatise on mathematics in 13 volumes.
  See: *Microsoft Encarta 1997 Encyclopedia*

FABRI Giacinto Bartolomeo (? – ?) was a Bolognese Anatomist who devoted himself to research. He was particularly concerned with the current controversy over Haller's doctrine as to the sensitivity of nerves and took part in the collection of the various opinions for and against Haller's views. [I am unable to verify the note on p. 111 of this book, which refers to him as a Professor of Medicine and Surgery. Ed.]
  See: (1) G. Fantuzzi, (ii), 1781–1794, Vol. IX, p. 94
      (2) M. Medici, (ii), 1857, p. 399

FARADAY Michael (Newington, London 1791 – Hampton Court 1867) was born of poor parents and had scant formal education in his early years, developing an interest in science during his apprenticeship to a book binder. Through wide reading, attending lectures, etc., he developed a considerable knowledge of electricity and was appointed assistant to Sir Humphry Davy at the Royal Insitution in 1813, becoming Director in 1825. He was the foremost electrical physicist in Britain in the 19th century discovering induced electricity and the laws of electrolysis.
  See: (1) L. Pearce Williams, *Michael Faraday,* London, Chapman and Hall, 1965
      (2) *Dictionary of Scientific Biography*, 1971, Vol. IV, p. 527

FONTANA Felice (Pomarolo 1730 – Florence 1805) was educated at Rovereto, Verona, Parma and Padua. In 1755 he went to Bologna where he worked with Caldani on irritability and sensitivity. In 1760 Fontana published his *Mémoires sur les parties sensibiles et irritabiles du corps animal* (Lausanne, 1760) defending Haller's views. In 1765 he was made Professor of Logic and a year later Professor of Physic in the University of Pisa. In the same year, Leopold I, Grand Duke of Tuscany, asked him to go to Florence in order to organise and develop the physic laboratory – a task which he accomplished with great success. In particular he supervised the making of a collection of superb wax teaching models, duplicates of which were housed in the Josephine Military Medico-Surgical Academy in Vienna. In 1775 he visited England and France, meeting leading scientists and exchanging ideas with them. His work was concerned with the irritability and function of muscles, microscopical investigations of nerves and blood vessels, biological studies of certain parasitic plants responsible for wheat blight and certain chemical works. He designed a eudiometer and an apparatus for oxygen therapy. His work on muscle irritability was published in *De irritibilitatis legibus nune primum sanctitis, et de spirituum animalium in movendis musculis inefficacia* (Lucca, 1767) revised and translated as *Richerche filosofiche sopra la fisica animale* (Florence, 1775). In this he showed insight into such properties of muscle as tetanic contraction, refractory period, fatigue, atrophy and disuse changes. Although initially unwilling to identify electricity with the nervous fluid, he eventually came to the conclusion that the nerves not only carry but generate such an electric change. By means of his microscopical investigations of nervous tissue he was able to demonstrate "the axon with myelin sheath and endoneural sheath" but also recognised the fluidity of axoplasm. He also showed that the regeneration of nerves is due to the growth of primitive nerve cylinders.

See: *Dictionary of Scientific Biography*, 1972, Vol. V, p. 55

FONTENELLE Bernard le Bouvier (Rouen 1657 – Paris 1757) was a mathematician educated in the Jesuit College in Rouen. He was elected to the French Academy and also to the Académie des Sciences in Paris, eventually becoming Secretary of the latter institution. He published papers on geometry and the theory of Cartesian vortices. He also wrote poetry and was a playwright of some considerable standing.

See: (1) *Poggendorf* (A–L), 1863, p. 770
     (2) *Dictionary of Scientific Biography*, 1972, Vol. V, p. 57

FOWLER Richard (London 1765 – Milford, nr Salisbury 1863) studied medicine in Edinburgh graduating in 1793. He was a member of the 'Speculative Society' and elected FRS in 1802. Apart from his interest in animal electricity, which he acquired during a visit to Paris (while still a student at Edinburgh) he turned his mind to the psychological problems of the blind, deaf and dumb, producing two small books on the subject. He was an active member of the British Association and contributed memoirs to their *Proceedings*, attending their meetings when well into his nineties.

See: *Dictionary of National Biography*, 1908, Vol. VII, p. 528

FRANKLIN Benjamin (Boston 1706 – Philadelphia 1790) owes his fame to his development of a theory of electricity on which future advances could be based. He showed that lightning is an electrical discharge and used this as the rationale for his grounded, pointed, lightning conductors. His other inventions included bifocals, the rocking chair and the Franklin Stove. His quantitative approach to electrical problems and his analysis of the working of the Leyden Jar are discussed in the text. Originally trained as a printer, he set up his own business in Philadelphia in the late 1720's. He soon became interested in scientific matters as a result of reading various expositions of Newton's philosophy, and it was upon this that he based the development of his thought about electrical phenomena. In 1747 Collinson sent a glass tube to the library committee of the Philadelphia Society of which Franklin was a member, with the suggestion that the Society should use it for making electrical experiments and this formed the starting point for Franklin's extensive researches in this field and for the association and regular correspondence which took place between Franklin and Collinson. Franklin's fame soon spread to Europe and in 1756 he was elected FRS having received the Copley medal in 1753. Franklin is remembered not only for his scientific achievements but equally for his place in American civil life. He was elected to the Pennsylvanian Assembly in 1751 and Alderman of Philadelphia and Deputy Postmaster General for the British Colonies in America (1753–1754).

See: (1) *Dictionary of Scientific Biography*, 1972, Vol. V, p. 129
(2) I. Bernard Cohen, *Franklin and Newton* . . .

GALEAZZI Domenica Maria Gusmano (Bologna 1686 – Bologna 1775) after an early education with the Jesuits he studied philosophy under the famous Lelio Trionfetti and obtained his laureate in medicine and philosophy in 1709. In 1711 he was elected Deputy Professor of Experimental Physics (the chair held by Beccari) and in 1734 was elected to the chair when Beccari took over the Chair of Chemistry. He visited Paris in 1714, meeting the leading scientists of the day and wrote long scientific letters to Beccari giving descriptions of instruments and contemporary theories and maintained contact with French scientific circles after his return to Bologna. He wrote on chemistry, physics, anatomy and medical practice and like other teachers of Galvani, was also a naturalist. His daughter, Lucia, married Galvani in 1760

See: M. Medici, (i), 1853

GALEN Claudius (Pergamon 129 – ?Rome 200) studied medicine in his native town under Satyrus. In 151 he visited Smyrna in order to study anatomy under Pelops and at this time wrote his earliest work which survives in translation as *Galen on Medical Experience* (Oxford University Press, 1944.) He later continued his study of anatomy under Numisianus in Alexandria where he stayed until 157. On his return to Pergamon he became physician to the gladiators, a post which afforded him excellent opportunities to learn anatomy at first hand when he attended the wounds of his patients. A few years later Galen settled in Rome and began practice where he soon established his reputation. He performed anatomical demonstrations and in 164 showed that arteries contained blood, not air. Four years later he was appointed physician to Commodus the son of Marcus Aurelius. While holding this post he was able to write many of his scientific works including *On the Natural Faculties, On Respiration* and *On the Use of Parts of the body*. In 176 he was appointed physician to the Emperor himself but four years later Marcus Ameleus died. Galen's anatomical and physiological writings became the standard classical works which were handed down through the centuries and formed the anatomical and physiological inheritance of the Renaissance. Unfortunately Galen's comprehensive and careful practical anatomy was carried out on apes a circumstance which led to certain misconceptions when his findings were accepted as being relevant to human anatomy.

See: Charles Singer, *Galen on Anatomical Procedures*, London, Oxford University Press, 1956, p. xiii

GALLI Giovanni Antonio (Bologna 1708 – Bologna 1782) was appointed to the first chair of obstetrics in Bologna University in 1757. He founded a practical school using for teaching purposes china, wax or terracotta models of the gravid uterus

containing the foetus at various stages of gestation. These models, for which he became famous, were bequeathed to the Institute. At his death in 1782 Luigi Galvani
succeeded to his chair.

See: (1) M. Medici, (ii), 1857, p. 397
     (2) G. Fantuzzi, (ii), 1781–1794, Vol. IV, p. 30
     (3) S. Mazzetti, (i), 1848, p. 136

GALVANI Camillo (Bologna 1753 – Bologna 1828) nephew of Luigi Galvani, gained
his Laureate in medicine in 1783. He was custodian of the Botanical Gardens associated with the Collegio delle Arte e Medicina and Professor of Natural History in the
University from 1801. He was a member of many scientific academies and gained
some reputation as a naturalist. He was a devoted admirer of his uncle and helped
with many of his experiments.

See: Candido Mesini, *Nuove Richerche Galvaniane*, Bologna, Tamari Editore, 1971,
p. 44

GEOFFROY Étienne Françoise (the elder) (Paris 1672 – Paris 1731) studied botany,
chemistry and anatomy in Paris and qualified as a pharmacist in 1693. He became
interested in chemistry as a result of meeting Homberg who was a friend of his
father. He was made FRS in 1698 during a visit to London as physician to the French
Ambassador Extraordinary. Eventually he completed his medical studies in Paris
where he graduated MD in 1704 and three years later began teaching in chemistry
at the Jardin du Roi, succeeding Fagon as Professor in 1712. He was an opponent of
Alchemy wherin he differed from Homberg. He thought (unlike Lemery) that the
iron contained in the ash of plants was not intrinsic but produced by the action of
fire. An adherent of the phlogiston theory (he was one of the first Frenchmen to
adopt it), he quoted Stahl's edition of Becher's *Physica Subterranea*. In his table of
affinities he quotes phlogiston as the "principe huilex ou Soufre Principe".

See: J.R. Partington, *A History of Chemistry*, 1962, Vol. III, p. 49

GHERARDI Sylvestro (Lugo 1802 – Florence 1879) gained his Laureate in philosophy in Bologna in 1822 and became professor of mechanics in the University in
1827. On account of his republican views he had to leave Bologna in 1849 and went
to Genoa where he eventually became a professor at the Naval Academy. Later he
obtained a chair at the University of Turin. Apart from his editing and historical
critique of Galvani's edited and unedited works (which is referred to in the text) he
was responsible for the publication of various manuscripts of Galvani's concerning
the torpedo fish, the action of noxious airs on the animal body as well as various
papers relative to Galvani's life. His other works were concerned essentially with
mathematical and electromagnetic problems.

See: *Poggendorf* (A–L), 1898, p. 12

GLISSON Francis (Rampisham 1597 – London 1677) was educated at Caius College
Cambridge, graduating MA in 1624. He was incorporated MA at Oxford three years
later and became a Fellow of the College of Physicians in 1635, being elected Regius
Professor of Physic at Cambridge in the following year. Here he lectured on
anatomy with great success and delivered the Gulstonian lecture at the College
of Physicians in 1640, becoming President of this body in 1667. He published
his famous tract on rickets under the title *De Rachitide sive morbo puerili, qui vulgo*
The Rickets dicitur (London, 1650, 2nd edn 1660, 3rd edn Leyden, 1671), and is

remembered for his demonstration of the fibrous envelope of the liver eponymously known as Glisson's capsule. In his *Tractatus de ventriculo et intestinis* . . . (London, 1677), he put forward his concept of the innate 'irritability' of all living fibres in the animal body. This was a new idea for biology since previously it was believed that all motion was the result of a stimulus brought to the fibres through the agency of 'animal spirits' carried in the nerves. Glisson's irritability was conceived as a property independent of consciousness or the nervous system.

> See: (1) Owsei Temkin, 'The classical roots of Glisson's doctrine of irritation', *Bulletin of the History of Medicine*, 1964, Vol. XXXVIII, p. 297
> (2) *Dictionary of National Biography*, 1908, Vol. VII, p. 1316

GODDARD Jonathan (Greenwich 1617 – London 1674) entered Magdalene College Oxford in 1632. He then went to Cambridge, where he graduated MB at Christ's College in 1638 obtaining his MD in 1643 at Catherine Hall. He was elected a Fellow of the College of Physicians in 1646. At this time he had lodgings in Wood Street where he used to meet Glisson, Wilkins, Ent and Wallis and discuss philosophy. In 1655 he became Professor of Physic at Gresham College and was one of the group responsible for the foundation of the Royal Society in 1663. An expert experimenter it is said that "Goddard used his laboratory to make numerous experiments for the Society (where any curious experiment was to be done, they made him their drudge till they could obtain to the bottom of it)."

> See: *Dictionary of National Biography*, 1908, Vol. VIII, p. 24

GRAY Stephen (Canterbury 1666 – London 1736) spent most of his life in Canterbury but lived for a while in London with Desaguliers being a 'poor brother' of Charterhouse where he made many of his electrical experiments. He was elected FRS in 1732, four years before his death. Towards the end of the 17th century there was no clear distinction made between bodies which could be made electric and those which could not, the general opinion being that given the appropriate degree of rubbing or heat all matter could be made capable of exerting electrical attraction. Electricians were trying unsuccessfully to make, what we now know as conductors, electric. At the beginning of the 18th century, Gray took up this problem but his experiments were also unsuccessful in that he failed to make metals electric. However, during the course of this work he discovered that electricity can be conveyed to non-electrics from an excited electric, although a non-electric cannot be charged by heat. As a result of these experiments the essential difference between conductors and non-conductors began to be recognised although Gray became more interested in the distance along which electricity can be conveyed and carried out numerous experiments to demonstrate this.

> See: (1) J. Priestley, *The History and present state of Electricity* . . ., 1966, Vol. I, p. 32 *et seq*
> (2) I. Bernard Cohen, *Franklin and Newton* . . ., 1966, p. 368 *et seq*

GROSSETESTE Robert (Suffolk ?1175–1253). As a teacher and Chancellor of the University of Oxford he transmitted the philosophy of Aristotle and wrote treatises on many subjects including astronomy psychology and physics.

> See: *Microsoft Encarta 1997 Encyclopedia*

GUERICKE Otto von (Magdeburg 1602 – Hamburg 1686) went to Leyden University after preliminary periods of study at Leipzig, Helmstedt and Jena. Here he studied mathematics and engineering as well as law. On his return to Magdeburg he was elected an Alderman of the city, representing his native city in many negotiations during the Thirty Years War. Much of his time was thus devoted to diplomatic matters, but his attendances at various courts brought him into contact with leading scientists and their ideas, in particular Cartesian Physics and Toricelli's work on the vacuum. Von Guericke's main scientific interest was with the nature of space. This led him to question Descartes' denial of a vacuum and to carry out experiments whereby he discovered the pumping capacity of air and invented 'the air pump'. As an example of the effectiveness of air pressure, he undertook his famous 'Magdeburg Experiment' whereby he showed the impotence of a team of horses to separate the two sealed halves of a copper cylinder which had been evacuated previously. Von Guericke's work stimulated such men as Boyle and Huygens in their studies with the air pump. His interest in space extended to the hypothesis of a celestial system in which the planets interacted as a result of magnetic forces and directed him to a study of astronomy.

See: *Dictionary of Scientific Biography*, 1972, Vol. V, p. 574

HALLER Albrecht von (Bern 1708 – Bern 1777) entered Tübingen University in 1723. Two years later he moved to Leyden where he became a pupil of Hermann Boerhaave who was at this time at the height of his powers. He graduated MD in 1727 and then spent some time travelling in Europe, becoming a friend of Sir Hans Sloane in England and studying under Jean Bernoulli, the mathematician in Basel. He then returned to Bern to practice medicine at the same time carrying out anatomical and physiological research. At this time his fame was beginning to spread and he was offered the Chair of Anatomy, Botany and Medicine at Göttingen University where he worked until his retirement to Bern. Haller's great work, *Elementa Physiologiae* (Lausanne, 1761) was a model textbook. Systematic, comprehensive and exact in its wording it represents one of the first modern textbooks of physiology, giving the reader Haller's extensive knowledge of the subject and adding the author's considered and experienced judgement of contemporary theories of the significance of his own and other experimental findings. His own research into the phenomenon of irritability has been dealt with in the text of this book (See Chapter 12).

See: Sir Michael Foster, *Lectures in the History of Physiology . . .*, 1970, p. 204

HARTLEY David (Halifax 1705 – Bath 1757) was educated at Bradford Grammar School and Jesus College Cambridge, graduating MA in 1729. He was induced to give up his original aim of taking Orders and became a physician although he did not take a medical degree. He moved to London and lived there for some time but eventually settled in Bath in 1742. He was elected FRS and had a wide circle of acquaintances among men of letters and science. He was a devoutly religious man who attempted to base the Christian ethic on rational principles. By 1738 he was involved with his major work, *Introduction to the History of Man* (London, 1749). He was a materialist in as much as he explained all mental phenomena in terms of vibrating particles but fervently denied that this in any way contradicted his Christian belief.

See: *Dictionary of National Biography*, 1908, Vol. IX, p. 66

HERACLITUS (Ephesus Asia Minor 540BC–475BC) was a Greek philosopher whose ideas stem from the Ionian School.

See: *Microsoft Encarta 1997 Encyclopedia*

HERING Karl Ewald Konstantin (Alt Gersdorg 1834 – Leipzig 1918) studied medicine at Leipzig under E.H.Weber, G.R. Fechner and Otto Funke. Between 1860 and 1865 he practised medicine and lectured in physiology. In 1861–1864 he published a study on space-perception which brought him into opposition with the great physiologist Helmholtz. In 1865 he succeeded Carl in Vienna. Here he continued his studies of space perception and binocular vision but turned also to the study of the innervation of the lungs. Working with Josef Breuer he discovered what is known now as the 'Hering-Breuer Reflex' – the reflex deflation of the lungs associated with inspiration and inflation associated with expiration. This regulatory mechanism for the lungs was one of the first feed-back mechanisms described in physiology. He also investigated the structure of the liver and variations in blood pressure associated with phases of respiration. When the Josephinium was abolished in 1870, he succeeded Jan Purkyně at Prague University. Here he continued his work on sensory perception and put forward a theory of colour vision. In 1895 he succeeded Karl Ludwig at Leipzig, spending his last years working in defence of his theory of colour vision.

See: *Dictionary of Scientific Biography*, 1972, Vol. VI, p. 299

HIGGINS Bryan (Collooney, County Sligo, Ireland 1737 – Walford, Staffs. 1820) went to Leyden University in 1765, graduating MD. He then returned to London where he established his medical practice and opened a school of practical chemistry in Soho. He became involved in a dispute with Priestley whom he had accused of having plagiarised some of his experiments on air. He published his various lecture courses under the titles, *A Philosophical Essay Concerning Light* (London, 1776) and *Experiments and observations relating to Acetous Acid Fixable Air . . . Oils and Fuel.*

See: (1) *Dictionary of National Biography*, 1908, Vol. IX, p. 817
     (2) *Dictionary of Scientific Biography*, 1972, Vol. VI, p. 382

HODGKIN Alan Lloyd (Banbury 1914 – Cambridge 1999) was educated at Trinity College Cambridge where, like A. Huxley, he met such men as Adrian, J.J. Thomson, Rutherford and Rushton. During the war he worked on aviation medicine, and on airborne radar. After the war he returned to Cambridge where he held a Readership in the Department of Physiology. Here he met Huxley and began the collaboration which led to their Nobel Prize in 1963. Hodgkin and Huxley did much of their research on giant squid axons at the Marine Biological Station at Plymouth. His Nobel Oration was entitled 'The ionic basis of Nerve conduction'. He was elected FRS in 1948 and was awarded their Royal Medal in 1958, being made President in 1970. He was knighted in 1972.

See: *Nobel Lectures . . .* 1963–1970, Amsterdam, Elsevier Publishing Company, 1972, p. 49

HOMBERG Wilhelm (Batavia, Java 1652 – Paris 1715) originally a practising lawyer, he taught himself botany and astronomy and while in Magdeburg he became friendly with Otto von Guericke with whom he carried out some experiments. Following this he studied medicine in Padua and Bologna, where he experimented on the Bologna Stone. In France he worked with Nicolas Lemery and in London with Robert Boyle. He graduated in Medicine at Wittenberg and then eventually returned to Paris where he worked with various chemists, particularly Lemery, to whom he was greatly attached. He was a practical chemist of considerable skill and believed in the possibility of the transmutation of metals. His various chemical papers were on such subjects as, the phosphorescence of the Bologna Stone, the evaporation and freezing of water under the vacuum pump, the extraction of cocoa butter, the imitation of gems by coloured pastes, the prevention of iron rust, the distillation of acids from blood, flesh, milk, vipers, flies and ants, and more, covering a wide range of interests. He became First Physician to the Duke of Orleans.

See: J.R. Partington, *A History of Chemistry*, 1962, Vol. III, p. 42

HUMBOLDT Friedrich Heinrich Alexander, Baron von (Berlin 1769 – Berlin 1859) studied at the University of Göttingen, then Frankfurt on Oder and Freiburg. A naturalist and explorer, he travelled widely, publishing the results of these journeys of scientific exploration as he did when he engaged on the subject of animal electricity. An intimate associate of Goethe and Schiller, Humboldt was in contact with the greatest intellects in Europe. In Paris he collaborated with J.L. Gay Lussac in chemical experiments on the constitution of the atmosphere and later in Naples these two worked together examining the properties of electric fishes. In 1827, he returned to Berlin at the request of the King of Prussia and began a series of lectures on "Cosmos or Physical Universe." This is the title of his major work which has received universal recognition as an important contribution to the history of science.

See: (1) Paul Fleury Mottelay, *Biographical History of Electricity and Magnetism*, London, Charles Griffen and Co., 1922, p. 330
(2) *Chambers Encyclopaedia*, 1959, Vol. VII, p. 285

HUXLEY Andrew Fielding (London 1917–) is the grandson of Thomas Huxley and half-brother to Sir Julian and Aldous Huxley. He went up to Cambridge to study physical sciences, taking mathematics, chemistry and physics as subjects in Part I of the Tripos. He then turned to the study of physiology when he came in contact with such men as Adrian, Rushton and Hodgkin and this caused him to become interested in the problems of electro-physiology and the nature of nerve conduction. In 1939 he joined Hodgkin at the Marine Biological Laboratory in Plymouth where, together, they succeeded in recording electrically from the inside of the giant squid axon. In 1941 he was elected a research Fellow at Trinity College, Cambridge teaching in the department of physiology and being elected FRS in 1955. In 1960 he moved to London where he became head of the Department of Physiology in University College. In 1969 he was appointed to a Royal Society Research Professorship. From 1945–1951 Huxley's main work was with Hodgkin on nerve conductors. In 1952 he turned to the problems of muscle contraction and developed an interference microscope for studying the striation pattern in isolated muscle fibres. He was awarded the Nobel Prize in 1963 for his analysis of excitation and conduction in nerves.

See: *Nobel Lectures . . .*, Physiology or Medicine, 1963–1970, Amsterdam, Elsevier Publishing Co., 1972, p. 70

IRVINE William (Glasgow 1743/1749 – Glasgow 1787) became lecturer in *materia medica* and chemistry in the University of Glasgow. He differed from Black in his views of latent heat, supposing that the heat absorbed when a substance melts, is due to the greater capacity for heat of water as compared with ice.

See: J.R. Partington, *A History of Chemistry*, 1962, Vol. II, p. 154

KATZ Bernard (Leipzig 1911–) studied medicine at Leipzig University, obtaining his MD in 1934. Leaving Germany in 1935 he came to London and worked under A.V. Hill at University College, receiving his PhD in 1938. He then went to Australia to work with J.C. Eccles and S.W. Kuffler on Neuro-muscular research. After his war service he returned to University College as assistant to A.V. Hill who was Director of Research. He was then appointed to the Chair of Biophysics. Katz's contribution to the understanding of neuro-physiology has been mainly concerned with the physico-chemical basis of neuro-muscular transmission. He was awarded the Nobel Prize in 1970 and received a knighthood in 1969.

See: *Nobel Lectures . . .*, Physiology or Medicine, 1963–1970, p. 493.

KEILL James (Scotland 1673 – Northampton 1719) the younger brother of John Keill, the mathematician, was educated at home and on the Continent coming to England to lecture on anatomy at Oxford and Cambridge. He obtained his MD from the latter university and settled in Northampton as a physician. He was an able mathematician and anatomist and a follower of the iatro-mathematical or mechanical theory of medicine. He applied mathematical methods to such problems of physiology as secretion, muscular motion, the force of the heart beat and the amount of blood in the body but his application was premature and his results wide of the truth.

See: *Dictionary of National Biography*, 1908, Vol. X, p. 1197

LAGHI Tommaso (Bologna 1709 – Bologna 1764) was an anatomist greatly concerned with the dispute over Haller's doctrine of the sensitivity of nerves. He carried out a great number of anatomical and physiological experiments on the subject of irritability, finding himself opposed to the opinion of the great physiologist. He gave public letters in anatomy and apart from his medical practice, devoted a great deal of time to the teaching of anatomy at his home. He was greatly respected and loved by his pupils.

See: (1) G. Fantuzzi, (ii), Vol. V, p. 3
     (2) S. Mazzetti, (i), 1848, p. 175

LAHIRE Gabriel Phillipe de (Paris 1671 – Paris 1719) was the elder son of Phillipe de Lahire. Destined at first for a medical career, he studied anatomy but his interests soon turned to mathematics. He was received as a member of the Académie des Sciences in 1699, succeeding his father as Professor of Architecture. He died young, before he was able to finish a work on the subject of cutting lenses for telescopes. He left a memoir in which he attempted to prove that the aqueous humour of the eye fulfils the same function as the vitreous humour.

See: *Nouvelle Biographie Générale . . .*, 1861, Tom. 28, pp 901–903

LANGRISH Browne (Hampshire ? – Basingstoke 1759) was educated as a surgeon but in 1734 began to practise as a physician. He was elected FRS in 1731. Apart from his publications on muscular motion he wrote on such topics as animal experimentation with a view to finding a means of removing bladder stone, small pox and a general textbook of medicine.

See: *Dictionary of National Biography*, 1909, Vol. XL, p. 556

LAPLACE Pierre Simon, Marquis de (Beaumont-en-Auge, Normandy 1749 – Paris 1827) was the son of a poor farmer. He studied at Caen, taught mathematics at the local military academy and then went to Paris where he attracted the attention of d'Alembert. This led to his appointment as Professor in the Royal Military School. He was elected a member of the Académie des Sciences in 1785. An outstanding mathematician and astronomer, he systematised the results of such workers as

Newton, Halle, Clairent and Euler. He helped to establish the Polytechnic and Normal Schools in Paris, was Minister of the Interior for a brief period and later Chancellor of the Senate and elected President of the Académie Française in 1817. Besides many treatises on the application of mathematical methods to lunar and planetary problems molecular physics, electricity and magnetism, he wrote four books among which his *Exposition du Système du Monde* (Paris, 1796, 6th edn 1824) and *Mécanique Cèleste* (Paris 1799–1825) are classics.

See: *Chambers Encyclopaedia*, 1959, Vol. VIII, p. 365

LAVOISIER Antoine Laurent (Paris 1743 – Paris 1794) was educated at the Collège Mazarin and although he was introduced to science at school, entered the University to study law qualifying as a licentiate in 1764. However, he maintained his interest in science studying geology, chemistry, astronomy, mathematics, botany and anatomy under leading French academicians. It was to chemistry however that he eventually turned as his major interest, his great contribution to the subject being his attack on the currently accepted phlogiston theory. He showed that Priestley's 'eminently respirable air' was converted to 'fixed air' by respiration and by burning candles and that it combined with non-metals to form acids. He renamed it therefore, 'principe acidifiant' or 'principe Oxygine'. This work brought about a revolution in chemical theory which necessitated a new definition of elements and a new nomenclature which Lavoisier first proposed in his work *Méthode de Nomenclature Chimique* (Paris 1787) and set out more fully in a revised form in the great *Traité Élémentaire de Chimie, presenté dans un Ordre nouveau et d'après les découvertes modernes* (Paris, 1789). He met his death at the guillotine having been convicted of treason by the Revolutionary Tribunal.

See: D. McKie, *Antoine Lavoisier, Scientist, Economist, Social Reformer*, London, Constable, 1952

LEEUWENHOEK Antonj van (Delft 1632 – Delft 1723). At the age of 16 he was sent to Amsterdam in order to learn the drapery trade. While in Amsterdam he is believed to have met Jan Swammerdam. Six years later he returned to Delft and set up business as a draper and was elected Chamberlain to the city. His entry into the scientific world coincided with a publication of some of his original observations in the *Philosophical Transactions* of 1673. This was in no small part the result of the correspondence between Henry Oldenburg, Secretary of the Royal Society and the Dutch Physician Regnier de Graaf (who was a fellow townsman of Leeuwenhoek). The Royal Society at this time was inviting European workers to communicate the results of their work and de Graaf wrote to Oldenburg telling him of Leeuwenhoek's great ability to make microscopes with which he observed various biological minutiae. From this time onwards his observations appeared regularly in the *Philosophical Transactions*. Among his most important communications was his observation of the capillary vessels in the tails of tadpoles, frog's feet, bat's wings etc. He described various blood cells and was able to distinguish spermatozoa and various bacteria and protozoa. He was elected FRS in 1680.

See: Clifford Dobell, *Antony van Leeuwenhoek and his "little animals . . ."*, New York, Dover Publications, 1960

LELLI Erco (Bologna 1702 – Bologna 1766) studied design but unfortunately his early pictures were of no great merit. Becoming discouraged he turned to the art of preparing wooden and wax models for the teaching of anatomy. Working with

Manzolini, he achieved great success and renown in this field, producing beautiful specimens for the Institute of Anatomy. He wrote a compendium of anatomy for painters and sculptors and was held in high regard by Pope Benedetto XIV.

See: *Nouvelle Biographie Générale . . .*, 1862, Tom. 30, p. 539

LEMERY Louis (Paris 1677 – Paris 1743) the son of Nicholas Lemery, was a physician who graduated MD in Paris in 1698. He gave a course of lectures on chemistry at the Jardin du Roi in 1708 and became Demonstrator in 1731. He published a large number of papers in the Mémoirs of the Academy. These deal with such diverse topics as the precipitation of iron, essential oils, the nature of various chemical precipitates and particularly the different colours of Mercury precipitate, the contraction on the solution of salts in water, sal ammoniac, the origin of nitre, borax, corrosive sublimate, alum and vitriols. He proved that iron is present in plants and is not generated by combustion as Geoffroy thought.

See: J.R. Partington, *A History of Chemistry*, 1962, Vol. III, p. 41

LESLIE Patrick Dugud (?1751 – ?1783) graduated from Edinburgh in 1781 and became physician to Durham Hospital. Unfortunately he died only two years later from pulmonary tuberculosis at the age of 32. His particular interest was the subject of animal heat.

See: *The Medical Register for the year 1783*, London, Joseph Johnson, 1783, p. 210

LEUCIPPUS (Abdera 450BC–370BC) was the Greek philosopher credited with founding the atomic theory later developed by Democritus.

See: *Microsoft Encarta 1997 Encyclopedia*

LOCKE Frank Spiller (1871–1949) was appointed lecturer in the Department of Physiology at King's College, London in 1910, under Professor Haliburton, FRS. In 1915 he was made a Reader but he resigned in 1922 on the grounds of wishing to devote more time to research. He is remembered for adding glucose to Ringer's solution which is used in physiological experiments (Locke's solution). His papers, many of which appeared in the *Journal of Physiology*, were concerned with the effect of various chemical solutions on muscular activity.

Pers. commun. from Dr Venetia France, King's College, London

LUCRETIUS (Titus Lucretius Carus) (?99BC–55BC) was the Roman poet whose poem *De Rerum Natura* presents the theories of Democritus and Epicurus.

See: *Microsoft Encarta 1997 Encyclopedia*

MACQUER Pierre Joseph (Paris 1718 – Paris 1784) graduated MD in 1742 and became Professor of Chemistry in the Jardin du Roi in 1771. He was an excellent teacher and his book *Elémens de Chymie Théorique* (Paris, 1749), became the standard textbook for students in France replacing Lemery's *Cours de Chymie* which had held this position for some time. His teaching was essentially from facts rather than philosophical theories and his book which was based on his lecture notes, was soon translated into other European languages so that his influence on the teaching of chemistry in Europe was considerable. Although he subscribed to the phlogiston theory and was alarmed by Lavosier's early suggestions that this was an erroneous concept he was ready to accept the new theory as soon as he was offered the practical evidence of Lavoisier's experiments.

See: J.R. Partington, *A History of Chemistry*, 1962, Vol. III, p. 80

MAHON Charles, third Earl of Stanhope (London 1753 – Chevening 1816) was both a politician and scientist. After early schooling at Eton, he came under the tutelage of G.J. le Sage in Geneva where his family had moved and at this stage his scientific interests were apparently developed. When only 18 he was awarded a prize by the Academy of Stockholm for a paper in French on the pendulum but quite soon after this he retired to England and became involved in politics rather than science. He became a close friend of William Pitt the younger and sat in the House of Lords. He urged the reform of parliament, an increase in polling places and a register of voters and was vehement in his attacks on corrupt practices. As a result of his scientific interests he was elected FRS in 1772 and was a member of the Philadelphia Philosophical Society. His main experiments related to the fire proofing of buildings by means of stucco. He was interested in steam propulsion and took out patents for steamships, his inventions receiving the approval of the Admiralty. He also devised various printing presses and perfected a process of stereo-typing. Apart from these major interests, he invented calculating machines and tuning instruments, developed microscope lenses, designed canals and many other novel things. He was, in fact, a polymath of considerable genius for all his electrical researches took but a small part of his time.

See: *Dictionary of National Biography*, 1909, Vol. XVIII, p. 888

MALEBRANCHE Nicolas (Paris 1638 – Paris 1715) was educated at the Collège de la Marche of Paris University, graduating MA in 1656. He then studied theology at the Sorbonne and entered the Congregation of the Oratory in 1660. As a result of reading the *Traitè de l'homme* of Descartes he grafted Cartesian ideas to his religious views, as evidenced by his *De la Recherche de la verité* (Paris, 1674–1712) which he began in 1668. He was interested in mathematics although he was by no means a mathematician of any great talent, his main importance historically being due to his role as a disseminator of the mathematical discoveries of both Descartes and Leibniz. In this respect he played a fundamental rôle in the reform of mathematics. His *Mémoire sur la lumière, les couleurs . . .* (Paris, 1699) won him entry to the Académie des Sciences in 1699.

See: *Dictionary of Scientific Biography*, 1974, Vol. IX, p. 47

MALPIGHI Marcello (Crevalcore 1628 – Rome 1694) entered Bologna University in 1645 in order to study philosophy but unfortunately his studies were interrupted owing to the death of his parents. However, he eventually returned to the study of medicine in 1651 and became an active member of the Corus Anatomicus – the name given to the group of younger professors who met regularly at the house of Bartolomeo Massari, the Professor of Medicine. This gathering of the most active minds among the Bologna anatomists was the inheritor of William Harvey's ideas and the meetings were devoted to discussion as well as experimental work on both dead bodies and living animals. Mapighi soon made his name in this group by virtue of his outstanding ability and obtained his MD in 1653. He took up medical practice and was granted a Chair of Medicine in 1656. For personal and family reasons, however, he moved to Pisa where Ferdinand II had created a special Chair in Theoretical Medicine (Physiology). Here he met Borelli and the two became close friends, the latter teaching Malpighi the new mathematics – physical ideas of the Galilean school, while Malpighi in turn, opened Borelli's mind to anatomical and biological problems. Again, owing to domestic problems, he left Pisa to return to Bologna and took up his old Chair. It was at this time that he did his work on the structure of the lung. The results of this work were published in *De pulmonibus observationes* *anatomicae* (Bologna, Baptista Ferronius, 1661). The two major discoveries which this important work contained were Malpighi's demonstration of the vesicular architecture of the lung substance, and the presence of a capillary network of vessels joining the arteries to the veins. After a brief spell in Messina, Malpighi returned once more to Bologna, publishing his work on the glandular nature of various organs, under the title *De viscerum structura exercibatio anatomica* (Bologna, 1666), his work dealing with the spleen, kidneys, liver and brain. (Unfortunately his interpretation of the structure of the cerebral cortex was erroneous.) His microscopical work also included a study of the taste buds of the tongue and the skin, his name being associated with the lower layer of the epidermis known as the 'Malpighian layer'.) His contributions to embryology as well as anatomy and zoology were outstanding and he ranks as one of the foremost biologists of all time.

See: Sir Michael Foster, *Lectures on the History of Physiology . . .*, 1970, p. 86

MANFREDI Eraclito (Bologna 1682 – Bologna 1759) was the brother of Eustachio Manfredi the Bolognese anatomist and Gabriello Manfredi the mathematician who was himself Professor of Mathematics, then the Professor of Medicine in the University of Bologna. The family was of great influence in the teaching of the new Galilean physics in Bologna. The link between the physical and medical sciences which created the intellectual background to the development of physiology in Bologna was in great part due to their influence.

See: (1) *Poggendorf* (M–Z), 1863, p. 31
　　　(2) G. Fantuzzi, (ii), 1781–1794, Vol. V, p. 182
　　　(3) S. Mazzetti, (i), 1848, p. 194

MARSIGLI Luigi Ferdinando Count (Bologna 1658 – Bologna 1730) came from a noble family, serving in the Army of Emperor Leopold I and attaining high rank. He was an inveterate traveller and gained a comprehensive knowledge of history, geography, politics and natural sciences. He was a disciple of Galileo's methods and this, together with his keen powers of observation, made him an able naturalist. He was particularly interested in the structure of mountains, seas, lakes and rivers, leaving many observations on the gypsum bearing strata of the Adriatic slopes of the Appenines. He published a study of the Bosphorus in 1681 and *Histoire physique de la mer* (Amsterdam, 1724) which was noted for his inclusion of Corals as plants. His works presaged the oceanographic exploration that was to follow, half a century later, with the famous voyage of the Endeavour, for his methods which he again used in his study of the physical and biological aspects of Lake Garda, indicated the way in which such comprehensive undertakings should be tackled. He is particularly well remembered as the founder in 1712 of Italy's Accademia dell Scienze dell' Instituto di Bologna. He was made FRS in 1722.

See: *Dictionary of Scientific Biography*, 1974, Vol. IX, p. 134

MARUM Martinus van (Delft 1750 – Haarlem 1837) was educated in Gröningen where he graduated in medicine in 1773 and was elected to the directorship of the new Museum of Natural History in 1784. He took over the care of a number of electrical machines in the Teyler Foundation, renovating and improving them, and building what was at that time the most powerful electrical machine known. He also constructed a very powerful battery with which he carried out extensive electrical experiments. He corresponded with the leading physicists and chemists of his day, conveying to them the results of his work. Among other things, he investigated the development of electricity during the melting and cooling of resinous bodies, the effects of electricity on animal and vegetable life and brought about the decomposition of water by means of electricity.

See: (1) *Biographisches Lexikon . . .*, 1932, p. 104

(2) Paul Fleur Mottelay, *Biographical History of Electricity and Magnetism*, London, Charles Griffin and Co., 1922, p. 452

MATTEUCCI Carlo (Forli 1811 – Leghorn 1868) studied at Bologna University and received his doctorate in mathematics in 1829. He later studied in Paris, returning to Bologna in 1832 when he began his electro-physiological studies, moving to Ravenna (where he was also director of a chemical factory), and then to Pisa University. In 1860 he was appointed Director of the Italian Telegraph System and later Director of the Meteorological Institute in Pisa. He was Minister for Culture for a short time and finally worked in the Institute of Science in Florence. His *Traité des phénomènes électro-physiologiques des animaux, suivies d'études anatomiques . . .* (Paris, 1844) was the starting point for Du Bois Reymond's work on the electricity of muscles and nerves. Although the latter spoke glowingly of Matteucci and his work when he first read it, some unfortunate remarks by Matteucci concerning Du Bois Reymond's experimental techniques led to a bitter resentment of the younger Swiss physicist and an unfortunate dispute and enmity developed between the two men.

See: (1) *Biographisches Lexikon . . .*, 1932, p. 116

(2) Emil Du Bois Reymond, *Jugendbriefe von E. Du Bois Reymond an Eduard Hallman*, Berlin, Dietrich Reimer, 1918, p. 120

MAUPERTUIS Pierre Louis, Moreau de (St Malo 1698 – Basel 1759) after private schooling went to Paris to study philosophy but disliking this, turned to the study of music. However, this was abandoned when he discovered a liking for mathematics which he studied under Guisnée and Nicole. He was elected to the Académie des Sciences in 1723 and began to publish papers on mathematics and biology. In 1728 he visited London when he became converted to the Newtonian mechanistic philosophy returning to France as a protagonist of these ideas which he defended against Cartesianism. He went on an expedition, aimed at measuring the length of a degree along the meridian of longitude (to be compared with similar measurements undertaken in Peru) since if as Newton postulated, the poles are flattened, these distances should vary. He was elected to the Académie Française in 1743 and two years later accepted Frederick the Great's invitation to go to the Academy of Sciences in Berlin where he attracted such men as Euler and La Mettrie among others. He was interested in the embryological controversy of preformation *versus* epigenesis, and was a firm adherent of the latter view, arguing that the embryo could not be pre-formed since characteristics could be passed on equally through the male or female parents. His *Système de la Nature* (Erlangen, 1751) a significant work, dealt with the question of bi-parental heredity. He investigated the family of a Berlin barber-surgeon who had polydactyly, and made the first explicit analysis of the transmission of a dominant heredity trait in man. As a result of this study, he postulated the existence of heredity particles in the semen of male and female parents corresponding to the various parts of the embryo they produced. Unfortunately Maupertuis became embroiled in various disputes, the most unpleasant of which was with Voltaire, whose verbal attacks were in great part responsible for him leaving Berlin.

See: *Dictionary of Scientific Biography*, 1974, Vol. IX, p. 186

MAYOW John (Morval, nr Looe 1641 – London 1679) was received as a Commoner of Wadham College, Oxford in 1658. He was elected to a Fellowship of All Souls two years later and having graduated in 1660, he became a noted medical practitioner in Bath. He was elected FRS in 1678, having been proposed by Hooke. His writings consisted of five treatises, two dealing with clinical subjects, *De respiratione* and *De rachitide*, both published in Oxford in 1668, and three concerned with chemical and biological subjects and published in 1674, *De sal nitro et spirita nitro-aereo; De respiratione foetus in utero et ovo* and *De motu muscularis et spiritibus animalibus.* In these latter treatises he anticipated the discovery of oxygen which was to come a century later. He perceived that only part of the air is concerned in respiration and combustion, two processes which he realised were chemically similar, demonstrating his ideas by ingenious experiments.

See: *Dictionary of National Biography,* 1894, Vol. XXXVII, p. 175

MENGHINI Vincento Antonio (Budrio 1704 – Bologna 1759) after his early schooling in Budrio, Menghini went to Bologna where he enrolled at the school of Teodosio Poeti, studying medicine and obtaining his Laureate in 1726. Ten years later he was appointed to the Chair of Logic and the following year to that of theoretical medicine, a post he held until his death. In 1725 he was admitted to the Academy of the Institute of Sciences, becoming its President in 1748. His most important scientific work was a study of the iron content of blood, although he published other works on urinary calculi, and on the medicinal use of Camphor. The results of his work, the first demonstration of the presence of iron in human blood, were published in two parts, the first *De ferrearum particularum sede in sanguine* (De Bononiensi scientiarum et artium Instituto atque Accademia Commentarii 1746), the second, *De ferrearum particularum progressu in sanguinem* (Ibid., 1747)

See: (1) Antonio Brighetti, 'Il Menghini et la scoperta del ferro nel sangue' *Pagine di Storia della Medicina,* 1968, 12; pp 63–80
(2) G. Fantuzzi, (ii), 1781–1794, Vol. VI, p. 8
(3) S. Mazzetti, (i), 1848, p. 208

MINES George Ralph (?Norfolk 1886 – Montreal 1914) went to school in Kings Lynn. He entered Sidney Sussex College, Cambridge in 1904 where he obtained first class honours in both parts of the Natural Science Tripos. He gained various university prizes including the Gedge Prize for research in physiology in 1911, the title of his paper being 'Researches on the physiological action of organic salts, chiefly in relation to the cardiac and skeletal muscles of the frog'. He was elected to a Fellowship at Sidney Sussex College in 1909. In 1914 he left England to take up the Chair of Physiology at McGill University in Montreal but died tragically the same year as a result of an accident in his laboratory.

From information kindly given by Dr Otto Smail, Sidney Sussex College, Cambridge.

MOLINELLI Pier Paolo (Bourbiana, nr Bologna 1702 – Bologna 1751) came to Bologna as a child and after his early schooling studied philosophy under Lelio Trionfetti, mathematics with Geminiano Rondelli and medicine with Matteo Bazzani. His main interest however was in medicine and in particular surgery which became his life's work. He wrote a number of works dealing with surgical pathology. At the early age of 19 he carried out a number of experiments on living animals before the Academy. These showed the convulsive effects of irritating the

right or left side of the brain. He studied surgery in Paris and Montpellier and on his return to Bologna he was appointed to the Chair of Operational Surgery. He became the leading Bolognese surgeon of his time.
See: M. Medici, (ii), 1857, p. 311 *et seq.*

MONRO Alexander (Secundus) (Edinburgh 1733 – Edinburgh 1817) the youngest son of Professor Alexander Monro (Primus) studied medicine at Edinburgh University showing an early interest in anatomy. His abilities were recognised and he was appointed joint Professor with his father, in 1754, the two sharing the load of teaching. He left Edinburgh to study with William Hunter in London, J.F. Meckel in Berlin and in 1757 enrolled at Leyden University, spending a year there and meeting Professors B.L. Albinus and Pieter Camper. His most important publication, *Observations on the Structure and Functions of the Nervous System* (Edinburgh, Creech, 1783) contains a description of the 'foramen of Monro' between the lateral and third ventricle of the brain, although he made no claim to priority in describing such a communication, acknowledging that Galen and many succeeding anatomists had noted it. However, he would not admit to a communication between the fourth ventricle and the spinal cord. He was Joint-Secretary of the Philosophical Society with David Hume.
See: R.E. Wright St Clair, *Doctors Munro*, London, The Wellcome Historical Medical Library, 1964, pp 69–95

MONTI Gaetano (? – ?) was a Bolognese anatomist who studied the reproductive physiology of various species.
See: M. Medici, (ii), 1857, p. 397

MORANDI-MANZOLINI Anna (Bologna 1716 – Bologna 1774) married the Bolognese anatomist Giovanni Manzolini who had worked with Erco Lelli preparing models for anatomical instruction. Anna Morandi soon joined her husband in this work, learning anatomy theory and becoming a highly skilled and very learned anatomist. Her models, which were placed in the Museum of Anatomy after her death, brought her widespread fame throughout Europe. It was at the dedication of this Museum that Galvani read an oration in her praise.
See: M. Medici, (ii), 1857, p. 356

MORTIMER Cromwell (Essex ? – Hatfield Peverel, Essex, 1752) went to Leyden to study medicine under Boerhaave, graduating MD in 1724. He became a Fellow of the Royal College of Physicians the following year and obtained his MD from Cambridge University in 1728. He practised in Bloomsbury Square, London, where he was in contact with Sir Hans Sloane and had the use of the superb collections of the latter. He was elected FRS in 1728 and was acting Secretary of the Society until his death. A vain man, he was not altogether popular with his professional colleagues. He edited Volume xxxvi to xlvi of the *Philosophical Transactions* and contributed numerous papers to them the most important of which dealt with distemper in cattle.
See: *Dictionary of National Biography*, 1909, Vol. XIII, p. 1014

NERNST Walther (Briesen 1864 – Ober-Zibell, nr Moscow 1941) studied at Zurich, Berlin, Graz and Wurzburg. He then worked in Ostwald's school in Leipzig eventually transferring to Berlin where he succeeded Lanholt at the Physical Chemistry Institute and to which, after a short break as President of the Physikalisch-

Technische Reichs Anstalt (1920–1922) he returned as Professor of Physics. His work was concerned with electrolytic dissociation, showing in 1889 that the production of an electromotive force in Galvanic cells could be explained in terms of 'solution pressure' of the metal electrodes, tending to throw off charged ions into solution and a counterbalancing osmotic force produced by the dissolved ions. He was awarded the Nobel Prize in 1921 for his work on thermodynamics and his enunciation of 'The Heat Theorem', commonly referred to as the third law of thermodynamics.

    See: (1) *Chambers Encyclopaedia*, 1959, Vol. IX, p. 763

        (2) J.R. Partington, *A Short History of Chemistry*, London, Macmillan, 3rd edn, 1957, p. 336

NEWTON Sir Isaac (Woolsthorpe 1642 – London 1727) after an early education at Grantham Grammar School, Newton went to Trinity College Cambridge, graduating in 1665. During the rest of 1665 and 1666 he spent a great deal of time at home as a result of the plague reaching Cambridge and at this time he conceived his ideas on gravitation, discovered the binomial theorem and formulated his method of fluxions direct and inverse. Also during this richly productive period he discovered the composition of white light and the specific refrangibility of its various components. He was elected FRS in 1672. His epoch-making *Philosophiae Naturalis Principia Mathematica*, appeared in 1687. He became master of the Mint in 1699 and President of The Royal Society in 1703. His *Opticks* was first published in 1704 and he was knighted in 1705.

    See: (1) Louis Trenchard More, *Isaac Newton*, New York, Dover Publications, 1962

        (2) I. Bernard Cohen, *Franklin and Newton* . . .

'**N.N.**' No details of the anonymous 'Padre Lettore N.N.' have been found.

NOBILI Leopoldo (Trassilico, nr Reggio 1784 – Florence 1835) was Professor of Physics in Florence. His main interest was in the relationship between electricity and magnetism demonstrated by Oersted and much of his work was concerned with the use of galvanometers in electrical investigation.

    See: *Poggendorf* (M–Z), 1863, p. 291

OERSTED Hans Christian (Rudkjöbing 1777 – Copenhagen 1851) attended Copenhagen University where he was appointed Professor of Physics in 1806. A man of great intellect he was unfortunately a particularly unskilled experimenter. It has been said that it was by accident that he discovered the ability of a current of electricity to deflect the magnetic needle. Be that as it may, this discovery which took place in 1819 was of fundamental importance to the development of Faraday's ideas and to the development of the galvanometer which was to be of such significance to electro-physiology in the 19th century. Oersted's discovery was thus of both theoretical and practical importance to the study of neuro-muscular excitation, since the theories of the first half of the 19th century were based on an analogy with Faraday's development of the relationship between electrical and magnetic forces.

    See: (1) Florian Cajori, *A History of Physics*, New York, Dover Publications, 1962, p. 231

        (2) L. Pearce Williams, *Michael Faraday*, London, Chapman and Hall, 1965, p. 137

        (3) Paul Fleury Mottelay, *Biographical History of Electricity and Magnetism*, London, Charles Griffen & Co., 1922, p. 452.

OSTWALD Wilhelm (Riga 1853 – Leipzig 1932) combined an artistic and scientific imagination with the ability to read widely, experiment skilfully and deduce rationally. In his youth he subordinated his artistic and literary talents completely to his rigid scientific method, although he was characterised by a desire to generalise from his results. He was always primarily interested in the fundamental laws demonstrated by any of his experiments and in later life became interested in the philosophy of science. As part of his university examination he discussed Julius Tomsen's work on thermo-chemistry and was struck by the fact that not only heat but other properties such as density could be used as a means of characterising and following chemical events in solutions. This idea led to numerous experiments, wherein he measured the densities and refractive indices of solutions. In 1832 he became Professor of Chemistry at Riga. The work of Arrhenius on electrochemistry stimulated him to researches resulting in a 'dilution law' for the electrical conductivity of acids in aqueous solutions. In 1887 he was elected to the Chair of Chemistry in Leipzig where he initiated a programme of physical chemistry. His great contribution to science was the concept of catalysis, for which he was awarded the Nobel Prize in 1909. Since this was a general concept, his award pleased him greatly and he considered this his most worthy piece of work. Late in life he became deeply interested in the concept of energy, fascinated by what he considered "the energy relationships between our sense organs and the world around us". As a result of this concept he denied atomism.

   See: (1) Eduard Farber, *Great Chemists*, New York, Interscience Publishers, 1961, p. 1021

   (2) *Biographical Dictionary of Scientists*, T.I. Williams (ed.), London, A. and C. Black, 1969, p. 398

PARMENIDES (around 500BC) was the Greek philosopher whose beliefs were the foundation of the materialistic explanations of the universe propounded by Empedocles and Democritus

   See: *Microsoft Encarta 1997 Encyclopedia*

PEMBERTON Henry (London 1694 – London 1771) received a good general education and then went to Leyden in 1714 where he studied medicine under Boerhaave and at the same time, "contemplated the best mathematical authors". A period in Paris followed during which he studied anatomy and he then went to St Thomas's Hospital in London. An industrious writer, he was soon elected FRS and became a friend of Newton, who employed him to superintend the publishing of the third edition of the *Principia* . . . In 1728 he became Gresham Professor. His main contribution to science was as populariser of Newton's work. He published *A view of Sir Isaac Newton's Philosophy* (London, 1728).

   See: *Dictionary of National Biography*, 1909, Vol. XV, p. 725

PETRINI Giorgio Vincenzo (? 1725 – ? 1814). The only reference found (shown below) was not available for consultation.

   See: Tommaso Vignas, *Index Bio-bibliographics, Matris Dei Scholarum piarum*, Roma, Tip. Vaticana, 1908–1911, 3 Vols, Vol. 3, p. 282.

PLATO (Athens ?428BC – Athens ?347BC) was the Greek philosopher who founded the Academy in Athens in 387BC. He wrote extensively on a wide variety of subjects. At the centre of his philosophy was the Theory of Forms which permeated all aspects of his philosophy.

   See: *Microsoft Encarta 1997 Encyclopedia*

PLOTINUS (Asyut, Egypt 205–270) was the Roman philosopher who founded Neoplatonism. He taught in Alexandria and Rome and wrote 54 treatises in Greek called the *Enneads*. These were edited by his student Porphyry.

See: *Microsoft Encarta 1997 Encyclopedia*

PLUTARCH (Chaeronea, Boetia ?46–120). Greek biographer and essayist who lectured in Rome and Athens. His biographies of great men have influenced other writers for generations.

See: *Microsoft Encarta 1997 Encyclopedia*

PRIESTLEY Joseph (Fieldhead 1733 – Northumberland, Penn. 1804) was brought up by his aunt who was a strict non-conformist and from whom he acquired his strong religious convictions. He studied for the non-conformist ministry at the dissenting Academy at Daventry. In 1751 he supplemented his small stipend as a minister by opening a school, acquiring an air pump and electrical machine – tokens of two of the areas of scientific study with which his name is remembered. He was elected FRS in 1766 – having written to Canton to say he wished this and the following years published his famous *History and Present State of Electricity* (London, 1767). (About this time Priestley had become acquainted with Benjamin Franklin, William Watson, John Canton and others who were actively engaged in electrical research.) With little other chemical knowledge beyond that gleaned from reading Boerhaave's *Elements of Chemistry* (Leyden, 1732) he began his own experiments, having become 'literary companion' to Lord Shelbourne, a post which gave him financial security and an environment in which he could devote himself to such work. He travelled on the continent with his patron and met Lavoisier and other French chemists. Working within the framework of the phlogiston theory, he discovered oxygen, noting that this fraction of the atmospheric air was particularly pleasant to breathe and would support a mouse for twice as long as the same volume of common air. He was also struck by the vigour with which a candle flame burned in his 'pure air'. He further observed that air which had been rendered unfit to support animal respiration could be revitalised by allowing green plants to grow in it but of course our present day interpretation of this phenomena of photosynthesis was explained by Priestley in terms of the phlogiston theory. After Lavoisier's masterful refutation of this, Priestley continued to defend it, his *Doctrine of Phlogiston Established . . .* (Northumberland, 1800) being his last stand against the new theory. He died in North America where he had moved in 1794 following the sacking of his home in Birmingham by rioters who objected to his freely expressed liberal political and religious sentiments.

See: J.R. Partington, *A History of Chemistry*, 1963, Vol. III, p. 237

RÉAUMUR René Antoine Ferchault, Sieur de (Rochelle 1683 – Bermondière 1757) having received an early education in law, gave up any intention of legal practice and studied science in Paris under Pierre Varignon. He became a member of the Académie in 1708 and was elected FRS in 1738. A man of considerable wealth he was somewhat of a polymath, able to indulge his interest and great natural talent in such fields as mathematics, natural history, chemistry and physics. He made a number of useful biological observations, perhaps the most notable being concerned with the digestive powers of the digestive juices of kites. His studies of insects resulted in his epoch-making book, *Mémoire pour servir à l'histoire des insectes* (6 vols, Paris, 1734–1742), his rich collection of natural history specimens being bequeathed to the Académie. He designed the Réamur thermometer, investigated the manufacture of porcelain and made valuable contributions to the steel industry in France as a result of his researches into the conversion of iron into steel.

See: J.R. Partington, Vol. III, p. 60

RINGER Sydney (Norwich 1835 – Lastingham, Yorkshire 1910) had a severe nonconformist upbringing. He studied medicine at University College, London, graduating in 1860 and obtaining his MD in 1863. An appointment as physician at University College Hospital followed and later at the Hospital for Sick Children. At University College he held successively the Chairs of Materia Medica, Pharmacology, Therapeutics and the Principles and Practice of Medicine and finally was appointed Holme Professor of Clinical Medicine. Having established himself in clinical medicine he turned his attention to physiological research, being especially interested in the influence of organic salts, particularly calcium on the circulation and heart beat. 'Ringer's solution' is still used universally in physiological experiments where an ionically balanced fluid is required for animal experiments. He was elected FRS in 1885.

See: *Dictionary of National Biography*, 2nd Suppl. 1912, Vol. III, p. 22

ROBINSON Bryan (? 1680 – Dublin 1754) was educated at Trinity College Dublin, obtaining his MB in 1709 and his MD two years later. He gave anatomical lectures for two years at Trinity (1716–1717) and in 1745 he was appointed Professor of Physic. He had a flourishing practise in Dublin and was three times President of the Royal College of Physicians of Ireland. His main interest was in animal electricity. However, his publications on this subject met with criticism.

See: *Dictionary of National Biography*, 1909, Vol. XVII, p. 4

SANDRI Jacopo (? – Bologna 1718).
See: (1) Chapter 13 of this book, Note 1
       (2) S. Mazzetti, (i), 1848, p. 280 and (ii), 1848, p. 75
       (3) G. Fantuzzi, (ii), 1781–1794, Vol. 7, p. 306

SCARPA Antonio (Mattadi Livenza c. 1750 – Bonasco 1832) after his early studies in mathematics with one of his uncles, he showed an interest in the study of medicine and his family sent him to Padua where he was taught by Morgagni who developed a great friendship with his young pupil whom he made his secretary. After a short time in Bologna, he returned to Padua to complete his studies, graduating in surgery at Modena in 1772. His early works on the anatomy of the ear date from this time and gave rise to the long drawn out debate between Galvani and himself as to priority in certain discoveries. In 1780, Scarpa undertook a voyage to England and France, studying the organisation of medical education. While in Paris he worked with Vicq d'Azyr among others and in London he became the pupil of Pott, Cruikshank and the Hunter brothers. In 1784 he went to Vienna with Volta and later visited many of the German universities, establishing a reputation throughout Europe as Italy's leading surgeon-anatomist. His anatomical and surgical works which are numerous dealt with nerve ganglia, the spinal and cardiac nerves, herniae, aneurysms and diseases of the eyes and bones.

See: *Nouvelle Biographie Générale* . . ., 1864, Tom. 43, p. 466

SCHULZE Johann Heinrich (Colbitz 1687 – Halle 1744) graduated in medicine at Halle in 1717 becoming Professor of Medicine three years later. He then went to the

University of Altdorf where he was Professor of Greek and Arabic. In 1732 he returned to Halle as Professor of Medicine. He was a correspondent of the Berlin Academy. Among his various papers which were almost all to do with chemical topics, is *Scotophorus pro phosphoro inventus: seu experimentum curiosum de effectum radiorum solarium* (Act. Acad. Nat. Cur. 1, 1727).

See: *Poggendorf* (M–Z), p. 862.

SLOANE Sir Hans (Killileagh 1660 – London 1753) studied medicine at Paris and Montpellier and learned history under Pierre Magnol and Tournefort. He graduated MD at the University of Orange in 1683. He had become acquainted with Robert Boyle and John Ray before going to France and resumed his friendship on his return. He was elected FRS in 1685. At this time he met Thomas Sydenham and went to live at the house of the famous physician. He was admitted to the College of Physicians in 1687. In the same year he sailed to the West Indies as physician to the Duke of Albemarle, Governor of Jamaica, and during a stay of nearly two years, made a wonderful collection of natural history specimens including eight hundred plants which he brought back to England with him. He settled in practice and bought a Manor House at Chelsea where he created a garden, stocked with many of his interesting and rare specimens. This garden founded in 1712 for the Society of Apothecaries, is still in existence. His publications included, *Catalogus Plantarum quae in insula Jamaica sponte proveniunt aut vulgo coluntur* (London, 1696) and *A Voyage to the Islands of Madeira, Barbadoes, Nieves, St Christopher's and Jamaica with the Natural History of the last* (London, 2 Vols, 1707 and 1725). He was elected a foreign member of the French Academy the Imperial Academy at St Petersburg and the Royal Academy at Madrid. On the death of Sir Isaac Newton in 1727 he was elected President of the Royal Society contributing various papers to the *Philosophical Transactions.* His medical practice was extremely large and successful and he numbered amongst his patients, the most influential and famous figures in English society. He was physician to Queen Anne and George II carrying out inoculations of the various members of the Royal family. Appointed physician to Christ's Hospital, he gave all his salary to the Foundation and was energetic in his appeals for financial aid on its behalf. It is said that he never refused to treat a patient who could not afford to pay his fees. Sloane's collection, which he bequeathed to the Nation was put in the care of Trustees who placed it in Montague House (1753). This collection formed the nucleus of what has grown into the British Museum. The Sloane Manuscripts containing letters by some of the most eminent physicians of the time form a highly valuable source of medical historical material.

See: (1) *Dictionary of National Biography*, 1909, Vol. XVIII, p. 379

(2) E. St John Brookes, *Sir Hans Sloane*, London, The Batchworth Press, 1954

(3) J.R. de Beer, *Sir Hans Sloane and the British Museum,* London, published for the Trustees of the British Museum by G. Cumberlege, Oxford University Press, 1953

SPALLANZANI Lazaro (Scandiano 1729 – Pavia 1799). After an early education at the Jesuit College at Reggio he entered Bologna University where he studied philosophy under his aunt Laura Bassi-Verati, having given up his original intention of becoming a lawyer. At the age of 26 he was appointed Professor of Belles Lettres and Philosophy at Reggio University but soon his interests were entirely directed to natural science. In 1760 he moved to Modena where he published papers on the action of the heart and blood vessels and the generation of hydra. At this stage he produced an Italian translation of Bonnet's *Contemplation de la Nature.* (Amsterdam

1764–1765). A great admirer of the French Naturalists he was flattered to be called the 'Buffon of Italy'. In 1770 he was appointed Professor of Natural History at Pavia, occupying himself with researches on the circulation, the natural history of infusoria and his famous experiments when he showed that digestion is a chemical rather than mechanical process and distinct from fermentation. He studied the senses of bats, demonstrated the necessity of the spermatozoon for fertilisation and was concerned with the problem of spontaneous generation, showing that boiled broth will not ferment if air is excluded. He travelled widely in the Mediterranean and Black Sea regions, writing on his observations of volcanoes and other geological features of interest. In 1797 Galvani addressed communications to Spallanzani on the subject of animal electricity.

See: (1) *Dictionnaire des Sciences Medicales . . .*, 1825, Tom. 7, p. 235
      (2) *Nouvelle Biographie General . . .*, 1865, Tom. 44, p. 282
      (3) *Chambers Encyclopaedia*, 1959, p. 15

STAHL Georg Ernst (Anspach 1660 – Berlin 1734) was one of the outstanding chemists of the 18th century. He studied medicine at Jena, taking his MD in 1683 and giving public lectures. In 1694 he went to Halle where he became second Professor of Medicine, a post he held for over 20 years. He was radically opposed to iatro-chemical ideas and although he taught medicine and chemical subjects he kept these entirely separate being of the view that chemistry can give no help in the understanding or explanation of vital functions. Like Becker he refused to base his chemical explanations on any known theory of matter (atomic or otherwise) and he insisted on practical chemical analysis as the only means of arriving at a true understanding of the essential chemical truths. His vitalism was extreme. He viewed all living things as differing from non-living objects in that they possessed a soul with (anima). This 'sensitive soul', which was of a completely abstract nature, however, worked directly on the chemical processes in the animal body. His great contribution to chemical theory was his introduction of the phlogiston theory which he developed into the system which dominated chemical thought until it was finally replaced by the new concepts established by Lavoisier at the end of the 18th century.

See: J.R. Partington, *A History of Chemistry*, 1969, Vol. II, p. 653

STENSEN (STENO) Nicolaus (Copenhagen 1638 – Schwerin 1686) was the son of a devout Lutheran, studied medicine in Copenhagen under Bartholin, in Leyden under Sylvius and then in Amsterdam under Blasius. While dissecting in the house of Blasius he discovered the duct of the parotid gland, which is commonly known as Stensen's duct and later completed this work by displaying the ducts of the sublingual, buccal and lachrymal glands. He published the results of his discovery in *Observationes Anatomicae* (Leyden, 1662). *Elementorum myologiae specimen* (Florence, 1667) was a significant publication. In this he described a muscle as composed of many muscle fibres, each of which is, in turn, composed of many minute fibrils. He grasped the essential fact that the fleshy part of the muscle is its true contractile element and that the tendinous part is purely passive, thus refuting the current view of the tendon as the contractile element, nourished by the fleshy part. Following this he travelled widely in Germany and France meeting the learned men of his time. While in Paris he delivered a discourse on the *Anatomy of the Brain* published in 1669, criticising the views put forward by Descartes. A spell in Italy as Court Physician in Florence followed and during this time he published a fundamentally important geological work, *De Solido intra Solidum Natur aliter contento dissertationes* *prodromus* (London, 1671). He became a convert to Catholicism and received the titular honour of Bishop of Titiopolis in Greece in 1677, being sent as vicar Apostolic to the northern countries of Europe in an attempt to convert them back to the Roman church. For a time he tried to combine anatomical teaching with his religious duties but this was unsuccessful and he gave up all scientific interests in order to devote himself to the Church and his work with it.

See: Sir Michael Foster, *Lectures in the History of Physiology* . . ., pp 70–71 and 106–108

STUART Alexander (London 1673 – ?London 1742) studied medicine in Leyden, graduating MD in 1711. He was admitted a Licentiate of the Royal College of Physicians in 1720. He became Physician in Ordinary to the Queen and was later a Fellow and Censor of the College. Apart from his clinical work at St George's and Westminster Hospitals, he devoted considerable time to the study of the problems of muscular motion and gained the Copley medal of the Royal Society for this. He delivered three Croonean Lectures before the Royal Society on this subject in 1739.

See: (1) *The Roll of the Royal College of Physicians of London*, Vol. II, London, The College, 1701–1800, p. 109
(2) *Dictionnaire encyclopédique des sciences médicales*, 3 série, Vol. 12, p. 451

SWAMMERDAM Jan (Amsterdam 1637 – Amsterdam 1680) was the son of Jacob Swammerdam (Dirkz) who was interested in natural history and had a magnificent collection of specimens which he had acquired from all over the world. Jan, who was originally intended for the church, turned to the study of medicine and was meanwhile entrusted with the cleaning and care of his father's museum. This proved to be the stimulus which led him to collect, dissect and catalogue as many specimens as he could find and soon added numerous new discoveries. Thus initiated in natural history, he entered Leyden University in 1661 to study medicine, graduating in 1663, having been taught by Franciscus de le Boë, Sylvius and Blasius. At Leyden he formed friendships with Nicolaus Stensen and Regnier de Graaf and lived with Stensen in Paris for some time. His extensive studies covered the fields of human anatomy, physiology, embryology, entomology and botany and his development of injection and other techniques for the preparation and preservation of specimens was of great significance in the progress of anatomical studies. In the field of anatomy he did important work on the female reproductive organs, was the first to describe the true anatomical pathogenesis of herniae, discovered the valves in lacteal and lymph vessels, was one of the first to see blood corpuscles in capillaries (along with Malpighi and Leeuwenhoek), was the first to demonstrate that the volume of a muscle does not increase when the muscle is active, and made many more new discoveries in his studies of various insects. His widespread studies resulted in a number of books, the most famous of which is his *Biblia Naturae* (Leyden, 1737–1738)

See: A. Schierbeck, *Jan Swammerdam, his life and works*, Amsterdam, Swets and Zeitlinger, 1967

TACCONI Gaetano (Bologna 1689 – Bologna 1782) was taught philosophy by Trionfetti and Bazzano. On graduation, his first major dissertation was concerned with the best methods of learning, teaching and practising medicine, an early indication of the breadth of his approach to his subject. He was appointed to the Chair of Philosophy in 1723. He took over the teaching of public anatomy four years after

Valsalva's death (1723) and later was promoted to the post of first surgeon at the hospital of Santa Maria del Morte. Here he was afforded ample opportunity for his primary interest, the study of pathological anatomy. His main topics of research included the pathology of fractures and the healing process in bone, gangrene, the chemistry of arthritis and gout, rickets and rabies. He was one of Galvani's teachers and was also in great part responsible for the scientific education of his protegée, Laura Maria Caterina Bassi.

See: M. Medici, (i), 1853

THALES (Miletus Asia Minor ?625–?546BC) was the founder of Greek philosophy and became famous for his knowledge of astronomy after predicting the eclipse of the sun which occurred on 28 May 585BC. He is also said to have introduced geometry into Greece.

See: *Microsoft Encarta 1997 Encyclopedia*

TRIONFETTI Lelio (Bologna 1647 – Bologna 1722) was granted his doctorate of philosophy at the early age of 15, lectured in the Bologna Academy the following year and was elected to the Chair of Philosophy in 1667. Eight years later he also became Professor of Natural History, taking charge of the specimens in the public gardens, a post previously reserved for medical men. To this post he brought his talents as a botanist and filled the post with great success. As a teacher of philosophy his influence (over nearly half a century) was enormous; he had as pupils men such as Galeazzi, Beccari and Tacconi, all of whom taught Galvani. Marsigli founded the Institute of Sciences and chose Trionfetti as the first President.

See: *Nouvelle Biographie Générale . . .*, Tom. 45, p. 638

VALLI Eusebio V. (Lucca 1755 – Havana 1816) studied in Pisa. He travelled widely in the Middle East and Orient, studying the nature and course of plague. As a result of experiments on himself, he became very ill and was forced to return to Italy in 1804. On his recovery he joined the army as a physician and later travelled to Spain as a member of a Military Medical Commission, studying an epidemic of Yellow Fever. He continued this work in Havana where he eventually died. Apart from this interest in infectious diseases Valli was, as we have noted, an ardent Galvanist.

See: *Biographisches Lexikon . . .*, Funfster Band, p. 698

VALSALVA Anton Maria (Imola 1666 – Bologna 1723) studied philosophy under Trionfetti and mathematics with Rondelli. However he became most interested in the study of anatomy and entered the school of Marcello Malpighi, obtaining his Laureate in philosophy and medicine in 1687. He became, by means of extensive experience in practical anatomy a remarkably dextrous experimenter and dissector. In 1705 he was elected Professor and Demonstrator of anatomy to the public, and was appointed surgeon to St Orsola's Hospital for incurables. His fame as an anatomist spread throughout Europe and he became President of the Bologna Academy and FRS. His major work was *De aure humana tractatus . . .* (Bologna, 1704). It is a comprehensive description of the human body and refers to his various discoveries.

See: M. Medici, (ii), 1857, p. 179

VARIGNON Pierre (Caen 1654 – Paris 1722) showed early talent as a mathematician, being influenced by the works of Descartes. He arrived in Paris in 1686 where he turned his mind to the problems of mechanics and at the instigation of Duhamel and de Lahire, wrote his *Project d'une nouvelle mécanique* (Paris, 1687). This work gained him recognition in scientific circles and he was admitted to the Académie des Sciences. He became professor of mathematics at the Collége Mazarin in 1688. He attributed the gravity of a body to the weight of the column of air pressing on it from above. He wrote on the subject of the calculus and in 1704 was appointed Professor of Philosophy at the Collége de France. He had a vast number of correspondents among the leading scientists in Europe.

See: *Nouvelle Biographie Générale . . .*, 1866, Tom. 45, p. 952.

VASSALI-EANDI Antonio Maria (Turin 1761 – Turin 1825) was a pupil of Beccaria and then professor of philosophy in Tortona from 1785–1792 before being elected professor of physics in Turin. Along with other scientific directorships he held the post of Secretary of the Academy of Science being elected in 1804. His experimental work was particularly concerned with electricity and the subject of Galvanism and his writings were prolific. He kept up a lively correspondence with Volta.

See: *Poggendorf* (M–Z), 1863, p. 1178

VOLTA Alessandro (Como 1745 – Como 1827) the great Ticinian physicist showed an interest in natural philosophy at school, learning French in order to keep abreast of current scientific work, writing his first paper on electricity at the age of 24. (*De vi attractiva ignis electrici . . .* a letter to Beccaria, 1769). In 1775 he was appointed Professor of Physics at Como and three years later he was appointed to the Chair at Pavia. In 1795 he was appointed Rector, but for political reasons he was dismissed and moved to Paris. While there he met Napoleon and when the latter took over Northern Italy Volta was reinstated at Pavia. His great achievement was the invention of the electric battery which put a tool of enormous power in the hands of scientific investigators. He was also responsible for the construction of the electrophorus in 1775. His great controversy with Galvani over the origin of the electro-motive agent responsible for muscular contractions has been dealt with in Chapter 21 of this book.

See: (1) *Biographical Dictionary of Scientists*, Trevor I. Williams (ed.), London, A. and C. Black, 2nd edn, 1974, p. 535

(2) Giovanni Cau, *Alessandro Volta, L'noma, la sua scienza, il suo tempo*, Milano, Casa Editrice Giacomo Agnelli, 1927.

(3) *Grand Dictionnaire Universal du XIXe Siècle . . .*, Par M. Pierre Larousse, Paris Admint. Du G.D.U., 1876. Tom. 15, p. 1180.

WALSH John (?Fort St George, India 1725 – London 1795) was the son of the Governor of Fort St George and entered the service of the East India Company, becoming paymaster of the troops at Madras. In 1757 Clive appointed him his private secretary. Four years later, Walsh took up residence in England and entered Parliament. His main interests however were scientific and he was elected FRS in 1770. His letter to Franklin which contained the first demonstration that the paralysing effects of the Torpedo fish are due to electricity was read before the Royal Society in January 1773. As a result of this and related papers he was awarded the Copley medal twice in 1774 and 1805.

See: *Dictionary of National Biography*, 1909, Vol. XX, p. 671

WATSON William (London 1775 – London 1787) was educated at the Merchant Taylors School. He was then apprenticed to an Apothecary, being at this time an ardent botanist and receiving the premium given annually by the Apothecaries Society for his proficiency in this subject. He became sufficiently recognised in scientific circles by 1741 to be elected FRS. Thereafter he contributed many original papers to the *Philosophical Transactions* these dealing in the main with electricity, natural history and medicine. In 1745 he was awarded the Copley Medal for his electrical researches. Sir Hans Sloane nominated him a Trustee of the British Museum in 1756. Among many distinguished positions he held the Vice Presidency of the Royal Society and was a Censor of the Royal College of Physicians. His electrical theory was very similar to that of Benjamin Franklin, a great part of his work being concerned with trying to determine the velocity of electricity. He was in correspondence with many leading European scientists.

See: *Dictionary of National Biography*, 1909, Vol. XX, p. 956

WHYTT Robert (Edinburgh 1714 – Edinburgh 1766) graduated MA at St Andrews in 1730 and then went to Edinburgh to study medicine. He devoted himself to the study of anatomy under Monro (Primus) going to London in 1734 to become a pupil of William Cheselden. Following this he travelled to Europe, attending lectures by Winslow in Paris, and Boerhaave and Albinus at Leyden. He took the degree MD at Rheims in 1736. On his return to England he was elected a Fellow of the Royal College of Physicians and began practice in London in 1738. Nine years later he was appointed Professor of the Theory of Medicine at Edinburgh University. In 1751, he published his book on the vital and other *Involuntary Motions of Animals* (Edinburgh, 1751) in which he attacked Stahl's views and ascribed such motions "to the effect of a stimulus acting on an unconscious sentient principle" He was elected FRS in 1752. In 1764 he published an important work, *On nervous, hypochondriac or Hysteric Diseases to which are pre-fixed some Remarks on the Sympathy of the Nerves* (London, 1764). He was elected President of the Royal College of Physicians of Edinburgh in 1763 – a post he held until his death.

See: *Dictionary of National Biography*, 1909, Vol. XXI, p. 174

WILCKE Johann Karl (Wismar 1732 – Stockholm 1796) studied in Uppsala living there between 1751 and 1757. He then followed Aepinus to Berlin where he introduced the latter to the rare mineral, tourmaline, which resulted in Wilcke's electromagnetic experiments. The two friends collaborated and their work resulted in the experimental demonstration of an air condenser, air being shown to act as a dielectric in a manner analogous to Franklin's glass in the Leyden Jar.

See: *Poggendorf* (M–Z), 1863, p. 1323

WILLIS Thomas (Great Bedwyn 1621 – London 1675) graduated MB from Christchurch, Oxford in 1646 and set up practice opposite Merton College. At this time he wrote *Diatribae Duae medico-philosophicae* which together with *Dissertatio Epistilaris de Urinis* were published in London in 1664. He worked with Richard Lower and Sir Christopher Wren, the latter being responsible for the illustrations of the anatomical dissections. This book contained a comprehensive account of the brain and nervous system and included a description of the blood vessels at the base of the brain (The Circle of Willis). He was involved with the meetings which led to the founding of the Royal Society and was elected FRCP in 1666. His later publications included *Affectionum quae diuntur hysterica et hypochondricae pathologia spasmodica* (London, 1670), *De Anima Brutorum* (Oxford, 1672) and *Pharmaceutice Rationalis* (Oxford, 1674) He was the first physician to distinguish the difference between diabetes mellitus and other conditions associated with polyuria.

See: *Dictionary of National Biography*, 1909, Vol. XXI, p. 496

XENOPHANES (active in Colophon Asia Minor late 6th and early 5th century BC) was the Greek poet and philosopher who founded the Eleatic school.

See: *Microsoft Encarta 1997 Encyclopedia*

ZANOTTI Francesco Maria (Bologna 1692 – Bologna 1772) studied at a Jesuit school and later at the Studio of Philosophy in the university. He was appointed to the Chair of Philosophy in 1718 and when Trionfetti died in 1723, Bazzani replaced him as President of the Institute and Zanotti took over Bazzani's post as Secretary. An accomplished classical scholar he made a deep study of the roots of medieval Aristotelianism; a convert to the new mechanistic philosophy, he was responsible for introducing the ideas of Descartes and then Newton to the school of philosophy in Bologna.

See: (1) Chapter 13, of this book
(2) G. Fantuzzi, (ii), 1781–1794

ZIMMERMAN Johann Georg (Brugg 1728 – Hannover 1795) went to Göttingen in 1747 to study medicine, graduating in 1755. He furthered his studies in Leyden and in Paris (where he worked under Senac) beginning medical practice in Bern in 1754 and writing *Leben des Herren von Haller* (Zurich, 1775). The dysentery epidemic which afflicted North Germany in 1763–1765 led to his travelling widely in order to treat patients. As a result of his experiences he published *Von der Ruhr unter dem Volke 1765 und dem mit der selben eingedrungenen Vorurtheilen* (Zurich, 1775 and 1787). However, he is best known through his friendship with the Kaiser and Kaiserin, Frederick and Katharine. The latter appointed him as a physician in 1784 and a long correspondence began between them. He attended Frederick at his death and published works dealing with his association with the Emperor and Royal Family in 1788.

See: *Biographisches Lexikon . . .*, 1934, p. 1042

LIST OF ABBREVIATIONS
USED IN THE BIOGRAPHICAL INDEX

Poggendorf (A–L) 1863 Erster Band.
Poggendorf (M–Z) 1863 Zweiter Band
Biographisch-Literarisches Handworterbuch zur geschichte der exacten Wissenschaften . . .
J.C. Poggendorf (ed.), Leipzig, Von Johann Ambrosius Barth, 1863

Biographischers Lexikon . . . 1934
Biographisches Lexikon der herrvorragerden Ärtze aller Zeiten und Volke, by various contributors, Berlin, Urban and Scharzenberg, 1934. Funf Bänder

I. Bernard Cohen, *Franklin and Newton . . .* 1966
I. Bernard Cohen, *Franklin and Newton, an enquiry into speculative Newtonian Experimental Science and Franklin's work in Electricity as an Example Thereof,* Cambridge, Mass. Published for the American Philosophical Society by Harvard University Press, 1966

Dictionary of Scientific Biography, Vol.-
Dictionary of Scientific Biography, Charles Coulston Gillespie (Editor in Chief), New York, Charles Scribner, Vols I–X, 1970–1974

Dictionary of National Biography, Vol.-
Dictionary of National Biography, Sydney Lee (ed.), London, Smith, Elder & Co., 1908–1909. 21 Vols and Supplements

Dizionaro Biografico degli Italiani, 1961, Vol.-
Dizionaro Biografico degli Italiani, 1961 Instituto della Enciclopedia Italiana fondata da Giovanni Treccani, Roma, Societa Grafica Romana, 1961. 13 Vols

Dictionnaire des Sciences Médicales . . . 1825 Tom.-
Dictionnaire des Sciences Médicales. Biographie Médicale. Paris, C.L.F. Pancoucke (ed.). 1825. 7 Vols

Dictionnaire de Biographie Française, 1936 Tom.-
Dictionnaire de Biographie Française, Paris, Letouzy, 1936. Eds: Tom. 1–3, J. Balteau, M. Barroux and M. Prevost; Tom. 4, M. Prevost and R. Amat

Dictionnaire encyclopedique des sciences médicales, Vol.-
Dictionnaire encyclopedique des sciences médicales. Directeurs A. Dechambre (1864–1865) et L. Lereboullet (1886–1889). 5 series in 100 Vols, Paris, Asselin & Masson, 1864–1889

G. Fantuzzi, (i)
G. Fantuzzi, *Elogio della dottoressa Laura Maria Caterina Bassi-Verati . . .* Bologna, Stamperia di S. Tommaso d'Aquino, 1778, con licencia di Superiori

G. Fantuzzi, (ii)
G. Fantuzzi, *Notize degli scrittori Bolognesi,* Bologna, Stamperia di S. Tommaso d'Aquino, 1781–1794. 9 Vols

S. Mazzeti (i)
S. Mazzeti, *Reportorio di tutti i Professori della Università e dell'Instituto delle scienze di Bologna,* Bologna, Tip. di S. Tommaso d'Aquino, 1848

S. Mazzeti (ii)
S. Mazzeti, *Alcune aggiunte e correzioni alle opere dell' Alidosi – del Fantuzzi . . .,* Bologna, Tip. di S. Tommaso d'Aquino, 1848

M. Medici (i)

M. Medici, *Della vita e degli scritti degli Anatomici e medici fioriti in Bologna*, Bologna, Tip. di S. Tommaso d'Aquino, 1853

M. Medici (ii)

M. Medici, *Compendio Storico della Scuola Anatomica di Bologna dal rinascimento delle scienze e delle lettere a tutto il secolo XVIII*. Bologna, Tipi Governativi della volpe e del Sassi, 1857

Nouvelle Biographie Général . . . 1861, Tom. -

Nouvelle Biographie Général etc. Depuis les temps les plus recules jusqu'à nos jours, avec les reseignements bibliographiques et l'indication des sources a consulter, Paris, M. Firmin Didot Frères, Fils et Cie, Editeurs, Imprimeurs-Libraires de l'Institut de France, 1861, Tom. 46

Nobel Lectures, **Physiology or Medicine**

Nobel Lectures, including Presentation Speeches and Laureate's Biographies, Physiology or Medicine, Amsterdam, published for the Nobel Foundation by Elsevier Publishing Co.

J.R. Partington, *A History of Chemistry,*

J.R. Partington, *A History of Chemistry*, London, Macmillan and Co. Ltd, 1962, 3 Vols

Appendix II

Electrical devices of the 18th century

The mid-18th century saw the development of a number of devices which were capable of producing a supply of electricity. During the mid-1740's, the prototype 'electric machine' was first described and brought into use by various German workers, for example, Bose and Winckler among others.[1] A good description of these is given by I. Bernard Cohen.[2] He says:

> *The electrical machines of the mid-forties usually consisted of a wooden frame with huge globes or cylinders on axles which were rotated by a cord passing around an axle pulley and a large wheel with a crank. The ratio of the diameter of the wheel to that of the axle was enough to permit one or more globes or spheres to be rotated at a very high speed . . . The sphere(s) or globe(s) were excited by having an experimenter hold his hand against them while they whirled; later a stuffed leather cushion was introduced to replace the hand and became known as the 'rubber'.*

With such a machine the 'charge' or 'quantity of electric fluid' produced greatly exceeded that formerly acquired by rubbing glass or ebony with various furs. Galvani's machine is a modification of this arrangement, as can be seen by his illustration to his *Commentary* (See Fig. 1, p. 161). The rotating sphere is represented by a glass plate which can be made to revolve in a vertical plane between the two pillars of its wooden frame, which stands on the table. The glass plate, on turning, rubs against four pads of some such substance as chamois leather, which are affixed to the opposing internal surfaces of the pillars. Leading from the glass plate are the two arms of the metallic conductor, which 'draws off' the charge induced in the plate. These two arms are united in a sphere which is depicted as resting on an elegant Venetian candlestick which acts as a support. The ball is extended as a stout rod which terminates in a second sphere, the whole projection being known as the 'prime conductor'. The machine was 'charged' by turning the metal crank-handle which passes through and is supported by the frame, before becoming attached to the glass plate, from which it is, however, insulated. Considered in mid 18th century terms, operating the crank-handle resulted in the accumulation of electrical fluid in the plate, this in turn being distributed to the prime-conductor which acquired a surplus of electrical fluid or was 'positively charged.' Meanwhile the pads, frame, crank-handle and operator acquired an equal deficit and became 'negatively charged.' If the operator were standing on the floor he was however considered as being in contact with an inexhaustible supply of electrical fluid so that the prime conductor was able to continue building up its supply of electrical fluid *via* the operator, until such time as it was so loaded with electrical fluid that it discharged this into the surrounding air. In the case of the operator being out of contact with the ground (insulated by a wax block) he would maintain his negative charge and a source of 'negative electricity' was produced in him. Thus when he touched a non-charged body with any conductor, he could draw electric fluid = 'positive charge' into his own body, thus tending to restore himself to an uncharged state, but causing the other body to be negatively charged or in deficit of electrical fluid. This was the commonly held Franklinian view.

The Leyden Jar was introduced during the early part of 1746 and rapidly came into use as a means of 'storing' electricity for various electrical experiments. The first discovery of the 'ability of glass to store up electrical fluid' which could be released at will, was made by Eward Georg van Kleist, Dean of Camin Cathedral, Pomerania on 4 November, 1745. He wrote to Doctor Lieberkuhn in Berlin telling him of his astonishing find and his account was recorded by the registrar of the Academy at Berlin. Van Kleist found that when he put a nail or a thick brass wire into a little apothecaries phial and then electrified the metal, an amazing effect occurred provided the phial was very dry and warm. Priestley quotes van Kleist from a translation of the Berlin records thus:

> As soon as this phial and nail are removed from the electrifying glass or the prime-conductor, to which it has been exposed is taken away, it throws out a pencil of flame so long, that with this burning machine in my hand, I have taken above sixty steps, in walking about my room. When it is electrified strongly, I can take it into another room and there fire spirits of wine with it. If while it is electrifying, I put my finger, or a piece of gold, which I hold in my hand to the nail, I receive a shock which stuns my arms and shoulders.

Van Kleist adds that if a little spirit of wine or mercury is placed in the bottom of the phial, "the experiment succeeds better". Various other German electricians came to know of the experiment and tried to repeat it but without success. However the same phenomenon was discovered a little later and quite separately in Holland by Professor Pieter van Muschenbroeck and his friends who were concerned with the problem of preventing electrified bodies from losing their store of electrical fluid by transmission to the conducting particles of the atmosphere. It seemed to them that if electrified bodies could be surrounded in some way by electrics *per se*, that is, non-conductors, this leaking of charge might be prevented. Their experiments consisted in electrifying water contained in a glass bottle by bringing the prime-conductor of their electric machine into contact with it *via* a metal wire dipping into it, the idea being that they could trap and build up a store of electrical fluid inside the bottle, the non-conducting glass preventing its dissipation into the atmosphere. During these manoeuvres, which took place in Leyden one of the assistants, Cuneus, was holding his glass bottle with its contained water in one hand through which he was thus in communication with the prime conductor. Thinking the water had received as much electrical fluid as it could, he reached up to take the communicating wire from the conductor with his free hand and thus remove the bottle, when he received a sudden shock in his arms and breast. The experiment was repeated by Muschenbroeck and others and with the publication of the astonishingly strong effects of the shock produced in this way, the glass bottle became known generally as the Leyden Jar after the Dutch city where Muschenbroeck was working.[3]

The Franklinian Square was yet another device for storing electricity. Benjamin Franklin carried out a great number of experiments involving the Leyden Jar. He was interested in finding out whether the ability of the Jar to store up electrical fluid and give an electric shock is a property of the glass itself or the non-electric conductors in contact with it's surfaces. Having demonstrated that this power rested in the glass itself,[4] he went on to see whether the shape of the glass had any influence on this property. This led him to try and produce a store of electrical fluid in a glass plate. He held a flat pane of window glass in one hand and laid a flat plate of lead on top of it. He then electrified the lead plate by bringing it up to the prime-conductor of his electric machine, and proceeded to obtain an electric shock when he touched the lead plate with his hand – a similar situation to that produced by van Kleist and Cuneus. Franklin then modified his glass 'store' further by placing a second lead plate on its under surface, the metal sheets being of rather smaller area than the interposed glass. The bottom plate was earthed and the upper plate electrified. On removing the two lead plates from the glass, he found that touching the glass with his finger yielded small pricking sparks. When the lead plates were returned to their former position and a person brought into the conducting circuit between them, he received as powerful a shock as before. The Franklinian Square thus supplied a ready supply of electrical fluid which could be tapped off by means of a conducting circuit between its upper and lower surfaces.[5]

The Electrophorus was invented by Alessandro Volta in 1775. This was yet another device involving the same electrical principles. It consisted of an electric slab made from wax and white spirit between a lower metal plate and an upper gold-plated wooden disc with a non-conducting handle attached to it. A negative charge was induced in the resinous central plate resulting in an equal and opposite positive charge in the metal plates. Touching the resinous plate momentarily caused it to lose its charge, so that lifting the upper plate by its handle enabled the operator to transfer positive charge to another conducting body. The process could be repeated a number of times.[6]

Notes

1   *Philosophical Transactions* (1744–1745) No. 476, pp 419–421 and No. 475, pp 307–3–4. Vol. 43; also Priestley J. (1966) *The History and Present State of Electricity . . .*, The sources of Science, No 18, Johnson Reprint Corporation, New York, Vol. I, Period VII, p. 87 *et seq.*
2   Cohen, I. Bernard (1966) *Franklin and Newton*, published for the American Philosophical Society by Harvard University Press, Cambridge, Mass., p. 384
3   Priestley J. (1966) *The History and Present State of Electricity . . .*, The Sources of Science, No 18, Johnson Reprint Corporation, New York, Vol. 1, Period VIII, p. 102 *et seq.*
4   Loc. cit. Note 2, p. 461, *et seq.*
5   Ibid., pp 461–462, *et seq.*
6   Volta, Alessandro (1816) *Collezione dell' opere*, Tom. 1, Par. 1, Firenze Nella Stampieri di Gugliemo Piatti, p. 106 *et seq.*

Index